WILLIAM BARNES

BORN 1801
DIED 1886

[*From a photograph given to the Author 1886*]

DORSETSHIRE FOLK-LORE

BY

JOHN SYMONDS UDAL, F.S.A.

(OF THE INNER TEMPLE)

HON. FELLOW OF THE ROYAL HISTORICAL SOCIETY; MEMBER OF COUNCIL OF THE FOLK-LORE SOCIETY; AND A VICE-PRESIDENT OF THE DORSET NATURAL HISTORY AND ANTIQUARIAN FIELD CLUB

WITH A FORE-SAY BY THE LATE

WILLIAM BARNES, B.D.

("THE DORSET POET")

A facsimile limited edition
with a foreword by R. N. R. Peers

Issued by subscription

DORSET BOOKS

First published in 1922
Third edition published by Dorset Books 1989

ISBN: 1 871164–04–4

British Library Cataloguing-in-Publication Data
Udal, John Symonds, *1849–1925*
Dorset folk-lore.
1. Dorset folk-lore
I. Title
398′ .09423′3

ISBN 1-871164-04-4

Printed and bound in Great Britain by BPCC Wheaton Ltd, Exeter

DORSET BOOKS

An imprint of Wheaton Publishers Ltd, a member of Maxwell Pergamon Publishing Corporation plc

Wheaton Publishers Ltd
Hennock Road, Marsh Barton, Exeter, Devon EX2 8RP
Tel: 0392 74121; Telex 42794 (WHEATN G)

SALES

Direct sales enquiries to Dorset Books at the address above.

LIST OF SUBSCRIBERS TO THE 1989 FACSIMILE EDITION

A

Mary Allen, *Duntish Cottage, Duntish Dorchester, Dorset.*
James M. Anderson, *"Wentworth", Damers Road, Dorchester, Dorset.*
Brenda and Douglas Ashdown, *6 Lime Close, Dorchester, Dorset.*
S. F. Austin, *Brooms Farm, Toller Porcorum, Dorchester, Dorset.*
Mike Ayton, *9 Birch Grove, Upper Halliford Road, Shepperton, Middlesex.*

B

Mrs Claire Baker, *20 Abbots Walk, Cerne Abbas, Dorchester, Dorset.*
Mr Colin Banfield, *10 Barrington Lodge, Princes Road, Weybridge, Surrey.*
Madeline A. Barber, *Waterloo Cottage, The Row, Sturminster Newton, Dorset.*
Mr K. and Mrs S. N. Barker, *Bookham Farmhouse, Alton Pancras, Dorchester, Dorset.*
William Barnes Collection, *Dorset Natural History and Archaeological Society, Dorset County Museum, High West Street, Dorchester, Dorset.*
Richard Bartelot, *Wareham, Dorset.*
John Bartlett, *30 Portalfield, Stalham, Norfolk.* (2 copies)
G. R. J. H. Beale, *Clarendon House, 39 Church Street, Bridgwater, Somerset.*
Mr and Mrs D. W. Bicheno, *Langton House, Blandford, Dorset.*
Olive Blackburn, *6 Mistover Close, Dorchester, Dorset.*
Anthony and Fiona Blad, *Bridles Cottage, Bloxworth, Wareham, Dorset.*
Susan Blake, *19 Shaston Crescent, Dorchester, Dorset.*
Mr and Mrs M. W. Blanchard.
William Henry Bond, *Holme Priory, Wareham, Dorset.*
Mike Bone, *"Sunnyside", Avon Close, Keynsham, Bristol.*
Hugh Brainett, *18 Lodge Road, Holt, Wimborne, Dorset.*
David Brewer, *22 The Grove, Teddington, Middlesex.*
Mrs Jean Bridge, *The Old Chapel, Redbridge Road, Nr Crossways, Dorchester, Dorset.*
Bridport Museum, *South Street, Bridport, Dorset.*
Buck and Julie Buckhurst *"Sunnydown", Gallows Gore, Worth Matravers, Dorset.*
Mr P. and Dr K. M. Budden, *The Old Post Office, Newmill, Penzance, Cornwall.*
Richard Burleigh, *The Old George, The Square Broadwindsor, Beaminster, Dorset.*

C

D. E. Chaffin, *17 Princes Street, Stirling.*
Professor Raymond Chapman, *London School of Economics, Houghton Street, London.*
Mr S. P. Chapman, *Forge Cross, Halstock, Yeovil, Somerset.*
Miss Violet K. M. Chinchen, *31 Spring Avenue, Rodwell, Weymouth, Dorset.*
Sqn Ldr P. F. Christopher MBE, DFC, *563 Ringwood Road, Ferndown, Dorset.*
Geoffrey and Mary Clacy, *"Crib Barton", Rivers Corner, Sturminster Newton, Dorset.*
Peter C. Clarke, *28 Heathwood Road, Weymouth, Dorset.*
Mrs L. A. Coe, *Barford House, Salisbury Road, Swanage.*
Mr Rodney D. N. Coffin, *106 Elmer Gardens, Isleworth, Middlesex.*
Arthur G. Cole, *"Holme", 10 Ashton Road, Weymouth, Dorset.*
Mrs D. Comben, *64 Avalanche Road, Southwell, Portland, Dorset.*
Mrs Margaret Complin.
Tony Cross, *9 Southview Rise, Alton, Hampshire.*
Barry Cuff, *27 Badgers Way, The Chimes, Sturminster Newton, Dorset.*
Mr Cecil N. Cullingford, *"Kampala", 15 Corfe Way, Broadstone, Dorset.*
L. A. Cushing, *4 St Martins Close, Broadmayne, Dorchester, Dorset.*

D

John Davis MBE, *2 Collyers Rise, Fontmell Magna, Shaftesbury, Dorset.*
K. A. Deacon.
M. D. Deas, *St Antony's College, Oxford.* (2 copies)
Kenneth F. Dibben, *Naish Priory, East Coker, Somerset.*
Mrs A. M. Dilke, *Valehouse Farm, Whitchurch Canonicorum, Bridport, Dorset.*
The Dorset Bookshop Ltd, *69 East Street, Blandford Forum, Dorset.* (3 copies)
Dorset County Museum, *High West Street, Dorchester, Dorset.*
F. J. Douch, *Oaklee Boundary Drive, Colehill, Wimborne, Dorset.*
Christopher Drury, *13 Guildford Road, Croydon, Surrey.*
Mr J. R. T. Dyer, *20 Barrow Close, Dorchester, Dorset.*

E

B. M. Edey, *55 East Street, Wareham, Dorset.*
Lady Edwards, *Nothe House, Weymouth, Dorset.*
Eldridge, Pope & Co., *Dorchester Brewery, Dorchester, Dorset.* (3 copies)
Marcia Evans, *7 Brierley Hay, Yetminster, Sherborne, Dorset.*
Alma Evers, *328 Pershore Road, Edgbaston, Birmingham.*

F

Mrs K. A. Falkner, *Rose Cottage, Stratford-Sub-Castle, Salisbury, Wiltshire.* (5 copies)
Raymond A. H. Farrar, *47 King's Road, Richmond, Surrey.*
Mr S. W. Feist, *8 Beverley Road, Littlemoor, Weymouth, Dorset.*
Roger Ffooks, *Priors Dean, Long Lane, Bothenhampton, Bridport, Dorset.*
N. H. Field, *The Croft, Croft Close, Corfe Mullen, Wimborne, Dorset.*
Donald W. Firth, *25 Greenacre Park, Hornsea, North Humberside.*
David A. Fisher, *21 View Point, Sandbourne Road, Bournemouth, Dorset.*
Folklore Society Library, *University College London, Gower Street, London.*
Ben Ford, *39 Icen Way, Dorchester, Dorset.*
Douglas Fox, *Tower House, St Peter's Hill, Stamford, Lincolnshire.*
Mr F. and Mrs E. Foy, *Greenfields, Henley, Buckland Newton, Dorchester, Dorset.*
G. and H. Frost, *Buckland Newton, Dorset.*
F. E. Fryer, *Shroton House, Blandford, Dorset.*

G

Mrs John Garnier, *The Old Rectory, Pulham, Dorchester, Dorset.*
F. P. Gerard, *Alton Mill, Alton Pancras, Dorchester, Dorset.*
Dr James Gibson, *4 Gore Mews, Canterbury, Kent.*
Magdelaine Gibson.
Zachary C. Graham, *"Laarbruch" Deans Drove, Lytchett, Matravers, Poole, Dorset.*
Lt Col G. E. Gray, *Wimborne, Dorset.*
Mr G. L. Green, *27 Ridgway, West Chinnock, Crewkerne, Somerset.*
Harry Green, *Bancroft Court, Longfleet Road, Poole, Dorset.*
Roy Greenfield, *6 The Fairway, New Barnet, Hertfordshire.*
A. R. Gurd, *"Little Hintock", Winsor Lane, Winsor, Hampshire.*

H

D. T. and K. M. Halfpenny, *Southbourne, Bournemouth, Dorset.*
Philip G. Hansford.
John Hanson, *The Malthouse, Lyme Regis, Dorset.*
Dennis Hardy, *Hardy Tours, 38 Chestnut Way, Dorchester, Dorset.*
P. D. G. Hares CBE, *"Honeywood", Lower Sea Lane, Charmouth, Bridport, Dorset.*
Mrs Cynthia Hart, *Wellbottom Lodge, Winterbourne Abbas, Dorchester, Dorset.*
Mrs Gabrielle Hatton, *10 Glendon Avenue, Kinson, Bournemouth, Dorset.*
Aileen Hawkins, *"Craigaras", Wavering Lane, Gillingham, Dorset.*
Desmond Hawkins, *Stanton Close, Blandford, Dorset.*
Trevor W. Hearl, *49 Noverton Lane, Prestbury, Cheltenham, Gloucester.*
Guy Hereward, *15 High Street, Toller Porcorum, Dorchester, Dorset.*
Shelagh Hill, *101 Acreman Street, Sherborne, Dorset.*
William Hoare, *18 Axwood, Woodcote Hurst, Epsom, Surrey.*
Mrs Betty A. Hodgson, *2 Came View Road, Dorchester, Dorset.*

Mrs Olivia Hole OBE, *"Lynchets", Higher Sea Lane, Charmouth, Dorset.*

Vernon Holleyoak, *"Quackers", 67 Dorchester Road, Maiden Newton, Dorset.*

Miss Elizabeth Howes, *12A The Street, Ashtead, Surrey.*

J

Anthony Jaggard, *Winfrith Court, Dorset.*

Hugh Jaques, *Dorchester, Dorset.*

Irene Jones, *"Lindenore", King's Mill Road, Stalbridge, Sturminster Newton, Dorset.*

K

Miss Pamela Kauders, *"Chumleys", Ice House Lane, Sidmouth, Devon.* (2 copies)

E. Maureen Keats, *7 Kingsbere Crescent, Dorchester, Dorset.*

L

F. M. Langford, *Weymouth, Dorset.*

Mrs D. J. W. Larkin, *West End Cottage, Belvedere Road, Swanage, Dorset.*

Professor C. J. S. Lock, *Department of English, Erindale College, University of Toronto, Canada.*

The Rev. K. N. J. Loveless FSA, FSA Scot, *3 Clothworkers' Cottages, Bishop Street, Islington, London.*

M

Miss Marion Makinson, *41 Casterbridge Road, Dorchester, Dorset.*

Mr and Mrs Anthony Manders, *10 Wayford Close, Longthorpe, Peterborough.*

Mrs Pamela Marley, *Swallowfield, Berkshire.*

Mrs J. M. Marriott, *221 Church Ope Road, Portland, Dorset.*

Rose and Jack Mawson, *21 Barclay Road, Westham, Weymouth, Dorset.*

Mr G. E. Mead, *Church Cottage, Tidenham, Nr Chepstow, Gwent.*

Mr and Mrs D. C. Mills, *32 Bullfinch Lane, Riverhead, Sevenoaks, Kent.*

Derek Mills, *Charity House, Cranborne, Dorset.*

S. M. Minhinnick, *"Little Maen", 37 Prince of Wales Road, Dorchester, Dorset.*

Mr C. Mintern, *Partridge Green Cottage, Woodhouse Lane, Broomfield, Chelmsford, Essex.*

R. M. Mitchell, *10 Britannia Way, Dorchester, Dorset.*

Mr and Mrs J. Moeran *West Bay, Bridport, Dorset.*

Pamla Morgan, *12 Chichester Road, Street, Somerset.*

Mr D. and Mrs W. J. Morris, *"Hestia", Buckland Newton, Dorchester, Dorset.*

Mrs I. A. Morris, *8 Widdicombe Avenue, Poole, Dorset.*

Daniel Moss, *Old Church Farm, Broadmayne, Dorchester, Dorset.*

O

J. Oliver, *Send Court Farm, Send, Woking, Surrey.*

Paul Oson.

P

Mr R. Parker, *17A Dean Park Road, Bournemouth, Dorset.*

Vanessa I. C. Parker, *Dairy Cottage, Owermoigne, Dorchester, Dorset.*

Lt Col T. G. Parsons, *31A Harrington Road, Dorchester, Dorset.*

R. N. R. Peers, *14 Church Street, Beaminster, Dorset.*

W. T. G. Perrott, *93 The Avenue, Muswell Hill, London.*

Pic's Bookshop, *11 South Street, Bridport, Dorset.*

S. H. Pickett, *71 Roman Road, Weymouth, Dorset.*

Harry William Polley, *16 Teesdale Gardens, Isleworth, Middlesex.*

Christopher J. R. Pope TD, JP, DL, *Wrackleford House, Dorchester, Dorset.*

Jeany Poulsen, *14 Front Street, Portesham, Weymouth, Dorset.*

Mr and Mrs A. Poulsom, *"Stannings", Colway Cross, Bishopsteignton, Devon.*

R

Edith Rawlinson, *"The Pleasance", 19 May Tree Close, Badger Farm, Winchester, Hampshire.*

Miss Gael Reed, *Marine Cottage, Brandy Row, 181 Chiswell, Portland, Dorset.*

Miss F. M. Reynolds, *150 Wet Bay Road, Bridport, Dorset.*

Christopher Ricks, *Lasborough Cottage, Lasborough Park, Nr Tetbury, Gloucester.*

Richard T. Riding, *17 Newark Way, Hendon, London.*

Peter Robson, *Vale House, Woolland, Blandford, Dorset.*

Mrs Joyce Ronald, *229 Westbury, Sherborne, Dorset.*

D. P. Russell, *33 Briantspuddle, Dorchester, Dorset.*

S

F. E. Saunders, *55 Crofters Way, Droitwich, Worcester.*

Mark Savage, *Holly Tree Cottage, Waytown, Bridport, Dorset.*

Mary Clare Sheahan, *23 Briantspuddle, Dorchester, Dorset.*

Mrs Hilary Shearman, *13 Quarry Lane, Long Burton, Sherborne, Dorset.*

G. Smallwood, *Child Okeford House, Blandford, Dorset.*

Mrs P. I. Stehr, *35A South Street, Dorchester, Dorset.*

Colin Bernard Stephens, *The Court Cottage, Frampton, Dorchester, Dorset.*

Judith Stinton, *70 Dorchester Road, Maiden Newton, Dorchester, Dorset.*

Sean Street, *Haddon House, 78 Feversham Avenue, Queens Park, Bournemouth, Dorset.*

Peter Strickland, *18 Wroxham Gardens, London.*

Mrs Audrey Elaine Sweet and Dr Hector S. Sweet, *Gothic Cottage, Lamb Corner, Dedham, Colchester.*

D. R. Symonds, *Stone Cottage, Marinstown, Dorchester, Dorset.*

T

Mr and Mrs S. R. Thomas, *Pilgrim Cottage, Plaisters Lane, Sutton Poyntz, Nr Weymouth, Dorset.*

Mrs Hilary Townsend, *"Silk Hay", High Street, Stalbridge, Dorset.*

Mrs P. A. Townsend, *Knapp Cottage, Rampisham, Dorcheter, Dorset.*

Mrs M. P. P. Troughton, *93 York Road, Broadstone, Dorset.*

Joan Tunstall, *Old Orchard, Holy City, Chardstock, Axminster, Devon.*

U

Susie and Michael Upton, *Victoria Grove, Bridport, Dorset.*

W

Colin Walls, *42 Burghley Road, St Andrews, Bristol, Avon.*

Mr E. J. Ward, *Rose Cottage, Ship Knap, Morcombelake, Nr Bridport, Dorset.*

W. Y. Warry, *Westrow House, Holwell, Sherborne, Dorset.*

S. Wayman, *2 Penally Terrace, Boscastle, Cornwall.*

Mr Charles Weld, *Chideock Manor, Bridport, Dorset.*

M. W. West, *19 Bramley Avenue, Aston, Sheffield.*

Belinda Wilding, *219 Mitchan Lane, Streatham, London.*

Richard Wilding, *175 Whitton Road, Twickenham, Middlesex.*

Mrs B. J. Whillock, *Court Farm, Litton Cheney, Dorchester, Dorset.*

Maj. Gen. E. A. W. Williams CB, CBE, MC, DL, *Herrington, Dorchester, Dorset.*

Mrs Teresa M. Williams, *87 Pasture Road, North Wembley, Middlesex.*

Mr and Mrs Donald J. Winslow, *23 Maple Street, Aubumdale, USA.*

Sam Woodcock, *"Hillside", Milton-on-Stour, Gillingham, Dorset.* (2 copies)

David and Lesley Wray, *"Milpool", Pud Brook, Milborne Port, Somerset.*

D. P. Wright, *Haileybury, Hertford.*

Kenneth G. Wright, *214 Bricknell Avenue, Hull, N. Humberside.*

Y

Mrs E. R. Yeo, *40 St Leonard's Road, Weymouth, Dorset.*

Rosie Young, *Oselhay Farm, Whitchurch Canonicorum, Dorset.*

LIST OF SUBSCRIBERS

A

The Lord Abercromby, *Edinburgh.*
Capt. J. E. Acland, F.S.A., *Dorchester.*
E. F. Adams, *Chelsea.*
Mrs. G. Alner, *Sturminster Newton.* [4 copies.]
G. Bryer Ash, *Winfrith House.*
Capt. H. W. Aston, *Iwerne Minster.*
E. H. Tindal Atkinson, *The Temple.*
H. Atwooll, *Portland.*
Australian Book Company, *London.*

B

Rev. A. H. Barnes, *Stockport.*
R. Barrow, *Exmouth.*
Rev. R. Grosvenor Bartelot, *Dorchester.*
Col. H. Cary Batten, O.B.E., *Yeovil.*
Major H. C. C. Batten, *Yeovil.*
B. Beale, *Bournemouth.*
F. Beale, *Weston-super-mare.*
W. O. Beament, *Beaminster.*
E. H. Beavan, *Swanage.*
Mrs. Beckett, *Fort Augustus* (*Scot.*).
J. H. Benyon, *Reading.* [2 copies.]
Maurice H. Berkeley, *Conservative Club, S.W.*
The Hon. Mrs. Slingsby Bethell, *Hove.*
E. C. Bignal, *Totton.*
Messrs. Bobby & Co., *Torquay.*
W. R. G. Bond, *Tyneham.*
H. Syndercombe Bower, *Fontmell Parva.*
Rev. F. W. Brandreth, *Buckland Newton.*
Bright's, Ltd., *Bournemouth.* [2 copies.]
Mrs. Bruton, *Wymering Mansions, W.*
E. J. W. Buckpitt, *Bridport.*
Mrs. Burnett, *Pulborough.*
G. M. Burt, *Weymouth.* [2 copies.]
W. G. Busk, *Wraxall.*

C

Cardiff Central Library, *Wales.*
G. R. Carline, F.R.A.I., *Pitt Rivers Museum, Oxford.*
H. A. Cartwright, *Handley.*
Major E. W. F. Castleman, *Chettle.*
W. E. Pitfield Chapple, *Axminster.*
Chicago University, *U.S.A.*
A. W. Chippindale, *Conservative Club, S.W.*
R. P. Chope, *Crouch Hill, N.W.*
R. Clark, *Street.*
W. J. N. Cleal, *Finsbury Park, N.W.*
W. V. H. Cobbett, *Richmond.*
A. C. Coffin, *Bradford.* [2 copies.]
Messrs. Cole & Co., *Brighton.*
Lieut.-Col. T. A. Colfox, *Bridport.*
Rev. E. Collett, *Retford.*
J. E. Cornish, Ltd., *Manchester.*
E. L. de Coverly, *Wimbledon Park.*
F. C. Coxhead, *Kensington.*
E. E. Cranton, *Fleet Lane, E.C.*
Rev. J. Cross, *Wimborne.*

D

J. M. J. Dacombe, *Bournemouth.*
Miss Violet Dale, *Verwood.*
M. Longworth Dames, *Guildford.*
N. W. Dartnell, *Salisbury.*
E. A. Dening, *Chard.*
Capt. the Hon. Gerald Digby, R.N., *Holywell.*
J. Dingley, *Sherborne.*
E. J. Domville, *Symondsbury.*
Warwick Draper, *Lincoln's Inn.*
Lieut.-Col. J. S. Drew, *Henstridge.*
J. Druitt, *Bournemouth.*
Mrs. Duke, *Godmanstone.*
Mrs. Dupuy, *Brookville* (*Ontario*).
R. H. Kortright Dyett, *Antigua, B.W.I.*

E

Sir Robert Edgcumbe, *Newquay.*
J. T. Edwards, *Sackville Street, W*
H. D. Ellis, *Roland Gardens, S.W.*
Arnold Evans, *Clifton.*
Exeter City and University Library.

F

C. G. Falkner, *Rusholme.*
Miss M. E. Ferguson, *Upwey.*
Rev. S. E. V. Filleul, *Wareham.*

LIST OF SUBSCRIBERS

A. J. Finch, *Fellows Road, N.W.*
Morgan Finucane, *Ashley Place, S.W.*
Mrs. Firth, *Clifton Maubank.* [2 copies.]
S. T. Fitzherbert, *Chepstow Villas, W.*
Dr. E. K. Le Fleming, *Wimborne.*
J. Foot, *Bethnal Green, E.* [2 copies.]
B. C. Forder, *Bournemouth.*
Mrs. Forrester, *Wareham.*
J. J. Foster, F.S.A., *Sutton.*
Major P. J. Foster, D.S.O., *Chatham.*
Sir James G. Fraser, *The Temple.*
B. E. Freame, *Gillingham.*
J. J. Freeman, *Shepperton-on-Thames.*
G. S. Fry, C.B.E., *Hove.*

G

Stanley I. Galpin, *Fleet Street, E.C.*
W. W. Gill, *Dalby* (*Isle of Man*).
C. G. Girling, *Cranborne.*
F. G. Green, *Carshalton.*
G. J. Gribble, *Kingston Russell.*
H. J. Grimsdell, *Weymouth.*
Sir Walter Grove, Bart., *Sedgehill Manor.*
H. J. Groves, *Weymouth.*
Guildhall Library, *London, E.C.*
Mrs. Gundry, *Honiton.*

H

G. Hamilton Fletcher, *Leweston Manor.*
Lieut.-Col. Cathcart C. Hannay, *Dorchester.*
Thomas Hardy, O.M., *Dorchester.*
W. Harrison, *Clifton.*
Miss F. Hayllar, *Margaret Street, W.*
W. Dunning Hayward, *Broadstairs.*
H. J. Hearn, *Church Stretton.*
Mrs. Hichens, *Sherborne.*
W. L. Hildburgh, F.S.A., *Society of Antiquaries, Burlington House, W.*
R. Hine, *Beaminster.*
Miss R. Hodgson, *Lichfield.*
Prof. Dr. E. Hoffman-Krayer, *Basle.*
H. Wilson Holman, F.S.A., *Topsham.* [2 copies.]
R. C. Hope, F.S.A., *Burnham-on-Sea.*
H. W. P. Hoskyns, *North Perrott Manor.*
Mrs. Hull, *Symondsbury.*
Mrs. E. W. Huson, *Weymouth.*
C. Hussey, *Croydon.*
E. R. J. Hussey, *Torquay.*

I

Sir Everard im Thurn, *Prestonpans.*
J. Ismay, *Iwerne Minster.*
Iwerne Minster Village Club.

J

Rev. T. Leonard Jenkins, *Leigh Vicarage.*
A. C. Jones, *Kenilworth.*
Mrs. A. C. Jones, *Kenilworth.*
Rev. J. F. Jones, *Winfrith Rectory.*
Miss West Jones, *Eckington* (*Sheffield*).

K

Reginald Kemp, *Chiswick.*
F. A. Kennett, *Symondsbury.*
C. W. Kitson, *Netherbury.*

L

F. E. Lacey, *Lord's Cricket Ground, N.W.*
Rev. Canon Langford, *Star Cross.*
C. H. Laycock, *Moretonhampstead.*
Mrs. H. H. Leas, *St. John's Wood Park, N.W.*
Miss Legge, *Bridport.*
H. M. Leman, *Nottingham.*
R. C. Leversedge, *Evercreech.*
W. A. Lindsay, K.C., *College of Arms, E.C.*
W. Llewellin, *Poole.*
Miss Lovell, *Highgate, N.*

M

P. W. Macdonald, *Radipole.*
A. S. Macmillan, *Yeovil.*
Rev. A. N. Malan, D.D., *Weymouth.*
E. C. Malan, *Bournemouth.*
Mrs. Mallock, *Dorchester.*
T. Manfield, *Northampton.*
Rev. Canon J. C. M. Mansel-Pleydell, *Chelsea.*
Dr. R. R. Marett, *Exeter Coll., Oxford.*
G. M. Mathews, *Fair Oak* (*Hants*).
F. B. L. Maunsell, *Bridport.*
Rev. Canon C. H. Mayo, *Gillingham.*
W. P. Merrick, *Shepperton.*
Major W. Middleton, *Sudan.*
F. C. Mills, *Limpsfield.*
W. R. Mitchell, *Seaborough Court.*
Mrs. Moorhouse, *Parnham.*

Mrs. Morgan, *Yetminster.*
E. H. Morris, *Abergwili* (*South Wales*). [2 copies.]
Rev. Canon C. Myers, *Salisbury.*

N

C. G. Nantes, *Bridport.*
Miss M. M. Nix, *Weymouth.*
North Devon Athenæum, *Barnstaple.*

O

Miss Olding, *North Gate, N.W.*
Vere L. Oliver, F.S.A., *Weymouth.*
Lieut.-Col. Uvedale Parry Okeden, *Turnworth.*
Miss Orme, *Newport, I. of W.*

P

G. E. Peachell, *Dorchester.*
E. Pearce, *Taunton.*
C. Penney, *Kensington Crescent, W.*
Lieut.-Col. P. R. Phipps, *St. James' Court, S.W.*
A. W. Pickard-Cambridge, *Ball. Coll., Oxford.*
Major G. A. Pinney, *Beaminster.*
Sir Reginald Pinney, K.C.B., *Racedown.*
Mrs. Pitfield, *Barnstaple.*
J. Pitfield, *Petworth.* [4 copies.]
T. A. Pitfield, *Ceylon.*
T. J. Pitfield, *Bournemouth.*
Miss Plumptre, *Hamilton Terrace, N.W.*
C. C. M. Plumptre, *Forest Hill, S.E.*
R. C. E. Plumptre, *Bridport.*
A. G. Pomeroy, *Melton Mowbray.*
C. L. Poole, LL.D., *Lytham.*
H. F. Pooley, *Hampstead.*
Alfred Pope, F.S.A., *Dorchester.*
Major A. Rolph Pope, *Dorchester.*
A. E. D. Prideaux, *Dorchester.*
W. de C. Prideaux, *Weymouth.*
The Viscountess Portman, *Bryanston.*

R

Northwood Rawlins, *Gray's Inn Square, W.C.* [2 copies.]
Sir C. Hercules Read, LL.D., Pres.S.A., *British Museum.*
Rev. W. T. Reeder, *Dunster.*
A. G. Rickards, K.C., *South Kensington, S.W.*
Mrs. C. J. Robin, *Jersey.*
Mrs. Cameron Robinson, *Mozufferpur.* [2 copies.]
Miss M. M. Roe, *Trent.*
G. Romilly, *Marnhull.*
Freeman Roper, *Forde Abbey.*
J. Rose, *Taunton.*
W. H. Rowley, *Barnet.*
Col. O. E. Ruck, *Aberdovey, N. Wales.*
Mrs. Russ, *Weymouth.*
John Ryland's Library, *Manchester.*

S

H. Savory, *Abbot's Leigh.*
H. Berkeley Score, *Ormskirk.*
H. S. Senior, *Sturminster Newton.* [2 copies.]
The Earl of Shaftesbury, K.P., *St. Giles' House.*
Sherborne School Library.
J. A. Sherren, F.R.Hist.S., *Parkestone.*
Rev. A. J. Shields, *Axminster.*
W. H. Simpson, *Conservative Club, S.W.*
R. H. Skelt, *Cullompton.*
Mrs. C. Small, *Chard.*
The Hon. Mrs. Aubrey Smith, *Roehampton.*
Mrs. R. Bosworth Smith, *Bingham's Melcombe.*
A. F. Somerville, *Wells.*
Messrs. H. Sotheran & Co., *Piccadilly, W.* [2 copies.]
H. B. Spencer, *West Moors.*
Major F. A. Stephens, *Holywell.*
E. Stevens, *Dorchester.*
H. Sturmey, *Coventry.*
Mrs. Leonard Sturdy, *Wareham.*
E. R. Sykes, *Iwerne Minster.*
G. S. Symes, *Weymouth.*
Major A. G. Symonds, *Dorchester.*
F. G. Symonds, *Sturminster Newton.*
H. Symonds, F.S.A., *Staplegrove Elm.*
W. P. Symonds, *Sturminster Newton.* [2 copies.]

T

Mrs. Tapper, *Chideock.*
Miss Hebe Templer, *Bridport.* [2 copies.]
Rev. J. Lethbridge Templer, *Maiden Newton Rectory.*

LIST OF SUBSCRIBERS

Mrs. J. A. Thompson, *Ludlow*.
Major G. Tolley, *Morecombelake*.
Toronto Public Library, *Canada*.
E. J. Trowbridge, *Swindon*.
Lieut.-Col. E. G. Troyte-Bullock, C.M.G., *Zeals House*. [2 copies.]
E. F. Turner, *Kensington, W*.
Mrs. Turner, *Colville Gardens, W*.

U

Mrs. Udal, 24 *Neville Court, N.W*.
A. Udal, *Hampstead, N.W*.
Major A. U. Udal, *c/o* 24 *Neville Court, N.W*.
Mrs. A. Udal, *c/o* 24 *Neville Court, N.W*.
E. Udal, *Clevedon*.
N. R. Udal, *Gordon College, Khartoum*.
W. Udal, *Richmond*.
United Service Club, *Lucknow*.
Rev. Canon T. E. Usherwood, *Parkstone*.

V

H. S. Vaughan, F.S.A., *Llangoedmore* (*S. Wales*).
Miss M. Vidler, *Stow Vicarage* (*Norfolk*).

W

R. Hensleigh Walter, M.B., F.S.A., *Stoke-sub-Hamdon*.
Miss F. Ward, *Oxford*.
Mrs. King Warry, *Portland*.
Washington Congress Library, *U.S.A*.
W. Watkins, *Bishopgate, E.C*.
W. G. Willis Watson, F.R.Hist.S., *Pinhoe*.
Lewis J. Upton Way, F.S.A., *Clifton*.
Lieut.-Col. W. F. Weber, C.M.G., D.S.O., *Montpelier Square, S.W*.
C. H. R. Weideman, *Dawlish*.
H. F. Weld, *Chideock Manor*.
Major M. J. Wheatley, *Upper Parkestone*.
C. Dampier Whetham, *Hilfield St. Nicholas*.
Rev. C. T. Wickham, *Twyford*.
E. J. Wilde, *Winchester*.
Mrs. C. L. Wilde, *Godalming*.
A. J. Williams, *Yetminster*.
Capt. Williams, *Herrington*.
Sir Robert Williams, Bart., M.P., *Bridehead*.
Mrs. J. Williams, *Bridport*.
J. W. Willis-Bund, C.B.E., F.S.A., *Worcester*.
Major H. S. Woodhouse, *Blandford*.

Y

Macleod Yearsley, F.R.C.S., *Welbeck Street, W*.
F. D. Yeatman, *The Temple*.
Mrs. Yorke-Davies, *Harrington Court, S.W*.
Wynne Yorke-Davies, *Harley Street, W*.
C. E. Baring Young, *Daylesford*.

INTRODUCTION TO THE 1989 FACSIMILE EDITION

THE preparation of John Symonds Udal's *Dorsetshire Folk-lore* reaches back to the 1870s, although the book was not to be published until 1922. Born in 1849, son of William Udal of Edgbaston, a member of an old Dorset family whose name was originally Uvedale, J. S. Udal was educated at the Queen's College, Oxford. He was called to the Bar by the Inner Temple in 1875, and went to the Western Circuit. During the time that he remained in England he made a close study of Dorset folklore, and for many years was engaged in the preparation of this book.

His researches were interrupted when he accepted the position of Attorney-General and Admiralty Advocate of Fiji, and his subsequent Colonial service compelled him to put his cherished book on one side. After a short period in Fiji he became legal assistant at the Colonial Office, but soon afterwards, in 1900, was appointed Chief Justice of the Leeward Islands, a post which he held until 1911. When he returned home he resumed his antiquarian interests with renewed zeal. In 1901 he had been elected a Fellow of the Society of Antiquaries of London.

Before he left England he had suggested to the editor of the *Dorset County Chronicle*, in 1881, that there should be a folklore column in that paper, and for a few years this was a spasmodic gathering-place for short articles. Amongst those early contributors William Barnes took a leading part. Gradually this venture came to a close through want of contributions rather than from want of readers' interest; for that which is everybody's business soon became nobody's. Lengthier and more serious papers on the subject by Udal were published in the *Proceedings of the Dorset Natural History and Antiquarian Field Club*, in *Somerset and Dorset Notes and Queries*, and in the *Dorset Year Book*. He had also written an article on Dorset folklore in the *Journal of the Folklore Society* in 1889.

When Udal began to collect items of the county folklore it was in an interleaved copy of Barnes' *Grammar and Glossary of the Dorset Dialect*, published in 1863, that he jotted them down until it became too small to hold them. Again, it was in the interleaved pages of the *Glossary* that he continued to enter any new dialect words he came across.

Although when he retired he lived for the most part in London, where he died on 13 March 1925, his ashes were buried in the churchyard at Symondsbury. Udal had lived for many years at the Manor House in that parish, and it was there that much of the original preparation of this volume took place. The *Bridport News*, when announcing his death in the issue of 20 March 1925, recorded, by the by, that whilst at Symondsbury he 'was greatly interested in local sport, and particularly in cricket, of which he was an ardent supporter. He frequently took part in the game and was a source of strength to the village club. His underarm lobs beguiled many an unsuspecting batsman, while in the batting department he was capable of putting up a useful score ... in the restoration of the Parish Church he displayed a keen interest, and generously defrayed the cost of one of the new windows that were placed in the sacred edifice ... as a county gentleman he was respected by all classes and nowhere will his death be more keenly felt than in West Dorset which he loved so well.'

It seems very likely that the idea of a folklore column in the *Dorset County Chronicle* was put into Udal's head by the Dorset antiquarian Charles Warne. When writing to William Barnes on 30 December 1881 Warne said 'I was pleased to see that a friend of mine has a letter in the DCC on the subject, what pleased me was that I had conferred with him on the subject, with which he became much interested. He is likely to become a good Antiquary and interested with Dorset. It is Mr – Udal I refer to, connected with the Udals and Simmonds' of the lower part of the County ..., the Mr Udal may be about 30 or 35 and is at the Bar. When here he called – and took all my works on Dorset.'

Udal apparently had come to know William Barnes in about 1876. Lucy Baxter when writing the life of her father, William Barnes (1801-1886), says 'Another visitor was J. S. Udal, Esq., a barrister who used to find time for a visit to the Rectory as often as his duties on circuit brought him near Came. Mr. Udal was of some assistance to the Dorset poet in sending him new words for the Glossary, which was always enlarging itself under his hand, and he returned the service by collecting legends and superstitions for Mr. Udal's contemplated work on the *Folk-lore of Dorsetshire*, for which, nearly ten years later, Barnes, at his request, wrote an introduction.'

Udal himself recounts in the *Dorset Year Book* for 1921 that when he was thinking of possible future publication he turned to Barnes 'with whom I was well acquainted' to ask him to write an introduction to the work. Barnes was then 'approaching his eighty-sixth year, and in very indifferent health, though his intellect was still keen and bright, and was mainly confined to his room, if not to his bed. He then wrote for me – without any knowledge of the actual materials I had collected, at his own leisure and in his own way, upon any odd ends or pieces of paper – what now forms his 'Fore-say' to my book – to my mind, by far the most interesting and valuable part of it.'

In 1885 Udal and Thomas Hardy took part in a meeting of the Field Club at the Iron Age hill-fort of Pilsdon Pen on 9 September. Udal was then living at the Manor House at Symondsbury, and had provided lunch for the Club that day. They did not know each other at the time, but Hardy wrote from Max Gate the next day 'Dear Sir, I had no opportunity of being introduced to you at the Field Club meeting yesterday, & did not write to say I was coming, I feel bound to send a line of thanks for your hospitality, & express my hope that at some future time I may have the pleasure of making your acquaintance.' Hardy's next surviving letter to Udal, on 23 July 1989, also refers to Field Club meetings, at Bridport and in Purbeck, and by that time they were on surname terms.

In a letter to Hardy, Udal wrote on 28 August 1910 'I am beginning to look forward in a few years to the quietude of retirement (I hope at Symondsbury) there I can at last settle down seriously to bring out my long contemplated work on Dorset Folklore, for which I still have poor old Barnes's 'Foreword', written for me in 1886 when he was lying on what turned out to be his deathbed! When I have retired I shall, I hope, be able to talk over these matters with you if not in Dorset then at the 'Athenaeum', by which time I ought to be up for election.' In this letter also he mentions that he had been 'put up for the Field Club by our old and common friend William Barnes ... at its outset.' When he died in 1925 Udal was one of the four original members of that Club.

Hardy and Udal continued to correspond, and in 1917 Hardy

wrote in answer to a letter seeking advice 'I see no objection to your using 'Dorsetshire' instead of 'Dorset' in the title of the Folklore book.'

The final preparations for publication made slow progress, but by 1920 Udal was able to write to the Rev. A. H. Barnes, grandson of the poet:

I am answering your card asking for a prospectus of my "D. F." in the hope & belief that you are the son of the Late Revd. W. M. Barnes (of Monckton & Dorchester) whom I knew well, & the grandson of the great William Barnes (the "Dorset Poet") whom I knew still better . . . I have been very chary in canvassing our clergy, knowing how severely they have suffered during the war & since. But I cannot resist the temptation of having one of the family of my dear old friend – your grandfather – as one of my subscribers . . . As you will see in the prospectus I attach the greatest importance to your grandfather's "Fore-Say" – & I think it should be a great "draw" for the book. How I wish it could have been published during his lifetime!

How have I fallen upon evil days indeed for it! No publisher I am told, would look at it under a guinea or 25/- a copy so, as I think that a very extravagant sum for such a book as mine, I am constrained to issue it by "subscription" & by dint of saving publisher's heavy commission & doing the distribution myself & other preliminary expenses, I am trying to issue it for the subscribers at 15/- a copy but at present prices of labour & material (& they seem to be rising still!) it will cost all *that, & every copy must moreover be sold, which is not at all likely to happen though I have no reason to be dissatisfied so far – & a good deal of ground remains still to be baited if I am not to be considerably "out of pocket".*

I do *want to have a photo of the Poet in it, as a frontispiece – but it all depends upon what happens. I have an awfully nice photo of your grandfather which he gave me himself, with his autograph on it, in 1886 – This is, I think, the same as the one appearing in* Thomas Hardy's *"selected" edition of the Poems, published in 1908. I wonder where he got it from! . . . Your father . . . told me if I recollect rightly – that he had the block of that photo: & also of the old thatched Rectory – which were quite at my service when the time came.*

I might be able to use one of them (the photographs) – your grandfather's – & I thought of getting it reproduced showing his poor, scrawling, but, to me, intensely interesting autograph at the foot of it.

The Society of Dorset Men were informed in an editorial note in 1922 of the early publication of *Dorsetshire Folk-Lore* by His Honour J. S. Udal. Subscribers were reminded that it was proposed, in the previous year, to issue an edition of 500 copies at the subscription price of 15/– each (plus postage) – the then estimated actual cost of publication. In the succeeding twelve months the cost had risen enormously. There were 274 subscribers ordering 295 copies. Udal had obtained a further estimate of what the cost of an edition of 350 copies only would be. This showed a loss of 7/6 per copy, or a fifty per cent increase in the price of every copy subscribed for. He therefore determined to close the subscription list as soon as it reached 300 volumes. The remaining 50 volumes were to be disposed of later, at a guinea each, in an attempt to recoup some portion of the heavy loss incurred on the subscriber's copies.

And so, some sixty years after conception, this remarkable record of the folklore of the county finally reached the shelves of predominantly private libraries. Only a third of the subscribers were in Dorset. Eleven were overseas, and the remainder in the United Kingdom, including one, Lords Cricket Ground, a most suitable subscriber in view of Udal's cricketing prowess.

R. N. R. PEERS

I am grateful to Laurence Keen for drawing my attention to the letter from Charles Warne to William Barnes.

CONTENTS

PAGE

Preface

Fore-say by William Barnes 1

Chapter I

Customs and Superstitions appertaining to Particular Days of the Calendar . . . 17

Chapter II

Customs appertaining to Particular Seasons of the Year 53

Chapter III

Local Customs 102

Chapter IV

Local Legends and Superstitions 142

Chapter V

Birth, Death, and Marriage Customs and Superstitions 177

Chapter VI

Witchcraft and Charms 201

Chapter VII

Superstitions relating to Natural History . . . 232

Chapter VIII

Weather-lore 262

PAGE

CHAPTER IX

MISCELLANEOUS CUSTOMS AND SUPERSTITIONS . . . 273

CHAPTER X

PROVERBS AND PROVERBIAL SAYINGS 288

CHAPTER XI

BALLADS AND SONGS 307

CHAPTER XII

CHILDREN'S GAMES AND RHYMES 333

INDEX 399

PREFACE

IT is not often, I should think, that an author carries about with him an introduction to a book now only just seeing the light written nearly forty years ago, and of which the writer was born more than 120 years ago! Yet, so it is. Not many months before he died in the autumn of 1886, William Barnes—usually known as the "Dorset Poet"—had at my request written an introduction—or "Fore-say", as he would have preferred to call it, for he scorned a Latin derivative—to a contemplated work of mine on Dorsetshire Folk-lore, for which I had collected a large quantity of material. This was a subject upon which he had never before written specifically (except in a few isolated instances in William Hone's works) but in which he had always greatly interested himself, as may be seen from his delightful dialect poems. This material of mine represented the gleanings of many years of inquiry and research, both in the county and elsewhere. To this "Fore-say", as I now call it,—it was an old term of his own,—(leaving to his great successor, Mr. Thomas Hardy, the use of the word "Fore-word", which he has for all time made peculiarly his own) I attach the highest value, as being, in my opinion, by far the most important part of my book. When one considers the circumstances in which it was composed—on what was practically his death-bed—by a man of great age and of feeble health, but of undimmed intellect—written upon any odd scrap of paper that came to hand—without knowledge of what material I had collected, though brimful of its elements—it is simply wonderful. As such I leave it, untouched by my hands and revered by me as his last and dying word of literary work.

A year or two after his death, and before I was able to complete my task, I left England to take up a Government legal appointment in the Colonies, from which I have not long retired. In the interim my work on folk-lore came practically to a standstill; though I may say that the delay brought some compensation as I was thereby enabled to add considerably to my collection of material, and had also the opportunity of contributing a good deal of it to the publications of our Dorset Field Club and the Folk-Lore Society.

On my retirement I commenced to put it all in order for publication. But shortly afterwards the Great War broke out, and again everything was delayed owing to the scarcity of labour and to the restrictions placed upon the use of paper. From these causes I found considerable difficulty in obtaining any publisher willing to undertake the publication of a book of this kind on his own responsibility. So in 1920 I made an effort to bring out the volume by way of subscription, and for this purpose issued a prospectus which was rendered abortive—at least temporarily—by the rapid rise in everything connected with the printing trade—more than 100 per cent over pre-war prices. At length, owing to the somewhat reduced figures of the last twelve months I have at last been enabled to bring it out—to a reduced number of subscribers, it is true, but nevertheless at the original subscription price.

And it was quite time I did so, for I found that in my long years of waiting several writers had helped themselves to much of the contents of my articles in the before-mentioned publications without the courtesy of the slightest acknowledgment of their indebtedness! Indeed, I am not at all sure that when this volume is issued I shall not be accused of plagiarizing from my own work! In works of a serious nature, such as anthropology and folk-lore, our best writers are always most particular to give chapter and verse for every statement made which is not their own. In my present volume this principle is fully carried out. I have given—principally in the text—the authority (there are more than a hundred separate ones) for every custom or superstition mentioned, every game described, every statement made. Where this is not attached my readers may rest assured that the statement is based upon my own personal inquiry and research or of those friends who have helped me in my collection. But it it is finished now. As I wrote in the *Folk-Lore Journal* in a long paper on Dorsetshire Children's Games in 1889 (which, with additions, forms the subject of my last chapter here) when speaking of the increasing difficulty one met with in obtaining exact information as to the games of our country children, and how they played: "If this is to be done, it must be done quickly; it is more than probable that *their* children will have none to tell."

No, such work cannot be done now. Our Board Schools have seen to that! Only very recently indeed have there been a few studied revivals in such matters. But the *survivals*—the genuine thing—no longer exist!

I claim no originality for my work. It is but a mere collection, a sheaf of gleanings, of what is left from old-time sources, with little or no attempt at any representation of comparative folklore. That will come from the folklorists of the future. My task to-day is to provide them with the materials for their studies—from a Dorset source and from a Dorset source alone.

It only remains for me to express my most grateful thanks to so many friends (whom it would be invidious to mention) who have so kindly helped me in my work—some for nearly half a century—and to the governing bodies of the Dorset Field Club, the Folk-Lore Society, *Notes and Queries* and the *Somerset and Dorset Notes and Queries* for their courteous permission to reproduce what I required from my various papers and articles in their publications.

For myself I am content. The fruits of my more than forty years' labour of love for our dear old county have at length been garnered in and put beyond all risk of loss. For this I am deeply indebted to the confidence and patience of my subscribers.

J. S. UDAL.

May, 1922.

FORE-SAY

BY

THE LATE REV. WILLIAM BARNES, B.D.
("The Dorset Poet").

FOLKLORE is a clear homely word for a wide field of homely knowledge, and lore is a good one in English word-making, for the Greek λόγος which has been so commonly brought into English speech for science, as in Biology—Lifelore; Dendrology—Treelore; Phytology—Wortlore; Philology—Speechlore; and for the names of other sciences for which λόγος has not been used, as Chemistry—Matterlore.

It may be that in the more common opinion of the upper ranks folklore is thought to be a narrower body of lore than it is in truth, and that it is a mislearnt body of mistaken faiths in cases of mind and matter, which should be all unlearnt as superstition or bad untruth.

Folklore, taken in broad meaning, is a body of home-taught lore, received by the younger folk from elder ones in common life, and in the forms of knowledge or faith, or mindskills and handskills; and so differing from the lore of schooling and books, which is often called by the people "book-learning", as they call a scholar a "book-learned man". Book-learning is that which is marked by the Greeks as *γραμματικὴ*—Booklore, from *γραμμα*—writ or a book, not our grammar or speech-craft. In Latin, "Literatura."

Much of the pure lore or knowledge that was formerly learnt as folklore is now given as booklore; but still, as bare theory is less trustworthy without practice, it is even now true that mindskills and handskills are better and more readily learnt by work under a skilled teacher than from a dead book. A chart alone does not fill the place of a pilot's home-won knowledge of a shore or haven; nor a map that of a Swiss guide up an Alp; and so a man's knowledge of his own neighbourhood is a kind of folklore of welcome help to a puzzled wayfarer. A geographical knowledge of the climates and of the breadth of the world-belts of sundry tribes of plants would not put a farmer, on coming to see a farm, above an old son of the parish in a knowledge of the growth-power of the soil of it; and a wayfaring stranger, well-schooled in geography, might be very glad to learn of such a villager the depth of the water, somewhat heightened by rain, at a ford of the parish, and the shortest way or best road to a town before him.

Folklore is of at least two levels of life, the level of the full-grown, and the level of boyhood or girlhood. Most of the lore of the work and life of the elders may be, and mostly is, learned of them by the youngers, rather after than ere their time of boyhood and girlhood; but there is a stream of lore which belongs more straitly to the life of the boy and girl, or the stripling, so that when children grow up to the years of that life they have the lore from their young mates who have already so learnt it.

This is the lore, among others, of children's games, and handskills in the making of tools, weapons, or toys, or fittings for their sports.

It may that as such things are now everywhere on sale in shops those handskills are less fully won than they formerly were. We, as boys, braided fishing lines of white horsehair, and made floats for them and hung them on a peeled withy wand, and made small rush baskets for our fish. Of a very roomy one we did not feel the want; and almost anybody could make a good whistle-pipe by drawing off the rind of a clean length of sappy ashen rod, and setting in a piece of the wood as a heading of the usual kind above the breath-hole. Our handskill did not reach so far as to cut a very good top without a lathe, but we knew that an eelskin would make a very good topwhip. To this level of folk-lore belonged the knowledge of the rules of children's games.

To folklore belong the customs by which folk may keep up the memory of the times and tides of the year, or of the thought-worthy haps which have befallen their forefathers. Thence some of our holidays or *festæ* (feasts), or, in old Saxon, *Freeols-daeges*, free days.

Christmastide is called "Yule", or "Yuletide", by a name of a festival of the heathen Anglo-Saxons. A.-Saxon *Geol*; Dan. *Yuul*; Swed. *Yul*; Satarland, *Yōl*; a wheel, or a wheel rolling, one rolling of the wheel of time, as a year; A.-Saxon *gear*.

Thence also " goal ", a starting and winning post of a race-course. The old Saxon " Yule " was New Year's Eve, the end and beginning of a year ; but our Christian fore elders shifted the " Yuletide " to the Nativity, which is very near to it. In old Dorset the tide seems to have been kept up with some customs of mirth and with a " Yule-log " or " Back brand ", a great log of wood burning against the back of the hearth, from within the old year into the new one ; a token, it may be, of the sun's new start for summer heat.

The Yuletide, as New Year's Eve, was, I suppose, personified in the Roman Janus with two faces, looking to both the old and new year. Janus is a masculine form of *janua*—a gate or gangway between the old and new year.

Christmas has still in Dorset, in some parishes and in some winters, the Mummers, who in tinsel and ribbons enact a little drama that sounds of the Holy Wars between the Christians and Turks. The waits—the old gleemen—and carol singers are less welcomed to folks' houses than they formerly were. The carol was, I suppose, so called as a night song, or " notturno ", sung under the window of the Beloved. Carol is from the Celtic *caru*, to love ; carol : belonging to love, a love-song. *Caróli* : to sing night songs, serenade.

Some years ago there was known in Dorset an old set of Twelfth Night lines somewhat of the form of " The House that Jack built ".[1]

In the time of the Saxon Ealdhelm, first Bishop of Sherborne, the mingled population of Saxons and Britons—which was more and more thickly British downward from Dorset to Land's End—could hardly have kept up Easter-tide with their Easter customs at the same time, since the British Christians kept the time of the Eastern church and the Saxons that of the Romish calendar.

From a book called " Jack-a-lent ", written by Taylor—the Water-Poet—it seems that in his time there was at the beginning of Lent a wonted procession with a thinly lean and ragged figure, betokening the Lenten feast and called Jack-a-lent ; and since a

[1] This was " The first day of Christmas my true love sent to me—" which was contained in the " Scrap-book " which Mr. Barnes handed to me a little time before his death in 1886. (See Chap. II, p. 80.)

scare-crow of a mock man in an old coat of rags and jags was formerly called in Blackmore Jack-a-lent, it is likely that the Lent Jack had had his day in Dorset.

Shrovetide was formerly marked in Dorset by a rough custom, called " Lent-crocking ", or the flinging of panshards at folks' doors, with a not over lowly petition for pan-cake or other fast day—if not unfasting—fare ; and among other kinds of fast day fare Dorset people were wont to eat " Firmety " (Frumentary). It is told of a poor woman of one of our parishes here in the west, when—as we can see by the old churchwardens' books—the celebrations of the Holy Communion were no more in a year than the three bidden by the canon, that on being asked how many sacraments there were, she answered, taking and mistaking the celebration for the sacrament, " Three—Easter, Christmas, and our Fair " (at Michaelmas).

Owing to the change of time brought into our calendar by the New Style, our month of May is earlier than was the merry month of May (a summer month) of our fore elders, and has its greensward less spangled with flowers, in less summerly hours, than had that on which they kept their May games, of which we have now few worthy of the name.

Dorset formerly had its maypoles ; but Shillingston, clustering round its softly rising knap, may now be the only Dorset village which keeps up the tall token of a merry May Day ; and the 29th of our May would hardly shine on oaks so leafy as was the one which hid King Charles II so wholly at Boscobel.

Whitsuntide is now a time commonly chosen for the yearly meeting of Friendly Societies—" Club-walkèn," as it is mostly called in Dorset. And Midsummer Eve does not yet in Dorset pass its few hours of twilight without some rites of divination among the girls to get a glimpse or two of their oncoming life as maid or wife.

Dorset had formerly some of the resources of mirth at friendly gatherings, the mazes or mizmazes, to be threaded by such as thought they would guide their feet to a more speedy outcoming than they could always find ; but the mazes are now levelled and lost with the May queens.

The Village wake—called in Dorset Feäst (*Festa*)—belonged mostly to the Christian seasons, as it was mainly holden at or near to the festival of the Saint to whom the village church was dedicated.

At some of these feasts, however, there was cudgel-playing; and I fear it cannot well be said that cudgel-fighting is the most fitting token of joy for the festival of St. Mary or St. John, albeit it be called play; but the feast brought to some houses of the parish merry meetings of friends with kindred and friends from elsewhere.

The 5th of November still gathers in some parishes of Dorset its fire-wielding youths to celebrate Guy Faux's night by flaring bonfires and flying fireworks, far more for fun than Faux, and rather as fire-worshippers than politicians.

Under the head of customs at set times we may give those of the *haining* [1] and stocking of common grass-fields at given days of the year. These customs of common field holdings and rights are some of the last belongings of the old Saxon (not to say British) village communities, who in Saxon times, under the law of folkland, held, for a common feeding of their cattle, land which the Norman kings changed into copyhold, and most of these commons have one by one been inclosed. At the stocking of Poundbury Field near Dorchester (now inclosed) on May Day, Dorchester folk were wont in the olden time, it is said, to go forth to its flowery and airy sward a-maying and to drink syllybub of fresh milk.

Proverbs.

Not the least of the branches of Folklore are Proverbs. A proverb—Latin: *Proverbium*. In A.-Saxon, *cwythe*—a saying, from *cwaethe*, to say. In German, Dutch, Swedish, its name means a saying or word. In Greek and Hebrew, a likening. In English, a saying, say or saw, from the A.-Saxon *saegan*, to say.

A proverb is a short form of words, giving for wisdom some so believed truth of good and evil as found in a long run of life in which

> "Long experience doth attain
> To something of prophetic strain".

The Saxon and English names of the proverb seem very good ones for it; as is the name "a likening" of the Greek and Hebrew.

[1] Laying up for grass.

It is also a " warn-saying " or a " waren-saw " for the warening (or making folk ware) of the likely outcome of a deed or behaviour.

Of English proverbs, earlier and later, there is a vast body; and many collections of them have from time to time been published, as that by Lydgate, 1385; R. Palmer, 1539; John Heywood, 1562; John Ray, whose collection may yet be the main one in its last edition. Monsr. Duplessis gives some proverbs of the Cavaliers on the Roundheads; and one of them on their want of reverence for holy things, is " As stiff as a Puritan's knee, which will not bend to him that made it ". Many forms of English folkspeech have a few proverbs of their own shires of England, as Dorset folk have some which they may have formed themselves from things of Dorset life, as:

" The vu'st bird, the vu'st eäs."
(The first bird, the first earthworm.)
First come, first served.

Two proverbs which give truths of man's life and mind, wherever he may dwell, may be found alike in sundry lands and tongues; or may teach the same truth as drawn from the behaviour of sundry things, as forecast may be taught from the emmet or bee, or from the bee or beaver. We say " Union is strength "; but Monsr. Duplessis gives an old and good English proverb which gives the same truth with a case in which it may readily be seen by any man in himself, " The fist is stronger than the hand " (for hitting or holding) " though it be only the hand."

A friend (Mrs. Hale), who lived some years in Jamaica, gathered a body of proverbs in the speech-form of the dark race, by whom they are in common use, and seem clearly to have been formed. I believe them worthy of our attention as they show what kind of a body of wisdom has been formed by the wit of poor souls who were through many generations unfree.[1]

Among the Iolo Manuscripts is a body of 160 British proverbs, or like-sayings, called the sayings of the wisemen (*Chwedlau'r Doethion*). They are given as the sayings of old Britons of mark, bards, holy men, princes, and others, and are put into verse of the form of the " Warriors' Triplet "—" Triban milwr "—a triad

[1] There were some two or three dozen of these in the scrap-book already mentioned.

or verse of three lines with endings of one rhime sound, which is deemed to be the earliest form of Bardic verse, as:

> "Hast heard the saying, ever right,
> Of some old giver-forth of light?
> 'Eager is truth to come to sight.'"

Truth cannot be hidden.

A saw of Cadwalader:

> "Hast heard the saw not ill express'd,
> Cadwalader's of high behest?
> 'The Fork that makes the plough's the best.'"

This is interesting, as it betokens the olden time when the plough (sull) was made of a fork of a length of a stem and of a limb of a tree. Calwalader thus praised tillage.

Of Cynllwg, a Bard:

"You have received good as long as you have not received evil." The good of mercy in freedom from evil.

Of Carátoc—the Caractacus of Roman history:

> "Hast heard the saying, good to scan,
> Of high Carátoc, son of Brân?
> 'Long theft to hanging brings a man.'"

Of Brân, the Blessed, Father of Caractacus:

> "There is none good but God alone."

This is very interesting as a confirmation of British history.

Brân, the father of Caractacus, is said in history to have brought the Christian faith to Britain from Rome where he had received it; and two of these triplets go to confirm British history, for one of them calls Caractacus the "son of Brân", and this one gives as a wise saying of Brân a Gospel text, the words of Our Lord—Matt. xix, 17. The triad of the three Blessed Kings of Britain gives Brân as the first of them, as he first brought a knowledge of the Christian faith to the Cymry from Rome, where he had been for seven years as a hostage for his son Caractacus.

Of Bengwlad: against reckless doings:

> "It is easier to burn a house than to build it."

There are some thirty of such triplets of the sayings of animals that speak in fables; and at the end of them it is said:

> "Happy is the man who is as wise as the pig."

The triplet of the pig's wise saw being,

> "Hast thou heard of the saying of the pig
> Keeping himself from filthy doings?
> 'There is none so loathsome as a drunkard.'"

In the words of Llywarch Hên (?), the Prince Bard of the fifth year-hundred is a set of proverbial triplets called "*Gorwynion*"—Glittering Things—as the first line speaks of the top of some tree or shrub:

> "Bright are the oak tops,
> Bitter are the ash tips,
> Sweet the hedge shelter,
> Loud the waves roar,
> The face cannot hide off
> The heart's painful sore."

It may be markworthy that the Italians have many and still form more little triplets of a form like that of the British *Gorwynion*, and beginning with the name of a flower or tree. These little triplets are called *Stornelli*, and are sometimes formed by simple land folk, and are mostly of very pretty thoughts, and make a nice body of folklore with a pattern of verses far better than much of the balderdash sometimes sent among us in valentine letters, as:

> "Blossom of lemon,
> You my first love have been,
> And again you shall be
> My last love as well
> If only you like me."

Duplessis gives some samples of thwarted proverbs (p. 389), as:

P. "Everything hath an end.
A. Not so. A ring hath not."
P. "The pride of the rich makes the labours of the poor.
A. Not so. The labours of the poor make the pride of the rich."

Of Persian proverbs many are found in the Gulistân (Rose Garden) of Sadi of Shiraz.

"Service to kings is like a voyage on the sea, gainful but hazardous." (p. 38.)
"To kindle a fire between two men is to burn yourself amid them."

Some of the Persian proverbs on self warding against foes

mark the strong difference between the Gospel and the worldly mind, or the Koran if they are drawn from it. One is:

"Whoever hath an adversary in his power and doth not kill him is a foe to himself."

"Allow not your foe to string his bow while you can pierce him with an arrow."

"He who spareth the life of a serpent wrongs the sons of Adam."

We need not wonder to find that the Italian—a later form of Latin, which itself was rich in proverbs—should have a full store of them; and the Spanish has a great wealth of that branch of folklore from which Sancho Panza is given as wise enough to speak forth so readily with the wisdom of others; and Duplessis, himself a Frenchman, handles very fully the rich store of French proverbs. In the speech of Gascony—which is one formed by the grafting of French or Latin on the Iberian, but which is more like French than is the Spanish—are many proverbs in rhiming couplets, longer or shorter.

"A paraules lourdes,
Aurelies sourdes."
(To witless words, heedless ears.)
"He who cannot dissemble cannot govern."

It is markworthy how some kindreds of men, though wide asunder, hold the same point of wisdom in the same saying, drawn from the same truth in nature; and others teach the same point by other saws from other truths.

"A rolling stone gathers no moss" is so in Gascony. For the Latin saw "Love and a cough cannot be hidden" the Gascon is "Love, a cough, and smoke cannot be hidden".

"Don't put all your eggs in one basket" is in Russian "Don't hang all on one nail". The French "The game is not worth the candle" is in Russian "The horse is not worth the oats".

"Many men, many minds," is found in Hindustani as well as English. "To kill two birds with one stone" is in Dutch "To catch two flies at one dab". "Many a slip between the cup and the lip," and "Sleep with dogs and rise with fleas", are found in Gascony. As a warning against high living the Gascon has "A fat kitchen, a lean will". In Russian—the speech of a folk mainly in serfdom—arose the proverb "Better be poor and free than a rich slave".

Mottos.

Mottos are mainly akin to proverbs, and some of them are purely so. Those of the higher kind are a form of heraldic man marks, giving, each one, the so shown strong bent of a man's mind and will. Hence they are called " symbols " or " tokens ", as mind-tokens. Many mottos are words of high wisdom and calls to righteous behaviour and noble aims, and form a good body of folklore worthy of keeping in mind ; and though many of them are used by the high and mighty, kings and nobles, as man marks to lead followers to honour by cry or banner, yet the common land folk have, almost each one, some pet principle which comes often from his lips, as :

" Upright an' downstrait vor me ; " or,
" Do what's right, and face the light."

Ulpii Traiani.

" Qualis rex,
Talis grex."
" Such the king,
Such the folk."

M. Aurelii Severi.

" Qui emit, vendat, oportet."
(He who buys, must sell—a good one against one-sided free trade.)

H. Magni Maximi.

" A peril is never overcome without a peril."

Frederici I.

" Qui nescit dissimulare, nescit regnare."

This is found as a Gascon proverb for a tyrant :—

" He who is feared, fears."

The Romans had some noble mottos :—

" Fiat justitia, ruat coelum."
" Quod non justum, non expediens."

The great motto of the British Bards :—

" Truth before the world and in the face of the sun."

Symbols.

In the olden time when there were no other books than handwritten ones, and they as such were of too high a cost for the shelves of the poor, the devising and knowledge of sight-tokens or symbols was a great branch of folklore ; and much knowledge of Christian history and faith was learnt from sight-tokens in the church, which taught the onlookers more clearly than would the names given in letters. The Cross was read the Christian Faith ; the Dove as the Holy Ghost ; Faith was known by her anchor ; St. Michael by his sword. The Bible and Crown betoken the Church and State. A beehive and a hand-in-hand on the flag of a Friendly Society would betoken to those who could not read work and forecast, and friendship or brotherhood ; and the three rays as of light in a Welsh newspaper is a call to read something of Bardship ; and some other eye-tokens bespeak something of Freemasonry.

Of course, everyone could not read every symbol. A lady friend had some time ago an emblem of geography in the shape of a woman with a globe in one hand and holding a pair of compasses on it with the other. A little boy, the son of a neighbour, having looked thoughtfully on it for some time, said : " What is that woman a-doing with that apple and the clothes-pin ? "

Charms.

Under the share of folklore which is mostly reckoned as superstition may be taken charms, witchcraft, and self-showing ghosthood. Charms or spells have seemingly always been a share of the folklore of Dorset, as of all of England.

A charm (Saxon : *cyrm*) is by its first meaning a mingled sound of voices of men or birds, and in folklore it seems to mean a form of muttered words ; and a spell was a form of words, and then also a message, whence Godspel—Go'spel, the Good-message. A telegram is indeed a wire spell, and a telegraph a spell wire.

It seems from the Latin word *incantatio* for a charm that among the Romans the charm was uttered in a singing voice. A very common work of charming in Dorset is that of the charming away of warts, which we must believe is an easy one for so mighty a form of magical might ; but it is sometimes tried on very bad, if not deadly, ailings in cattle.

The following is a very old charm of our race—a charm against a worm—from the old Saxon [1] :—

[1] From the *All- und Angel-sachsisches lesebuch*, by Max Rieger.

The following is a translation :—

"Go out, worm,
With bad little worms ;
Out from the marrow
to the bone ;
From the bone
to the flesh ;
Out from the flesh
to the hide ;
Out from the hide (or skin)
to this arrow.
O Lord, be it so.—"

Witchcraft.

There are still, I believe, in Dorset many folk who believe that they have been or may be somewhat the worse for witchcraft, whatever they may have done on the teachings of old folklore to thwart the witches' power. From an old deposition on witchcraft in Dorset, we find that at some meetings which the witches held at night on a common they made a waxen man-shape and christened it (*christened* it, forsooth !) with the name of some unhappy man who was to be bewitched ; and thereafter he was to be bewitched and his likeness was to be pricked with pins, which would give him the pangs of thorns in his flesh ; or his waxen other self was to be holden before a fire, so that at the melting of it he himself would pine away. And we find in the answer of the witch of Horace, Canidia, that she was wont to use the same like wicked mystery with waxen statuary.[1]

The Dorset name for the dragon-fly is " hoss tinger "—horse tinger—and homely Dorset folk are sometimes laughed at by others who are rather more highly schooled for the ignorance in which they can believe that the dragon-fly " stingers " horses. However, carters, who have never seen a dragon-fly sting a horse, may understand the word ; our fore elders did not give it as meaning a " horse-stinger ", or stinger of horses ; it is a " horse-tinger ", or " horse-tanger ". A " ting " or " tang " is that which " tings " out long, as the tang of a buckle or knife-blade, or " tang ", the long sea-weed ; and " horse " means coarse or big, and " horse-tinger " means the big, very long fly. " Horse "

[1] *Canidiæ Responsio*, Epodon xvii.

does not mean the animal, but coarse or big, as "horse-chestnut", "horse mushroom", "horse radish." A horse was, I suppose, so called as being big with our forefathers, where they had no elephant, nor the great wild buffalo—"Reem" of the Bible.

A like mistake seems to be shown in the spelling of the name of the bird "wheatear", as if our fore elders had thought it like an ear of wheat. I suppose the Saxons called it the *hwitaer*, "white rump", as our boys now call it. Not unlike that mistake is another of the "ear wig", which some believe was so called from a silly belief that it is wont to crawl into a man's ear. I suppose the Saxons called it "Eor-wicga" or "Ear-wigga", as being "eor" or "ear"—longeking: "wigga,"—worm. "Eor" or "ear" for an ear of a dog or of corn means that which ekes more or less out.

Soothsaying by the behaviour of animals, which may not be an ill-grounded lore, as weather wisdom may broaden out into a belief that they show trustworthy tokens of oncomings of good or evil haps in the life of folk who meet with them as such.

I cannot say that a dog could never smell, or that some other animal could never feel, ere men may be aware of it, the foulness in the air which might cast into his blood the heat of the fever or other sickness; or that it may never betoken by its behaviour under its forefeeling of coming foul morning.

Augury—or soothsaying from the behaviour of birds—which with Etruscans and Romans was deemed worthy of a priesthood, is not without faith in Dorset folklore of the forefeeling of a coming storm by birds, which therefrom gave a foretoken of it though it was not understood. A landowner of Ireland, Sir John Lesley, gave me a sample. He had, near his house, a wood which was a night home of a body of rooks which had seemingly the right of grubbing in a streech [1] of land for some miles around it. (We have in this neighbourhood such a night home of a community of rooks—Rokewood—Roc being the old Saxon form of rook, and showing that it was in Saxon times the rooks' night home, whence they went out in flocks round the neighbourhood and came back to it in the evening to roost.) So

[1] The space taken in at one *striking* of the rake. See *Glossary*, p. 91.

some years ago the Irish rooks came home one evening, but instead of roosting in the trees of the wood they squatted for the night on the ground near to it, and in the night many of the trees in which they would otherwise have roosted were wrecked by a furious storm.

Game Rhimes.

Game rhimes used by children in their round games are a kind of folklore of the lower level of life, though they are mostly called " nursery " rhimes, as some of them are wont to be sung by mothers and nurses to children in the lap.

I am ready to believe that those which are clearly rather game verses than nursery rhimes were made by clever children ; since if the girl is mother to the woman, there is wit in girls or boys as in their elders, and many play-games that are good may as such have come down in the stream of childhood folklore, while others may have been lost.

Justus Halbertsma says in his *Lexicon Frisicum* that Friesic children, on beginning a many-mated game, pitch—just as ours—for fairness on the one who is to be the beginner by a kind of lot. One of them goes round by the others in a ring, singing a verse of play rhimes, and touches each in row, one at each word or syllable ; and the last one so touched is the first to begin the game, and is called by the Friesic children the " Bokke " (Buck). He gives the ending of a play-rhime—not far unlike our " Hiccory, dickery, dock ", etc.—and which, he says, he was wont as a boy to say almost daily :

" Ikkè, likkè, mikkè,
Tik, tak, tè,
Wile, wolle, wè."

Some lullabies composed as such might have been chosen by children for game rhimes, and many lullabies might have been composed by nurses, mothers, or girls ; but it seems to me from much of the wording of game rhimes that they were composed by children and as lot rhimes for pitching, as by a kind of lot, on the " Buck " or first player, so as to show no unfair choice as of one more worthy than the others.[1]

[1] Mr. Barnes gives several versions of " counting out " or " lot " rhymes in his scrap-book before mentioned, which are later referred to in my chapter on " Children's Games " (xii), and in this " Fore-say "

Wortlore.

There were in the wortlore of the physicians of olden time two things which may have come down to the folklore of the wise women ; a belief that herbs were, each one, under the dominion of one of the planets from which it had some power, and that many worts bore somewhere in their bodies some shape (signature) or hue of the limb or ailing which it was meant to heal.

A. Culpepper's *English Physician* (1799) tells what planet governeth every wort or tree, and says of " Pilewort " that it is so called as being healsome to piles. He says : " If you dig up the root of it, you shall perceive the perfect image of the disease which they commonly call the piles."

" Liverwort," so called from the liver shape of the " thallus " (a signature) used for disease of the liver (Prior).

" Lungwort " (*pulmonaria*) was thought to have in its spotted leaves a signature of a diseased lung, and to be healsome to it.

Herblore.

The herblore of the wise women with our fore elders was a branch of folklore of which most mothers took some care to get some knowledge ; and their belief in the healing power of worts cannot well be called superstitious or idle, since the most learned physicians now use them, who can now afford to laugh at the old wives for their use of burnt sponge in cases now handled with iodine, which is drawn from sea worts. Nobody then knew iodine by body or name, but its power was found without a name in sponge.

Time and tide brought round the great fairs of the olden time, when each fair, one after another, was for its neighbourhood a great mart of wares brought round on the backs of strings of pack-horses; and it was the custom of the folk to buy in a stock of goods, as far as they wanted or could afford them, for

he refers to a letter he had received from an American gentleman in 1874 who had published a paper on Folklore and Children's Games in a Massachusetts newspaper. Mr. Barnes says :—

" The letter seems interesting to me as it shows how truthful in form much of the folklore of Old England, and above all that of the games, had been taken over to New England by the children of the early settlers and how well it has been given down by young to young."

the year, even in some cases of butchers' meat to salt down for the winter. There was no great run of years of many generations between the last train of pack-horses and the first railway train between Liverpool and Manchester.

The feasts of Harvest-Home—in which the work folk were invited to

" The hall
where beards wagged all,—"

to share of mirth and meat under the smiles of the master and mistress, as tokens of approbation of their work, are now less customary than they formerly were, as in these commercial days it seems to be felt that the clock measures all the workman owes his master, and the paytable all that the master owes to him.

It should not be understood that we ought not to give, in a body of Dorset folklore, any that, as such, reaches beyond it into other shires. Neither folklore, nor a form of folk speech, is confined by the outline of a county ; and if no piece of Dorset folklore should be given in a book of Dorset folklore because it is found also in Somerset, Devon, Wilts, or Hants, then it should not be given in a book of the folklore of either of those shires, because it is found in Dorset ; and so, as there is not likely to be any shire the folklore of which does not reach into a neighbouring one, there should not be published any book of English folklore at all. It may be very well to know that Dorset had any one piece of lore of its own, but this would fall very short of broad work of the study of man's mind in his folklore ; which is to find how far the children of men have sundry forms of such lore in common and how far sundry races differ in their ratings of what we may deem weighty truths and high wisdom.

CHAPTER I

CUSTOMS AND SUPERSTITIONS APPERTAINING TO PARTICULAR DAYS OF THE CALENDAR

To the plain and homely definition of the word "Folk-lore" given by the late Rev. William Barnes, B.D.—our "Dorset Poet"—in his "Fore-say" to this book—a meaning expressive of the fullest scope of my work—I would like to add that of another Dorset writer, even another Dorset schoolmaster, one whose chief recreation in an active and busy life has been the study of bird life and lore, a study carried on mainly in his own county—the late R. Bosworth Smith of Bingham's Melcombe. In his most delightful book *Bird Life and Bird Lore* (published in 1909, mainly from papers contributed to the *Nineteenth Century Review* and other journals) occurs this most happy expression: "Folk-lore is the débris of paganism, often colouring, or coloured in its turn by Christian legends or traditions." This definition, I feel sure, may be extended to many of the customs of our ancestors that have survived to us.

Perhaps no better subject upon which to commence a work upon local folk-lore could be found than the customs and superstitions which appertain or belong to the days and seasons of the year. It is the system adopted by that early writer upon our "popular antiquities", John Brand—there was then no such comprehensive term known as "folk-lore"—whose work (itself founded upon Rev. Henry Bourne's studies [1]) revised and enlarged by modern commentators is still the model which most of us plain folk would, I think, desire to follow rather than the more scientific syllabus tabulated by the Folk-lore Society in its *Handbook of Folk-lore.* But in so doing I have felt some difficulty in deciding as to which is the better plan or scheme of division of this subject, for it seems to me too wide to deal with as a whole. So I have thought it better to make two chapters of it, the first relating solely to the customs and

[1] *Antiquitates Vulgares,* Newcastle, 1725.

superstitions appertaining to particular days in our national church calendar, leaving for the second those customs which belong to particular times and seasons of the year, in each case arranged in chronological order.

In this first division as to calendar customs and superstitions it is not surprising, perhaps, that I have not been able to obtain any very large amount of material, when one considers that Dorsetshire, as one of those western counties which from the sturdy part it took in the religious movements of the day, could scarcely be expected to give any strong adhesion to those customs or superstitions which revolved round the particular saints or events enumerated in the church calendar of the old faith. I think that I may fairly assume, therefore, that such of these as still exist are mostly of pre-Reformation origin, and of which some again have survived from the days of paganism, tolerated by the early church or absorbed in its rites and ceremonies.

Before commencing the subject I should like to call attention to a suggestion I made more than forty years ago (I find that it was in 1881) that a " Folk-lore Column " should be started in the *Dorset County Chronicle*, the leading county newspaper, for the collection and preservation of all items that came under the term " Dorset Folk-lore ".

The editor gave a ready assent, and the idea was cordially supported by the Dorset public generally; amongst the contributors being the late Rev. William Barnes—better known, perhaps, as the " Dorset Poet "—Miss M. G. A. Summers, and other well-known Dorset writers; I myself also supplying material from time to time. After the death, however, of the Dorset poet in 1886 and my own departure from England a few years afterwards the project appeared to languish, though the columns of the *Dorset County Chronicle*, which has always taken a great interest in all that concerns the antiquities of the county, have always been open to any contribution of the kind.

Some excuse, moreover, may be found in the fact that the publications of the Dorset Field Club and the *Somerset and Dorset Notes and Queries* were beginning to form a receptacle for lengthier and more serious articles on the subject. To all these three publications students of Dorset folk-lore must ever be indebted for much valuable assistance.

New Year's Day

It was from this source then, namely, a correspondent of the *Dorset County Chronicle* in December, 1891, that I am able to give the following item which being more extensive than mere " weather lore "—a subject which I deal with later [1]—may claim, I think, to come under this chapter also.

It reads like a prophecy from *Old Moore's Almanac* or one of Mother Shipton's, and there is certainly an old-world savour about it, but I cannot give the actual source whence it was taken. It treats upon what we may expect should New Year's Day fall upon a Thursday.

" Winter and summer windie. A rainie harvest. Therefore we shall have overflowings; much fruit; plentie of honey; yet flesh shall be deare; cattel in general shall die; great troubles; warres."

Twelfth Day
(*6th January*)

So called from its being the twelfth and last day of Christmas, counting from the Nativity. It is sometimes called " Old Christmas Day ". It is considered to be the last day upon which it is lawful to eat mince- or minced-pies, which are essentially a Christmas dish. To eat one on each of the twelve days of Christmas is said to ensure for the eater entire happiness for the ensuing year, or, failing that, one happy month for each mince-pie so eaten. In some parts of Dorsetshire, however, it is said that to procure the desired result each mince-pie must be of a different person's " make ", or must be eaten at a different house.

As to the " Wassailing "—or drinking the health—of apple trees on the Eve of Twelfth Day, see Chapter VII, p. 251.

Candlemas Day
(*2nd February*)

Evidently so called from the candles or lights which were distributed and carried about in olden times upon that day.

William Hone, in his *Every-Day Book,* vol. i, p. 107 (1826), gives the following from a Dorset source. He speaks of a gentleman having communicated a custom which he had witnessed at Lyme Regis in his juvenile days. To what extent

[1] See Chapter VIII.

it prevailed he was unable to say, his knowledge being limited to the domestic circle wherein he was included. He says :—

" The wood-ashes of the family being sold throughout the year as they were made, the person who purchased them annually sent a present on Candlemas-day of a large candle. When night came the candle was lighted, and, assisted by its illumination, the inmates regaled themselves with cheering draughts of ale and sippings of punch, or some other animating beverage, until the candle had burnt out. The coming of the Candlemas candle was looked forward to by the young ones as an event of some consequence ; for, of usage, they had a sort of right to sit up that night and partake of the refreshment till all retired to rest, the signal for which was the self-extinction of the Candlemas candle."

Candlemas Day—or Eve—was the great occasion in Dorsetshire, as in other counties, when all Christmas decorations, such as holly, mistletoe, and evergreens, should be taken down in accordance with Herrick's well-known lines :—

" Down with the rosemary and bays,
Down with the mistletoe," etc.

But care should be taken that they are not thrown away as ordinary rubbish, but should be entirely destroyed in the fire. If otherwise, it portends death or misfortune to some one of the household before another year is out.[1]

In Dorsetshire, apparently, Candlemas Day is mostly known to the rustic public as affording portents or omens of what the weather is likely to be for the rest of the winter, as shown by what it is on Candlemas Day. But as this more properly comes under the subject of " Weather-lore ", which forms Chapter VIII of this work, I will reserve any further observations for that section.

St. Valentine's Day
(14*th February*)

Amongst my Dorset notes for this day I find one from the *Illustrated London News* in February, 1880, which states that on St. Valentine's Day the maids suspend in the kitchen a nosegay of early flowers tied up with a " true-lover's knot " of blue ribbon. It is not stated, however, what was the object or purpose of this

[1] Conf. *Shropshire Folk-lore*, p. 245.

act; though it is not difficult, I think, to believe that it indicated some manifestation or expression connected with the young women's attitude towards those subjects to which the lover's Saint's day is dedicated.

Somewhat akin to this, perhaps, is the belief that it is unlucky if a male is not the first visitor that comes to the house on St. Valentine's Day.

Formerly in Dorsetshire, as elsewhere, large numbers of "valentines" were exchanged between young people, a practice to which this day gave special licence; some of these, especially those sent in ridicule, being both vulgar and wanting in good taste. A great improvement has, however, set in in late years with regard to this; and now the custom is mostly confined in regard to "valentines" to the exchange or sending of presents of a more useful or valuable nature.

Hone, in his *Every-Day Book*, vol. i, p. 118, records a custom which prevailed many years since in the West of England, and may well, therefore, be known in Dorsetshire, although I am not myself personally acquainted with it:—

"Three single young men went out together before daylight on St. Valentine's Day, with a clapnet to catch an old owl and two sparrows in a neighbouring barn. If they were successful and could bring the birds to the inn without injury before the females of the house had risen they were rewarded by the hostess with three pots of purl in honour of St. Valentine, and enjoyed the privilege of demanding at any house in the neighbourhood a similar boon. This was done, it is said, as an emblem that the owl, being the bird of wisdom, could influence the feathered race to enter the net of love as mates on that day, whereon both single lads and maidens should be reminded that happiness could alone be secured by an early union."

Shrove Tuesday

Lent-crocking.—Also known as Pancake Day. Dorsetshire was not behind other counties in the usual festive observances commemorative of this day. That especially applicable to its name of "Pancake Day" was the custom of "Lent-crocking"—the name speaks for itself—which obtained in many parts of the county.

The earliest reference to "Lent-crocking" that I can find

from a Dorset source is from the pen of the Dorset poet himself, the Rev. William Barnes, in Hone's *Year Book*, p. 800 (ed. 1832), which, as it gives a very graphic description of the custom, racy as the soil, I give in full :—

" In some of the villages of Dorsetshire and Wiltshire the boys, at Shrovetide, still keep up a custom called *Lent-Crocking*, which originated in the carnival of Roman Catholic times, and consists in going round in the evening to pelt the doors of the inhabitants with pieces of broken crockery.

" In Dorsetshire the boys sometimes go round in small parties, and the leader goes up and knocks at the door, leaving his followers behind him armed with a good stock of potsherds—the collected relics of the washing-pans, jugs, dishes, and plates that have become the victims of concussion in the unlucky hands of careless housewives for the past year. When the door is opened the hero, who is perhaps a farmer's boy, with a pair of black eyes sparkling under the tattered brim of his brown milking-hat, covered with cow's hair and dirt like the inside of a blackbird's nest, hangs down his head, and, with one corner of his mouth turned up into an irrepressible smile, pronounces, in the dialect of his county, the following lines composed for the occasion, perhaps, by some mendicant friar whose name might have been suppressed with the monasteries by Henry VIII :—

' I be come a shrovin,
Vor a little pankiak,
A bit o' bread o' your biakin,
Or a little truckle cheese o' your own miakin.
If you'll gi' me a little I'll ax no more,
If you don't gi' me nothin I'll rottle your door.' [1]

" Sometimes he gets a piece of bread and cheese ; and at some houses he is told to be gone, when he calls up his followers to send their missiles in a rattling broadside against the door. In Wiltshire the begging of pancake and bread and cheese is omitted ; and the Lent-crockers pelt the doors as a matter of course.

" The broken pots and dishes originally signified that, as Lent was begun, those cooking vessels were of no use, and were supposed to be broken ; and the cessation of flesh-eating is understood in the begging of pancakes and bread and cheese."

In 1872 F. C. H. (the well-known Rev. Dr. F. C. Husenbeth) in *Notes and Queries* (Ser. IV, ix, 135) referred to a Dorset custom

[1] In later editions of his poems Barnes softened down the vowels " ia " of the rich Doric of the Blackmore Vale into " eä ". See Chapter II, p. 65 (n.).

of boys going about at Shrovetide with potsherds to throw at people's doors. These were tolerated, but they were not allowed to throw stones. As they called at the various houses they used to sing this doggerel :—

"I'm come a-shroveing,
For a piece of pancake,
Or a piece of bacon,
Or a little truckle cheese
Of your own making.
Give me some or give me none,
Or else your door shall have a stone."

I replied (p. 208) calling attention to the interesting account of this custom given in Chambers' *Book of Days* (1864, vol. i, p. 239), and there spoken of as existing in Dorset and Wilts. I added a second verse, as given in Chambers, which savours more of the old vernacular speech. Chambers also gives a first verse which varies somewhat from that furnished by F. C. H.

The second verse is as follows :—

"A-shrovin, a-shrovin,
I be come a-shrovin,
Nice meat in a pie,
My mouth is very dry!
I wish a wuz zoo well-a-wet
I'de zing the louder for a nut.

Chorus: A-shrovin, a-shrovin,
We be come a-shrovin."

I may say that at that time I was not aware that the account in Chambers, though not the verses, was taken directly from Barnes's description in the *Year Book* given above.

Many years ago the late Rev. W. K. Kendall, of East Lulworth, sent me some MSS. containing various references to Dorset customs and superstitions which he had met with. His remarks as to this particular custom are well worth giving. He says :—

"I am told by a Portlander that it is still the custom for boys on Shrove Tuesday to go round the villages throwing stones, etc., at the doors of the houses. The following doggerel is sung :—

'Slit, slat, sling,
If you don't give me a pancake
I'll make your doors ring.'

"On this account Shrove Tuesday is called 'Pansherding Day'. This custom has been observed also at West Lulworth until very lately.

"In the parish of Berwick St. James also the children go a-shroving. On Shrove Tuesday they sing the following verses from house to house :—

'We are coming shroving,
For a piece of pan-cake,
For a piece of chuckle cheese,
Of your own making.
Is the pan hot,
Is the pan cold,
Is the peas in the pot,
Nine days old ?
Is the knives and forks whet ?
Is the bread and cheese cut ?
Is the best barrel tapped ?
For we are come shroving.' "

The following account of the custom as occurring at Stalbridge, in the northern part of the county, is taken from the Rev. W. S. Swayne's pamphlet on the *History and Antiquities of Stalbridge* (1889), p. 36 :—

"On Shrove Tuesday evening the boys of the parish were accustomed to pelt the doors of the inhabitants with shards and tiles ; this was called keeping Pan-shard night.

"The traditional account was that when King Alfred raised his banner at Stourhead the inhabitants of the neighbouring villages were in this way summoned to join him. This custom died a natural death soon after the passing of Sir Robert Peel's new Police Act."

The Rev. Herbert Pentin, late Vicar of Milton Abbey, in the northern part of the county, contributes an interesting account of this custom as still practised in that parish to the *Proceedings* of the "Dorset Field Club" for 1904 (vol. xxv, p. 4). After telling us that the sports in Old Milton were badger-baiting under the cedar trees in the Abbey churchyard, cock-squailing, cock-fighting, and playing of fives outside the west end of the church, whilst bowls were played on the bowling-green and ringing was very popular, Mr. Pentin goes on to say :—

"During Lent the children went 'Shroving' and 'Lent-crocking'. On Shrove-Tuesday the children, carrying sticks, knocked at the doors of the principal residents and repeated this doggerel verse :—

'Please I've come a-shroving
For a piece of pancake
Or a little ruckle cheese
Of your own making.
If you don't give me some,
If you don't give me none,
I'll knock down your door
With a great marrow bone
And away I'll run.'

"The result of this threat was that the children were given half-pence, apples, eggs, a piece of pancake, or a piece of ruckle cheese. A ruckle cheese was a small sour-milk home-made cheese weighing about a pound. It could be rucked, i.e. rolled along the ground. Hence its name.[1] In the evening the 'Lent-crocking' began. Those people who had not given the children anything when they came 'a-shroving' were then rewarded by having pieces of broken crockery and pans and other missiles thrown at their doors. In this way real damage was often done.

"The practice of shroving still exists in the present village of Milton; it is one of the customs which have survived the demolition of the old town. It exists in other parishes, but is gradually dying out."

See also a similar account by the same writer in *Memorials of Old Dorset* (1907, pp. 111–12).

Sometimes, it would appear, an attempt was made by the owner or occupier of the house whose door was so battered to derive some personal advantage out of "Lent-crocking" by a selfish limitation or variation of the old custom.

A correspondent (T. B. G.) in the *Somerset and Dorset Notes and Queries* (1889, vol. i, p. 158), states that in the early days of the century a schoolmaster at Cerne was accustomed to permit each boy to hurl against the school door a log of wood, no matter what the weight; and great were the efforts to break through, or, at least, crack the venerable oak, well studded with iron. But nothing of the kind happened; the only tangible result being the accumulation of a handsome pile of fuel for future use of the wily pedagogue.

But in later days, apparently, all owners of houses are not inclined to take so quietly the often unpleasant results that follow the attacks of disappointed "Lent-crockers" and appeal

[1] More generally known, perhaps, as "truckle-cheese". (See Barnes's *Glossary*.)

to the law for protection ; and, of course, however much one may regret from a folk-lore point of view that it should be so, when the law is invoked with that object custom must give way.

At all events this would seem to have been the result of the following case which I find amongst my notes, taken, I believe, from the *Bridport News* sometime in the " eighties " :—

" PANCAKE DAY

" Eliza Jane Horn and Fanny English, young women, were summoned by Elizabeth —— of Allweston, for wilfully injuring a door, doing damage to the amount of eight shillings.

" Complainant was the owner of a cottage occupied by a widow named Harriet Cooper, and about ten o'clock on the night of Shrove Tuesday defendants, in obedience to old-established custom, were full of the fun and frolic associated with the day of pancakes and fritters. Accordingly they sallied forth with a large stone jar as the ' pan-shard ' to use in the event of meeting with no response to the cry of ' Gie us some pancake O ! '

" Arriving opposite the house the widow was alarmed with a bang and crash at the front door and shook with fear. It was a long time before she could muster up enough courage to go and see the cause of the crash ; and when she arrived at the front door, the panel of which was broken with the blow, she saw at her feet the remnants of the jar ; and in the road close by were the defendants, hugely delighted with their achievement.

" Defendants now denied that they did the mischief ; but four witnesses were called who stated that they saw them close by the house at the time it was done, and that no one else was there.

" The Bench thought that sufficient evidence had been given to prove guilt, and fined defendants six shillings and costs, as well as ordering them to pay eight shillings damages. After some protest the money was paid."

Cock-squailing.—I do not suppose that the rural population of the western counties was more cruel or brutal in its amusements than those in other counties,—particularly in the midland or northern counties, where bull-baiting, dog and cock-fighting seems to have been very prevalent,—but the age was a rough one and the manners of the people uncouth. What wonder then if their amusements and customs sometimes followed suit !

The particularly cruel and barbarous amusement of " throwing at cocks ", or " cock-squailing ",—as it is called in the Dorset dialect,—was a common pastime on Shrove Tuesday and sometimes also, it is said, at Whitsuntide.

A spirited engraving of this so-called sport is shown in Hone's *Every-Day Book* (vol. i, p. 129), in which the bird,—a hen in this case,—is depicted lying wounded on the ground, tethered to a stake, and upbraiding, like Balaam's ass, those who had struck her.

George Roberts, the well-known Dorset historian and writer upon social subjects, in speaking of the cruelty of the seventeenth century and how it was fostered, alludes in his *Social History of the Southern Counties* (1856) to this custom. He says (p. 422) :—

"When a young couple were blessed with offspring the mother, while early instilling the rudiments of virtuous instruction, did not fail to procure the means for early capability of keeping Shrove Tuesday in an orthodox manner. The village tailor made a cloth representation of a cock, which, being lined with lead, regained an erect position upon being knocked down by the juvenile cock-squailer. To practise upon a living bird was but the next step in the art."

Cock-fighting. — "Cock-fighting" was another form of pastime,—less brutal and degrading, perhaps, than the last,—commonly practised at this time.

It seems to have been largely followed in the old grammar schools, and Roberts speaks (p. 423) of "cock-pence" being still paid in some grammar schools to the master as a perquisite on Shrove Tuesday.

Hutchins also (*History of Dorset*, iii, 197) refers to the custom of cock-fighting on Shrove Tuesday having been long established at Wimborne Grammar School, and only discontinued at the beginning of the last century; but as it is there dealt with at some length as rather constituting a local custom at Wimborne, I will reserve further notice of it for my chapter on Local Customs.

"*Kicking the Ball.*"—"Kicking the ball,"—to which the modern and highly scientific game of "football" was in the olden days entirely restricted,—was a pastime customary to Shrove Tuesday in certain parts of Dorsetshire,—though not, I believe, to any large extent.

From time immemorial, however, it would seem to have been indulged in at Corfe Castle by the quarrymen of Purbeck;

but is so identified with their life and customs that I have thought it better to deal with it in my chapter later upon Local Customs rather than treat it here as a calendar custom merely.

Lent

I have already mentioned (p. 21) the custom of "Lent-crocking", but I can find no trace existing in Dorsetshire of the old Lenten custom or pastime of throwing cudgels at "jack-o'-lents",—puppets usually stuffed with straw.

Barnes, indeed, in his *Glossary* (1863), p. 65, defines them as "a scarecrow of old clothes, sometimes stuffed", and refers to Fielding,—"who was sometime in Dorset,"—as using the name in his *Joseph Andrews* (chapter ii). Barnes's reference here would appear to indicate that he knew of the word being used only as a scarecrow, and not as a pastime; for Fielding in this passage, in which he alludes to "Jack-o'-Lent" being the modern appellation of the god Priapus, can scarcely have used it as referring to any of that deity's attributes other than an agricultural one,—in this instance that of a "bird-keeper".[1]

That the pastime, however, must at one time have prevailed in Dorsetshire is clear from an extract which the late Mr. Thomas Wainwright has given from the "Cofferers' Accounts" for the year 1574–5 in his *Bridport Borough Records* (1898), p. 33:—
"Itm paid to Owyn for the making of Jack-a-lent and his hors hire—4.s."

Brand, too, gives references to this practice from various Elizabethan and later dramatists.

One of these, from Quarles' *Shepheards' Oracles* (1646), p. 88, gives the word as used in both senses:—

> "How like a Jack a Lent
> He stands, for Boys to spend their Shrovetide throws,
> Or like a puppit made to frighten cows."

I have no evidence as to how this pastime was carried out in those days; though it is not improbable that it was the direct ancestor of our own modern, and still universally indulged in, amusement of "Aunt Sally".

[1] See also Barnes's observations in his Fore-say (*ante*) as to "Jack-a-lent", p. 3.

MOTHERING SUNDAY
(*Mid-Lent Sunday*)

Without attributing to Dorset folk the ideas of some old writers in giving this name to the fourth Sunday in Lent, namely, that whilst Roman Catholicism was the established religion in England it was customary for people to visit their Mother church on Mid-Lent Sunday and to make their offerings at the high altar,[1] yet there are traces of a less ecclesiastical practice that at one time prevailed in some parts of the county at this time. The eating of " furmity " (fr. *frumentum*) a dish composed of steeped wheat, milk, currants, spice, etc. and boiled together—whether at the house of parents whom it was usual in some parts of England to visit on this day and to take them some little present of nice eatables, or otherwise—was customary at this time to some extent in Dorsetshire. We have the authority of the late Sir Frederick A. Weld, K.C.M.G.—at one time Prime Minister of New Zealand and, later, Governor of the Straits Settlements—for saying [2] that in his own home at Chideock, in West Dorset, " furmity," made of boiled wheat and raisins, was eaten on their village feast day. I myself, many years ago, accepted some of this savoury dish at the hands of an old West Dorset lady, now dead, at this time of the year.

I have had no support from any Dorset source for the suggestion of certain scriptural writers [3] that this eating of " furmity " on Mothering Sunday may have taken its rise from the miraculous " feeding of the five thousand " by our Saviour as recorded in the Gospel for that day, or, perhaps, from the entertainment by Joseph of his brethren as related in the first lesson.

PALM SUNDAY

See Chapter III, *s.v.* Cheselborne, for custom of " Treading in the wheat " at Cheselborne on this day.

GOOD FRIDAY

Good Friday Bread.—It is generally believed that the bread baked on Good Friday never gets mouldy; and in some parts it

[1] See Brand, i, 92.
[2] *Notes and Queries*, Ser. v, v. 76.
[3] See Brand, i, p. 93 (n.).

is used as a charm or talisman in order to make other bread "keep".

The late Rev. Canon C. W. Bingham, a well-known writer upon Dorset antiquities, and who rendered most useful work to the Continuators of the third and last edition of Hutchins' *History of Dorset*, stated in *Notes and Queries*[1] (1865) that he had recently seen in a cottage a very small toy-loaf hanging over the chimneypiece, and on inquiry was told that it had been baked on Good Friday, and that if it were carefully preserved it would prevent the good wife's bread from being "reämy", that is, stringy, during the whole year.

The same preservative effect,—that is, to prevent mouldiness or heaviness in bread,—is said to be obtained if a cross is pricked with a fork on the loaves before they are baked. In Dorsetshire the cross generally consists of five pricks or points, thus . . .

The practice also obtained of making a cross in the flour before baking, and on the malt before mashing up before brewing, to keep it from being bewitched.[2]

I think it was this form of pricked cross that usually figured on the "hot-cross-buns" so generally consumed on this day.

A correspondent in the *Somerset and Dorset Notes and Queries* (1904), vol. ix, p. 113, speaking of "Good Friday Bread", says that this was a large plain bread cake made at the same time as the buns for Good Friday, and marked with a cross. It was stored for the year and used as a remedy for sick cattle. It was supposed to be especially good for calves suffering from quarter-evil. When required for use a portion of the bread was crumbled, mixed with cider, and given as a drench. The correspondent adds that another peculiar use of the sign of the cross was that in the weekly making of bread for the household, and when the "leaven was laid" overnight (*i.e.* the yeast mixed with a part of the flour and left to ferment) a cross was marked in it to prevent the witches from dancing over it.

The Dorset editor of this periodical (Rev. Canon C. H. Mayo) added a footnote that a lady parishioner of his at Holnest, who

[1] Ser. III, viii, 146.

[2] Conf. *Shropshire Folk-Lore*. p, 167.

died in 1895, was a firm believer in the virtues of Good Friday Bread. When grated it was taken as a remedy for diarrhœa. In some parts it is believed that it will cure any ailment.

Doles of loaves of bread, large and small for adults and children, were formerly distributed in the parish churchyard at Corfe Castle; but as that custom seems to have partaken more of a local character I have reserved any further account of it for my chapter on Local Customs.

Plants.—The late Rev. Canon Bingham mentions [1] that a very fine Brompton stock was recently presented to him from a cottage garden in Dorsetshire, with the assurance that its flourishing condition was due to the fact of the seed from which it grew having been planted on Good Friday.

This testimony as to the efficacy of stock seed being sown on Good Friday is confirmed by the belief in some parts of the county that the flowers will in that case be double.

Bees.—Many people, I am told, make a practice of examining their hives on Good Friday, and salting the floor of the hives.

Nails.—It is believed in Portland that finger-nails must not be cut on Good Friday or you will suffer from toothache throughout the year.

Soapy water.—Another writer in the *Somerset and Dorset Notes and Queries* (1911), vol. xii, p. 232, states that an old Dorset woman, aged about 86, told him that she had been taught by her grandmother never to throw away soapy water on Good Friday. No reason was assigned for this except that it was said to have " something to do with our Saviour ".

An editorial footnote confirmed the existence of this belief, and added that it was also said that soapy water thrown away at this time turns to blood.

Several of these customs and superstitions referable to Good Friday have been noted by the late Mr. R. Bosworth Smith, of Bingham's Melcombe, in his *Bird Life and Bird Lore* (1909), p. 363; and it is not difficult, I think, to believe that he gathered much of his information from the same source that I have, namely, from the late Canon C. W. Bingham of that parish. He says:—

[1] *Notes and Queries*, Ser. II, vii, 451.

"Good Friday is one of the most important days of the year, from a secular as well as a religious point of view; the secular, doubtless, owing to the religious. Many of the villagers still make a point of baking a batch of bread on that day, and of setting apart a miniature loaf to be carefully kept, hung up by the fireside, throughout the year. It will prevent the bread of other bakings from turning 'vinny'[1] or sour. A few crumbs of it, soaked in milk, are a sovereign specific for most of the ailments to which children's flesh is heir.

"In like manner they sow gilly flower seed at precisely 12 o'clock on Good Friday, in the belief that the flowers will come up double. Potatoes 'set' on that day, irrespective of the question—rather an important one, it will be admitted—whether Easter be early or late in the year, will have an important influence on all the other 'settings' of the season.

"The weather, indeed, of Good Friday and Easter Day is as important a factor in the growth of the hay crops, as is that of St. Swithin elsewhere:—

'Rain Good Friday or Easter Day,
Much good grass, but little good hay.'

Another Dorset writer, Mr. Wilkinson Sherren, in his *Wessex of Romance* (1908), p. 17, mentions the fact that in Moreton Church sprigs of English willow and pieces of yew-tree are placed at the end of every seat on Palm Sunday and Good Friday, and that no one in the village remembers the time when this custom was not observed.

Easter

Of the many ceremonies and customs that formerly existed at this time the distribution of Easter cakes was probably as common in Dorsetshire as in other counties. A Dorchester correspondent of the *Dorset County Chronicle*, writing in April, 1858, after referring to the old nursery rhyme of "Pat-a-cake, pat-a-cake, baker's man" (which he calls "Batty Cake"), says:—

"Hot cross buns have their own holy mark, which requires no further observation than that the ecclesiologist has pronounced it to be a Grecian and not a Latin cross. Easter cakes, however, have not any ecclesiastical distinction, although intimately connected with church officials. The parish clerk, time out of mind, has had the privilege of calling at each house at Easter to treat the inmates with 'figgy' cakes at a remunerative cost. (When were currants and raisins first termed 'figgy'?)

[1] Mouldy.

"The Churchwardens and sidesmen (Synodsmen) are also great patrons of Easter customs, holding a special meeting for their celebration when inaugurated into office.[1]

"Moreover, in this county, at Easter, 'furmity,' a diet composed of wheat and milk,—was sold by the plate or cup full, especially at the Easter sessions, at Sherborne. . . And in country places 'skimmer cake' (dough cake boiled in a 'skimmer', used commonly by dairy folk in Dorsetshire on festival occasions) was formerly much given to rustics as a treat instead of the household loaf. . . But the School-Children's treat of Easter cakes, from the Lady Bountiful of the parish, was always customary in Dorset as in other parts of England."

For an account of the inhabitants of Stalbridge playing "crookern" and "hunting the buck" on Easter Monday, see Chapter III, p. 133.

Hock- or Hoke-tide

(*The second Monday and Tuesday after Easter*)

Hocking.—Several of our writers upon popular antiquities have referred to the existence of the custom of "hocking" as having been practised on these two days in certain counties. The only reference that I can find as to its having survived in Dorsetshire is contained in two meagre entries recorded by Hutchins in his account of the Borough of Blandford (vol. i, p. 221):—

"1607. Received of the wives at Hocktyde . £1 6s. 6d.
"1616. Received of the women what they got on Hock Monday . £1 2s. 10d."

These entries would seem to have been taken from some MS. collections relating to the county made by an anonymous author and now preserved in the Cotton Library in the British Museum. No doubt most of the Blandford municipal and other records were destroyed in the great fire of 1731.

Hutchins then refers to Cowel's statement that "it was customary in several manors in Hampshire for the men to hock the women on the Monday and the women the men upon the Tuesday; that is, on that day the women in merriment stop the ways with ropes, and pull the passengers to them desiring something to be laid out in pious uses in order to obtain their freedom".

[1] The churchwardens of each parish, in Dorsetshire as well as elsewhere, were always elected at the old vestries held on Easter Monday.

From the nature of these entries Hutchins deduces the fact that " something of the kind took place at Blandford ". That is all that he can tell us.

So recently, however, as May, 1905, the *Bridport News* published a letter in *T.P.'s Weekly*, in which " A Dorset Yokel " describes the custom as it was once observed in many Dorset towns and villages on the second Monday and Tuesday after Easter, which follows and somewhat amplifies the account given by Hutchins from Cowel. At the end he cites the two entries given above from Hutchins, giving 1610 instead of 1616 as the date of the later entry. To this entry the correspondent attaches the remark " *sic* " to " Hock *Monday* " ; and rightly so, for the women's contribution always had reference to the *Tuesday*, which was the principal or " Hock day ". I am somewhat surprised to find that this custom existed at Blandford at so recent a date as these entries would seem to indicate ; for similar entries by these earlier writers mostly refer to pre-Reformation periods. One can scarcely imagine the later clergy of the West of England adopting such means for replenishing their funds *ad pios usus* ! " A Dorset Yokel " ends his communication by stating that Hocktide appears to have been originated to commemorate the destruction of the Danes in the time of Ethelred.

The procedure given above would seem to be very similar to that recorded elsewhere, and does not seem to have partaken at all of the boisterous quality of the " Heaving " or " Lifting " of the two sexes, alternately, on a following Monday and Tuesday, which was a very common practice at Eastertide in some of the more northern counties. The origin both of the term and of the custom itself would seem to be obscure ; the suggestion that it was in any way commemorative of the slaughter of the Danes in Ethelred's reign is shown by Brand and other writers to be very improbable.

Holy Thursday, or Ascension Day

Beating the Bounds.—It was the general custom in olden days, and is still observed in many parishes in Dorsetshire, for certain persons to go round, or perambulate the boundaries or limits of their own particular parish in Rogation Week, or,—to be more precise,—on one of the three days before Holy Thursday or

Ascension Day, though more often, I think, on Holy Thursday itself. Upon these occasions, as Brand (i, 168) tells us, "the minister, accompanied by his churchwardens and parishioners, were wont to deprecate the vengeance of God, beg a blessing on the fruits of the earth, and preserve the rights and properties of the parish."

In Dorsetshire the last of these objects would seem to be the one principally or solely considered at the present day. This perambulation is known as "Beating the Bounds".

Before I proceed to the "perambulations" of particular parishes, I would like to produce in full the most amusing account of this interesting and useful custom contributed by William Barnes to Hone's *Year Book* (p. 589) as existing in Dorsetshire in his younger days. He says :—

"A Perambulation, or, as it might be more correctly called, a circumambulation, is the custom of going round the boundaries of a manor or parish, with witnesses, to determine and preserve recollection of its extent, and to see that no encroachments have been made upon it, and that the landmarks have not been taken away. It is a proceeding commonly regulated by the steward, who takes with him a few men and several boys who are required to particularly observe the boundaries traced out, and thereby qualify themselves for witnesses in the event of any dispute about the landmarks or extent of the manor at a future day. In order that they may not forget the lines and marks of separation they 'take *pains*' at almost every turning. For instance, if the boundary be a stream, one of the boys is tossed into it ; if a broad ditch, the boys are offered money to jump over it, in which they, of course, fail, and pitch into the mud, where they stick as firmly as if they had been rooted there for the season ; if a hedge, a sapling is cut out of it and used in afflicting that part of their bodies upon which they rest in the posture between standing and lying ; if a wall, they are to have a race on the top of it, when, in trying to pass each other, they fall over on each side, some descending, perhaps, into the still stygian waters of a ditch, and others thrusting the 'human face divine' into a bed of nettles ; if the boundary be a sunny bank, they sit down upon it and get a treat of beer and bread and cheese, and, perhaps, a glass of spirits. When these boys grow up to be men, if it happens that one of them should be asked if a particular stream were the boundary of the manor he had perambulated, he would be sure to say, in the manner of Sancho Panza 'Ees, that 'tis, I'm sure o't, by the same token that I were tossed into't, and paddled about there lik' a water-rot till I wor hafe dead.' If he should be asked whether the aforesaid pleasant bank were a boundary : ' O, ees it be,' he would say, ' that's where we squat down and tucked in a skinvull of vittles and drink.' With regard to any boundary perambulation after that he would most likely declare, ' I won't be sartin ; I got zo muddled up top o' the banks, that don' know where we ambulated arter that.' "

Melcombe Regis.—The late Mr. H. J. Moule, sometime curator of the Dorset County Museum at Dorchester, and a learned writer upon the county's antiquities, in his account of the " Weymouth and Melcombe Regis Borough Records ", which he edited in 1883, gives (p. 9) several extracts from a small folio volume, chiefly of law minutes, comprising depositions taken about the middle of the seventeenth century, recording a " perambulation " of the parish of Melcombe Regis about that time, in which one of the deponents, an old woman of 82 years of age, speaks of having joined in a " Procession " round the bounds of Melcombe Regis nearly three-quarters of a century previously, and deposes to an " old elderne stubb " (stump) at Washford as having been one of the boundaries.

Radipole.—The same deponent also testified that the minister of the adjoining parish of Radipole, with his parishioners, used to go round their bounds on the same day ; and at a pound on the bounds (" in the place of which pound a dairy house was sithence builded ") he read a chapter and " alsoe a psalm there to be sung ". After this the perambulation was continued, the villagers on the west side of some rails then standing and the townsmen on the east side.

West Lulworth.—There is also in the same volume (C. p. 232) a reference to still earlier depositions (Elizabethan), in which an old man gives evidence as to his having often " after he was of remembrance " gone on procession, as the custom then was, with the minister and parishioners to take " view " of the boundaries of the parish of West Lulworth. The witness describes the route, ending at Furzeymill Pitt, " where they had usuall Beere and Cake-bread."

Chideock.—A very complete account of the " perambulation " of the bounds of a parish and manor as entered in old records is that of Chideock, in West Dorset, which took place before the steward of the manor and many inhabitants of the parish. It is given by the Rev. T. Worthington in his *History of Chideock*, and copied by the late H. N. Cox in his account of that parish, contributed in a series of papers to the *Southern Times* in 1886. Mr. Cox also, like Mr. Barnes, alludes to the various steps that were sometimes taken to impress upon the memory of the boys who accompanied the perambulation the exact situation of the boundaries.

Bridport.—Although the main incidents of these several "perambulations" may have been very much the same, yet occasionally they have been varied by others of a more interesting or amusing character. A modern instance of the latter, fortunately attended by no serious result, occurred on the occasion of "beating the bounds" of the borough of Bridport in 1891, which was reported in several West Country papers. The following account, taken from the *Bath Daily Chronicle* of 24th October, 1891, appears in the *Somerset and Dorset Notes and Queries* for December, 1891 (vol. ii, p. 305) :—

"The historic function of walking the boundaries of the Borough of Bridport by the Mayor and Corporation and the principal inhabitants was the occasion of an amusing *contretemps*. In the course of the perambulation the city fathers came to a large millpond, which marked the boundary of the town. It was necessary to the performance of the ceremony that the pond should be crossed, and the Mayor, the Borough Surveyor, and another embarked on a large raft, on which they were to be towed across. They had not been long afloat when the raft was submerged by their weight, and the trio were standing up to their knees in water. When half-way over, to make matters worse, the rope became entangled, and, amid the laughter of the townspeople, the Mayor toppled over into the pond, and his two fellow-citizens were also precipitated into the water. They quickly regained the raft, but were as quickly thrown again into the muddy pool. The Mayor promptly described the boundary by swimming ashore, and his example was followed by one of his companions, but the Borough Surveyor remained alone on the raft, and was eventually towed to land completely drenched."

Marnhull.—The Rev. Canon Mayo publishes in the *Somerset and Dorset Notes and Queries* (vol. xv, pp. 19–21 and 29–31), 1917, a long account of a perambulation held for the Manor of Marnhull on 7th and 8th June, 1808, and made by the then Lord of the Manor, John Hussey, Esq., his steward, and the principal inhabitants of the parish. A copy had been furnished to the Dorset editor of that periodical of the perambulation contained in a MS. book of Rentals and Quit Rents relating to the Manor.

As Canon Mayo says: "It has a value as being a record of local boundaries, and illustrates a custom which at one time was universal in our county."

Wyke Regis.—For account of the annual visit paid by Portlanders to the Boundstone on the Chesil Beach on Holy Thursday, see Chapter III, p. 141.

MAY DAY

"It was anciently the custom for all ranks of people to go out a-Maying early on the first of May," says Brand; but I do not think that there exist now in Dorsetshire many traces of the old merry dances and games, such as the Maypole dance, the Morris dancers, the milkmaids, the chimney-sweeps, the maidens' garland or flower dances and processions, which used to be so prevalent in many parts of England on May Day.

Flower and Maypole Dance, Chardstock.—In some parts of Dorsetshire, however, some few such observances still take place. For instance, in the parish of Chardstock, on the Somerset and Devon border, according to the *Dorset County Chronicle* in May, 1884, the children of the parish brought round garlands as usual on May Day; in the afternoon upwards of seventy of them sat down to a feast at which the local squire, the vicar, and other gentlemen and ladies were present. "Dancing round the Maypole concluded the keeping up of this old English custom."

Crowning the May Queen and Maypole Dance (*Bridport*).—The *Dorset County Chronicle*, in June, 1918, gives a very recent instance of this as occurring in the West Dorset town of Bridport:—

"On Thursday the girls of the National Schools had their annual festival of crowning the May Queen and dancing round the Maypole. There was a very good attendance of the general public, the ceremony taking place in the school-yard. Favoured with fine weather, the scene was a very picturesque one, and the proceedings were watched with the greatest interest and pleasure. The children, as is their custom, were dressed in white, and with their Queen (Vera Meech), who is elected by the votes of her schoolmates, they paraded the Rope Walks, St. Michael's Lane, and Gundry Lane, and returned to the playground. Here the Maypole was set up and the Queen was then enthroned. She recited a verse of Tennyson's *May Queen,* and then the Rector 'crowned' her with a wreath of flowers. Some very pretty Maypole dances were then gone through, and some nicely rendered songs gave variety to the programme, while at the close a collection, which realized £4, was made to defray the cost of a new set of strings for the Maypole."

I have since been told that this is not a genuine folk-lore survival, but rather a sham revival, having been introduced from Whitelands College by the National Society of School teachers, taught by Ruskin. The recitation of Tennyson's *May Queen* would seem to confirm this ; but even if this be so, it is a decided improvement upon the usual School Board methods of recent years, which tend to destroy all traces of local folk-lore in the young people of the present age.

Maypole: Cattistock.—There is an interesting reference in H. N. Cox's serial *History of Cattistock,* published in the *Southern Times* in 1886, to the " old custom of the Maypole ", which would appear to have been regularly kept up in that village until 1835. Mr. Cox alludes to a decree of Parliament in 1644, which ordered every Maypole in England and Wales to be taken down and none afterwards to be erected. Presumably Cattistock obeyed the mandate, at all events until the Restoration. Mr. Cox goes on to say that probably as time passed on the Maypole festivities were bereft of many of their ancient customs, but even at the last there was an immense assemblage of people, and the merry dance around the gaily decked pole with its thousands of May flowers was indulged in by all parties. He remembers on one occasion the Maypole being " set up " in the open space near to the main entrance to the church and rectory, but that generally it was opposite " The Fox ", no doubt one of the principal hostelries in the village. Cattistock is still to this day an important hunting centre. Mr. Cox is of opinion that the custom was permitted to die out, not because the people disapproved of it, but that the expense of getting good music for the dance was not met by the subscriptions.

Maypole: Cerne Abbas.—Dr. Colley March, F.S.A., in his paper on " The Giant and the Maypole of Cerne " in the Dorset Field Club's *Proceedings* (1901), vol. xxii, p. 105, speaks of the ordinance of the Long Parliament in April, 1644, whereby all maypoles were to be taken down and removed by the constables, churchwardens, and other parish officers; but it met with no little resistance.[1] After the advent of Charles II the Maypole was set up again, and had a long life. Dr. March quotes from an old sexton at Cerne, who well remembered it:—

"It was made," he said, "every year from a fir-bole, and was raised in a night. It was erected in the ring just above the Giant. It was decorated, and the villagers went up the hill and danced round the pole on the 1st of May."

This hill was Trendle Hill, situated about half a mile from the town, upon the steep southern declivity of which the famous figure of the giant was cut in the chalk.

According to authorities cited by Dr. March, "the festival of the maypole" was not unattended by scenes that "called forth ample invective". Philip Stubbes, in his *Anatomic of Abuses*, 1583, refers to a custom when

"hundreds of men, women, and children go off to the woods and groves and spend all the night in pastimes, and in the morning they would return with birche boughes and branches of trees to deck their assembles withal. And they bring home with great veneration the Maie-pole, their stinking idol rather, covered all over with flowers and herbes, and then fall they to leaping and dancing about it, as the heathen people did. I have heard it crediblie reported by men of great gravity that, of an hundred maides going to the wood, there have scarcely the third part of them returned home again as they went."

Maypole: Shillingston.—William Barnes in his Fore-say (*ante*) speaks of this decline in the old maypole customs. He says: "Dorset formerly had its maypoles, but Shillingston, clustering round its softly rising knap, may now be the only Dorset village which keeps up the tall token of a merry May Day."

In the *Life of William Barnes*, by his daughter, Mrs. Lucy E. Baxter, published in 1887 under the pseudonym of "Leader Scott", she gives (p. 150) a poem of her father's, hitherto unpublished, called "Our Early Landscape",—in which the poet alludes to the maypole at Shillingston in the following lines:—

[1] Dr. March states, p. 105 (n.), that the Cerne maypole was destroyed in 1635.

"And Shillingston, that on her height
Shows up her tower to op'ning day,
And high-shot Maypole, yearly dight
With flow'ry wreaths of merry May."

Stocking of Poundbury Field, Dorchester.—William Barnes in the above Fore-say also refers to the annual stocking of Poundbury Field, near Dorchester, on May Day under the head of customs at set times or given days of the year. The field is now enclosed, but "Dorchester folk were wont in olden time, it is said, to go forth to its flowery and airy sward a-maying and to drink syllybub of fresh milk". (See Poundbury, Chapter III, p. 124.)

Flower Service: Bridport.—The town of Bridport in West Dorset has for many years been prominent in keeping up an old flower custom on May Sunday—the first Sunday in May. The *Bridport News* in May, 1885, gave an interesting account of the ceremony, where on "May Sunday" the children, to the number of 312, assembled at the schools in Gundry Lane, and having been duly marshalled in procession, marched to the parish church, carrying flowers. They came up South Street as far as the old castle, and going down the east side of the street crossed again by the rectory, and entered the church by the west door, occupying seats in the nave, which were given up to them for the occasion by the parishioners who generally used them. The children were accompanied by their superintendent and also by their teachers. Divine service followed, and in the afternoon the usual children's service was held. The bells were rung spiritedly at intervals during the day and a flag was hoisted, as usual, on the church tower.

Again, in May, 1890, the *Bridport News* recorded that, in accordance with the usual custom, the first Sunday in May was kept by the scholars of the Bridport Parish Church Sunday Schools by the usual special and joyous services. Shortly after 7 a.m. the bells of the parish church (St. Mary's) pealed forth to herald in the school anniversary, and at 8 o'clock there was a full choral celebration of the Holy Communion. In his sermon the Rector, the Rev. E. J. B. Henslowe, alluded to the origin of May Sunday celebrations in Bridport, and to the fact that it was an institution not celebrated to his knowledge in any other town, but was peculiar to Bridport. He said that years ago there was no proper school, but classes were held by different people in their own houses; these classes used to meet once a year, and have a procession and go to church.

In the afternoon the usual flower service was held. The scholars formed in procession and again marched to the church. The rector officiated. The service commenced with a hymn, and then the scholars passed up to the chancel steps and presented their floral offerings. While another hymn was being sung flowers were presented by members of the congregation. The service was then proceeded with. The flowers were afterwards packed and forwarded to London for some of the hospitals.

Again, in May, 1905, the *Bridport News* contributed a long leading article on the subject which it styled "May Sunday: A Link with the Past". It dealt fully with the origin of the present flower-custom in Bridport, and referred to the institution of Sunday Schools in Bridport in connexion with St. Mary's Church in 1788. At that time the procession formed almost a complete "perambulation" of the parish boundaries, and many visitors would come in from the country "to see the children walk". The writer of the article thinks that this "walking" may have been but a survival of a much older custom—that of "beating the bounds"—which prevailed in many parishes at Rogation-tide; and that "May Sunday" occurring near the same time of the year the one custom had at the end of the eighteenth century merged into the other. As we have seen, the custom of "walking" still continues, but only to a very limited extent.

For a flower custom obtaining amongst the fishermen at Abbotsbury on Old May Day, see Chapter III, p. 104.

Oak Apple—or Royal Oak—Day

(29*th May*)

This is also known as Restoration Day, being the anniversary of the Restoration of Charles II in 1660. It is also said to have been his birthday. Brand and other writers speak of the common people, especially in the north of England, still wearing in their hats the leaves of the oak, which is sometimes covered with leaf-gold, and of others decorating their doors, etc., with green oak branches in commemoration of his escape by means of that "miraculous divergence"—as it has been called in Dorsetshire—through the county after the battle of Worcester in September, 1651. But in Dorsetshire itself one might almost look in vain for any such observances at the present day, though, perhaps, more interest has been taken of late years in the subject by reason of the recent books and articles that have been written upon King Charles's wanderings.

George Roberts, in his *History of Lyme Regis*, writing in 1834, refers to the growing disuse of this old-time practice. He says :—

"The practice of decorating the doors of houses with oak boughs on May 29th has within the last few years somewhat grown into disuse, owing to the means adopted by the proprietors of land to prevent depredations from being committed on their trees by the apprentices, etc.

"Fifteen years ago scarcely a door was without its branch. At the doors of some persons might be seen, early in the morning, a bunch of nettles by the inmates when they arose. Dissenters who in Charles II's reign did not celebrate his restoration by putting up oak boughs, or pay those who had put them up during the night, were served in this manner. I have not seen any nettles at doors for several years; party feeling as to the Restoration seems now extinct. None save the lower orders wear oak leaves in their hats; the boys continue to gild their oak apples, and apply an approbious name to those who have not an oak leaf displayed, or who wear it after twelve o'clock. For the origin of this appellation, by which noncomformists were commonly distinguished, Granger accounts, vol. iii, p. 316, in a truly ludicrous manner."

Mr. Edmund Gosse contributed a very interesting article, compiled from the unpublished papers of his father, the late Philip H. Gosse, F.R.S., depicting the latter's childhood at school in Poole in 1818, to *Longman's Magazine* in March, 1889, from which I take the following extract :—

"The 29th May, Oak Apple Day, was called 'Shicsack Day', when all loyal urchins were expected to display a bit of oak in their hats or caps. A mere twig of oak-leaves was sufficient, but if an oak-apple was attached it was better; while those who wished to be altogether 'the cheese' wore leaves or apples on which a fragment of gold-leaf was gummed. There was a considerable demand for gold-leaf just before the day at the stationers' shops, and for boys whose 'tin' was scarce there was an inferior kind of foil provided called Dutch gold; while in the little hucksters' shops bits of oak duly gilt could be obtained 'for a consideration'."

Mr. Gosse added that Mr. Thomas Hardy had told him that the day was still called "Sic-sac-day" by the peasantry; but that he had no idea what the words meant.[1]

The following account of this custom—as obtaining, presumably, in the adjoining county of Wilts—is given by that close observer of natural history, the late Richard Jefferies, in his *Wild Life in a Southern County* (ed. 1902, p. 83):—

"In May the ploughboys still remember King Charles, and on what they call 'shick-shack-day' search for oak apples and the young leaves of the oak to place with a spray of ash in their hats or button-holes; the ash spray must have even leaves, and an odd number is not correct. To wear these green emblems was thought imperative even within the last twenty years, and scarcely a labourer could be seen without them. The elder men would tell you,—as if it had been a great calamity,—that they could recollect a year when the spring was so backward that not an oak-leaf or an oak-apple could be found by the most careful search for the purpose. The custom has fallen into disuse lately; the carters, however, still attach the ash and oak leaves to the heads of their horses on this particular day."

Midsummer Eve
(*Eve of St. John the Baptist*)
(23*rd June*)

Dorsetshire does not appear to have followed the example of many other parts of England and of other European countries in the ceremonies which marked the advent of the summer solstice as recorded by Brand and other writers, such as, piling up and dancing round or through bonfires, and other recognized festivities. It seems to have contented itself with those simple and domestic practices that are so dear to the heart of the village maidens, who seek by "divination", or some form of "matrimonial oracle", to learn what is to be their own fate or chance of happiness in the married state.

William Barnes, writing in Hone's *Year Book* in 1832, refers to one of the commonest or best known of these. After

[1] Halliwell (*Dict. of Archaic and Provincial Words*, 1852) gives "Shick-shack-day" as a term for the 29th May, or Royal Oak Day, used in Surrey.

mentioning some of the various means and practices which were resorted to in his childhood in order to attain this object, and which required no particular day or season in order to be effective, he tells us (p. 588) :—

Hemp-seed throwing.—" Midsummer Eve, however, is the great time with girls for discovering who shall be their husbands; why it is so, more than any other, I cannot tell, unless, indeed, the sign *Gemini*, which the sun then leaves, is symbolical of the wedding union. But, however that may be, a maiden will walk through the garden at midsummer, with a rake on her left shoulder and throw hemp-seed over her right, saying at the same time :—

> 'Hemp-seed I set, hemp-seed I sow,
> The man that is my true-love come after me and mow.'

" It is said by many who have never tried it, and some who have without effect, that the future husband of the hemp-sowing girl will appear behind her with a scythe, and look as substantial as a brass image of Saturn on an old time-piece."

Barnes also weaves this superstition or charm into "Mrs. Mary's Tale" in *Erwin and Linda*, one of his *Poems of Rural Life in National English*" (1846), pp. 11 and 12 :—

> " For once, when summer's shortest night
> Came round, so slowly letting fall
> Its sparkling dew below the light
> The moon cast down upon the wall;
> The while the slowly-clanging bell
> Struck twelve o'clock, and giggling maids
> Stole out to try the well-known spell
> That brings their unknown husbands' shades;
> Young Linda too was scatt'ring wide
> Her hemp-seed, crying 'This I sow
> 'That he who takes me for his bride
> 'Should now come after me and mow.'
> And turning round her fair-neck'd head
> With timid smile, and backward look,
> She saw—and seeing, felt half dead—
> A shape come slowly o'er the brook;
> And when she saw his scythe-blade's bow
> Behind him gleaming by the moon,
> She sank with one convulsive throe,
> Against an elm-tree in a swoon."

Thomas Hardy gives a delightfully realistic account of the observance of this custom by the village maidens of the Hintocks in *The Woodlanders* (vol. ii, chapter iv), where, as they left their homes for the woods in which they were to try their fate, " a handful " (of hemp-seed) " was carried by each girl ".

Mr. Hardy—who is a keen observer of all that is archaic and quaint in the life of the Dorset peasantry—at the same time alludes incidentally to a somewhat similar species of divination by which girls were enabled to learn what were the trades of their future husbands, namely, by " hole-digging " at noon on the following day, St. John the Baptist's or Midsummer Day. No further details are given; and as I have not myself come across this particular form of divination I cannot give any information as to how it was actually carried out, beyond saying that it would seem to bear some kinship to that mentioned by Brand (i, 267), who cites Aubrey's *Miscellanies* (1696) for the statement that " on the day of St. John Baptist " as he was walking in the pasture at 12 o'clock he saw a group of young women on their knees " very busie, as if they had been weeding ".

" A young man told him that they were looking for a coal [1] under the root of a plantain, to put under their heads that night, and they should dream who would be their husbands. It was to be that day and hour."

Crossed Shoes.—Barnes also gives another well-known " matrimonial oracle ", which consists in a girl, on going to bed on Midsummer Eve, putting her shoes at right angles to each other in the shape of a T, and saying :—

" Hoping this night my true love to see,
I place my shoes in the form of a T."

When she will be sure to see her husband in a dream, and perhaps in reality, by her bed-side.

According to the Rev. Canon C. H. Mayo this couplet sometimes takes the form of a quotation :—

" I place my shoes in the form of a T,
Hoping this night my true-love to see,
In his apparel and in his array,
As he goes forth on every day."

Letters of Alphabet.—There is still another one mentioned by Barnes. " A girl, on going to bed, is to write the alphabet on

[1] Or " cole " : an old, blackened root, often found under mugwort or plantains.

small pieces of paper and put them into a bason of water with the letters downward; and it is said that in the morning she will find the first letter of her husband's name turned up, and the others as they were left."

Death Omen.—Miss M. G. A. Summers, of Hazelbury Bryan, contributed to the "Folk-lore Column" of the *Dorset County Chronicle* in 1881 several interesting items relating to Midsummer Eve.

She stated that a curious old custom was still firmly believed in Dorsetshire, that if you sit in the church porch on Midsummer Eve you will see those who are to die during the ensuing year enter the church and not come out again; whilst those who will have a serious illness will go in and return again.

Also that she had been informed by a Dorset woman "with a most solemn face" that if you put some yarrow gathered off a young man's grave under your pillow on Midsummer Eve you will surely see your future husband.

Miss Summers further remembered hearing a young woman in a neighbouring village say that she had laid out some bread and cheese and had sat up, as she had "heard tell how her young man's spirit would come and take some".

This last is evidently that alluded to by Thomas Hardy in his *Under the Greenwood Tree,* where at the Christmas party given by the tranter Reuben Dewy, depicted in Part I, Chapter VIII, Mrs. Penny speaks of the occasion when one Midsummer Eve, when she was a young woman, she had sat up, according to the time-honoured custom, to watch for the spirit of the man who was to be her future husband. She says: "I put the bread and cheese and cider quite ready as the witch's book ordered, and I opened the door and waited till the clock struck twelve. When the clock had struck, lo and behold I could see through a little small man in the lane wi' a shoemaker's apron on. In he walks and down he sits, and, O my goodness, didn't I flee upstairs, body and soul hardly hanging together!"

Though this was not the figure she approved or desired, as her conduct on this occasion showed, so effectual was the charm that she had prepared that she nevertheless in due course of time became his wife.

Allhallowtide or Hallow E'en
(31*st October*)

Bell-ringing: Blandford.—Hone is responsible for the statement that "At Blandford Forum, in Dorsetshire, 'there was a custom, in the papal times, to ring bells at Allhallow-tide for all Christian souls.'"[1]

This assumes that this custom existed practically alone at Blandford. Hutchins does not notice it; and I have very grave doubts myself whether this statement of Hone can be accepted as justifying this assumption. Brand states (i, 310) that "it is stated in Kethe's sermon preached at Blandford Forum in Dorsetshire, January 17th, 1570, p. 19, that 'there was a custom, in the papal times, to ring bells at Allhallow-tide for all Christian souls'." He thus shows the authority for Hone's statement, which is contained in a sermon *preached at Blandford* in which this allusion to a very general custom appears to have been made.

Guy Faux Day
(5*th November*)

The Guy Faux Day celebrations by fireworks and bonfires have always been very popular in Dorsetshire, particularly in the county town, where on more than one occasion disturbances have taken place because the populace has considered that its ancient privileges had been interfered with or its looked-for amusements on this night curtailed.

I well remember on one occasion some thirty or forty years ago in Dorchester when the military had to be called out in order to assist the civic authorities in quelling the riots. These celebrations appear now to be shorn of much of their former importance and, apparently, significance.

Barnes, in his "Fore-say" says that "the 5th of November still gathers in some parishes of Dorset its fire-wielding youths to celebrate Guy Faux's night, by flaring bonfires and flying fireworks, far more for fun than Faux, and rather as fire-worshippers than politicians". He himself gives us a dialect poem on "Guy Faux's Night" (p. 99).

[1] *Every-Day Book*, i, 711.

Portland Bonfire Custom.—The late Rev. W. K. Kendall once lent me a MS. notebook in which he had recorded a very curious form which the customary bonfire celebration in the Isle of Portland on the night of 5th November had taken.

When the bonfire was lighted the following custom was observed. A man taking up one of the children in his arms gave the signal, and then all the others followed him in single file round the fire, over which he leaped with the child in his arms. When the fire began to burn low the children also jumped over it. The following doggerel was sung :—

> " Wood and straw do burn likewise,
> Take care the blankers [1] don't dout your eyes."

This would appear to partake more of the characteristics of the old Midsummer fires.

St. Thomas's Day

(21*st December*)

Christmasing.—Christmas being the principal season of the year for feasts and other festive rejoicings—when people, too, were generally supposed to be more charitably disposed towards their fellow-beings than at any other time—many of the poorer class would seek by visiting in good time the houses of their richer neighbours to obtain the means of taking some share in these rejoicings themselves. This was generally called " Christmasing ".

In 1872 I sent to *Notes and Queries* (Ser. IV, X, 494) a short account of this custom, as follows :—

" A few days before Christmas, the women, children and old men in a parish would visit by turn the houses of their wealthier neighbours, and in return for and in recognition of Christmas greetings and their general demand of ' Please, give me something to keep up a Christmas ' (or ' for keeping up o' Christmas ') would receive substantial pieces or ' hunks ' of bread and cheese, bread and meat, or small sums of money. The old and infirm of either sex were generally represented by their children or grandchildren, those only being refused the dole who did not belong to the parish."

This, I should have stated, always took place on or about St. Thomas's Day, the 21st of December.

[1] Or " flinders " = flying particles.

This custom appears to be somewhat akin to that known to Brand (i, 350) as " *going-a-gooding* on St. Thomas's Day ", which there seems to have been carried out by women only. He suggests that it may have been only another name for the northern custom of going about and crying " Hagmena ". There would appear to be other variants.

Tithe Custom: Thornford.—The *Standard* newspaper, sometime in 1878, gave an account of a custom which is said to have prevailed some years ago in Thornton, near Sherborne, amongst the tenants of the Manor of depositing five shillings in a hole in a certain tombstone in the churchyard, a ceremony which precluded the lord of the manor from taking the tithe of hay during the year. This had always to be done before twelve o'clock on St. Thomas's Day, or the privilege fell through.

Again, in December, 1887, the *Antiquary* (xvi, p. 225) refers to this custom in almost the same words, citing Hampson's *Mediævi Kalendarium*, p. 83, for its authority.

It is, however, clear from the *Somerset and Dorset Notes and Queries* for 1894 (vol. iv, p. 122) that Thornton in both these journals is a mistake for Thornford, which is a village near Sherborne. Here the custom is again detailed, with a slight variation in phraseology, on the authority of the *Salisbury and Winchester Journal* of 2nd November, 1829. An editorial note is added referring to a statement by Hutchins that a tomb in the churchyard at Thornford was called the " Prebendal Tomb ", because in a hole on its cover the modus in lieu of tithe on the prebendal lands due to the rector was formerly paid on St. Thomas's Day. This curious modus, Hutchins tells us (vol. iv, p. 302), led to a dispute between the then rector and the lord of the manor, which being carried into the law courts ended in the defeat of the rector. Beyond this Hutchins makes no reference to the alleged custom.

Christmas Eve
(24*th December*)

In a paper on " Christmas in Dorsetshire " which I contributed to *Notes and Queries* in December, 1880 (Ser. VI, ii, 504), I stated that it was customary in many farmhouses on Christmas Eve for a large block of wood (in fact, a very Yule log) to be brought into the kitchen, and, an immense fire having been made up, the farm labourers would come in and sit round it, or as many as were able would crowd into the chimney corner, and drink beer and cider. This was what was usually called a Christmas " brown ".[1]

William Barnes, in his " Fore-say " speaks of this custom. He says :—

" The old Saxon ' Yule ' was New Year's Eve, the end and beginning of a year ; but our Christian fore elders shifted the ' Yuletide ' to the Nativity, which is very near to it. In old Dorset the tide seems to have been kept up with some customs of mirth and with a ' Yule-log ' or ' Backbrand ', a great log of wood burning against the back of the hearth, from within the old year into the new one ; a token, it may be, of the sun's new start for summer heat."

This is similar to the bringing in the " Yule Clog " or " Block " on Christmas Eve in many parts of England, especially in the north, as related by Brand (i, 359).

Miss Summers, of Hazelbury Bryan, writing in the *Dorset County Chronicle* in 1881, says that

" there is a popular notion amongst the ignorant that the powers of darkness can have no evil influence on mankind on Christmas Eve. The cock is thus supposed to crow all night long, and so to scare away all malignant spirits. Bread which is baked on Christmas Eve, they also say, will never get mouldy. There is another old superstition which is often palmed off on children in this neighbourhood. They are told if they hang up their stockings at the foot of their bed on Christmas Eve Old Father Christmas (who naturally appears in the person of some friend or relative) will come and fill them with toys, money, sweets, etc. The early rising and wild exclamations which ensue on the following morning are, I hear, quite ludicrous. They are also told Old Father Christmas never visits or takes any notice of them after they are twelve years old."

Christmas Eve was always, and still is, considered the proper time for putting up the Christmas decorations of holly, mistletoe, etc. So, also, amongst strict observers of old customs in Dorsetshire, no one would think of eating a mince-pie before Christmas Eve or later than Twelfth Night, so keeping within the twelve days of Christmas.

[1] Or " bron' " = brand. A large log of wood put on at the back of the fire, particularly at merry-makings in winter. (Barnes's *Glossary*.)

The following picturesque account taken from the *Journal of Mary Frampton from the year* 1779 *to* 1846 (pp. 365–6), published in 1885, gives a very good idea of the way in which Christmas festivities were ushered in in well-to-do houses in Dorsetshire in bye-gone days.

" Our Christmas was passed with a large family party at Moreton. The house was unbarred and unblockaded, with the exception of one large window on the staircase. The carol singers from Mr. Frampton's own parishes ushered in Christmas Eve and Christmas Morn as usual, but no mummers were allowed to perform their ancient drama of the wonderful recovery of a man killed in battle by a little bottle of elixir drawn from the pocket of the doctor of the piece, or to personify the 'Senses' from the ancient mysteries, with their Latin names, 'Tactus,' 'Visus,' etc. The yule-log, however, burnt on the large hearth of the entrance hall. The peacock in full plumage, with its fiery mouth, was placed on the dinner-table, with, of course, the boar's head; the immense candles were well covered with laurel, the hare appeared with the red herring astride on its back; and the wassail bowl and lamb's wool were not inferior to former years."

CHAPTER II

CUSTOMS APPERTAINING TO PARTICULAR SEASONS OF THE YEAR

Sheep-shearing

There are many traces in our older writers, both of prose and verse, of the festivities that formerly ruled at sheep-shearing time. Both Brand and Hone deal at some length with this subject, the former remarking (i, 452) that in England they prevailed " particularly in the southern parts, for these festivities were not so common in the north ". Sheep-shearing was, as we may readily suppose, one of the topics considered by the old Elizabethan poet, Thomas Tusser, in his " Five Hundred points of Husbandry ". It was also a favourite theme with more modern poets, *e.g.* Thomson, in his " Summer ", and John Clare, the Northamptonshire peasant poet,—who owed so much to Thomson,—in his " Shepherd's Calendar " speaks somewhat sadly of the decay of these homely old customs.

If this decadence was becoming so evident then—a century ago—can we wonder that so little now remains of the customs and usages that formerly attended these gatherings ?

In Dorsetshire, however, being so largely a pastoral county, one might, perhaps, expect to find that this " passing away " has been more gradual than in the more northern counties.

Originally, in most counties, sheep-shearing festivities partook more of the character of a " harvest-home " ; the same songs, for instance, being sung indiscriminately at one or other of these feasts. Some of these verses sung at Dorset " harvest-homes " seem peculiarly adapted for sheep-shearing gatherings. Here is one which Mr. T. H. Garland sent to the *Dorset County Chronicle* in 1873.

" Here's a health unto the shepherd,
His clip and his dog,
Thinking on the dumb creatures
While they feed in the field ;
With other dumb creatures
Their fruit they do yield.

For their dung serves the corn ground,
And the wool clothes the poor.
So drink up your liquor
And fill up some more."

The refrain in the principal toast—that of the "meäster", —given at a Dorset "harvest-home" at which I was present [1] :—

"So drink, boys, drink !
And see that you do not spill ;—
For if you do
You shall drink two ;
'Tis by your master's will.—"

is stated by a correspondent in *Notes and Queries* in 1878 (Ser. v, x, 375) to have been heard by him some forty years previously at a sheep-shearing feast in the lower part of Dorsetshire (presumably the western division) when each man was supplied with a small cup, of about the third of a pint, to drink the toast in.

The following fragment of an old sheep-shearing song comes from one of the members of the "Mellstock Quire", as told in the opening pages of Thomas Hardy's *Under the Greenwood Tree :*

"With the rose and the lily
And the daffodowndilly,
The lads and the lasses a-sheep-shearing go."

I regret Mr. Hardy did not give us the remainder of it.

It would seem to have been the custom—so far as I have been able to ascertain from old and reliable informants—up to about the middle of the last century for the young farmers of the neighbourhood to go and help their friends in their shearing, who, of course, would be aided by the shepherds and other labourers of the farmer to whose assistance they had gone. In the evening a good supper would be provided for them ; after which the families and friends of those who came to help were invited to join in games of cards, dancing, or other amusements. I am speaking now more particularly of West Dorset.

This arrangement gradually gave way to gangs or companies of paid workmen, who used to go round to various farms in a district, as it was considered more convenient to the employers, and also cheaper and more satisfactory to pay so much a score for the sheep that were shorn. The shearers were paid and fed

[1] See *post*, p. 70.

according to agreement. There was no "feast", or festival supper, when their work was completed, but a substantial meal consisting of hot meat, vegetables, and plum pudding,—and in some places, as an "extra", roly-poly gooseberry pudding,—was spread out for them on the "sheet" (a winnowing-sheet) on the floor of the barn, or, if the weather permitted, on the turf, which they preferred owing to the draught caused by the large open doors of the barn. In the absence of any festival supper, amusements—other than a few songs, perhaps—were not often indulged in.

The farmers liked their sheep shorn by the end of May, if possible; but, if it was later, then the fat sheep and the "hogs" [1] were also done, the ewes coming last of all. This would sometimes entail the return of the men to finish their work. A big sheep would naturally take longer to shear than a "hog" or a lamb; but a good man would shear about thirty sheep in a day. A man has been known to shear as many as forty; but probably such very expeditious work would often cause the cry of "Snip!" usually used when it was seen that some poor animal had suffered from too hasty a contact with the shears.[2] No fine or other penalty was imposed for these "snips", for they were very general; for if the sheep was not laid or resting so that the skin was properly strained "on the round", as it was called, the skin was apt to get loose and catch the points of the shears, and a "snip" would result. An immediate application of some kind of spirits of tar, which was always forthcoming, would assist the healing and tend to keep the "fly" from the wound.

The "gangs" would usually keep together for the season, though they might vary in number according to the size of the flock at any particular farm, and would stay from one to six days at a place according to the number required to be shorn. They were composed chiefly of thatchers, hedgers, hurdle-makers, under-shepherds and thrashers (in the days before thrashing-machines when the "flail" only was used).

[1] Sheep one year old.

[2] As I write I notice in the *Dorset County Chronicle* for 5th June, 1916, that a Devonshire farmer has created an interesting record by taking the fleeces of 110 of his sheep in one day with the aid of a sheep-shearing machine!

The month of May would seem to be rather early for sheep-shearing; but it must be remembered that this part of Dorset has a long southern seaboard, and the seasons are usually early; whilst the lambing season of the "Dorset horns" is much earlier than that of the flocks to the north of them.

Readers of the Wessex novels will scarcely need to be reminded of the Dorsetshire sheep-shearing scene and the feast that followed it, so graphically described by Mr. Thomas Hardy in chapter xxii—"The Great Barn and the Sheepshearers"—of his book *Far from the Madding Crowd*. The picture is a charming one, for where Mr. Hardy has an old country custom to chronicle,—especially if set in an architectural background—he is always at his best.

"The large side doors were thrown open towards the sun to admit a beautiful light to the immediate spot of the shearers' operations, which was the wood threshing-floor in the centre, formed of thick oak, black with age, and polished by the beating of flails for many generations, till it had grown as slippery and as rich in hue as the state-room of an Elizabethan mansion."

Here, then, the shearers—who comprised a "master-shearer", and some half-dozen others, together with an assistant shearer and a general supervisor—knelt with their polished shears, and beneath each of them lay a captive sheep, for the animal, having been flung down on to its back by a dexterous twist of the right arm, was controlled and kept in its place by the shearer's knees until his task was completed, when the animal, restamped with its owner's initials, was allowed to rejoin the flock. Nothing is omitted; no detail of the preparations for the shearing left out.

"The spacious ends of the building answering ecclesiastically to nave and church extremities, were fenced off with hurdles, the sheep being all collected in a crowd within these two enclosures; and in one angle a catching-pen was formed, in which three or four sheep were continuously kept ready for the shearers to seize without loss of time."

In the background were the women ready to gather up the fleeces, and to twist ropes of wool with a wimble for tying them round. No incident is missed, not even to the cutting, or "snipping" of a sheep; nor the ready means of stanching the blood always at hand in the shape of some tar or other antiseptic liquid; not even the time within which it was considered good work to complete the shearing of a sheep. Anything under the half-hour appears to have been thought good for Weatherbury in those days; but that rate must have continued for fifteen hours to have compared favourably with the times I have mentioned!

"For the shearing supper a long table was placed on the grass-plot beside the house, the end of the table being thrust over the sill of the wide parlour window, and a foot or two into the room. Miss Everdene sat inside the window looking down the table. She was thus at the head without mingling with the men."

Supper being ended, songs followed, when, presently, Bathsheba retired within the house, leaving the party to itself, which, soon after, broke up. There does not appear to have been any "health-drinking", or other recognition of their hostess's hospitality; presumably because the "supper" was one of the terms of the sheep-shearer's engagement, of whom, moreover, the majority were probably more or less strangers to their employer.

William Barnes in his dialect poem "The Shepherd o' the Farm" (p. 35) gives an interesting picture of a Dorsetshire sheep-shearing a century ago.

. . . .

"An' I do goo to washèn pool,
A-sousèn over head an' ears
The shaggy sheep, to cleän their wool
An' meäke 'em ready for the sheärs.

An' when the shearèn time do come
Then we do work vrom dawn till dark;
Where zome do shear the sheep, and zome
Do mark their zides wi' meäster's mark.

An' when the shearèn's all a-done
Then we do eat, an' drink, an' zing
In meäster's kitchen till the tun[1]
Wi' merry sounds do sheake an' ring.

Oh! I be shepherd o' the farm,
Wi' tinklèn bells and sheep-dog's bark,
An' wi' my crook a-thirt my eärm
Here I do rove below the lark."

[1] The chimney-top from the ridge of the house.

Whitsuntide

Club-walking

Whitsuntide was, no doubt, in the old days a time of some considerable festivity amongst a certain class of Dorset folk; although I cannot find that the old "Whitsun Ales",[1] so common in many counties, had—at least under that name—any prominence in Dorsetshire.

It appears, however, from a sermon made by William Kethe at Blandford Forum in 1570 that it was the custom at that time for the "Church Ales" to be kept upon the Sabbath-day, which holy day "the multitude call their revelyng day; which day is spent in bulbeatings, bearebeatings, bowling, dycing, carding, daunsynges, drunkennes, and whoredom, in so much as men could not keepe their servauntes from lyinge out of theyr owne houses the same Sabbath-day at night".

This does not afford a very pleasant picture of the way Dorset folk spent their Whitsuntide in Elizabethan times, and affords some evidence of the brutal sports that were practised amongst them at Whitsuntide as well as on Shrove-Tuesday. But whatever may have been the amusements which the Dorset "multitude" indulged in at that time, it is some satisfaction to find that their only survival to-day is that of the parish, or village, club-walking.

Nearly every village has, or, until recently, had its "club". The old time club was not framed upon the modern provident type, such as those excellent institutions of "Odd Fellows" and other associations founded upon the Friendly Societies' Acts, but "broke" every seven years or so, when the funds then standing to its credit were distributed amongst the members. It was customary in the old clubs that when a member died all the others were called upon to pay 2s. 6d., as a contribution for "death-rate pay". If it was a member's wife who died the contribution was only a shilling.

This system, it can easily be seen, was far more favourable to the local tradespeople and shopkeepers than to the members to

[1] Or "Ale-feasts", which, according to Halliwell, were festivals or merry makings at which ale appears to have been the predominant liquor.

whom more extended credit was given as the time drew near for the " breaking ". In most places now I think it will be found that the old club has been replaced by more benevolent institutions, which provide much better terms in case of the sickness or death of their members. In some parishes the old and new societies have amalgamated, though, of course, those members of the old club who were above a certain age would not be able to join one of the modern Odd Fellows' Societies. They would often, too, join forces for the celebration of the Feast-day. In the parish of Symondsbury, in West Dorset, there has been no " club-walkèn ", or procession, for some thirty years or more. There the old club day was the second Tuesday in May ; but in most places Whitsun week was the favourite time. The members would don their sashes, rosettes, etc., and with flags and banners and preceded by a band would start about 9 a.m., walking generally four abreast in procession, the outer one of each four—usually an older man—carrying a pole, to call at the principal houses in the parish where they would be likely to obtain refreshments and sometimes money. Cider would be brought out to them in big jugs ; and after being refreshed they would move on to some other farmhouse or kindly neighbour, taking care to be back in time for divine service in the parish church at noon.

The poles carried in these processions, generally painted blue with white bands running round them, are often handsomely ornamented with metal tops or points screwed on to a round wooden knob painted yellow, something in the style of the old halberds, and are much prized in the villages to which they belong. I am informed that an elderly lady living in a West Dorset village still keeps a couple of these poles at her house, which were formerly used in the local procession. If I remember rightly, too, the borough officials at Lyme Regis possess quite a number of them ; whilst a very fine collection of Somersetshire ones is preserved in the county museum at Taunton.

The " feast " was provided in a large tent or marquee erected in a field usually lent by one of the principal farmers in the parish, at which a large company assembled, the rector of the parish usually presiding, with several of the local gentry and farmers in attendance.

The dinner—which was paid for by the members—over, the speeches usual on such an occasion followed, the loyal toasts always being heartily received. The rest of the afternoon was spent in various amusements, games for the children, and dancing for the young people. There were generally a few " standings " for the selling of cakes, sweets, and toys, together with an " Aunt Sally " or a shooting gallery rigged up for the occasion. The field was frequented by a large number of visitors, who looked forward to meeting once a year at this pleasant gathering.

I may add that though I have attended these " feasts " on more than one occasion I have not noticed anything in the conduct of the people such as is animadverted upon in the Blandford sermon. It is certainly significant of the improvement in rustic morals in this respect that the modern parson only deemed it necessary to warn his hearers against the possible occurrence of some of those very delinquencies which his Elizabethan predecessor roundly accused them of having committed.[1]

In his " Fore-say " (*ante*) William Barnes alludes to these festal gatherings, where he says that " Whitsuntide is now a time commonly chosen for the yearly meeting of the Friendly Societies' ' club-walkèn ', as it is called in Dorset ", and mentions amongst the " resources of mirth " formerly existing at these celebrations " the mazes or miz-mazes, to be threaded by such as thought they would guide their feet to a more speedy outcoming than they would always find ; but the mazes are now levelled and lost with the May queens ".

He continues :—

" The village wake, called in Dorset ' Feast ' (*Festa*) belonged mostly to the Christian seasons, as it was mainly holden at or near to the festival of the Saint to whom the village church was dedicated. At some of these feasts, however, there was cudgel-playing ; and I fear it cannot well be said that cudgel-fighting is the most fitting token of joy for the festival of St. Mary or St. John, albeit it be called ' play ' ; but the feast brought to some houses of the parish merry meetings of friends with kindred and friends from elsewhere."

[1] See Barnes's poem " Whitsuntide an' Club walkèn ", *post*, p. 61.

A fitting conclusion is afforded to this subject by Barnes's very interesting dialect poem descriptive of what took place on these occasions—probably half a century before I ever saw them—which I here give in full :—

"WHITSUNTIDE AN' CLUB WALKÈN."

"Ees, last Whit-Monday I an' Meäry
Got up betimes to mind the deäiry ;
An' gi'ed the milkèn päils a scrub,
An' dressed, an' went to zee the club,
Vor up at public-house by ten
O'clock the pleäce wer vull o' men,
A-dress'd to goo to church, an' dine,
An' walk about the pleäce in line.

Zoo off they started, two an' two,
Wi' painted poles an' knots of blue,
An' girt silk flags,—I wish my box
'D a-got em all in ceäpes an' frocks,—
A-weäven wide an' flappèn loud
In pläysome winds above the crowd ;
While fifes did squeak an' drums did rumble,
An' deep beäzzoons did grunt an' grumble,
An' all the vo'k in gathrèn crowds
Kick'd up the doust in smeechy[1] clouds,
That slowly rose an' spread abrode
In streamèn äir above the road.

An' then at church there were sich lots
O' hats a-hangèn up with knots,
An' poles a-stood as thick as ever
The rushes stood beside a river.
An' Mr Goodman gi'ed em warnèn
To spend their evenèn lik' their mornèn ;
An' not to pray with mornèn tongues,
An' then to zwear wi' evenèn lungs ;
Nor vu'st sheäke hands, to let the wrist
Lift up at last a bruisèn vist ;
Vor clubs were all a-meäned vor friends,
He twold em, an' vor better ends
Than twitèn vo'k an' picken quarrels,
An' tipplèn cups an' emptèn barrels,—
Vor meäkèn woone man do another
In need the kindness ov a brother.

[1] Dusty, like smoke.

An' after church they went to dine
'Ithin the long-wall'd room behine
The public-house, where you remember,
We had our dance back last December,
An' there they meäde sich stunnèn clatters
Wi' knives an' forks, an' pleätes an' platters;
An' waiters ran, an' beer did pass
Vrom tap to jug, from jug to glass;
An' when they took away the dishes,
They drink'd good healths an' wish'd good wishes
To all the girt vo'k o' the land,
An' all good things vo'k took in hand;
An' woone cried *hip, hip, hip*! an' hollow'd,
An' t'others all struck in an' vollow'd;
An' grabbed their drink wi' eager clutches,
An' swigged it wi' sich hearty glutches,[1]
As vo'k, stark mad wi' pweison stuff,
That thought theirzel's not mad enough.

An' after that they went all out
In rank ageän, an' walk'd about,
An' gi'ed zome parish vo'k a call;
An' then went down to Narley Hall
An' had zome beer, an' danced between
The elem trees upon the green.
An' down along the road they done
All sorts o' mad-cap things vor fun;
An' danced, a-pokèn out their poles,
An' pushèn bwoys down into holes;
An' Sammy Stubbs come out o' rank
An' kissed me up ageän the bank,
A saucy chap; I han't vor-gi'ed en
Not yet,—in short, I han't a-zeed en.
Zoo in the dusk ov evenèn zome
Went back to drink, an' zome went hwome."

Hay-making

The season of hay-making would seem never to have been such a period of gaiety and festivity in Dorsetshire as was the case with the "harvest-home" gatherings later in the year. The success of the hay harvest, however, was a very important matter to so large a pastoral community as the county comprised; and without doubt some celebration by way of reward for and appreciation of services loyally rendered, often in long extended hours of work when the weather was uncertain, was indulged

[1] Gulps.

in at the conclusion of that harvest. Extra money payments, as in the corn harvest, have largely taken the place of social gatherings and festivities amongst the labourers in which their employers once freely joined. Still in many places at the in-gathering of the hay an extra jar of cider or ale would be brought out, and the men would sit down and have a chat amongst themselves and, perhaps, a song or two; whilst at the close hats would be raised and "hip, hip, hurrahs" would be given.

In later years, both in hay and corn harvesting, machinery has taken a very active part in reducing the amount of manual labour employed in these operations, which at its introduction went sorely against the conservative feelings of the Dorset peasant. This feeling was just as strongly expressed as in the great industrial centres in the North where labour-saving appliances were ever on the increase; and sometimes took the form of reprisals by way of burning hay and corn ricks as well as the occasional destruction of the offending machinery.

Under these influences in course of time the very names of the old haymakers' several occupations would be lost. In William Barnes's early days—a century ago—these were numerous and distinctive. We are fortunate in having him to record what they were. Here is a description which he gives in his *Glossary* (1863) of what haymaking was like in his time (*s.v.* Häymeäken).

"Hay-making consists of several operations which with fine weather, commonly follow each other in Dorsetshire, thus: The mown grass—in *zwath*, swath,—is thrown abroad—*tedded*, and afterwards turned once or twice; in the evening it is raked up into little ridges—*rollers*,—single or double, as they may be formed by one raker, or by two raking against each other; and sometimes put up into small cones or heaps, called *cocks*. On the following morning the rollers or cocks are thrown abroad in *passels*—parcels,—which, after being turned, are in the evening put up into large ridges—*weäls*; and the weals are sometimes *pooked*, put up into larger cones—*pooks*,—in which the hay is loaded. In raking grass into double rollers, or pushing hay into weäls, the fore raker or pickman is said to *rake in* or *push in*, or *row* or *roo*, and the other to *close*."

Barnes had already preserved many of these terms in two of his charming dialect poems, one on "Häy-meäkèn", and the other on "Häy-carrèn" (pp. 51–2), which afford so delightful a picture of rustic life in the hay-field that one feels inclined to say, too:

"I do long to toss a pick,
A pitchèn or a-meäkèn rick."

Harvest Home

The celebration of the ingathering of the corn harvest is common to all our counties and to most countries. Full accounts of these festivals and their significance may be found in Brand's, Hone's, and Chambers's works, as well as in those of less known writers.

It is to the late William Barnes that we might expect to look for a fitting description of a Dorset harvest-home feast, or supper, and we find it in an account,—as particular and as life-like as a painting of an old Dutch interior—of what usually took place on these occasions, which he contributed to Hone's *Year Book* (p. 586), from which I take the following extract:—

"*Harvest Home*, formerly celebrated with great mirth but now a declining usage, was a feast given by the farmer at the end of harvest, or when his hay and corn were got in . . . Some years ago the 'harvest home' in my native county, Dorset, was kept up with good old English hospitality.

"When the last load was ricked the labourers, male and female, the swarthy reaper and the sun-burnt hay-maker, the saucy boy who had not seen twelve summers and the stiff horny-handed old mower who had borne the toil of fifty, all made a happy groupe, and went with singing and loud-laughing to the harvest-home supper at the farmhouse, where they were expected by the good mistress, dressed in a quilted petticoat and a linsey-wolsey apron, with shoes fastened by large silver buckles which extended over her foot like a pack-saddle on a donkey.

"The dame and her husband welcomed them to a supper of good wholesome food, a round of beef, and a piece of bacon; and perhaps the host and hostess had gone so far as to kill a fowl or two, or stick a turkey, which they had fattened in the wheat-yard. The plain English fare was eaten from wooden trenchers, by the side of which were put little cups of horn filled with beer or cider. When the cloth was removed one of the men, putting forth his large hand like the gauntlet of an armed knight, would grasp his horn of beer, and standing up on a pair of legs which had long out-grown the largest holes of the village stocks, and with a voice which, if he had not been speaking a dialect of the English language, you might have thought came from the deep-seated lungs of a lion, he would propose the health of the farmer in the following lines :—

> 'Here's a health unto our miaster
> The founder of the feast,
> And I hope to God wi' all my heart
> His soul in heaven mid rest ;
>
> That everything mid prosper
> That ever he tiak in hand,
> Vor we be all his sarvants,
> And all at his command.'

" After this would follow a course of jokes, anecdotes, and songs, in some of which the whole company joined, without attention to the technicalities of counterpoint, bass, tenor, and treble, common chords and major thirds ; but each singing the air and pitching in at the key that best fitted his voice, making a medley of big and little sounds, like the lowings of oxen and the low beatings of old ewes, mixed up with the shrill pipings of the lambs at a fair.

" The conversation commonly turned on the incidents of the summer ; how the hay-makers overtook the mowers, or how the rain kept the labour back ; how they all crept in a heap under the waggon in a thunderstorm ; how nearly some of them were crushed under the load that was upset ; who was the best mower or reaper in the village ; which field yielded the best crop ; and which stack was most likely to heat."

Later Barnes devoted two of his charming dialect poems to a similar description, which form such a delightful complement to the whole subject that I have no hesitation in reproducing them here in full. They are to be found at pp. 78–80 of the first collected edition of the poems published by Kegan Paul & Co. in 1879, and again in 1888.[1]

[1] The first edition of *Poems of Rural Life in the Dorset Dialect* was in 1844, whilst the earlier edition of Hone's *Year Book* in which Barnes's contribution first appeared was published in 1832. A change of spelling in some of the dialect words,—particularly the " vowel sounds ",—(*e.g.* " ia ", in " miaster ", or " tiak ", to " eä ") will be noticed in the earlier and later editions of the poems ; a scheme not involving so much a change of pronunciation, perhaps, but, as justified by Barnes in the preface to the third edition of his " first collection " of poems, published in 1862, on the ground that " while it affords the Dorset forms of the words to Dorset readers it may make them of more English look and more legible to others ".

Harvest Hwome

The vu'st peärt. The Supper

"Since we wer striplèns näighbour John,
The good wold merry times be gone:
But we do like to think upon
What we've a-zeed an' done.
When I wer up a hardish lad,
At harvest hwome the work-vo'k had
Sich suppers, they were jumpèn mad
Wi' feästèn an' wi' fun.

At uncle's I do mind, woone year,
I zeed a vill o' hearty cheer;
Fat beef an' puddèn, eäle an' beer,
Vor every workman's crop;
An' after they'd a-gi'ed God thanks,
They all zot down, in two long ranks,
Along a teäble-bwoard o' planks,
Wi' uncle at the top.

An' there, in platters, big and brown,
Wer red fat beäcon, an' a roun'
O' beef wi' gravy that would drown
A little rwoastèn pig;
Wi' beäns an' teäties vull a zack,
An' cabbage that would meäke a stack,
An' puddèns brown, a-speckled black
Wi' figs, so big's my wig.

An' uncle, wi' his elbows out,
Did carve, and meäke the gravy spout;
An' aunt did gi'e the mugs about
A-frothèn to the brim.
Pleätes werden then ov e'then ware,
They ate off pewter, that would bear
A knock; or wooden trenchers, square,
Wi' zalt-holes at the rim.

An' zoo they munch'd their hearty cheer,
An' dipped their beards in frothy beer,
An' laugh'd, an' jok'd—they couldden hear
What woone another zaid.
An' all o'm drink'd, wi' woone accword,
The wold vo'ks' health: and beät the bwoard,
An' swung their eärms about, an' roar'd,
Enough to crack woone's head."

Second Peärt. What they did after Supper

" Zoo after supper wer a-done,
They clear'd the teäbles, an' begun
To have a little bit o' fun,
As long as they mid stop.
The wold woones took their pipes to smoke
An' tell their teäles, an' laugh an' joke,
A-lookèn at the younger vo'k,
That got up vor a hop.

Woone screäped away, wi' merry grin,
A fiddle stuck below his chin;
An' woone o'm took the rollèn pin,
An' beät the fryèn-pan.
An' t'others, dancèn to the sound,
Went in and out, an' droo an' roun',
An' kick'd, an' beät the tuen down,
A-laughèn, mäid an' man.

An' then a mäid, all up tip-tooe,
Vell down; and woone o'm wi' his shoe
Slit down her pocket-hole in two,
Vrom top a-most to bottom.
An' when they had a-danced enough,
They got a-pläyèn blindman's buff,
And sar'd the mäidens pretty rough,
When woonce they had a-got em.

An' zome did drink, an' laugh, an' roar,
An' lots of teäles they had in store,
O' things that happened years avore
To them, or vo'k they know'd.
An' zome did joke, an' zome did zing,
An' meäke the girt wold kitchen ring;
Till uncle's cock wi' flappèn wing,
Stratch'd out his neck an' crow'd."

To these Barnes has added " A Zong of the Harvest Home " (p. 80), of which the refrain to each of the six verses is:

" The happy zight—the merry night—
The men's delight—the Harvest Hwome."

Again, many years later, in his " Fore-say " to this work, Barnes speaks of the decline of the old-time celebrations of this festival. He says:

" The feasts of Harvest-Home in which the work-folk were invited to

'the hall
where beards wagged all,—' [1]

to share of mirth and meat under the smiles of the master and mistress, as tokens of approbation of their work, are now less customary than they formerly were, as in these commercial days it seems to be felt that the clock measures all the workman owes his master and the paytable all that the master owes to him."

As Brand says (i, 443), " Different places adopt different ceremonies " ; but that which seems to me to conform most to the Dorset ritual on these occasions is that of " crying the knack ", or " neck ", in the neighbouring counties of Devon and Cornwall, and in which there seems not only a strong affinity but traces of considerable antiquity.[2]

In 1873 I contributed an article to *Notes and Queries* (Ser. IV, xii, 491), describing " A Dorsetshire Harvest-Home " in West Dorset, which I had recently attended, and this I now reproduce :

" It was my good fortune to be present in September last at one of those old-fashioned gatherings in the West of Dorset, a harvest-home, and I thought that perhaps an account of such a quaint and time-honoured custom might not be unacceptable to some among the readers of ' N. and Q.', especially as these congenial meetings are becoming scarcer year by year and ere long bid fair to rank amongst the things that have been. Small sums of money are now in many places given to the men, women, and boys instead of the usual supper, a practice that I am sorry to say seems to be on the increase, and which I here offer up my voice to protest against.

" I say ' sorry ', first, because it denotes a departure from old customs, and, secondly, because the purpose for which the alteration is intended is, it seems to me, but very imperfectly carried out. At the time of such a general holiday in the parish the labourers of one farm do not seem willing to disperse quietly to their own homes and husband the few shillings they may have received as ' largess ', whilst their fellows are enjoying themselves on another farm ; but rather to keep up a harvest-home of their own in the village ale-house, though, I need scarcely say, not of so orderly a character as that of the *bonâ fide* supper ; and which, to tell the truth, they themselves much prefer, for a ' Dorsetshire labourer ', though he may be poor, is none the less Conservative.

[1] Thomas Tusser : *Five Hundred Points of Good Husbandry.*

[2] Conf. *Shropshire Folk-lore*, pp. 372–3.

" On the day appointed for the celebration of the harvest, the labourers from the several farms attended afternoon service in the parish church, dressed in their best clothes, the church being decorated in the usually seasonable manner. The entrance-gates of the principal farms were likewise decorated with an arch of evergreen, flowers, corn, etc., crowned with a sickle and scythe swathed in bands of wheat and barley, the whole surmounted by appropriate mottoes.

" In the evening tables were laid out in the kitchen of a size sufficient to accommodate the men, women, boys and girls employed on the farm, the ' master ', assisted by such members of his family as might be, sitting at their head and carving a grand rump of Old English beef.

" As soon as the company had partaken of as much beef and plum-pudding as was considered desirable an adjournment was made to a large tree that stood near the homestead, where the following quaint custom—peculiar, I was informed, to the west of Dorset[1]—took place.

" The men formed themselves into a circle, and each taking off his hat and holding it out in front of him, stooped to the ground; then, led by one standing in the centre, chanted the words: ' We have 'em ' (or ' 'en '). The first word, ' We,' is commenced in a very low tone, the men the while slowly and gradually raising themselves up, and so prolonged till they have almost reached their full height. They close the sentence by saying ' have 'em ' more quickly. This is done three times. They then shout ' Huzza ! ' once. Again they stoop down and go through the same performance; finishing up this time with two ' huzzas '. This is repeated once more, and finally wound up by huzzaing three times. As soon as the men have finished the women come forward and go through the same ceremony. This, when well performed, has a not altogether unimpressive or unmusical effect. The words, I believe, bear reference to the conclusion of the harvest and the sheaves of corn being satisfactorily ' had ' in.

" The discharge of small cannon, (the peculiar care of the boys) likewise gave considerable *éclat* to the whole proceeding. This over, the party returned to the house and entered upon a course of singing and drinking, not unmixed with dancing in the back kitchen.

" The first song was, of course, in honour of the ' meäster ', and unenriched by the Dorset vernacular indulged in by the toast-master, was in the following words :—

[1] " It would seem to be somewhat similar, however, to the custom of ' crying the knack ', which obtains in Devon and Cornwall."

'Here's a health unto our master,
The founder of the feast,
And when that he is dead and gone,
I hope his soul may rest.
I wish all things may prosper,
Whatever he takes in hand,
For we are all his servants
And serve at his command.
So drink, boys, drink!
And see that you do not spill.
For if you do,
You shall drink two,
'Tis by your master's will.'

"This song is repeated till everybody present has drunk the health.

"Then follow the 'healths' of the mistress and various members of the family, to the following words:—

'Here's Mrs' (or Mr's) good health!
Let the glass go round
And the trumpet sound,—
Huzza! huzza! huzza!
Down fall all the re-bels,
We long to see the day,—
Con-fusion unto them
That set 'em up again!
Huzza! huzza! huzza!
Confusion etc.'

"This, like the last, was repeated till all had drunk.

"Then followed the curious and laughable custom of 'drinking to your love over the left arm'. Each man, while the following verse was being sung, was obliged to drain his mug or horn-cup of ale by holding it in his right hand, and passing it outside of and over his left arm, which would be thrown across the chest. Great merriment was afforded when some of the older hands, through age or other infirmities failed to accomplish this in a satisfactory manner. The words sung were the following:—

'As I was a-riding over a mountain so high
I saw a pretty girl that plea-sed my eye,
She plea-sed my eye, but pla-gued my heart;
From this cup of liquor we never will part;
'Twill do us no good,—'twill do us no harm.
"Here's a health to my love, over left arm, over left arm!"
Here's a health etc.'

"This was continued till all had satisfactorily passed the crucial test. Songs of a more general character and sundry speeches followed; and eventually the proceedings were brought to a close about midnight by the whole company joining in the National Anthem, 'God Save the Queen.'"

The following version, similar but less ornate, of the " whooping " ceremony,—as it was called in the district,—was given me as having been performed at a farmhouse in the same neighbourhood as the last. At the end of the harvest a jar of cider or ale and two small cups were taken just outside the yard, when all the labourers would gather in a circle round the jar, which is presided over by the oldest man amongst them, and, taking off their hats and standing in a stooping position, would bow slowly down to the ground, whilst singing in a low, guttural, drawling tone, " We-e-e-e have 'en ! " They then stand upright again and holloa " hurrah " once. This is gone through a second time, when the " hurrah " is given twice. Again, a third repetition, when three " hurrahs " are given. They then have a drink all round ; after which they return mostly for songs or dances after supper. I have been told that these cheers were often heard at a distance of a mile or two !

At the time I sent the above account to *Notes and Queries* I was not acquainted with Jacob Grimm's *Teutonic Mythology*—or, rather, Stallybrass's translation of it,—in four volumes, which were not published till 1880–8. After I had read it I was struck by the very strong resemblance to the Dorset " whooping ", as it is called, that exists in the custom of the people in Lower Saxony invoking their great god Woden at the conclusion of the harvest. Grimm states (i, 154) that it is usual to leave a clump of corn standing in a field to Woden for his horse.

He then describes (p. 156) a custom in Schaumburg where the people, having finished the mowing of the corn, or having purposely left only a small strip standing which they could cut down at a stroke, then at the finish would raise their implements aloft, beating the blades three times with the strop, while each would spill a small quantity of beer on the ground and then drink himself. They would then wave their hats and beat their scythes three times and cry aloud, " Wôld-wôld-wôld," which, Grimm says, a Schaumburg man pronounced as " wauden ". They would then march home shouting and singing. If the ceremony were omitted the next year would bring bad crops of hay and corn.

It is a pity that Grimm did not know of the custom as existing in western Dorsetshire, which I have described above. I wonder whether he would have agreed with the suggestion that I now venture to make, that the Dorset labourers' cry in this corner of old Wessex of "We hav'en", repeated three times, is but a survival of the old invocation to the great god Woden of their Saxon ancestors, still continued from time immemorial at these harvest celebrations but of which the real significance and meaning have been lost.

Shortly before I left England in 1889 I was anxious to test this resemblance still further, so I invited certain of the farm labourers belonging to the same West Dorset parish—Symondsbury—in which the ceremony had been performed in 1873, after they had attended the now usual harvest festival service at the old parish church, to do their "whooping" on the lawn in front of the Manor House close to the church. They went through it all in much the same way as their predecessors had done, and again the close affinity to what Grimm had related was borne in upon me. Out of compliment to him I added a further Teutonic association that was by no means unacceptable to the performers. I made the men drink the healths from a tall seventeenth century pewter tankard, or loving-cup, with covered lid (of which there were one or two similar ones in the Victoria and Albert Museum at South Kensington), of a capacity of several quarts, which had formerly been the property of some civic company or guild in some German town (to judge from the inscription), this being the first opportunity I had had of putting it to anything approaching its former use. It would be a strange but not inappropriate incident if it should again, after so many years, have assisted in the survival of an ancient Teutonic festivity.

I have since obtained from locally printed sources and otherwise a few songs or verses that were sung at harvest-home gatherings. Several of these, as I have already pointed out, may also have been sung at sheep-shearing feasts in the days when these feasts were more worthy of the name. The main toasts were evidently the same. In particular the one [1] sent by Mr. T. H. Garland to the *Dorset County Chronicle* (which had reprinted my paper from *Notes and Queries*), wherein he added that he was a West Dorset man and had for many years witnessed the old customs to which I had alluded.

[1] See *ante*, p. 53.

The following verse appeared in the *Bridport News* in 1874 as having been sung at the same place as my account referred to:

> "When the wheat is all ripe the harvest begin,
> The farmer the fruits of the earth gather in;
> In the mornings as soon as the reap hooks are grind
> We repair to the field for to reap and to bind."

Another couplet ran :—

> "When the harvest is over to our master's we will steer,
> And wet a good supper with a drink of strong beer."

The following toast was given by a farm labourer at a harvest home at Blandford in 1849 [1] :—

> "Horses strong, sheep healthy,
> Barns full, money plenty."

A correspondent in *Notes and Queries* in 1878 (Ser. v, x, 375) speaks to his having heard, some forty years previously, the same refrain

> "Drink, boys, drink, and see you do not spill;
> If you do you shall drink two,
> For 'tis our master's will."

at a sheep-shearing feast in the lower part of Dorsetshire, when each man was supplied with a small cup of about the third of a pint to drink the customary healths in.[2]

Forfeits.—Amongst the amusements at harvest home suppers forfeits appear to have been sometimes indulged in (though such games were usually set apart for Christmas), when songs or rhythmic jingles were sung with the object of entrapping the unwary. The following were given me as having been used at harvest homes in the parish of Stoke Abbott, also in West Dorset.

One of the company leads off with the following rhythmic jingle, followed by the others :—

> "Green grow the leaves on the hawthorn tree,
> Some grow high and some grow low;
> With my ringo and my jingo
> We seldom disagree,
> And the tenor of my song goes merrily—
> And the tenor of my song goes merrily."

[1] "N. & Q.," Ser. v, x, 306. For a more correctly rhyming Worcestershire variant see the same volume, p. 375.

[2] See *ante*, p. 54.

The leader alone then sings :

"Twenty, nineteen, eighteen—"

The next one in rotation :

"Seventeen, sixteen, fifteen—"

The next, in their order :

"Fourteen, thirteen, twelve—"
"Eleven, ten, nine—"
"Eight, seven, six—"

The last in rotation chimes in with "Five, four, three"—and they all add :

"And the tenor of my song goes merrily."

When this is done the person next to the leader begins it over again, and it goes on as before, except that when he comes to the figures he starts with "Seventeen, sixteen, fifteen"—the next to him taking it up as before, and so on to the end. This over, the third person in rotation commences the strain, beginning the figures at "Fourteen, thirteen, twelve"—and so on as before until the whole is exhausted.

Should anyone make a mistake in repeating his portion he must pay forfeit, which, on these occasions, generally consists in being made to drink something.

Here is another one from the same place :—

"O splice the cable-rope,
The rope it is so fine ; [1]
And with a sugar loaf we'll have
A glass of currant wine ;
And if the wine is sharp
The sugar makes it sweet ;
What greater joy in all the world
When two sweethearts do meet !
With my Rider, Ready, Rum,
My Rider, Ready, Rum,
So drink *half* your liquor, boys,
And say no more than 'Mum'.
So drink *off* your liquor, boys,
And say no more than 'Mum' !"

[1] Possibly a covert allusion to the excellent quality of the hemp grown in the neighbourhood. So highly was it esteemed that a statute, 21 Henry VIII, provided that cables intended for the use of the Royal Navy should be made from hemp grown within a certain radius of Bridport, within which radius the parish of Stoke Abbott is situated.

The above rhyme is sung by all the company together, after which the leader, and any one who may be initiated in the game, endeavour to entrap the person sitting next them into answering more than the permitted " Mum " by accusing him, truly or otherwise, of having made a mistake in singing or in drinking more than half the liquor at the wrong time, so as to entail a forfeit. The verse is then gone through again, and the next person is interrogated with the like object, and so on in rotation until all have been subjected to the ordeal.

CHRISTMASTIDE

The season of Christmas may be said to be the principal one for festival celebrations in all English counties. The customary festivities, which extended from Christmas Eve until Twelfth Night (the " twelve days of Christmas ") in Dorsetshire embraced all kinds of amusements and games, indulged in by old and young alike, some of these being of considerable antiquity.

In December, 1880, I contributed an article to *Notes and Queries* (Ser. VI, ii, 504) on " Christmas in Dorsetshire ". Amongst others I there mentioned the custom of " Going a-Christmasing " a few days before the great festival; but as I have already fully alluded to that under " St Thomas's Day "[1] there is no occasion to refer to it further here. I also mentioned the old custom of bringing in the " Christmas 'brown' (or 'bron') " or yule-log, already sufficiently treated of under " Christmas Eve ".[2] I then referred to the playing of " forfeits ", a subject which I treated of at some length, and gave one or two forfeit-rhymes as illustrations.

Forfeits.—Since writing that article to *Notes and Queries* I contributed a long paper to the *Folk-Lore Journal* for 1889 (pp. 202-64), on " Dorsetshire Children's Games ", in which I dealt at much greater length with the subject of " forfeits " and gave several more forfeit-rhymes. By dealing with the playing of " forfeits " here,—being more particularly a Christmas amusement,—I shall be able later on to appreciably lighten my long chapter on " Children's Games ".

[1] See Chapter I, p. 49.
[2] See Chapter I, p. 50.

This is what I said in the *Folk-Lore Journal* (p. 239) :—

" Playing forfeits was a very favourite amusement with Dorset folk during the long winter evenings, and more particularly at Christmas-tide, when the family circle had generally more than its usual complement. There should be, if possible, twenty or thirty present to play forfeits properly, who arrange themselves round the room as conveniently as possible, and should be careful to be provided with some trifling article wherewith to pay the forfeits should any be incurred.

" In some places the players sit in two lines opposite each other, each holding in his or her hand a piece of paper, or pencil, or thimble, or some such slight article, wherewith to pay their forfeit in case they should make a mistake in answering.

" A common form of playing forfeits was that of a game which involved a question and answer. Two persons sat in front of the party, one of whom says as follows : ' Here's a poor old sailor just come from the sea, pray what have you got to give him ? ' Whoever is called upon to answer the question must be careful not to mention the word ' red ', ' white,' ' blue ' or ' black ', or even, sometimes, give the name of any colour at all ; and must not say ' yes ' or ' no ',—in default of which she or he will have to pay a forfeit. The questioner then passes on to the next one, and says : ' Here's a poor old sailor just come from sea, pray what have you got to give him ? ' The one questioned must be careful only to answer, ' Nothing at all.' The other replies, ' Nothing at all ! ' and with an insinuating attempt to obtain an answer that will subject the speaker to a forfeit will add, ' Not a red coat ? ' or ' Not a blue hat ? ' On the person interrogated persisting in replying ' Nothing at all ', the other moves on, in the hope of getting a more favourable response out of another player ; and so on, until the questioner has gone all round. After this has been done, any forfeits that may have been obtained have to be redeemed by those persons who have been so unfortunate as to incur them.

" Another form of playing forfeits was called ' Yes, No, Black, and White ', these being the four words which must not be mentioned in the answer. In this game any kind of question was permitted.

" This was sometimes called ' The old soldier ', when each of the party in turn must take a poker in the right hand and knock, and, passing it to his neighbour with the left, say : ' An old soldier is come to town, what will you please to give him ? ' You may answer whatever you like, except ' yes ', ' no ', ' white ', or ' black '. The object is to induce the person interrogated to use one or other of these words, when a forfeit occurs.

" Another form the game would sometimes take was that of a ' word puzzle ', when an outlandish single word, or a curiously involved sentence had to be repeated several times (seven or nine was the usual number) without a mistake ; on failure of which a forfeit was exacted.

" The following is a specimen of such a word :—

' Aldibirondifosdiforniosdikos.'

and this of a sentence :—

' Of all the saws I ever saw saw, I never saw a saw saw as that saw saws.'

" Here is another of a slightly different character in a versified form :—

' A twister of twist once twisted a twist,
And the twist that he twisted was a three-twisted twist ;
But in twisting the twist one twist came untwisted,
And the twist that untwisted untwisted the twist.'

" The redemption of the forfeits takes place in the following way. Two persons, as before, remain in front of the others, the one sitting in a chair facing the party, the other kneeling down and laying his or her head in the lap of the other, with the face downwards. The person sitting in the chair will hold the forfeited article that is about to be redeemed over the bent head of the person kneeling in front of her, and will say as follows : ' Here's a thing, and a very pretty thing ! What must the owner of this pretty thing do to redeem it again ? ' Or, ' What must the owner do to receive it again ? ' Whatever the person who has his or her head in the other's lap (and who, of course, cannot see what or whose is the article held up) says the owner of that article must do, or the forfeit cannot be redeemed, let it never be so much prized. The penalties of redemption sometimes oblige the ordeal of crawling up the chimney, or, at least, attempting to do so ; or giving a sweetheart's name ; or she or he may be told to ' run the gauntlet ', or ' to go through purgatory ', both of which have specific penalties attached to them by Dorset players ; or to sing in one corner of the room, cry in another, laugh in another, and dance in another.

" Sometimes the task imposed is either something which is apparently impossible to perform, such as being told ' to bite an inch off the poker ', or ' to put yourself through the key-hole ' ; or else it is designed to make the victim ridiculous.

" There are many other ways and means suggested by which the forfeits may be redeemed, and much amusement is frequently caused before the articles can be reclaimed. The game is often kept up with spirit for hours."

William Barnes, in his *Glossary of the Dorset Dialect* (1863), describes a game of forfeits to which he gives the name of "Snappèn tongs". Those playing it stand up in a room in which are seats for all but one of them ; and when the tongs are snapped all run to sit down, and the one who fails to get a seat pays a forfeit.[1]

"A favourite form which the game of forfeits will sometimes take is that of making persons in turn repeat in their proper order various lines of a jingle or rhyme, when if it were not correctly rendered a forfeit was claimed. The following is an example [2] :—

"One of the company who knows the game (all being seated round the fire) commences by saying :

'Ragged-and-tough.'

"And this having gone the circuit of the company, he or she begins the second round with :

'Not Ragged-and-tough, but Huckem-a-buff,
First cousin to Ragged-and-tough.'

"This being duly honoured, he or she begins again :

'Not Ragged-and-tough, nor Huckem-a-buff, first cousin to Ragged-and-tough, but Miss Grizzle, maiden-aunt to Huckem-a-buff, first cousin to Ragged-and-tough.'

"This is continued through the following rounds :—

'Not Ragged-and-tough,
Nor Huckem-a-buff, first cousin, etc.
Nor Miss Grizzle, maiden-aunt, etc.
But Goody Gherkin, grandmama to Miss Grizzle, etc.

'Not Ragged-and-tough,
Nor Huckem-a-buff, first cousin, etc.
Nor Miss Grizzle, maiden-aunt, etc.
Nor Goody Gherkin, grandmama, etc.
But little Snap, favourite dog of Goody Gherkin, grandmama, etc.

'Not Ragged-and tough,
Nor Huckem-a-buff, first cousin, etc.
Nor Miss Grizzle, maiden-aunt, etc.
Nor Goody Gherkin, grandmama, etc.
Nor little Snap, favourite dog, etc.
But the whip which tickled the tail of little Snap,
Favourite dog of Goody Gherkin,
Grandmama of Miss Grizzle,
Maiden-aunt of Huckem-a-buff,
First cousin to Ragged-and-tough.'

[1] This is evidently akin to the modern games of "General Post" or "Musical Chairs", in which latter the piano takes the place of the tongs.

[2] This and the following rhymes also formed part of my paper on "Dorsetshire Children's Games" in the *Folk-Lore Journal* already mentioned.

"Each person, in turn, has to repeat this jingle, gradually increasing in length, going backwards through the list, a new character being introduced each round; so that by the time the last lines have been reached someone's memory is sure to become confused and a mistake be made in the repetition, for which, amidst general laughter, a forfeit is claimed.

"Another form of rhyme or jingle is the following, which I first learned, as a child, from my mother, and is repeated in the same way as 'Ragged-and-tough':—

'A gape-mouth (or gaping) wide-mouthed, waddling frog;
Two pudding ends won't choke a dog;
Three monkeys tied to a log;
Four mares stuck in a bog;
Five puppy-dogs and our dog "Ball"
Loudly for their breakfast call;
Six beetles on a wall,
Close to an old woman's apple-stall;
Seven lobsters in a dish,
As good as any heart could wish;
Eight cobblers, cobblers all,
Working with their tools and awl;
Nine comets in the sky,
Some are low and some are high;
Ten peacocks in the air,
I wonder how they all got there,
You don't know and I don't care;
Eleven ships sailing on the main,
Some bound for France and some for Spain,
I wish them all safe back again;
Twelve hunters, hares, and hounds,
Hunting over other men's grounds.' [1]

"Here is another similar rhyme of an alliterative character, repeated in the same way:—

'One old ox opening oysters;
Two toads totally tired trying to trot to Tewkesbury;
Three tame tigers taking tea;
Four fat friars fishing for frogs;
Five fairies finding fire-flies;
Six soldiers shooting snipe;
Seven salmon sailing in Solway;
Eight elegant engineers eating excellent eggs;
Nine nimble noblemen nibbling non-pareils; (*apples*)
Ten tall tinkers tasting tamarinds;
Eleven electors eating early endive;
Twelve tremendous tale-bearers telling truth.' [2]

"The following Christmas lines, of a similar character to the foregoing, were contributed by the late William Barnes to the *Dorset County Chronicle* in February, 1882:

[1] *Conf.*: A slight variant in Halliwell's *Nursery Rhymes* (ed. 1846, No. ccli).

[2] *Conf.*: A different variant in Halliwell's *Nursery Rhymes* (No. ccxxvii).

'The first day of Christmas my true love sent to me:
(1) The sprig of a juniper tree.[1]
The second day, etc.
(2) Two turtle doves, and No. 1.
The third day, etc.
(3) Three French hens, and Nos. 2 and 1.
The fourth day, etc.
(4) Four coloured birds, and Nos. 3 to 1.
The fifth day, etc.
(5) Five gold rings, and Nos. 4 to 1.
The sixth day, etc.
(6) Six geese a-laying, and Nos. 5 to 1.
The seventh day, etc.
(7) Seven swans a-swimming, and Nos. 6 to 1.
The eighth day, etc.
(8) Eight hares a-running, and Nos. 7 to 1.
The nineth day, etc.
(9) Nine bulls a-roaring, and Nos. 8 to 1.
The tenth day, etc.
(10) Ten men a-mowing, and Nos. 9 to 1.
The eleventh day, etc.
(11) Eleven dancers a-dancing, and Nos. 10 to 1.
The twelfth day, etc.
(12) Twelve fiddlers a-fiddling;
Eleven dancers a-dancing;
Ten men a-mowing;
Nine bulls a-roaring;
Eight hares a-running;
Seven swans a-swimming;
Six geese a-laying;
Five gold rings;
Four coloured birds;
Three French hens;
Two turtle doves, and
The sprig of a juniper-tree.' [2]

"The last should be said all in one breath. Mr. Barnes remarks that the gift of the tenth day in this version of 'Ten men a-mowing' would seem to be an untimely one for Christmas and suggests that it might have been 'Ten men a-mumming'.

"It is to be noted that these illustrations of forfeit rhymes, or jingles, are very similar in their cumulative or backward repetition or refrain to the widely known 'The House that Jack built', a system of games or rhymes to which we may attach considerable antiquity, if we believe the statement that the original of our old friend (in the style of the well-known 'Old Woman and her Pig') is to be found in the Chaldean language, and that another of the same is in existence in a Hebrew MS."

[1] In one version the first day's gift is "A peacock in a pear tree".
[2] *Conf.* A variant in Halliwell's *Nursery Rhymes*, No. ccxl.

At the end of these forfeit rhymes (all of which I contributed to the *Folk-Lore Journal*), I added one given to me by the late William Barnes not long before he died, which, except for the backward repetition or refrain bears more of the impress of a carol or song than a forfeit rhyme. I mentioned that I had also been given the music or score in MS. with two versions of the libretto.

Mr. G. C. Boase, writing in *Notes and Queries* in 1885 (Ser. VI, xii, 484) had claimed a similar version of it as a carol sung " from time out of mind " in East Cornwall. An editorial note to Mr. Boase's article stated that in a version that used to be sung at Oxford suppers more than thirty years previously, and might sometimes still be heard in London, some of the mystic allusions were said to be referable to Talmudic legends.

Miss R. H. Busk, again (*Notes and Queries*, Ser. VII, i, 96), mentioned that she had heard a similar version, but with a different " burden " or refrain, sung in Wiltshire at harvest time; whilst I (p. 315) showed that it had been sung by Dorset children in their youthful games. Although I was not aware that its use was restricted to any particular time, yet in all probability it was more generally used in game rhymes or forfeits at Christmas. So I may more fittingly include it here, adding in brackets where my versions differ.

First voice:

" Come and I will sing to you."

Second voice:

" What will you sing to me ? "

First voice:

" I will sing you one-o."

Second voice:

" What may [will] your one-o be ? "

First voice:

" One and one are [is] all alone,
And evermore shall be so."

These lines are repeated at the commencement of every verse, with the alteration of " one-o " into " two-o ", etc., and as each succeeding verse is reached the preceding ones are gone through again until the twelfth and last is arrived at. Then the whole song or carol becomes complete :—

"Twelve are the twelve apostles;
Eleven and eleven go to Heaven;
[Eleven the eleven that went to Heaven]
Ten are the ten commandments;
Nine and nine are the brightest shine [so bright that shine];
Eight are [the] Gabriel angels [gable rangers].
Seven are the seven stars in the sky;
Six are the six bold waiters;
[The other version is incomplete];
Five are the flamboys [framboises] under the brow [bough];
Four are [the] gospel preachers;
Three of them are drivers [thrivers];
Two of them are little [lily] white babes,
A-clothed all in green-o;
One and one are [is] all alone,
And evermore shall be so."[1]

These lines have been made the subject of two very interesting papers in *Longman's Magazine* for January and June, 1889, the former ("At the Sign of the Ship") by Mr. Andrew Lang, an ex-President of the Folk-Lore Society, the latter ("A Chant of Arcady") by Dr. Augustus Jessop. Mr. Lang considers these lines attributable to a nautical and Cornish origin, containing a "rude *memoria technica* of Catholic doctrine, or even something older than that, a reverberation from Celtic legend". Dr. Jessop differs from this conclusion, and whilst giving a version of the chant (as he calls it) as sung in Norfolk at harvest homes, considers that it represents some ancient summary of things to be believed and received by the lay folk, and for their use drawn up in the vernacular perhaps ages ago.

Dr. Jessop further alludes to a paper by Mr. Everard Green, F.S.A., read before the Society of Antiquaries in 1885, on the words "O Sapientia" in the calendar, and refers the origin or source of this chant to the "Great O's of Advent", and to the collection of *Antiphons*, which were in general use in the earlier centuries of the Christian Church.

Carol-singing.—Carol-singing at Christmas time seems never to have lost its popularity for Dorset folk and their children; the older and simpler carols, common to many counties, still

[1] Two other versions of this, called respectively "The Twelve Apostles" and "Green grow the Rushes, oh!" were contributed by the Rev. H. Pentin, in a paper on "Old Dorset Songs", to the *Proceedings* of the Dorset Field Club in 1906 (vol. xxv, p. 24).

maintaining their freshness and old-world fragrance, though in some localities later ones appear to have vied with, if not superseded, the old traditional ones.

William Barnes would seem to be of opinion [1] that the waits, the old gleemen, and carol-singers are less welcomed to folks' houses than they formerly were. The carol was, he supposes, so called as a night-song (*notturno*) sung under the window of the beloved ; " carol " being from the Celtic *caru* to love,—hence a love-song.

Thomas Hardy, in chapter iv of *Under the Greenwood Tree*, gives the words of the four eight-lined verses of an old Christmas carol, commencing :

" Remember Adam's fall,
O thou man ! "

as sung by the members of the Mellstock Quire, which he describes as " an ancient and time-worn hymn, embodying Christianity, in words orally transmitted from father to son through several generations down to the present characters ".

The Rev. Canon C. H. Mayo (Dorset editor of the " S. and D. N. and Q."), in the pages of that periodical in 1893, gives several instances of hitherto unpublished carols, which he stated had been sung by Christmas carol-singers in the parish of Long Burton, near Sherborne, for generations. (They are to be found in vol. iii, pp. 63, 113, 179, and 227.)

Mummers.—Chief amongst the amusements and customs of this festive season—as, no doubt, it was one of the most ancient—were the " Mummers ", or, as they were sometimes called, " guisers " or " maskers ". Earliest amongst Dorset authorities to give any description of them was William Barnes, who, in his *Glossary* (1863) *s.v.* " Mummers ", alluded to them as " a set of youths who go about at Christmas, decked with painted paper and tinsel, and act in the houses of those who like to receive them a little drama, mostly, though not always, representing a fight between St. George and a Mohammadan leader, and commemorative, therefore, of the Holy Wars. One of the characters, with a hump-back and bawble, represents ' Old Father Christmas '."

Mr. Barnes adds that the *libretto* of the Dorset mummers is

[1] See his " Fore-say " *ante*, p. 3.

much the same as that of the Cornish ones, as given in *Specimens of the Cornish Provincial Dialect,* published in 1846. He no doubt referred to the collection made by " Uncle Jan Trenoodle " (W. Sandys) and published in that year.[1] A reference to Mr. Sandys's publication shows that some portion of the dialogue mentioned by Mr. Barnes is certainly very similar to that in the versions known to me. In the Cornish play, however, are introduced two characters, " the Dragon "—who fights with and is defeated by St. George—and the " King of Egypt's daughter ", both of whom are strangers to my versions. Another peculiarity to be noted in the Dorset versions is that whilst in nearly all the others that I am aware of the actors are represented as asking for " room " to perform in, in these one of the actors assumes the character of " Room " itself.

I think the following very interesting observations made by Professor J. C. Bridge, D.Mus., F.S.A., in a paper read before the Society of Antiquaries in February, 1912 (*Proceedings,* Ser. II, vol. xxiv, pp. 117–24), referring to the " Christmas Mumming Play " are worth reproducing here. He speaks of a duet by " St. George " and " Slasher ", a solo by " the Doctor ", and another by " Little Devil Doubt ", of which the music presented was taken down in the north of England some thirty-five years previously from an old man, eighty years of age, and was undoubtedly of great antiquity. The first opening theme was note for note the same as a troubadour song of 1245, given by Burney from a MS. in the Vatican. The last song was founded on a Church mode.

Dr. Bridge said :

" There was not a county in England without a performance of this play at Christmas time. The versions differ but little, and must have a common origin. What is that origin ? My own theory is that the wandering troupes of minstrels in the middle ages saw what an enormous profit was made out of the crowds who came to see the old miracle plays in cities such as Chester and York, and that they produced a secular play of their own which they could, and did, perform to the country rustics throughout England. The characters of the play differ but very little. Sometimes a fresh public character like Lord Nelson

[1] In the *Glossary* appended these Christmas plays are called " giz "— or " guise "—dances.

is tacked on for a time, but as a rule we have a reference to Egypt and the Crusades in the persons of St. George, a King of Egypt, and a Turkish Knight. The dragon is sometimes added. Then we have the learned doctor (as in the Chester play of ' The Three Kings ') not a Doctor of Divinity, but a Doctor of Medicine who can cure all ills with his bottle of Elicumpane. Then we have one or two roystering spirits under the name of Slasher, Slacker, Alexander, etc., and at the very end the Devil, who is always popular, enters and gives a dramatic finish to the play.

" It is a remarkable fact that the characters do not enter together, but are introduced by a character, such as Old Father Christmas, who thus acts the part of the Expositor in the Chester plays."

In 1874 I first seem to have taken an active interest in Dorset Mumming plays, for I find that I sent to *Notes and Queries* (Ser. v, ii, 505) a list of characters in two plays—the plays being too long to reproduce there—as performed by mummers at Christmas time in two distinct parishes in West Dorset, copies of which had been given to me by an old lady long since dead. It will be seen that there is a considerable variation not only in the numbers but also in the names of the performers in the two parties. In the second, too, the English champion is represented by the sovereign—instead of by the saint—George ; no doubt a modern innovation.

No. 1. Old Father Christmas.
Room.
Anthony, the Egyptian King.
St. George.
St. Patrick.
Captain Bluster.
Gracious King.
General Valentine.
Colonel Spring.
Old Betty.
Doctor.
Servant-man.

No. 2. Old Father Christmas.
Room.
Turkish Knight.
King George.

Marshalee.
Valiant Soldier.
Cutting [1] Star.
Doctor.
Old Bet.

I had there ventured to claim for Dorset mummers the introduction of " Old Bet " or " Betty ", the wife of " Old Father Christmas ", the character being taken by a boy possessed of a shrill voice and dressed as a very old woman in a black bonnet and red cloak. But I was later informed that a similar character had been introduced in a mumming representation in Derbyshire.

" Father Christmas " himself was sometimes mounted on a wooden horse, covered with trappings of black cloth, from which the old man was generally more than once thrown. The rest of the party was decked out as befitted the character each was intended to assume, garnished with bows, coloured strips of paper, caps, sashes, buttons, swords, helmets, etc. The representation of the play concluded with a song.

In 1880 I had an opportunity of giving fuller details of these two plays by reading a paper upon " Christmas Mummers in Dorsetshire " before the then newly formed Folk-Lore Society, which was subsequently printed in the *Folk-Lore Record* (vol. iii, p. 87), in which I gave each of these two plays in full. The plays were preceded by a general introduction to the subject, in which numerous authorities and references to plays in other counties were cited, and was followed by a very interesting discussion, which was also printed. To this I would refer any of my readers who may be interested in the subject of mumming plays from more than a mere Dorset point of view.

Further, in 1904, in answer to a request by a correspondent for a copy of the dialogue formerly used by the mummers in the neighbourhood of Beaminster, in West Dorset—a custom which he stated was then almost extinct in the neighbourhood—I contributed an additional play to the *Somerset and Dorset Notes and Queries* (vol. ix, p. 9), which had been acted at Christmas time at my own home at Symondsbury, in West Dorset, in the mid eighties. Similar performances had been given there by boys, and by others quite adults.

[1] Cutting = swaggering. (See Beaumont & Fletcher's *Scornful Lady*.)

In all these versions, whilst varying in details, there is a strong family likeness; so I will select one for reproduction here which, I think, represents most fairly and gives the best idea of what a Dorset Mumming play is like. It is the first of the two I read before the Folk-Lore Society, and is very similar, both in the characters and diction, to the version I subsequently sent to the *Somerset and Dorset Notes and Queries*. Of course, it must be remembered that in most of these versions, as originally rendered by the performers, are contained numerous traces of the rich Dorset vernacular or dialect language. This I have thought it better not to reproduce here in order that readers of literary English, as opposed to dialect, may find nothing to mar their full comprehension of the play. I have also made a few emendations in the text which later discoveries have shown to be necessary.

I give again the *dramatis personæ*:

Old Father Christmas.
Room.
Anthony, the Egyptian King.
St. George.
St. Patrick.
Captain Bluster.
Gracious King.
General Valentine.
Colonel Spring.
Old Betty.
Doctor.
Servant-man.

SCENE: *The servants' hall or kitchen of the mansion or farmhouse in which the performance is to take place. The actors are grouped together at the back of the stage, so to speak, and each comes forward as he is required to speak or to fight; and at the conclusion falls back upon the rest, leaving the stage clear for other disputants or combatants. This is the "enter" and "exit" of the mummers.*

Enter OLD FATHER CHRISTMAS

Here comes I, Father Christmas, welcome or welcome not,
I hope Old Father Christmas will never be forgot.

Although it is Old Father Christmas he has but a short time to stay;
I am come to show you pleasure and pass the time away.
I have been far, I have been near,
And now I am come to drink a pot of your Christmas beer;
And if its a pot of your best,
I hope in heaven your soul will rest.
If it is a pot of your small
We cannot show you no Christmas at all.
Walk in, Room, again I say.
And pray, good people, clear the way.
Walk in, Room.

Enter ROOM

God bless you all, ladies and gentlemen,
It's Christmas time, and I am come again.
My name is Room, one sincere and true;
A merry Christmas I wish to you.
King of Egypt is for to display,
A noble champion without delay.
St. Patrick too, a charming Irish youth,
He can fight or dance, or love a girl with truth.
A noble Doctor I do declare, and his surprising tricks bring up the rear
And let the Egyptian King straightway appear.

Enter EGYPTIAN KING

Here comes I, Anthony, the Egyptian King,
With whose mighty acts all round the globe doth ring;
No other champion but me excels,
Except St. George, my only son-in-law;[1]
Indeed that wondrous knight whom I so dearly love,
Whose mortal deeds the world dost [well ?] approve,
That here whom no dragon could affright,

[1] This may be explained by the following lines in another version, spoken by "King" George:—

"I fought the dragon boldly,
And brought him to the slaughter.
'Twas thus I gained the fairest maid of all,
The King of Egypt's daughter."

From Mr. Sandys's Cornish version I find that she was named "Sabra".

A whole troop of soldiers couldn't stand in sight.
Walk in, St. George, his warlike [ardour ?] to display,
Walk in St. George.

Enter ST. GEORGE

Here am I, St. George, an Englishman so stout,
With whose mighty warriors I long to have a bout;
No one could ever picture me the many I have slain,
I long to fight, it's my delight, the battle o'er again.
Come, then, you boasting champions,
And hear that in war I doth take pleasure,
I will fight you all, both great and small,
And slay you at my leisure.
Come haste, away, make no delay,
For I'll give you [some lusty thumps]
And like a true-born Englishman
I'll fight you on my stumps.
And now the world I do defy
To injure me before I die.
So now prepare for war, for that is my delight.

[*Enter* St. Patrick, *who shakes hands with* St. George.

ST. PATRICK

My worthy friend, how dost thou fare, St. George?
Answer, my worthy knight.

ST. GEORGE

I am glad to find thee here;
In many a fight that I have been in, travelled far and near,
To find my worthy friend St. Patrick, that man I love so dear.
Four bold warriors have promised me
To meet me here this night to fight.
The challenge I did accept, but they could not me affright.

ST. PATRICK

I will always stand by that man who did me first enlarge,
I thank thee now in gratitude, my worthy friend, St. Garge;
Thou did'st first deliver me out of this wretched den,
And now I have my liberty I thank thee once again.

Enter CAPTAIN BLUSTER

I'll give St. George a thrashing, I'll make him sick and sore,
And if I further am disposed I'll thrash a dozen more.

ST. PATRICK

Large words, my worthy friend,
St. George is here.
And likewise St. Patrick too,
And he doth scorn such men as you ;
I am the match for thee.
Therefore prepare yourself to fight with me,
Or else I'll slay thee instantly.

CAPTAIN BLUSTER

Come on, my boy ! I'll die before
I yield to thee, or twenty more.

(*They fight, and* St. Patrick *kills* Captain Bluster.)

ST. PATRICK

Now one of St. George's foes is killed by me,
Who fought the battle o'er ;
And now for the sake of good St. George,
I'll freely fight a hundred more.

ST. GEORGE

No, no, my worthy friend,
St. George is here,
I'll fight the other three ;
And after that with Christmas beer
So merry we will be.

Enter GRACIOUS KING

No beer or brandy, Sir, I want my courage for to rise,
I only want to meet St. George or take him by surprise ;
But I am afraid he never will fight me ;
I wish I could that villain see.

ST. GEORGE

Tremble, thou tyrant, for all thy sin that's past,
Tremble to think that this night will be thy last.
Thy conquering arms shall quickly by thee lay alone,
And send thee passing to eternal doom.
St. George will make thy armour ring ;
St. George will soon despatch the Gracious King.

GRACIOUS KING

I'll die before I yield to thee or twenty more.

(*They fight.* St. George *kills the* Gracious King.)

Enter GENERAL VALENTINE

ST. GEORGE

He was no match for me, he quickly fell.

GENERAL VALENTINE

But I am thy match, and that my sword shall tell.
Prepare thyself to die, and bid thy friends farewell.
I long to fight such a brave man as thee,
For it's a pleasure to fight so manfully.
[Thou art no coward, but a man so brave]
Rations so severe [I long] to [receive ?]
So cruel, for thy foes [are] always killed !
Oh ! what a sight of blood St. George has spilled !
I'll fight St. George, the hero, here,
Before I sleep this night.
Come on, my boy, I'll die before
I yield to thee or twenty more.
St. George, thou and I'll the battle try,
If thou dost conquer I will die.

(*They fight.* St. George *kills the* General.)

ST. GEORGE

Where now is Colonel Spring ? He doth so long delay,
That hero of renown, I long to show him play.

Enter COLONEL SPRING

Holloa ! behold me, here am I !
I'll have thee now prepare,
And by this arm thou'lt surely die,
I'll have thee this night beware.
So see what bloody works thou'st made,
Thou art a butcher, sir, by trade.
I'll kill [thee] as thou didst my brother,
For one good turn deserves another.

ST. GEORGE

Come, give me leave, I'll thee battle,
And quickly make thy bones to rattle.

COLONEL SPRING

Come on, my boy, I'll die before
I'll yield to thee or twenty more.
St. George, thee and I
Will the battle try.

(*They fight.* St. George *kills the* Colonel.)

ST. PATRICK

Stay thy hand, St. George, and slay no more; for I feel for the wives and families of those men that you have slain.

ST. GEORGE

So am I sorry. I'll freely give any sum of money to a doctor to restore them again. I have heard talk of a mill to grind old men young, but I have never heard of a doctor to bring dead men to life again.

ST. PATRICK

There's an Irish doctor, a [fellow-] townsman of mine, who lived next door to St. Patrick, he can perform wonders. Shall I call him, St. George?

ST. GEORGE

With all my heart. Please to walk in Mr. Martin Dennis. It's an ill wind that blows no good work for the doctor.

[*Enter* Doctor.

If you will set these men on their pins, I'll give thee a hundred pound, and here is the money.

DOCTOR

So I will, my worthy knight, and then I shall not want for whiskey for one twelvemonth to come. I am sure the first man I saw beheaded I put his head on the wrong way. I put his mouth where his poll ought to be, and he's exhibited in a wondering nature.

ST. GEORGE

Very good answer, Mr. Doctor. Tell me the rest of your miracles, and raise those warriors.

DOCTOR

I can cure love-sick maidens, jealous husbands, squalling wives, brandy-drinking dames, with one touch of my peple (triple?) liquid, or one sly dose of my Jerusalem balsam; and that will make an old crippled dame dance the hornpipe, or an old woman of seventy years of age conceive and bear a twin.

And now to convince you all of my exertions, rise Captain Bluster, Gracious King, General Valentine, and Colonel Spring! Rise, and go to your father!

(*On the application of the medicine they all rise and retire.*)

Enter OLD BET

Here comes I, Dame Dorothy,
A handsome young woman, good morning to ye.
I am rather fat, but not very tall,
I'll do my best endeavours to please you all.
My husband he is to work, and soon he will return
And something for our supper bring,
And perhaps some wood to burn.
Oh! here he comes!

[*Enter* Jan *or* Old Father Christmas.

Well, Jan!

OLD FATHER CHRISTMAS

Oh, Dorothy!

OLD BET

What have you been doing all this long day, Jan?

OLD FATHER CHRISTMAS

I've been a-hunting, Bet.

OLD BET

The devil a-hunting is it! Is that the way to support a wife? Well, what have you catched to-day, Jan?

OLD FATHER CHRISTMAS

A fine Jack hare, and I intend to have him a-fried for supper; and here's some wood to dress him.

OLD BET

Fried! No, Jan, I'll roast it nice.

OLD FATHER CHRISTMAS

I say I'll have it fried.

OLD BET

Was there ever such a foolish dish!

OLD FATHER CHRISTMAS

No matter for that, I'll have it done; and if you don't do as I do bid I'll hit you in the head.

OLD BET

You may do as you like for all I do care,
I'll never fry a dry Jack hare.

OLD FATHER CHRISTMAS

Oh! you won't wooll'ee? [will you]

(*He strikes her and she falls.*)

Oh! what have I done! I have murdered my wife!
The joy of my heart and the pride of my life!
And out to the gaol I shall quickly be sent,
In a passion I did it, and no malice meant.
Is there a doctor that can restore?
Fifty pounds I'll give him, or twice fifty more.

[*Someone speaks*

Oh! yes, Uncle Jan, there is a doctor just below, and for God's sake let him just come in. Walk in Doctor.

[*Enter* Doctor

OLD FATHER CHRISTMAS

Are you a doctor?

DOCTOR

Yes, I am a doctor—a doctor of good fame. I have travelled through Europe, Asia, Africa, and America, and by long practice and experience I have learned the best of cures for most disorders instant (incident?) to the human body; find nothing difficult in restoring a limb, or mortification, or an arm being cut off by a sword, or a head being struck off by a canon ball, if application have not been delayed till it is too late.

OLD FATHER CHRISTMAS

You are the very man I plainly see
That can restore my poor old wife to me.
Pray tell me thy lowest fee.

DOCTOR

A hundred guineas I'll have to restore thy wife.
'Tis no wonder that you could not bring the dead to life.

OLD FATHER CHRISTMAS

That's a large sum of money for a dead wife!

DOCTOR

A small sum of money to save a man from the gallows! Pray what big stick is that you have in your hand?

OLD FATHER CHRISTMAS

That is my hunting-pole.

DOCTOR

Put aside your hunting-pole, and get some assistance to help up your wife.

[Old Bet *is raised up to life again*

OLD FATHER CHRISTMAS

Fal, dal, lal ! fal, dal, lal ! my wife's alive !

[*Enter* Servant-man, *who sings*

Well met, my brother dear !
All on the highway
Solemn (?) I were a walking along ;
So I pray you come tell to me
What calling you might be,
I'll have you for some servant-man.

OLD FATHER CHRISTMAS

I'll give thee many thanks,
And I'll quit thee as soon as I can ;
[But ?] vain did I know
Where thee could do so or no ;
[So show me ?] the pleasure of a servant-man.

SERVANT-MAN

Some servants of pleasure
Will pass time out of measure ;
With our hares and hounds
They will make the hills and valleys sound ;
That's a pleasure for some servant-man.

OLD FATHER CHRISTMAS

My pleasure is more than that,—to see my oxen grow fat,
And see them prove well in their kind,
A good rick of hay, and a good stack of corn to fill up my barn,
That's a pleasure of a good, honest husbandman.

SERVANT-MAN

Next to church they will go with their livery fine and gay,
With their cocked-up hat and gold lace all round,
And their shirt so white as milk,
And stitched so fine as silk,
That's a habit for a servant-man.

OLD FATHER CHRISTMAS

Don't tell I about thee silks and garments that not fit to travel the bushes.
Let I have on my old leather coat,
And in my purse a groat,
And there, that's a habit for a good old husbandman.

SERVANT-MAN

Some servant-men doth eat
The very best of meat,
A cock, goose, capon and swan.
After lords and ladies dine,
We'll drink strong beer, ale and wine;
That's a diet for a servant-man.

OLD FATHER CHRISTMAS

Don't tell I of the cock, goose, capon, nor swan; let I have a good, rusty piece of bacon, [or] pickled pork in the house, and a hard crust of bread and cheese once now and then; that's a diet for a good, old, honest husbandman.
So we need must confess
That your calling is the best,
And we will give you the uppermost hand;
So no more we won't delay,
And we will pray both night and day,
God bless the honest husbandman.

SERVANT-MAN

Well done, old Father Christmas, and that is the best of all,
I wish you "Merry Christmas", and "God bless you all" [*To the audience.*]

(*There follows a song, after which exeunt omnes.*)

The play over, and the actors regaled with such good cheer as the hospitable hearts of Dorset folk seldom refused, the mummers passed on to the next parish, where to a fresh and ever-delighted audience they went through a repetition of their performance; and though if the night were wet and the wind cold they experienced rough usage at times, yet their welcome was all the warmer at their next halting-place; so that no one could doubt for a moment but that they came in for no small share of the delight of a "Merry Christmas".

I am unable to find in the representations of the mummers that I have come across any trace of the personation of animals, by means of masks, that at one time would seem to have prevailed in these Christmas revels. As we know, the mummer is really a masker—the old name of these performers in Dorsetshire, "guisers," tells us this—the word being derived from the Danish *mumme*, or the Dutch *momme*, which signifies disguise in a mask.[1]

Strutt, in his *Sports and Pastimes of the People of England* (1831), p. 251, states that the mummeries practised by the lower classes of the people usually took place at the Christmas holidays, and that such persons as could not procure masks rubbed their faces over with soot or painted them. And at p. 250 he says :—

"There was a sport common among the ancient which usually took place on the kalends of January, and probably formed part of the *Saturnalia*, or feasts of Saturn. It consisted in mummings and disguisements ; for the actors took upon themselves the resemblance of wild beasts or domestic cattle, and wandered about from one place to another . . . those concerned in it were wont to clothe themselves with skins of cattle and put upon them the heads of beasts."

And on p. 160 he gives two illustrations of these players wearing various animals' heads, taken from a beautifully illuminated MS. in the Bodleian Library at Oxford, of the time of Edward III.

But though nothing of this kind is to be observed in our present day Christmas mumming (with the exception, perhaps, of the characters dressed up to represent *Father Christmas's* "hobby-horse") it is very interesting to learn that the practice of wearing masks of animals' heads for some purpose must have existed until comparatively recent times, for in an article in the *Somerset and Dorset Notes and Queries*, vol. ii, p. 289 (1891), the Dorset editor of that periodical (Rev. Canon Mayo) gives a description and a photographic illustration of "the Dorset Ooser", which is defined in Barnes's *Glossary* (1863), p. 73, *s.v.* "*ooser*" or "*oose*" (a corruption of "*wurze*" or "*wu'ze*", a name of the arch-fiend) as "a mask with opening jaws, put on with a cow's skin to frighten folk".

[1] See my paper on "Christmas Mummers in Dorsetshire", in the *Folk-Lore Record*, vol. iii, p. 87 (1880).

Mr. Mayo says :—

" The object itself is a wooden mask, of large size, with features grotesquely human, long flowing locks of hair on either side of the head, a beard, and a pair of bullock's horns, projecting right and left of the forehead. The mask or ooser is cut from a solid block, excepting the lower jaw, which is movable, and connected with the upper by a pair of leathern hinges. A string, attached to this movable jaw, passes through a hole in the upper jaw, and is then allowed to fall into the cavity. The Ooser is so formed that a man's head may be placed in it, and thus carry or support it while he is in motion. No provision, however, is made for his seeing through the eyes of the mask, which are not pierced. By pulling the string the lower jaw is drawn up and closed against the upper, and when the string is slackened it descends."

This mask, Mr. Mayo goes on to say, belonged to Mr. Thomas Cave, of Holt Farm, Melbury Osmond, in whose family it had been preserved time out of mind.

Even so recently as 1917 a lady correspondent from University College, London, asks in the same periodical (vol. xv, p. 182) as to the present whereabouts of this " Ooser ".

In this connection the story of "The Cutler and his Apprentices" in William Howitt's delightful *Boys' Country Book* (1839), p. 188, and its accompanying illustration (p. 197) would lead us to believe that some idea of animal personation must have been as prevalent amid the Derbyshire peaks or the Yorkshire dales as on the Wessex downs.

I do not like to leave the subject of the mumming plays without referring to the very interesting account given of one by Thomas Hardy in *The Return of the Native* (vol. i, pp. 271, *et. seq.*), as performed in a cottage amidst the gloomy wilds of " Egdon Heath ". In it, apparently, the performers form two parties—one " on the side of Christendom ", the other " on the side of the Moslem "—but from what I can gather from the rather fragmentary description given both of the characters and of the dialogue I should say that Mr. Hardy's version is not far removed from one of our West Dorset ones. These latter, indeed, would seem to be a compromise with, or a development of, an older and simpler play representative of the Crusades—a comic element being introduced in the character of " Old Bet "—in order to keep in touch with more recent national military events, the characters of Buonaparte and other warlike heroes appearing in some of them.

Mr. Hardy does not appear to see in the play any cheery or humorous expression of the jollities of a Christmas festivity such as I have always considered it to typify. He characterizes his players as being by no means enthusiastic in their performance, and as though they were "moved by an inner compulsion to say and do their allotted part whether they will or no."[1] Nor does he credit their audience with any greater exhibition of feeling or interest. "The play ended . . . nobody commented. . . . They took the piece as phlegmatically as did the actors themselves. It was a phase of cheerfulness which was, as a matter of course, to be passed through every Christmas; and there was no more to be said. They sang the plaintive chant which follows the play, during which all the dead men rise to their feet in a silent and awful manner. . ."

And he preludes this by declaring that "A traditional pastime is to be distinguished from a mere revival in no more striking feature than in this, that while in the revival all is excitement and fervour, the survival is carried on with a stolidity and absence of stir which sets one wondering why a thing that is done so perfunctorily should be kept up at all. This unweeting" (unwitting) "manner of performance is the true ring by which, in this refurbishing age, a fossilized survival may be known from a spurious reproduction".

Be this as it may, Mr. Hardy possesses such a marvellous insight into all that concerns the psychology of the Dorset peasant that I will not venture to gainsay his deduction. I can only say for myself that I have noticed no such perfunctoriness in the spirited little performances that I have witnessed down in West Dorset; yet I hold as firm a belief—derived from less occult standards of folk-lore, perhaps—as Mr. Hardy himself that the mumming plays are, indeed, an ancient "survival", and not any "spurious reproduction" of more modern times. Any occasional want of vivacity or self-abstraction in a performer I have put down in great measure to the unaccustomed burden of having to commit so many lines to memory; for, be it remem-

[1] This criticism is again reflected in the Preface to his great epic drama, "The Dynasts", part i, p. xii.

bered, these were the days before the School Boards, which now, perhaps, may be trusted to cause this defect to disappear, if they do not cause the mumming plays themselves to disappear at the same time !

I cannot close this chapter on seasonal customs more fittingly than by a couple of extracts from two of William Barnes's dialect poems, descriptive of some of the amusements indulged in by simple Dorset folk at this time of the year, the " Chris'mas Invitation " and the " Keepèn up o' Chris'mas ". The one follows the other in his " Winter " pieces ; and, indeed, they may be read together as one, being alike in subject if not altogether in metre.

Chris'mas Invitation

. . . . . .

" We got a back-bran',[1] dree girt logs
So much as dree ov us can car ;
We'll put 'em up athirt the dogs,
An' meäke a vier to the bar.

An' ev'ry woone shall tell his teäle,
An' ev'ry woone shall zing his zong,
An' ev'ry woone wull drink his eäle
To love an' frien'ship all night long.

We'll snap the tongs,[2] we'll have a ball,
We'll sheäke the house, we'll lift the ruf,
We'll romp an' meäke the maïdens squall
A catchèn o'm at blind-man's buff.

Zoo come to-morrow night ; an' mind
Don't leäve thy fiddle-bag behind ;
We'll sheäke a lag, an' drink a cup
O' eäle, to keep wold Chris'mas up."

Keepèn up o' Chris'mas

" An' zoo you didden come athirt,[3]
To have zome fun last night ; how wer't ?
Vor we'd a-work'd wi' all our might
To scour the iron things up bright,
An' brush'd an' scrubb'd the house all drough ;

[1] Or back bron'. Sometimes called a Christmas " brown ". A large log of wood put on at the back of the fire, particularly at merry-makings in winter. See Chapter I, p. 51.

[2] Snappèn tongs : A game of forfeits. See Chapter II, p. 78.

[3] Across.

An' brought in vor a brand, a plock[1]
O' wood so big's an uppèn-stock,[2]
An' hung a bough o' misseltoo,
An' ax'd a merry friend or two,
To keepèn up o' Chris'mas.

. . . . . .

We pläy'd at forfeits, an' we spun
The trencher roun', an' meäde such fun!
An' had a geäme of dree ceärd loo,
An' then began to hunt the shoe.
An' all the wold vo'k zittèn near,
A-chattèn roun' the vier pleäce,
Did smile in woone another's feäce,
An' sheäke right hands wi' hearty cheer,
An' let their left hands spill their beer,
A keepèn up o' Chris'mas."

[1] A large, hard block of wood.

[2] A horse-block; a large block fastened into the ground, and cut in steps to get on horseback from.

CHAPTER III

LOCAL CUSTOMS

Abbotsbury.

(i) *Wishing at St. Catherine's Chapel.*—In the *Bridport News* in February, 1886, appeared an extract from the *Family Herald* of 16th September, 1865, giving an account of a visit paid by the Archæological Institute to Dorsetshire in 1865, when a party of that Society visited the little Norman Chapel of St. Catherine at Abbotsbury, which, now in ruins, stands on a high hill about half a mile from the town. Two engravings of this old chapel are given in Hutchins (vol. ii, p. 721) showing the still massive proportions of its buttresses. The late Canon Bingham, the well-known Dorset antiquary, who accompanied the party, spoke of the traditionary custom of the young women of Abbotsbury and the neighbourhood on a certain day in the year going up to the chapel and there invoking the aid of the Saint in the following prayer :—

" A husband, St. Catherine ;
A handsome one, St. Catherine ;
A rich one, St. Catherine ;
A nice one, St. Catherine ;
And soon, St. Catherine ! "

The paper relates that one of the party, Mr. Beresford Hope, modestly proposed that all gentlemen and married ladies should retire from the church so as to afford the young ladies present the opportunity of using so desirable a prayer.

Some years subsequently to this I attended a meeting of the Dorset Field Club at Abbotsbury, when a visit was paid to St. Catherine's Hill and its ruined chapel. The customary prayer or invocation to the Saint was alluded to, and the wishing holes in the stone, both for hands and knees—the latter much worn, if I remember rightly—pointed out. Mr. J. J. Foster in a note to p. 118 of vol. vi of the *Folk-Lore Journal* alludes to these " wishing-holes ". He says : " They are in the south doorway. You put your knee in one hole and your hands in two others, and *wish.*"

A very similar custom seems to have prevailed at Milton Abbey (*q.v. post*).

(ii) *Fishing Customs.*—Hutchins (vol. ii, p. 724) gives a very interesting account of certain customs which prevailed amongst the fishermen of Abbotsbury, and for which the editor of the last edition was indebted to a late vicar of the parish, the Rev. William Jenkins. He says :—

" They have some old and very peculiar customs which are strictly adhered to. In the season, before the first launching of the boat in every week, when the net and all are ready the Captain says : ' Let us pray ! ' when the whole crew, bareheaded, fall on their knees around the boat and join in silent address to the Almighty, recommending themselves and their undertaking to his protection and favour. Having gone through this ceremony they rise, and all saying : ' In the name of God,' their united efforts thrust the boat from the shore.

" The fish are disposed of to dealers, who convey them to London, Bath, etc., or to those who supply the neighbourhood. Of these in a plentiful season great numbers attend, so that the beach resembles a country fair.

" The captain of the boat has the sole disposal of what is taken, and accounts for the profits of the week's labour every Saturday evening, when the amount is divided after this manner : they assemble at the captain's house, where on a table is placed a quantity of beer, which they call their ' flaggon ', with biscuits or bread and cheese and pipes and tobacco, in proportion to the success of the preceding week. Opposite to each person is laid his allotted share of the gains ; then, before they presume to take the money or refresh themselves, they kneel around the table and thank Heaven for its favours ; and adding this emphatic expression, ' The God who gave us this can give us more ! ' they rise and merrily partake of the cheer provided for them. Whenever it happens that they catch more fish than the purchasers take off their hands, or so few that the dealers do not think them worthy of their notice, they have this singular method of dividing them. They part the whole into as many shares as there are persons to partake ; when all are satisfied with the quality of the lots one of the crew is blindfolded ; and another, the rest looking on, touches at his option either of the lots, and asks the blinded person, ' whose it shall be ? ' The person named by him immediately takes the lot, and the same question is repeated and an answer given till an owner is fixed on for every one. These fish they salt and barrel, or dry in the manner of red herrings, for their winter's food."

It would appear that a small annual sum was paid by each boat to the lord of the royalty, who likewise had a claim to certain fish called " prize-fish " ; but he was entitled to only one fish of each sort, and that the first or best which was taken by each boat every day.

The editors of the last edition of Hutchins add in a footnote (p. 725) that many of these customs have now fallen into disuse ; indeed the prayers on the beach and in the flagon-houses were such manifest formalities, not unusually followed by profanity and drunkenness, that they were very properly laid aside. And they further stated that as Mr. Jenkins's account did not represent the state of the case at the date of the last edition (1863) some additions and footnotes have been made for that edition.

(iii) *Flower Custom* (*Garland Day*).—They refer to a pleasing custom which still obtains on Old May Day (13th May). The children belonging to the crew of each boat build up a large garland of handsome flowers upon a frame, and carry it from house to house, usually getting a few pence apiece from those who can afford it. The people throng the beach, weather permitting, in the afternoon, when the garlands are taken out in boats and thrown into the sea. The late Lord Ilchester, the lord of the manor, had of late years provided an entertainment for the children, often close upon 200 in number, and was accustomed to attend them to the beach, where the vicar read a suitable portion of scripture, a psalm was sung, and prayer offered for the general welfare.

This custom is alluded to at somewhat greater length by Canon Mayo in a communication to *Somerset and Dorset Notes and Queries*, vol. iii, p. 231 (1893), entitled " Garland Day ", in which he states that it is also observed in the neighbouring villages of Swyre and Puncknoll, but that in them only one garland is provided, not one for each boat.

Bishop's Caundle.

Church Penance.—I have no doubt that on many occasions in olden time the customary penance for ante-nuptial incontinence, namely, standing during divine service clothed in a linen sheet, has been exacted in many Dorset churches. An instance of this is recorded in *Somerset and Dorset Notes and Queries*, vol. iv,

p. 133, as having occurred in comparatively recent times at Bishop's Caundle, near Sherborne, and is contributed under the initials of the Dorset editor of that periodical.

It was written on a fly-leaf at the beginning of the second volume of the Register of that parish, and is as follows :—

" On Sunday, the 23rd Day of October, 1785, Susannah Philips, who lives near Colonel Bridge (more properly Kernel or Cernel Bridge) in this parish of Bishop's-Caundle, did Penance in this Church by standing, during the whole time of divine Service near the Reading Desk, in a white linen sheet, and immediately after the second Lesson repeating words after the Minister to the following effect. Here the note terminates and the recited words are not recorded. The occasion which gave rise to this act of Penance may be seen on referring to the Baptismal Register on 15th June, 1785, when an entry appears of the baptism of Job, base-born son of Susannah Philips, at Colonel Bridge, aged three months."

Blandford.

Hock-tide Custom.—See Chapter I, p. 33.

Bridport.

(i) *Flower Service.*—See Chapter I, p. 41.

(ii) *Robin Hood Ale.*—The late Mr. Thomas Wainwright, curator of the " North Devon Institute " at Barnstaple, and formerly of Bridport, in his *Bridport Records and Ancient Manuscripts*, p. 43, reprinted from the *Bridport News* (1898), gives a reference (K. 18) to the Receipts and Expenditure of the Robin Hood's ale fund (" Robyn-hode-ale ") for one year, 1555. He says :—

" From this account we learn that ' ales ' [1] were kept at Bridport as elsewhere. They served the twofold purpose of affording social intercourse in days when opportunities for enjoying them were rare, and of raising funds for various purposes. The malt, wheat, and other requisites for the feast were collected from the parishioners, and the ale, bread, etc., made therefrom sold to the visitors on the festival days.

" There were several different kinds of ' ales ', Church Ales, Whitsun Ales, Lamb Ales, Clerk Ales, Bride Ales (whence we get the word *bridal*, Robin Hood Ales, etc. The latter formed a portion of the May games. Robin presided as lord of the May ;

[1] So called from the liquor drunk at these festive gatherings.

a female called the Maid Marian, his faithful mistress, was the lady of the May.[1]

"Bishop Latimer, in a sermon which he preached before King Henry VI,[2] relates the following anecdote which proves the great popularity of the May pageants. 'Coming,' he says: 'to a certain town on a holiday to preach, I found the church door fast locked. I taryed there for half an hour and more, and at last the key was found, and one of the parish comes to me and sayes: "Syr, this is a busy day with us, we cannot hear you; it is Robin Hoode's day; the parish are gone abroad to gather for Robin Hood. I pray you let (prevent) them not.' I was fayne, therefore, to give place to Robin Hood; I thought my rochet would have been regarded, but it would not serve; it was faine to give place to Robin Hoode's men.'

"Various public works and charities benefited by these 'ales'; the profits of the Robin Hood's ale at Bridport in 1555 were, it appears, devoted to repair roads and bridges.

"In course of time these festivities degenerated into scenes of debauchery and riot, and were suppressed. From a sermon preached at Blandford in 1570 by William Kethe it appears that it was the custom at the time for the Church Ales to be kept upon the Sabbath Day, 'which holy day', says our author, 'the multitude called their revelyng day, which day is spent in bulbeatings, bearbeatings, bowlings, dicying, cardyng, daunsynges, drunkenness', and other vices, 'insomuch as men could not keep their servantes from lying out of theyr owne homes the same Sabbath Day at night.'"[3]

Broadway (near Weymouth).

Candle Auction.—The practice of "Candle Auction", or the sale of or letting property by "inch of candle", prevailed in many parts of the west of England in days when the modern niceties of sale by auction were unknown; and in some places no doubt continue to the present day. They mostly, one may believe, referred to the annual letting of municipal property where the conditions would probably be known to the purchasers, who often were restricted to the inhabitants of the borough or township where the property was situated. There would seem to have been two forms of this: one where the candle used was

[1] *Conf.* account given by Mr. Roberts, of the Lyme Regis Cobb Ale, *post*, *s.v.* Lyme Regis. [2] ? Henry VIII.

[3] See Chap. II, p. 58.

only an inch long; the other where only an inch of the whole candle used was consumed, the line of demarcation being usually marked off by a pin.

A correspondent in the *Western Antiquary*, vol. i, p. 122, gives an interesting account of this practice as occurring at the annual letting of the parish meadow of Broadway, near Weymouth, where (in 1873) an inch of candle was placed on the edge of a knife and lighted by one of the parish officers. The biddings were taken down, and the chance of taking the meadow was open to all while the candle was burning, the last bidder before the light went out being declared the incoming tenant.

The same correspondent referred to a similar practice of letting by "match and pin" as in vogue in some parts of the country, the "match"[1] being a spill of wood soaked in brimstone or other inflammable substance, and the letting continued until it had burnt down to a point where a pin was stuck in, the fall of the pin being equivalent to the present auctioneer's hammer.

The *Dorset County Chronicle*, in January, 1892, mentions that the annual letting of the "parish mead" at Broadway recently took place with the customary ceremonies at the Swan Inn in the presence of a number of parishioners, when in consequence of the candle toppling over before being burnt out the letting failed to realize as much as the previous year by 30 shillings. After the letting some little time was spent convivially, the health of the local M.P., who had sent a contribution towards the evening's festivity, being drunk with the greatest cordiality.

This custom at Broadway is also referred to in *Notes and Queries* (Ser. IX, xi, 188) as still obtaining in 1903; and later, by the *Bridport News* in January, 1907, which speaks of the custom as one dating back to the fifteenth century. It is there stated that the "parish meadow", which was two acres in extent, was, under the will of one John Gould, to be bid for by parishioners during the burning of an inch of candle.[2]

The following references to this custom of selling by auction

[1] One definition of "match" in Halliwell's *Archaic Dictionary* is the "wick of a candle".

[2] See also *Notes and Queries* (Ser. XI, i, 404), where an account appeared of a similar letting of a piece of land at Tatworth, near Chard, co. Somerset, though under rather more restricted conditions.

are to be found in the late Mr. Moule's *Weymouth and Melcombe Regis Borough Records*, 1883 :

" Orders : Nov. 3, 1619. Order for the cellar under Melcombe Regis Town-hall to be ' graunted by a candle ' for seven years to the highest bidder. C. pp. 50–51."

Again, No. 59, on p. 144 :

" Memoranda : Nov. 13, 1663. Speed's Chronicle, distrained for Capt. J. Arthur's town rent, was ' soul'd by a peece of candle ' to Mr. J. Studley for 29s. He also took ' Thames Well ' from the Borough at 2s. per annum (Tems Well, Greenhill). C. pp. 287–8."

Came (Winterborne).

Induction Service. — The late Mrs. Baxter (" Leader Scott ") in her *Life of William Barnes*, published in 1887, at p. 198, speaks of the curious ordeal of induction which her father, " the Dorset Poet," had to undergo at Came Church on his appointment as rector of the parish in 1862, when he was presented with a sod of earth, and had to ring the church bell, besides other ancient ceremonials.

It is a pity that Mrs. Baxter did not tell us what those " other ancient ceremonials " were, as I can find no trace of them in Hutchins's account of the parish.

Cattistock.

(i) *Feast Day.*—The late Mr. H. N. Cox, of Bridport, in one of those very interesting, if somewhat discursive, little histories of certain West Dorset parishes in the neighbourhood of Bridport, which he published from time to time in the *Southern Times* during the years 1885–7, writes in December, 1886, that Cattistock was one of the few places that had kept up the old custom of the " village feast " ; and he speaks of having seen some fifty years previously the pewter plate on the dresser of a very old inhabitant removed ; and on its removal there was found a bill of the proceedings at Cattistock feast in the early part of the century, recording races for ponies, donkeys, etc., wrestlers, bell-jingling, wheeling barrows blindfolded, and other amusements, one in particular being " grinning through a horse collar ". The feast at Cattistock would seem to have been from time immemorial an important event ; and it was for years the custom to make it a feast indeed for the poor, who had a splendid tea provided for them, and games and amusements were kept up until the small hours in the morning. Mr. Cox mentions that in modern days Cattistock feast was very rationally observed, and that the old amusements were not altogether gone—the dance on the green, for instance—and recalls that fifty or sixty years previously Cattistock feast was the great event of the year and that people from miles around assembled to meet their old friends, and family reunions and greetings were always observed.

I had at one time a pamphlet containing three sermons preached on the anniversary of the " Dorset Feast Day "—held in London—for the years 1690, 1691, and 1692. This, no doubt, was the forerunner of our modern " Society of Dorset Men in London ", which, founded some dozen years ago, is now strongly established and doing most excellent work, besides holding a " feast " in May and other meetings in each year, and publishing a most excellent annual volume, the *Year Book*, for its members.

(ii) *Maypole Custom.*—For account of Maypole custom at Cattistock see Chapter I, p. 39.

Cheselborne.

Treading in the Wheat.—A correspondent in the *Somerset and Dorset Notes and Queries*, vol. iv, p. 89, speaks of a custom at Cheselborne which formerly prevailed, but which had by that time fallen into desuetude, of the village maidens, dressed in white, walking through the fields on Palm Sunday for the purpose of " Treading in the Wheat ".

Chideock.

For account of the perambulation of the parish and manor of Chideock, see Chapter I, p. 36.

Combe Keynes.

Manorial custom.—Hutchins (vol. i, p. 347) gives the following curious customs appertaining to the manor of Combe Keynes.

" The tithing-man of Combe Keynes is obliged to do suit at Winfrith-Court ; and after repeating the following incoherent lines, pays 3d. and goes out without saying another word :—

'With my white rod,
And I am a fourth post,
That three pence makes three,
And the Lord's of the Manor is the fourth,
God bless the King and the Lord of the Franchise.
Our weights and our measures are lawful and true,
Good morrow, Mr. Steward ; I have no more to say.' "

Tradition says that by default of any of these particulars the court-leet of Combe is forfeited.

Corfe Castle.

(i) *Quarrymen's customs.* — One of the oldest and most interesting amongst the customs of the Isle of Purbeck is that connected with the quarrymen of the district—the "Purbeck Marblers", as they were anciently called. These quarrymen, who were resident in the districts of Corfe Castle and Swanage, were formed into a strong company or guild, to whom was granted a charter confirming all their rights and privileges. These were evidenced by a series of Articles of Agreement. Corfe Castle was the proper metropolis of the quarriers' country; though Swanage, being the place of shipment of the stone, the business tended more to that quarter. At one time, it is said, the general meeting was opened at Corfe, and adjourned to Swanage, but afterwards the meetings were held at Corfe and Langton respectively.

Hutchins (vol i, pp. 682–4) gives an account of the Marblers' Company and of the articles of their charter, which account was taken from a paper by the late Mr. Oliver W. Farrer, which appeared in that interesting but short-lived—and now very scarce—publication, *The Purbeck Papers,* in 1859. Hutchins states that the early history of the company is involved in obscurity, the ancient records having been destroyed in a fire at Corfe Castle. They were governed by certain rules or articles of agreement, which it seems to have been customary to renew at intervals, for several copies, varying only in orthography, are extant. To one of these, in the possession of the only member of the company then resident in Corfe Castle, and one of the wardens, was attached a seal, purporting to be the seal of the Company of Marblers, but it was a heraldic device, viz. *On a pale three roses slipped proper.*[1]

[1] The Roses of Kempstone in Corfe Castle bore " on a pale three roses slipped ".

To this account of Mr. Farrer's I would refer those who desire a fuller account of the company and its constitution.[1] In the *Standard* newspaper of 10th March, 1886, appeared a very good and succinct account of a meeting of the Purbeck quarrymen at Corfe Castle on Shrove Tuesday (their customary day of meeting) of that year. This account I, many years after, sent to the *Somerset and Dorset Notes and Queries* (1907), vol. x, p. 249, with references to Mr. Farrer's article in the *Purbeck Papers*; and as it expresses all that it seems to me necessary to state here about the Company and its customs, I reproduce it.

" A curious old custom among the quarrymen of the Isle of Purbeck was observed yesterday at Corfe Castle. There is among the quarrymen a charter bearing the date 1551, which is rigorously obeyed in order to keep the working of the stone quarries in the Isle of Purbeck in the hands of the freemen. To be able to take up one's freedom one must be the legitimate son of a freeman. He must be 21 years of age, up to which time his wages belong to his parents.

" Once during the year the quarrymen used to meet at Corfe Castle Town Hall and there read the charter, and on that occasion, viz. Shrove Tuesday, ' free boys ' claim and take up their freedom. Yesterday morning a large number of quarrymen assembled in the Town Hall, Corfe Castle, and proceeded to the election of officers, after which about twelve freemen were sworn in. Each man has to sign the roll of freemen, pay a fee of 6s. 8d., provide a penny loaf made on purpose by the baker of the place, and buy a pot of beer. The man thus sworn in becomes his own master. Should any of the freemen desire to marry during the next year he has to pay to the stewards a ' marriage shilling ', and should he neglect to do this his wife loses all interest in the quarry and cannot take an apprentice to work for her. After the above business was transacted the ceremony of ' kicking the ball ' commenced. The ball is provided by the man who was last married among the freemen, and is presented in lieu of the ' marriage shilling '. If it should happen that no freeman has married since the previous Shrove Tuesday the old football is used. The ball was taken from the Town Hall to a field at Corfe Castle, and there kicked about by any one who wished.

" These very novel proceedings terminated by the ball and a pound of pepper being taken to the lord of the manor as an

[1] References might also be made to Biggs's *Isle of Purbeck*, pp. 27–8; and for privileges and customs of Corfe to the late Mr. Thomas Bond's *History of Corfe Castle* (1883), p. 125.

acknowledgement to him in respect of the way to the River Ower."

(ii) *Kicking the Ball.*—The custom of kicking the football "to be provided by the man who was last married amongst the freemen", is alluded to in the above account. In a later set of rules provision was made for the carrying of the ball to Ower—I believe on the following day, Ash Wednesday. I have seen it stated somewhere that in these degenerate days it was carried, not kicked, to its destination. The *Bridport News* in March, 1884, speaks of the annual custom of the Swanage Freemen "kicking the ball" as having taken place at Corfe on Shrove Tuesday. It says that the custom was one that had been kept up annually for generations past. The ball was taken to Corfe Castle, and kicked from the Castle grounds through Corfe on towards Swanage.[1]

(iii) *Charity customs.*—Mr. J. Webber wrote in the *Dorset County Chronicle* on the 25th March, 1890, as follows :—

"Some charities are given away within or near the parish church, and on each side of the pathway leading to the north entrance of our church stood an ancient tomb built with large slabs of Purbeck stone. On one of these tombs the inscription stated that he who lay beneath 'gave 23 povnes to the poore at his death'. The inscription on the other tomb was obliterated by time, and both are no longer to be seen. On every Good Friday large quantities of bread were placed on these tombs, every child in the town under a certain age receiving a penny loaf, and every adult above a certain age a twopenny loaf.

"Seventy-six years ago the price of bread was double the amount now paid; the penny loaf was extremely small, but we felt more proud of our tiny loaf than a larger, and refused other food while it lasted. This custom has for some years been discontinued.

(iv) *Harden's Charity.*—"Another small charity consisting of bread was given on St. John's Day to twelve Marblers living in the town, each person receiving a loaf value 1s. left by John Harden, a Marbler, being the proceeds of one acre of land; this custom no longer exists.

"The charities here are amalgamated and applied to purposes not originally intended by the donors.

[1] See reference to "kicking the ball" on Shrove Tuesday, Chapter I, p. 27.

" Corfe Castle within the last century has become notable for the abolition of ancient rights and customs. Good Friday at the present day differs but little from any other day, whereas the insignificant gift of a penny loaf to children formerly stamped an impression on the youthful mind never to be erased, whilst the visible element forcibly reminded the thoughtful of Him who on Good Friday distributed impartially the bread of life."

Ibberton.

Curfew Plot[1].—Hutchins (*History of Dorset*, vol. iv, p. 361), in speaking of the church at Ibberton, says :—

" Eight acres of ground were formerly given for the repairing of the church, and one acre for ringing the eight o'clock bell."

And adds in a note :

" De manibus reginæ amovendis de tribus clausis pasturæ vocatæ Curfew Grounds in Everton (Ibberton) in com. Dorset, ae gardianis ecclesiæ de Everton in jure ejusdem liberandis.

Pasch. Rec. 5 Eliz. rot. 30."

Lulworth (West).

(i) *Feeding custom.*—In the *Weymouth and Melcombe Regis Borough Records*, edited by the late Mr. H. J. Moule in 1883, appears (No. 88) a declaration (31st August, 1652) by Mr. Mayor Pley that J. Hanwell and T. Vey have deposed that from 1588 and about 1610 respectively, they kept sheep by day and night and all the year on West Lulworth Down, now claimed by Winfrith Newburgh Parish, except inasmuch as the Lulworth people have a " slight "[2] within this down for their cattle to feed up to 11 a.m.

(ii) *Perambulation of Bounds.*—For a reference to the perambulation of the parish boundaries of West Lulworth see Chapter I, p. 36.

Lyme Regis.

Cobb Ale Feast.—One of the most interesting, and certainly one of the most ancient, of the customs connected with the borough of Lyme Regis was that with reference to the Cobb or Pier, which for so many centuries has endeavoured to afford some protection for its scanty shipping against the heavy buffetings of the south-westerly gales from the Channel.

[1] See *post, s.v.* Mapouder and *s.v.* Stoke Abbott.

[2] Or " slait " = a sheepleaze. (See Barnes's *Glossary*.)

Hutchins (ii, 64) gives some account of this little harbour, the most prominent feature of Lyme Regis—for which he is considerably indebted to George Roberts, the local historian of that borough—but tells us nothing of the Cobb Ale Feast, which Roberts in his later work, *The Social History of the Southern Counties* (1856), pp. 327 *et seq.*, deals with at some length.

The origin or building of the Cobb itself is involved in obscurity, though it certainly existed in early Plantagenet days.

It can easily be imagined that owing to its exposed position the Cobb was in need of continuous repair ; and, indeed, on some occasions it has been practically destroyed for a time. Funds were continually being required for its repair or restoration, and certain dues were levied with this object on shipping entering the port. But the amount was never sufficient for its need, so assistance had be to invoked outside shipping circles. Sometimes, indeed, grants, imperial or otherwise, were made for its upkeep, but local assistance was always invited and was always forthcoming. One of the most popular ways of effecting this was by the " Cobb Ale " or " Feast ", by which means money was raised in much the same way as by a modern charity entertainment or banquet.

According to Mr. Roberts, an " ale " meant four or five centuries ago some good malt liquor, brewed to be drunk in good fellowship by neighbours of the same parish ; but as good drinking is said to require good eating so an *ale* came to mean a *feast* — a Church or Whitsun Ale, a Church or Whitsun Feast. There were " drinkings " in Lent, to which private persons and parishes contributed. Two persons were chosen previously to the meeting of the Whitsun or Church ale to be lord and lady of the ale, who dressed as suitably as they could to the character they assumed. These feasts were the prototypes of the " Cobb Ale "—the great feast of Lyme Regis — which probably dated from the destruction of the harbour in 1376. But no " accompts " exist before the time of Henry VIII in which any mention of it can be found. The first entries are those of Thomas Ellesdon, Mayor, in 1547. " Item, more, I made of Cobb Ale 3*l*. 6*s*. 4*d*." As is seen, the funds of the Cobb Ale were duly carried to account.

Mr. Roberts goes on to say that the " ales " originated from the " wakes ", and that particulars of the festivity when it was only an " ale "—if ever such and not a " feast "—are wanting. The managers of the Lyme Feast were dignified by the title of the " Wardens of the Cobb Ale ", and were chosen yearly at the Guildhall; the mayor for the time was the Lord of the Cobb Ale. Mr. Roberts gives an account of the festivities in the " Cobb Hall "—the name of the hall appropriated to the feast—usually a large empty barn, or some such building, fitted up with seats for the accommodation of the company, where they assembled to dance and regale themselves in the best manner their circumstances and the place would afford. Each young fellow would treat his girl with a ribbon or flower; the lord and lady, with their retinue, honouring the hall with their presence.

Mr. Roberts concludes his interesting account by saying:

" We cannot learn how long the feasting or dinner lasted each day. There was in those ancient festivities no precipitancy. Neighbours, perhaps, saw no termination to the consumption of good cheer which the enchantments of vocal and instrumental music and jesting made to appear short." [1]

Mapouder.

Curfew Plot.[2]—Hutchins (*History of Dorset,* vol. iii, p. 729), under the heading of " Lands given to the church of St. Peter and Paul at Mapouder, in pure and perpetual alms by John Filham, patron of that church," (*inter alios usos*) " to find a man to ring the morning and evening curfew bell throughout the year."

Melcombe Regis.

For " perambulation " of parish boundaries see Chapter I, p. 36.

Milton Abbey.

(i) *Annual Fair.*—The Rev. H. Pentin, M.A., now for many years Honorary Secretary of the Dorset Field Club, in an interesting paper published in vol. xxv of its *Proceedings* (1904) upon " The Old Town of Milton Abbey " at p. 4, says:

" The annual fair was on St. Sampson's Eve and Day, July 27th and 28th, St. Sampson being the chief patron saint

[1] *Conf.* account given by T. Wainwright of the " Robin Hood Ale " at Bridport, *ante, s.v.* Bridport.

[2] See *ante, s.v.* Ibberton, and *post, s.v.* Stoke Abbott.

of the Abbey Church. This fair, like the market, was granted by King Athelstan, but it was practically discontinued when the old town was pulled down.

" The sports in old Milton were badger-baiting under the cedar trees in the Abbey church-yard, cock-squailing, cock-fighting, and playing fives outside the west end of the church. Bowls were played on the bowling green, and ringing was very popular.

" The weekly market was well-attended, and was held around the market cross. The market cross was one of the finest in the kingdom, quite worthy of its position near the Abbey Church, and had an ascent of no fewer than thirty steps. Its site is marked in the present Park by a stone which is said to be a portion of the original cross. Our registers tell us that during the days of the Commonwealth banns of marriage were published ' in the market.' "

(ii) *King Athelstan's Chapel.*—In *Memorials of Old Dorset* (1907), pp. 103–5, the same writer, speaking of King Athelstan's Chapel at Milton Abbey (in which publication appears an excellent little woodcut of the chapel)—of which St. Catherine of Alexandria was the patron saint as well as of spinsters, and in days gone by was supposed to have the power of finding a husband for those who sought her aid—refers to a similar custom as that obtaining at Abbotsbury,[1] the invocation taking the following forms, which Mr. Pentin says may be the echoes of mediæval doggerel rhymes.

" St. Catherine, St. Catherine,
O lend me thine aid,
And grant that I never
May die an old maid.
A husband, St. Catherine,
A *good* one, St. Catherine,
But ar-a-one better than
Nar-a-one, St. Catherine."

or

" Sweet St. Catherine,
A husband, St. Catherine,
Handsome, St. Catherine,
Rich, St. Catherine,
Soon, St. Catherine. "[2]

[1] See *ante, s.v.* Abbotsbury.

[2] To show that this superstitious custom is not confined to Dorsetshire, or even to England, Mr. Pentin refers to Mr. Baring Gould's *A Book of Brittany* (1891), where he states, at p. 76, that unmarried girls, with the

Moreton.

Palm Sunday and Good Friday Church Decorations—For account of willow and yew tree decorations in Moreton Parish Church on Palm Sunday and Good Friday see Chap. I, p. 32.

Piddlehinton.

Christmas Dole.—Hutchins (ii, 807) states that " there is an ancient custom for the rector to give away, on old Christmas Day, annually, a pound of bread, a pint of ale, and a mince pie to every poor person in the parish."

This is apparently taken, word for word, from H. Edwards's *Collection of Old English Customs*, etc. (1842), p. 6, which states, in addition that " this distribution is regularly made by the rector to upwards of three hundred persons."[1]

In the hope of obtaining some fuller particulars of this charitable custom, I inquired in the Folk-lore column of the *Dorset County Chronicle* in the early eighties of the last century, if this dole was still distributed, and an interesting correspondence thereupon ensued.

Mr. T. H. Squire wrote stating that the dole was last given on Old Christmas Day, 6th January, 1837, by the then rector, Rev. Thomas Carter. As a native of Piddlehinton, and as one who had received the dole himself, he could vouch for the custom, and that the pies originally were worth calling by that name, being large enough to be cut in four, each quarter being sufficient for one person. The bread, he states, was originally given to counteract the richness of the mince meat. The pastry and bread used to be baked in an oven built especially for the purpose at the rectory, and he believed that it was still in existence.

I also mentioned that I had received a direct answer to my inquiry from " An old Parishioner " of Piddlehinton, who stated that the custom was for the dole to be given to every individual of the parish, both old and young, rich and poor, to the number of about 400. He said that about the year 1841 the Rev. T. T. Carter, who was then the rector, to the great displeasure of the

same object, used to resort to a side chapel at Guincamp in Brittany, in which was an image of St. Catherine, into which they would stick pins.

[1] See *Denham Tracts* (published by the Folk-lore Society in 1895), vol. ii, p. 91, in which a reference is given to the Charity Commissioners' Reports, vol. xxix, p. 108.

parishioners, broke the custom under the plea of giving to the *poor* of the parish the same amount in blankets. He added that not long afterwards the rector left the parish, and from that time the custom had been discontinued.

Mr. Squire's letter drew forth a reply from Mr. T. M. Colson, who pointed out that Mr. Squire was in error in assigning the year 1837 as the date of the discontinuance of the custom, for at that time his grandfather, the Rev. J. M. Colson, was rector of Piddlehinton, and he knew that the custom was not given up during his lifetime. As, however, he died in December of that year, it was quite possible that his successor, the Rev. Mr. Carter, might have discontinued it a year or two later.

Mr. Colson confirms Mr. Squire's opinion that in his grandfather's time the pies were " worthy of the name ", as he could just remember seeing them ; and he gives his father's opinion, who was then in charge of the adjoining parish of Piddletrenthide, that the dole was abused by parishioners applying for it who were perfectly well able to provide pies for themselves.

So that under these circumstances we can scarcely regret the discontinuance of the custom, more especially if it has been replaced, as alleged, by a distribution of blankets to the poor of the parish.

Portland.

(i) *Bonfire custom.*—As to Bonfire custom at Portland, on 5th November, see Chapter I, p. 49.

(ii) *Reeve-staff.*—More than thirty years ago I presented to the Dorset County Museum at Dorchester a Reeve-staff or pole formerly used in the Manor Court of the Island of Portland, and I contributed to the *Somerset and Dorset Notes and Queries*, vol. i, pp. 6–8 (1888) the description of this Reeve-staff and its history so far as I was able to gather it. I said :

" The reeve-staff or pole was formerly used for keeping the accounts of the quarry-lands, etc. in the manor ; and the one I had was apparently made of old Spanish mahogany ; and was about 8 feet 6 inches in length and nearly an inch and a half square, and covered with a variety of cuts and notches like a huge Exchequer tally, of which more anon. It had been in the possession of the family of the gentleman from whom I purchased it for many years, whose ancestors had formerly been quarry owners in the island. Through the kindness of this gentleman I have been furnished with the following extracts from the rules of the Court of the Island and Manor of Portland (of which Her Majesty the Queen is the Lady) when the Court was closed on the 7th July, 1846, the last occasion of its being held:

" 'We present our Manor to be ancient demesne and land of inheritance, descendable as lands in gavel-kind, with appurtenances, paying a certain yearly rental of £14 14s. 3d., which is collected by a Reeve, taken in course by the Jury from the Rent Roll at each annual Michaelmas Court, which is paid at such Court to the Steward for the use of Her Majesty, being Lady in Chief.

" 'We also present that all tenants in our Manor are Freeholders, and our rent is certain and collected in the manner before mentioned, according to a staff called the *Reeve-Staff*, which is annually cut from the Rent Roll as will appear from such staff.'

" The marks on the staff represent every acre of land, for which 3d. has to be paid; half an acre 1½d.; and for every house ¼d. had to be paid. If twenty-four houses were built on an acre 6d. would be the court rent. A person could only be *reeved* once; that is, a different person every year would have to collect the rents and pay them over to the steward; he would be what they called *reeved*, or reeve-man."

I also furnished diagrams or symbols of the divisions cut on the staff, which represented the five following villages, Weston, Wakeham, Easton, Chesil, and Southwell. I, however, failed to find the symbol representing the last village on the staff. I believe it should be an O.

I then gave a reference to the Reeve-staff which occurred in Commins's *Improved Weymouth Guide* (*circa* 1846), p. 55.

" At the *Portland Arms* (where George the Third generally dined when on a visit to the Island), Mrs. Winter will show the Reeve-Pole, which exhibits the ancient mode of keeping accounts; it is said to be of Saxon origin, by which the bailiff of the Island collects the manor dues, as on the pole is described every acre of land the place contains."

I also asked if only one such staff was in use by the steward of the Manor Court, or was a new one furnished at every Court. My curiosity has not yet been gratified. My informant told me that he knew of the existence of no other staff but mine; but I have heard of one being in the possession of a gentleman at Weymouth.

Mr. Wilkinson Sherren in his book *The Wessex of Romance* (1908), p. 100, states that this mode of keeping the manorial accounts by means of a reeve-staff is said to be of Danish origin.

(iii) *Marrying the Land.*—A correspondent of the *Somerset and Dorset Notes and Queries* (1894), vol. iv, p. 62, sends the following interesting account of a land transfer custom obtaining in the Isle of Portland, taken from a book called *Angels, Cherubim, and Gods*, published by Wertheim & Co., London, in 1861.

"The custom of *marrying the land* is to the present time observed in the Isle of Portland, Dorsetshire. The inhabitants, who say that they are Phœnicians, have never, until lately, allowed any English, or 'foreigners', as they term us, to hold land in their territory, but have kept themselves a distinct people. About twenty or thirty years ago the English Government, wishing to erect a prison there, offered so large a sum of money for a building site that some of the inhabitants were tempted to do away with the old rule, while others so contended for its continuance that it was three years before they would agree to sell the property. And though since then other purchases have been effected they are of rare occurrence, and the old inhabitants have as little intercourse as possible with the 'new comers'.

"Before this time they had two modes of conveying land among themselves, one of which was called 'marrying the land', and was thus described a few years ago to a friend of the writer, when in the island, by a native quarryman. The contracting parties meet at the church, and the rite is performed by the clergyman at the altar, where one party taking the hand of the other (the quarryman here exemplifying his statement by taking the hand of our informant within his own), says: 'I, Uncle Tom' (they never use the surname), 'give to thee, Cousin Tim,' such a land of so many inches. The clergyman lays his hand on theirs, and the contract is concluded. The inches refer to the space between certain notches on a pole called the rood or reed pole, on which every man who has land has a notch cut at a longer or shorter distance, according to the quantity he possesses. The pole or stick (which our friend saw) is kept either at the church or the public-house, and is annually examined, to make such additions or alterations as may be needed.

This mode of holding land, which the inhabitants, who have no title-deeds, affirm to have been from time immemorial, is evidently of eastern origin and early date, as in Ezek. xxxvii, 16, we find sticks were to be cut and kept as tokens that Judah and Israel were again *to possess their own land.*"

There is added in a footnote :—

" Some doubts having arisen as to the truth of the above statement, the author has made fresh inquiry on the subject, and is informed that the clergyman has nothing to do with the ceremony, but that both parties affix their names to a document on the communion-table. Probably the custom is becoming obsolete, and the form therefore slightly varies from that formerly observed ; but the custom itself is remarkable, and the variation as to form does not invalidate its application with reference to the passage of scripture in question.

" The passage of scripture in question is Isaiah lxii, 4, containing the words, ' thy land shall be married.' "

(iv) *Transfer of land by " Church Gift "*.—The above custom of " marrying the land " would seem to be the same as, or very much akin to, that mode of transferring land in Portland, known as " Church Gift ".

In the *Somerset and Dorset Notes and Queries* (1901), vol. vii, p. 322, the Dorset editor of that periodical, the Rev. Canon Mayo, gives an account of a trial that had recently taken place in the Probate Court in which reference was made to this ancient custom of land transfer in the Isle of Portland. The account of the proceedings was taken from the *Western Gazette* of 19th July, 1901, which states :

" On the opening of the case Sir Richard Howard, solicitor and town clerk of Weymouth, was called, and gave evidence as to the testator's instructions for the will. He had acted as the testator's legal adviser for many years, but not in transfers of land, as the testator usually adopted the local custom of ' church gift '. For hundreds of years it used to be the custom at Portland for persons buying or selling land to go to the Parish Church, and there make a verbal declaration to that effect, and this was held a valid transfer. After the passing of the Act of 1845, requiring transfers of land to be by deed, people asked a schoolmaster to go to the church, and there draw up on a sheet of foolscap paper a recital of a transfer by ' church gift ', and this had until recently been considered legal and valid.

" Later on in the proceedings the form of ' church gift ' was stated to be as follows :—

" '(Stamp 5s.) Memorandum. That on the — day of — in the year — I — of —, Portland, in the County of Dorset, came into the Parish Church dedicated to St. George, and did then and there, according to an ancient custom of the island, time out of mind, in the presence of the undersigned witnesses, freely give, transfer and convey unto — and this I acknowledge to be my free Church Gift. In witness whereof I have set my hand and seal this said day and year above written.

" Signed. (Seal) Witness. Witness.' " [1]

(v) *Land System.*—The following remarks made by Mrs. King Warry in a paper on " The Status of Peasantry in Portland " in the Dorset Field Club *Proceedings*, vol. xxx, p. 78 (1909), on the old English land system as still in force in Portland are interesting.

" The Old English land system was mainly communal, in spite of certain private rights. The arable land was cultivated in strips, separated from neighbouring acres by thin fringes of unploughed turf, called ' balks '. These strips were sometimes hereditary, sometimes allotted. After the crops were gathered the fields became common pasture land, and individual rights were lost for the time. Up to the passing of the Tithes' Commutation Act in 1836 this Old English system remained partly in force in Portland Isle, the fields having what were ' open ' and ' closed ' years. During the ' closed ' period the owners planted and gathered their crops in the usual way, but the following or ' open ' year the fields were treated in ' common ' and opened to all cattle of the island, irrespective of ownership.

" With regard to meadows, a valuable asset in village life, it was usual to put them under prohibition until Lammas Day,[2] when the grass was cut and made according to certain rules, after which the land became the undivided pasture of the community.

" According to present-day legal opinion the constitution of the Court Baron proves that there must have been free tenants to constitute a manor. The Court Leet represented arrangements that were in full force in Saxon times, but were fitted into the Feudal system later.

" This Court Leet is still summoned twice a year at Portland under the same old methods of procedure, and the various officers

[1] This case was also reported in the *Standard* newspaper of 12th July, 1901, and references made to it in *Notes and Queries*, Ser. IX, viii, 81, 248, 432.

[2] The first day of August.

still comprise the steward, bailiff, reeve, chief constable, affeerors,[1] and haywards. Also the rights of pasturage appear to be the same as in Saxon times; and the old methods of land disposal, namely, by Church-gift, by Surrender in Court, or by last will or testament, are still favoured by the inhabitants, though Surrender in Court has well-nigh died out."

(vi) *Courtship and Marriage customs.*—For courtship and marriage customs prevalent amongst the Portland quarrymen, see Hutchins ii, 820. And also Chapter V, p. 198.

(vii) *The "Jump".*—Like their fellows in Purbeck, the Portland quarrymen are tied and bound by many old rules and curious customs, of which the following is still practised in the Island. It is mentioned by Mr. A. M. Wallis in a paper on "The Portland Stone Quarries" contributed to the Dorset Field Club's *Proceedings*, vol. xii, p. 193 (1891).

"On the return of a newly-married man belonging to the quarry to his work arrangements are made for the *pay off*. It was compulsory at one time for the men to pay five shillings or to *jump*; now it is a matter of choice whether he will do either, but as a rule he will not get much peace until he has complied with the general custom. When a *pay off* is to take place notice is given to the men of the neighbouring quarries. Sometimes five or six sets of quarrymen will assemble and dine together. As soon as dinner is over preparations are made for the *jump*. A piece of thin wood is held at one end by the man who was last married, and at the other end by the man who is likely to be married next. The piece of wood is held at a convenient height to jump it with ease, the married man standing on one side and the unmarried man on the other. A man stands by the side of each man who holds the board armed with a stick, whose duty it is to strike him while he is jumping. Before he begins another man stands forward, and with his hat off he reads the law, as it is termed, the custom, which is as follows:

'Young men and bachelors, I bid you all adieu;
Married men and Kohers I come unto you.'

"The jump is to be made while the last sentence is uttered. This is generally repeated. He then reads the law relating to those who do not observe the rules, such as omitting to take their hats off, talking, or otherwise out of order. The afternoon is then spent in a genial manner."

[1] As to their duties see Halliwell's *Archaic Dictionary*, *s.v.* "Affeer."

Mr. Wallis considers that the above originated from some ancient marriage custom, probably Celtic or Saxon, for there are many Celtic words, he says, in common use in Portland.

(viii) *Binding Day*.—Mr. Wallis then describes another custom, now obsolete, termed *Binding Day*, which persons now living can remember. He says:

"It was observed on the Wednesday of the seventh week after Christmas Day, when men and women took anything they could lay their hands on from their neighbours, including wearing apparel, which could be redeemed by paying a small tribute. On that day there was no law to interfere. The custom is said to have originated from an attack upon the islanders by some foreigners, who killed all the men they could find on the island and saved the women alive. Many hid themselves, and when the foreigners thought they had gained the confidence of the women and were safe they and the men who were hidden rose and killed the foreigners."

Poundbury (Dorchester).

As to the annual stocking of Poundbury Field, near Dorchester, on May Day, see Chapter I, p. 41.

Pucknoll.

For "Garland Day", see *ante, s.v.* Abbotsbury.

Purbeck.

(i) *Purbeck Marblers*.—For an account of the "Purbeck Marblers" see *ante, s.v.* Corfe Castle.

(ii) *St. Aldhelm's Chapel* (*Wishing and Flower customs*).—In a paper by the Rev. J. H. Austen, read before the Purbeck Society at a meeting at St. Aldhelm's Head in July, 1857, and published in the *Purbeck Papers* (1862–9), p. 135—in which two engravings of the Chapel, exterior and interior, appear—the author, referring to its popular designation as "The Devil's Chapel", states that

"there is a peculiar veneration which has continued to be attached to the Chapel to the present time, for it is still the custom with the young women of the neighbourhood to drop a pin into a hole in the centre pillar and wish for a husband, or at least the happy consummation of whatever they have most at heart."

He also mentions that

"On Whit Thursday annually the villagers of Worth proceed with music to the head, dress the Chapel with flags and dance within it, when many an offering is doubtless made, accompanied by many a whispered wish."

A correspondent in *Folk-Lore*, vol. xix, p. 92 (1908), gives an extract from the *Church Times* of 13th September, 1907, wherein the writer, after mentioning the custom last alluded to, on the authority of the late Mr. H. J. Moule, goes on to say :—

"There was an old custom, still maintained, of placing a pin in an opening of the central shaft, accompanying the action with a silently expressed wish. When visiting the building on two occasions last August about a dozen pins were noticed in the aperture, which is not to be wondered at since all the cheap guide-books exploit its fame in this direction. On my last visit a young lady, apparently of some refinement and education, entered the fabric, at once proceeded to the pin-hole and deposited her contribution, at the same moment closing her eyes with a rapt expression of countenance, whilst her lips moved as she mutely made her wish."

Radipole.

Perambulation.—For account of the perambulation of the boundaries of the parish of Radipole, see Chapter I, p. 36.

Rempstone.

Right of way. — The *Bridport News* in February, 1894, stated that in order to preserve a right of way for the quarrymen of the Isle of Purbeck over the lands of Rempstone Manor a football and a pound of pepper had to be carried every year on Shrove Tuesday to a certain house and deposited there.

This no doubt had reference to what has been stated before *s.v.* Corfe Castle, as to the custom of "kicking the ball" on that day by the Purbeck quarrymen.

Shaftesbury.

The Bezant. — The very interesting ceremony of the "bezant" or "prize-besom", by which the inhabitants of Shaftesbury formerly obtained their supply of water for the town from wells at Enmore in the adjoining parish of Motcombe, is almost a matter of historic interest.

The earliest account of it that I can find is in a small book that I once possessed, *A Compleat History of Dorsetshire*, c. 1716. This account I contributed to the Folk-lore column of the *Dorset County Chronicle*, about 1883, and it was as follows :—

" This town, being seated upon a high Hill, is destitute of Water, which how it is supplied with, according to custom, is not unworthy our Observation. There are a quarter of a Mile from the Town three or four large wells in the Parish of *Melcomb* within the liberty of *Gillingham*, a Manor belonging to Edward Nicholas, Esq., from which this Town has been supplied Time out of mind, being brought on Horses Backs, or upon the Head in Pails, at a certain Price ; but the Town is obliged to make this Acknowledgment to the Lord of the Manor for their Water. The Mayor and Burgesses of *Shaftesbury* the *Monday* before *Holy Thursday*, dress up a Prize-Besom, as they call it (somewhat like a *May Garland* in Form) with Gold and Peacocks Feathers, and carry it to a broad Green half a mile below the Hill in the parish of *Melcomb* and present it to the Lord of the Manor as an Acknowledgment for his Water, together with a raw Calves-Head, and a pair of Gloves, which his Steward receives distributing at the same time among the People twelve Penny-Loaves and three dozen of Beer. This ceremony being over, the Prize-Besom (which is usually worth 1,500£, being adorned with Plate and Jewels borrowed of the neighbouring gentry) is restored to the Mayor and brought back again to the Town by one of the Officers with great solemnity."

I there asked for information as to when this custom had been abandoned. By a correspondent I was referred to Chambers's *Book of Days*, vol. i, p. 585, for fuller information, and I was told that " the festival has ceased in 1830 ", water being then supplied by a new artesian well in the town itself.

He went on to say that :

" The curious trophy formally presented to the lord of the Manor in return for the water supply was called a ' bizant '—your correspondent's authority makes natives call it a ' prize-besom '. A frame four feet high was covered with ribbons, flowers, peacocks' feathers, jewellery, and gold and silver coins, from which last the name was taken, a ' bizant ' being an ancient gold coin, and the amount, probably, of the original water-tax."

At the same time I had received a direct reply from a friend, resident at Shaftesbury, which confirmed Chambers's account of the discontinuance of the custom. My friend had ascertained from one of the " oldest inhabitants " of the place that the custom had been abolished by the late Marquess of Westminster, when he purchased the Motcombe (or Melcombe) Estate about 1830. Probably in this year on the Monday before Whit-Monday (that is the Rogation Monday of Chambers) was the last instance of this custom having been carried out.

He also added (which Chambers does not) that on the Tuesday and during the week after the custom, a fair was held in Enmore-green, a hamlet of Motcombe, in which the wells were situate, and, further, that the people filled up the wells with rubbish, being disgusted that the custom was abolished. In conclusion, he said that Shaftesbury, which was then supplied with water from a deep well sunk by the late lord about thirty years previously, was famous for three things, viz. more strong beer than water ; the churchyard higher than the church ; more rogues than honest men.

Another friend has supplied an alternative to this last : " More whores than married women."

In 1907 Shaftesbury followed the custom of so many other towns about that time by holding an " Historic Pageant ",[1] and amongst the tableaux that were given illustrating the ancient history of the town was that of the " Bezant ".

The *Dorset County Chronicle* of 18th April of that year gave the following account of it :—

" The last episode was the Byzant ceremony, which was observed towards the end of the eighteenth century.

" It represented the Mayor and Corporation going down to Enmore Green and making presents of bread, ale, a calf's head, and gloves to the Lord of the Manor for allowing the inhabitants to draw water from the wells of Enmore Green. The Mayor (Dr. Harris) and several aldermen and councillors marched on to the stage preceded by the mace-bearers and Byzant, where they were received by the Lord of the Manor. The custom of handing over the bread etc. was duly observed, and a document setting forth the reasons for the observance was read by the Mayor, after which he declared that dancing should be the order of the day. The Mayor, aldermen, and councillors then led off the dance. This was an excellent representation and was highly successful."

[1] These Pageants were first set on foot by the excellent one given at Sherborne Castle a few years previously under the superintendence of Mr. Louis Parker.

In its issue for the 9th May following the same paper contained a statement that

"Lady Theodora Guest of Inwood House, Henstridge, has presented the town of Shaftesbury with the old 'Byezant' which was used in one of the representations at the recent display of historical *tableaux*. In a letter to the Mayor, read at Wednesday's council meeting, the donor said that she felt it was an interesting relic of the past, and that, as such, it ought to be preserved in the town to which its history belonged. The Corporation have decided to keep the relic in a cabinet in the Mayor's parlour."

Hutchins also (iii, 44) gives a very good account of this custom, to which I would refer my readers. Also to Lady Theodora Grosvenor's *Motcombe : Past and Present* (1873), pp. 51–3. See also *Somerset and Dorset Notes and Queries*, vol. ii, p. 235, and iii, p. 297 (where an excellent representation of the "Bezant" is given) and *Notes and Queries*, Ser XI, iii, 170.

Sherborne.

(i) *Bell-tolling custom.*—A correspondent in Hone's *Every-Day Book* (vol. ii, p. 628) states that the 23rd September has obtained in Sherborne, Dorset, the name of "Tolling Day", in commemoration of the death of John, Lord Digby, baron Digby of Sherborne and Earl of Bristol in 1698, and in conformity with his will under which the yearly sum of £10 was to be paid by his successors to the churchwardens of the parish church at Sherborne at Michaelmas and Lady Day respectively, in equal portions, to be employed by them towards the repair of the church, with the proviso (amongst others) that the largest bell in the tower should be tolled for six full hours (there specified) in every year on the day of the month upon which he should happen to die. The correspondent adds :

"This custom is annually observed, but not to the extent intended, the tolling of the bell being limited to two hours instead of six. It begins to toll at six o'clock and continues till seven in the morning, when six men, who toll the bell for church service, repair to the mansion of the present Earl Digby with two large stone jars, which are there filled with some of his lordship's strong beer, and, with a quantity of bread and cheese, taken to the church by the tollers and equally divided between them, together with a small remuneration in money paid by the church-wardens as a compensation for their labour. At twelve o'clock the bell is again tolled till one, and in the evening divine service is performed at the church, and a lecture suited to the occasion delivered from the pulpit; for which lecture or sermon the vicar is paid thirty pounds, provided by the will of the above donor."

Hutchins (iv, 268) also gives abstracts from the will of the above Earl of Bristol, embodying these two bequests.

(ii) *Pentecost Money.*—The value of this vicariate would seem to be somewhat uncertain, depending much on surplice fees, fair tolls, and voluntary subscriptions. Hutchins (iv, 263) gives the names of twelve parishes who pay tribute or "Pentecost money" to the vicar, but amounting in the whole to only 9s. 3d. There is no glebe, he says, nor has the vicarage been augmented by Queen Anne's Bounty.

W. Carew Hazlitt in a paper on "Uncollected Tenures and Manorial Customs", published in *The Antiquary*, vol. xii, p. 112. (1885), alludes to this Pentecost Money as being collected at Sherborne in Hutchins's time.

(iii) *Christmas Pence for Children.*—The *Dorset County Chronicle* in January, 1890, stated that "in accordance with old-established custom a large number of children from Sherborne and surrounding villages presented themselves at the Castle Lodge on Christmas morning, and were each presented with two new pennies". Again, in December, 1917, the same paper records the due observance of the old custom of going "up to Lodge" on Christmas morning, and adds: "As usual, all the children unable to walk were either pushed in prams or were carried."

(iv) *Furmity Eating.*—For a statement by a correspondent in the *Dorset County Chronicle* that "furmity" was formerly sold by the plate or cupful at Sherborne, especially at Easter, see Chapter I, p. 33.

(v) *Pack Monday Fair.*—Hutchins (iv, 209), speaking of the three annual fairs held in the town of Sherborne,—the first on St. Thomas à Becket's Day, O.S., upon the green near the site of St. Thomas à Becket's Chapel; the second in St. Swithin's Street on St. Swithin's Day, O.S.—continues:

" The third, outside the Abbey Close, on the first Monday after the feast of St. Michael, O.S.

" This last is the most considerable, and is a great holiday for the inhabitants of the town and neighbourhood. It is ushered in by the ringing of the great bell at 4 a.m., and by the boys and young men perambulating the streets with cows' horns at a still earlier hour, to the no small annoyance of their less wakeful neighbours. It has been an immemorial custom in Sherborne for the boys to blow horns in the evenings, in the streets, for some weeks before the fair. It is commonly known as Pack Monday Fair, and there is a tradition that Abbot Peter Ramsam and his workmen completed the nave of the abbey and kept a holiday on that day in 1490, and that the name was derived from the men packing up their tools. These fairs are chiefly for cattle, horses, and sheep. At the last woollen cloths and all sorts of commodities are sold. The tolls of St. Swithin's belong to the Vicar ; those of the others to the lord of the Manor."

In September, 1826, a resident in Sherborne sent to Hone's *Every-Day Book* (ii, 654) the following very full description of what goes on at Pack Monday Fair. He says :

" This fair is usually held on the first Monday after the 10th of October, and is a mart for the sale of horses, cows, fat and lean oxen, sheep, lambs, and pigs, cloth, earthenware, onions, wall and hazel nuts, apples, fruit trees, and the usual nick nacks for children, toys, ginger-bread, sweetmeats, sugar plums etc. etc. with drapery, hats, bonnets, caps, ribands, etc. for the country belles, of whom, when the weather is favourable, a great number is drawn together from the neighbouring villages.

" Tradition relates that this fair originated at the termination of the building of the church, when the people who had been employed about it packed up their tools, and held a fair or wake in the churchyard, blowing cows' horns in their rejoicing, which at that time was perhaps the most common music in use. . . .

" The fair has been removed from the churchyard about six or seven years, and is now held on a spacious parade in a street not far from the church. . . .

" To the present time Pack Monday fair is annually announced three or four weeks previous by all the little urchins who can procure and blow a cow's horn parading the streets in the evenings, and sending forth the different tones of their horny bugles, sometimes beating an old sauce-pan for a drum, to render the sweet sound more delicious, and not infrequently a whistle-pipe or a fife is added to the band.

"The clock's striking twelve on the Sunday night previous is the summons for ushering in the fair, when the boys assemble with their horns and parade the town with a noisy shout, and prepare to forage for fuel to light a bonfire, generally of straw obtained from some of the neighbouring farmyards, which are sure to be plundered, without respect to the owners, if they have not been fortunate enough to secure the material in some safe part of their premises.

"In this way the youths enjoy themselves in boisterous triumph, to the annoyance of the sleeping part of the inhabitants, many of whom deplore, whilst others, who entertain respect for old customs, delight in the deafening mirth. At four o'clock the great bell is rang for a quarter of an hour. From this time the bustle commences by the preparation for the coming scene: stalls erecting, windows cleaning and decorating, shepherds and drovers going forth for their flocks and herds, which are depastured for the night in the neighbouring fields, and every individual seems on the alert. The business in the sheep and cattle fairs (which are held in different fields, nearly in the centre of the town, and well attended by the gentlemen farmers of Dorset, Somerset and Devon) takes precedence, and is generally concluded by twelve o'clock, when what is called the in-fair begins to wear the appearance of business-like activity, and from this time till three or four o'clock more business is transacted in the shop, counting-house, parlour, hall and kitchen than at any other time of the day, it being a custom of the tradespeople to have their yearly accounts settled about this time, and scarcely a draper, grocer, hatter, ironmonger, bookseller, or other respectable tradesman but is provided with an ample store of beef and home-brewed October, for the welcome of their numerous customers, few of whom depart without taking *quantum suff*: of the old English fare placed before them."

"Now," Hone's correspondent goes on to say,—"is the *town alive*." And he tells us of the usual merry sights of a country fair—the giant, the learned pig, the giantess and dwarf, the conjuror, the managerie of wild beasts, the merry-go-round, the lucky bag, the Sheffield hardwareman with his wonderful display of cheap cutlery, the inevitable Cheap Jack offering everything for next-to-nothing—for fuller details of which I would refer my readers to his account. And he concludes with the following remarks:—

" This is Pack Monday fair, till evening throws on her dark veil, when the visitors, in taking their farewell, stroll through the rows of ginger-bread stalls . . . By this time the country folks are for jogging home, and vehicles and horses of every description on the move, and the bustle nearly over, with the exception of what is to be met with at the inns, where the lads and lasses so disposed, on the light fantastic toe, assisted by the merry scraping of the fiddle, finish the fun, frolic, and pastime of Pack Monday fair."

Some sixty years later Mr. E. Archdall Ffooks—the present clerk of the peace for the county of Dorset, and then a resident in the neighbourhood of Sherborne—at my request for information as to the modern proportions of the fair, wrote me a letter in which he says : " The old custom of horn blowing has now, through the aid of the police, been reduced to reasonable limits. A few years ago small boys blew horns at all hours of the day and night until their bed-time for more than a month before Pack Monday Fair. Then the inhabitants complained of the nuisance, and the police were instructed to prevent it and to take away the horns, with the result that now only a few occasional horns are heard for about a week beforehand. On Sunday evening about 10 p.m. on October 12th (1884) a few horns in different parts, calling together those who were to take part in the march round, were heard ; and these gradually increased in number and became mingled with an occasional tin tray etc. until 12 o'clock, when the whole body of about 300 assembled at the Antelope Hotel moved off in no particular order and marched once all over the town, starting down Cheap Street and then passing through as many as possible until all the most important had been visited, keeping up an incessant din the whole time with horns, bugles, and all sorts of tin trays etc. that would make a noise. About 2 a.m. the town is allowed to go to sleep.

" This is what is left of the old custom, and seems likely to last in about its same proportions until something puts an end to Pack Monday Fair itself."

Shillingston.

Maypole custom.—For a reference to Maypole custom at Shillingston, see Chapter I, p. 40.

Stalbridge.

(i) *Lent-crocking.*—For account of Lent-crocking custom at Stalbridge see Chapter I, p. 24.

(ii) *"Crookern" and "Hunting the Buck" Customs.*—The Rev. W. S. Swayne in a pamphlet on *The History and Antiquities of Stalbridge* (1889), p. 37, speaks of a custom which the inhabitants of Stalbridge were wont to indulge in on Easter Monday. He says:

"There is a custom at Stalbridge for the inhabitants to play "crookern" on the Ring at Easter-Monday. About four o'clock in the afternoon a body of men and women would congregate on the Ring to the number of about fifty. They first joined hands and played a game called "Hunting the Buck"; one member of the party was selected as "Buck", and others knelt down at intervals to represent obstacles. After a certain period the whole party joined hands and danced a species of country dance down the Stalbridge High Street, and on until they reached the Virginia Ash at Henstridge, where every person had a pint of beer, and so homewards."

I can find no other reference to this custom, which has an ancient savour about it, and bears the nearest resemblance to the Cornish "Furry-dance" that I can find in Dorsetshire. It is noteworthy that in the "Furry Day Song" the invocation is made "To chase the buck and doe", which would seem to be here personified by the Stalbridge folk in their preliminary game of "Hunting the Buck".

I initiated a discussion in *Notes and Queries* (Ser. XII, ii, 470, iii, 16, 99, 158) (1916–17) in the hope of obtaining some information as to the origin of this game but hitherto without success. So may I ask now what is the etymology of this word "crookern"? Can it have had anything to do with the old town of Crewkerne in Somerset (frequently spelt "Crookhorn" in old maps), on the borders of which county the parish of Stalbridge abuts? Or it may with more probability have something to do with "Crookern Stoke", a hamlet in the parish of Lydlinch, which adjoins Stalbridge.

Stoke Abbott.

(i) *Flax Horn.* — Mr. Richard Hine, of Beaminster, in *Somerset and Dorset Notes and Queries* (1902), vol. viii, p. 180, asked for information as to the origin of what he believed to be a very old custom of the flax dressers, and still observed in the neighbourhood of Stoke Abbott, of carrying a flax horn, which was always sounded at meal times and on commencing and leaving their work.

I think that Mr. Hine is in error in supposing that this custom was in existence at the time he wrote (1902), for in answer to inquiries that I have made I have been told that it was discontinued some twenty-five or thirty years before that, when machinery did away with the working of flax by hand. I have been informed by a friend at Stoke Abbott, from inquiries made from one or two old flax dressers who are still living in the village, that they, being the head ones, used to blow the horn from their bedroom window as soon as they had risen from their beds, to call the other members of their party so as to be up and ready to meet and go together when the horn sounded again. It was also sounded at every meal, or when they had a horn of cider between meals, and also on leaving work and on arriving back at the village.

I was afforded no information as to the origin of the custom; but I wonder if it can in any way have arisen from the fact that Stoke Abbott was well within the statutory radius from Bridport, where the flax and hemp—so good were they—were by statute [1] reserved for making cordage for the use of the Royal Navy; to which use certain customs and privileges may have been attached.

(ii) *Curfew Plot.*—In the second edition of Hutchins's *History of Dorset* (1796) (vol. i, p. 467) mention is made of a small piece of land in the parish of Stoke Abbott, called the "Curfew Plot", lying on the west side of the street opposite the parsonage barton, which is said to belong to the clerk of the parish for the time being for ringing the Curfew bell. The donor is uncertain.[2]

In the year 1870 a very interesting question arose as to the ownership of this particular piece of land. In the October County Court held at Bridport an action (*Barrett v. Gill*) was brought by the churchwardens and overseers on behalf of the parish of Stoke Abbott to recover possession of the "Curfew Plot" (measuring 32 perches and numbered 544 on the parish

[1] 21 Hen. VIII, c. 12.

[2] There is no mention of this "Curfew Plot" in the account given of the parish in the latest edition of Hutchins (1863).

Tithe Commutation Map) from an inhabitant of the parish who had obtained possession of it.

It was stated that the piece of land had been held by the parish from time immemorial, and that it had been permitted to be held by the parish clerk and bellringer in part payment of his salary, amongst his duties being that of ringing the curfew bell. The commencement of such a custom was not known ; all deeds, if any ever existed, had been lost. The bell was now only rung in the morning, during the summer months, at 5 o'clock. It appeared that the piece of land had been in the possession of a family who had filled the office of parish clerk since the year 1790. The defendant had been a purchaser at a sale of some of the old parish clerk's property, amongst which this particular piece of land had been included ; and the question was in whom was the ownership of this piece of land.

The above statement in Hutchins was endeavoured to be put in as evidence on the part of the parish, but was objected to on the part of the defendant. Several of the principal and oldest inhabitants of the parish were called as witnesses, including the then rector of the parish, whose evidence bore out the statement made by Hutchins, so far back as 1796, that the plot of land had always been occupied by the parish clerk for the time being in part payment of his salary for the duties he performed as clerk and bellringer.

The result of the trial was in favour of the parish, and possession of the land was ordered to be given up to the churchwardens.[1]

Some years later when I happened to be acting for the County Court judge in this district, and being interested in the parish of Stoke Abbott was anxious that its old customary rights should not again be infringed, I obtained an official copy of this judgment and sent it to the rector to be kept with the other documents belonging to the parish.

At the time I saw it—some few years after the trial—I believe the rector of the parish rented the " Curfew Plot " from his clerk and used it as a garden. I have since been informed that the " Curfew Plot " is rented from the churchwardens by the

[1] For a detailed account of the trial see the *Bridport News* of 28th October, 1870.

rector at £3 a year, which sum is paid to the clerk for ringing the Curfew bell at 5 a.m. from 1st May till December.[1]

Sturminster Marshall.

(i) *Smoke-hole* (*or hold*) *tenure.*—The following indications of a very curious customary tenure—if tenure it be—are made by a correspondent in the *Somerset and Dorset Notes and Queries*, vol. iv, p. 69 :—

" A cottage in Sturminster Marshall, held by Israel Gallop, was burnt down about 1850. When it was being rebuilt Gallop lived inside the walls, day and night, till the chimney was sufficiently formed to allow of a fire being lighted. He feared lest his elder brother, or indeed anyone else, might be before him and by lighting a fire get a title to the place."

I can find no reference to any such a tenure in Hazlitt's *Tenures of lands and customs of Manors*, or in any such work ; and I am inclined to believe that the action of the burnt-out occupant of the cottage was due more to some superstitious belief, or to the terms of some capricious family bequest than to any legal compliance with the tenure of his occupation.

(ii) *Land customs.* — In an article in the *Somerset and Dorset Notes and Queries*, vol. ii, pp. 41–7 (1890) by its Dorset editor, upon a survey of the parish (1819) which had been placed in his hands by the vicar of the parish for examination, the Rev. Canon Mayo remarks that it is interesting as illustrating the manner in which the open fields—all traces of which have disappeared since the Inclosure Award in 1845—were divided into small strips or portions amongst various proprietors, and as indicating the numerous rights of common which were attached to the separate estates or " livings ".

There appear to have been five open arable fields (there named) which were cultivated, as stated by Mr. Ahuzzath [2] Legg on a three years' system (there stated). The cultivation of these strips in the open fields occasionally gave rise to disputes between the

[1] Also see *s.v.* Mapouder and *s.v.* Ibberton, and for other similar curfew customary rights see Edward's *Old English Customs* (1842), pp. 223–7.

[2] Where is this name taken from ? I cannot find it in any list of Biblical proper names that I am acquainted with.

several occupiers, which disputes were arranged by a jury of twelve men serving in the Court Leet.

In addition to the arable fields there was a grass meadow called " Sturminster Mead ", where were numerous strips usually marked off by stones set at intervals.

The other point of interest presented by this survey arises with reference to the ancient commonable rights attached to the various holdings. These rights at Sturminster Marshall existed in the Common, in the first swathe of Shapwick Marsh, and in the second swathe of the same, or, as it is usually termed in the survey, so many rights were owned in *First Marsh*, and so many in *Second Marsh*. The nature of these rights is thus explained :—

" No hay was ever made in Shapwick Marsh ; (so named from its situation near the parish of that name which lies on the opposite side of the river) but the Marsh was thrown open twice a year, first in June for three weeks and three days—fully long enough for the consumption of all the grass growing there—and secondly on the grand event of the neighbourhood, Woodbury Hill Fair, 18th Sept., and it then remained open till 14th February following,—Old Candlemas. These open periods were severally called First and Second Swathe. Within the former of these, when the cows had been about nine days or a fortnight feeding upon the grass, a feast of Sillabub was held. This was a joint-stock merrymaking, to which one person would contribute the milk of one cow, another the milk of two, and so on, according to his ability, and Dr. Heath (Vicar 1805–1822) would send a bottle of wine as his contribution to the festivity. The sillabub [1] was made in the milking pails, and drunk after milking time.

" Two curious customs were connected with Shapwick Marsh and Sturminster Mead.

" The Trenchards, as owners of the Newton property, had the right of running a horse in Shapwick Marsh after the Marsh was ' broke ',[2] on the condition that it might be used in sending for the midwife (latterly, for the parish doctor). This condition, even if it were anything but a jocular tenure, was never known to be acted on, as the time and trouble consumed in catching the horse would be better employed in sending a foot messenger into Wimborne, for the necessary assistance.

" Mrs. Grosvenor, of Charborough Park, also had the right (attached to what is now the Reading Room) of running a mare

[1] A dish made of mixing wine or cider with cream or milk, and thus forming a soft curd.

[2] *i.e.* thrown open for cattle.

and foal in Sturminster Mead, on the condition that the former might be used in sending for assistance in case of fire."

The common in the moors was open throughout the year. (The rights of those who had authority to run cattle there are set out).

Canon Mayo continues :

" The whole of this system of agriculture and pasturage was abolished when the Enclosure Award was settled in 1845, and the land of the parish divided afresh among several proprietors.

" The customs here narrated could no doubt be more fully and accurately described if reference could be made to the Court Rolls of the principal manor in the parish, but in the meantime it will be advisable to place on record the mass of information gathered from the early recollections of Mr. Legg, who is now,[1] in all probability, the only man living who is familiar with the conditions under which farming was in olden time carried on in the parish where he has so long resided."

Swanage.

As to the custom of the Swanage marblers kicking the football on Shrove Tuesday at Corfe Castle, see *ante, s.v.* Corfe Castle.

Swyre.

For " Garland Day ", see *ante, s.v.* Abbotsbury.

Thornford.

For account of tithe custom in this parish on St. Thomas's Day, see Chapter I, p. 50.

Upwey (near Weymouth).

Auction by Candle.—Upwey furnishes another instance of auction by candle in the neighbourhood of Weymouth.[2] A writer in the *Globe* newspaper of 12th January, 1917, in an article on " Auction by Candle ", after giving a description from Pepys's *Diary* for 3rd September, 1662, of one of these auctions, says :

" Here and there bidding by candle is still carried on, generally be it said in connection with the letting of land, usually charity or parish lands—according to the custom of centuries. No doubt the best known of all these candle auctions is that at Upwey, not far from Dorchester, in Dorset, which takes place every

[1] Mr. Legg died in March, 1890.

[2] See *ante, s.v.* Broadway.

January. In 1624 one William Gould left two acres of meadow for the poor of the parish, and the candle auction is held for the letting of this. Perhaps it is as well for a busy age that there are not more of these auctions as much valuable time would be consumed in carrying them on as the ceremony may be a lengthy one. A few years ago Upwey complained that the candle used was merely a common dip, an article hardly fitting for so ancient a custom. The complaint was duly taken to heart, for the following year a fine piece of wax candle was lit by the parish clerk; it burnt steadily, but slowly, and the lessee for the twelve months was not decided until an hour had elapsed." [1]

Wareham.

Borough custom.—In a detailed account of churches, chapels, and chantries formerly existing in Wareham contained in the *Dorset County Chronicle* in January, 1891, occurs the following passage:—

"The church of All Hallows, or All Saints, North Street, probably a chapel of ease to St. Martin's, . . . is said to have been desecrated and used as a warehouse or barn. Stables occupy the site. All Saints' Day was formerly observed at Wareham. In the ancient constitution of the borough 'it is constituted and ordered that all officers, magistrates and ministers that do sute and service at the Court where the Maior setteth judge, shall accompany the Maior to and from the church on the feast of All Saints . . . upon pain that every one being absent without lawful cause shall pay twelve pence to the use of the poor'."

Wimborne.

(i) *Cock-fighting.*—Hutchins (iii, 197), in speaking of the custom or practice of cock-fighting as being prevalent amongst schoolboys on Shrove Tuesday as far back as the time of Henry II, says:

"From this time at least this diversion, however cruel and absurd, was continued in many of the schools in this kingdom; in that of Wimborne in particular, where it annually took place till the beginning of the present century, when it was very properly abandoned. The theatre (the cockpit) it seems was the school, and the master the comptroller and director of the sport. The master presided, having the names of the boys inserted in paper billets, and huddled together in his hat.

[1] In the same article mention is made of two places in the adjoining county of Somerset, namely, Chedzoy and Tatworth, where similar auctions are occasionally held.

"The names of any two boys being first drawn and announced, their respective cocks were brought into the pit and fought till one of them was dead; a second couple was then drawn, then a third, and then a fourth, till such time as one half of the original cocks lay dead; when the remaining ones were, in the same manner as before, brought to a second contest, till one only of the whole was left alive, the owner of which was distinguished by the glorious name of victor, with many other privileges annexed to it, such as never to be subjected himself during the whole time of Lent to the disgrace of flagellation; but, what was still more, when any other boy was on the point of undergoing that punishment, he was at liberty if he pleased to exempt him from it by only clapping his hat on the culprit's posteriors, and thereby saving him from the lash." [1]

(ii) *Cake custom.*—Hutchins (iii, 255) states that the Minster authorities at Wimborne are in possession of several volumes of churchwardens' accounts, commencing in 1475 (which he describes), and which furnish us with curious and valuable information respecting matters connected with the church. Under the head of receipts appears the following:—

"*Sale of Cakes.*—Two women, 'the wives,' seem to have been appointed to sell cakes for the benefit of the church, one for the town, 'the wife of the town'; the other, 'the wife of the country.' This seems to have been periodically inaugurated by some kind of procession or ceremony; the following, from an old presentment, related to this matter:

"'1599. Item, we present that on Sownday last the great cacke was brought throwe the churche accordyndge unto the olde custum after devyne servyce by Stephen Hapgood and Davye Williams, at wch tyme ther was an infaunt a chrystenynge unknowen unto us, whereof we crave favour of the court.'"

These old churchwardens' accounts seem to be of great interest; and it is to be hoped that some day one of our local antiquarian societies may be able to publish them, and so save them and their valuable contents from the risk of being destroyed.

Wool.

(i) *Smoke-pence.*—Hutchins alludes (i, 349) to an ancient custom of collecting what was termed "smoke-pence" on the annual court day of the Manor of Wool. The payment seems to have been made by the occupiers of every dwelling-house or

[1] See Chapter I, p. 27.

chimney. It was probably an acknowledgment that the property belonged to the manor. The money was collected by the constable, who was obliged to bring 20*d.* into court or make up the money himself. The custom, says Hutchins, has fallen into disuse for many years past.

(ii) *Dog fair.*—In a note to the same page Hutchins, referring to the annual cattle-fair held at Wool in May, speaks of another one, termed the "Dog-fair", which takes place in September, at which time the boys of the village consider themselves at liberty to whip and drive away any dogs that they may find at large in the streets. The origin, he says, of this custom has not been ascertained; and the fair, although, according to the parishioners, formerly of more consequence, has now nearly fallen into disuse.

Wyke Regis.

The Bound Stone.—The following account of the annual visit paid by Portlanders to "The Bound Stone" on the Chesil Beach at the Fleet appeared in the *Bridport News* in May, 1893, under the heading of "Wyke Regis: The Bound Stone":—

"The Portlanders seem determined to keep up their rights, which they annually maintain by an official visit to the well-known 'bound stone' on the Chesil Beach. Holy Thursday, or Ascension Day, is, as by custom, the day on which the ceremony takes place. This year the number attending seems to have been augmented for some reason or other; perhaps the fact of a new stone being used added importance to the affair. Be that as it may, there were many visitors, both by sea and land.

"It is said the rights of the Portlanders extend to the new bound stone opposite Fleet, but the public would like to be enlightened as to the nature of those rights. There is one right at all events which does not extend beyond the Portland side of the stone, that is, we are informed that the lord of the manor of Abbotsbury, or rather the Earl of Ilchester, does not interfere with or claim the foreshore. Not that such a right would be of any use whatever, seeing the difficulty of telling where it is. The shingle shifts with the weather, and with it the foreshore, if ever such existed except in fertile imagination."

CHAPTER IV

LOCAL LEGENDS AND SUPERSTITIONS

Bagley House : (Baglake ?) (Bridport).

Ghost Story.—I take the following rather weird story from a review in the *Dorset County Chronicle* in August, 1883, of Miss M. F. Billington's paper on "Dorsetshire Ghosts" contributed to *Merry England* for that month.

"Bagley House, near Bridport, has very gloomy legends attaching to it. Tradition (for the stories are traced back to the last century) says that 'Squire Lighte, who then owned the place, had been hunting one day, and after returning home had gone away again and drowned himself. His groom had followed him with a presentiment that something was wrong, and arrived at the pond in time to see the end of the tragedy. As he returned he was accosted by the spirit of his drowned master, which unhorsed him. He soon fell violently ill, and never recovered, one of the consequences of this illness being that his skin peeled entirely off. Shortly after 'Squire Lighte's suicide his old house was troubled by noisy disturbances, which were at once associated with the evil deed of self-destruction. It was suggested that the spirit should be formally and duly 'laid' or exorcised. A number of the clergy went therefore for that purpose, and succeeded in inducing the ghost to confine itself to a chimney in the house for a certain number of years,—it is not known exactly now for how long.

"For many years after this, however, the place remained at peace; but on the expiration of the power of the charm very much worse disturbances broke out again. Raps would be heard at the front door; steps in the passage and on the stairs; doors opening and closing. The rustle of ladies dressed in silk was audible in the drawing-room, and from that room the sound was traced into a summer-house in the garden. The crockery would all be violently moved, and at certain rare intervals a male figure, dressed in old-fashioned costume, is said to have made itself visible and walked about the house. The neighbours say that these extraordinary occurrences continued for many years. They believe in them most fervently; and are of opinion that as long as the house stands it will be thus troubled. An element worthy of notice in this story is the time-honoured faith in the power of the clergy over evil spirits."

Batcombe.

Batcombe Down Cross.—The following account of the legend attaching to the monolith or cross on Batcombe Down was furnished to the *Folk-Lore Journal*, vii, 25 (1889), by the late Mr. H. J. Moule, Curator of the Dorset County Museum at Dorchester, and by him subsequently sent to the *Somerset and Dorset Notes and Queries*, vol. i, p. 247 (1889) :—

" On Batcombe Down, Dorset, is a stone about three feet high, evidently part of a cross, and called Cross Hand Stone. Why should a cross be set up, away there on the down ? Well, this ' be teäle twold o't '. Back in the middle ages, one dark, wild winter night, Batcombe priest was sent for to take the *viaticum* to a dying man, two or three miles off. Taking pyx and service-book, he sallied out with a brave heart on his dark, lonely way over Batcombe Down, and safely reached the sick man's house. But on getting in, and producing what was needed for his ministration—where was the pyx ? It was lost. He had dropped it on the way, and its fall on the turf of Batcombe Down—in the howling wind too !—had not been heard. Back he toiled, into the darkness and the storm, on his almost hopeless quest. Hopeless ? The easiest search ever made. Up on Batcombe Down there was a pillar of fire, reaching from heaven to earth, and steadily shining in the storm. What could this be ? He struggled on faster and faster, with strange, half-formed hopes. He came near to the spot over which stood the calm beam in the gale. He saw numbers of cattle of various kinds, gathered in a circle—kneeling—kneeling round the pyx.

" Well, this seemed to me to be the mediæval legend, rendering a reason for Batcombe Cross being set up there, away on the down, where, though time-worn, it yet remains. But (*me judice*) in the last century a rider was added, as follows :

" The priest was much astounded at what he saw, yet not so much so but that he observed among the live-stock a black horse, kneeling, indeed, like the rest, but only on one knee. The priest said to this lukewarm beast, ' Why don't you kneel on both knees, like the rest ? ' ' Wouldn't kneel at all if I could help it.' ' Who, then, are you ? ' ' The devil.' ' Why do you take the form of a horse ? ' ' So that men may steal me and get hung, and I get hold of them. Got three or four already.' "

Mr. Moule added that he was indebted to the late Rev. C. R. Baskett for this legend, who also told him of a pinnacle belonging, indeed, to Batcombe church tower, but which by no means could be made to stand in its place thereon " since conjuror Minterne's horse kicked it off ". Two vain attempts to erect the pinnacle had been made of late years.

Mr. Thomas Hardy gives the legend of " The Lost Pyx " [1] in much the same terms as Mr. Moule had done, and, in a letter to which I have referred later in this chapter (*s.v.* Wool), agrees with his fellow-townsman that the incident of the " black-hooved animal ", which declined to kneel with the rest of the cattle, is an accretion to the mediæval legend.

Apropos of " conjuror Minterne ", Hutchins (iv, 423) speaks of the half of an old tomb which formerly touched the outer wall of the Minterne aisle in Batcombe church. The village legend says that it covers the grave of " Conjuring Minterne ", who vowed that he would be buried neither in the church nor out of it. Hence the position and shape of the monument.

Beaminster.

Ghost Story.—The following account of the legend or ghost-story attaching to Beaminster school, which originally appeared in the *Gentleman's Magazine* in 1774, is given in J. H. Ingram's *Haunted Homes* (*First Series*), 1884, p. 10, and was also reprinted in the *Bridport News* on 4th September, 1891.

" In 1774 the *Gentleman's Magazine* printed the following narrative, prefacing it with these words: 'The following very singular story comes well authenticated.' In many respects the story may be deemed unique in the history of the supernatural. The apparition appears in broad daylight, and is seen of five children, one of whom did not even know the individual it represented when alive, and yet proved its identity by a wonderful piece of circumstantial evidence. The intense pathos of the unfortunate and evidently murdered lad, reappearing amidst the scenes of his childish occupations, and where he had been wont to play with those boys who now could only look upon him as a passing shadow, is most suggestive.

" The school of Beminster, says the account, is held in a gallery of the parish church to which there is a distinct entrance from the churchyard. Every Saturday the key of it is delivered to the clerk of the parish by one or other of the schoolboys. On Saturday, June 27th, 1728, the master had dismissed his lads as usual. Twelve of them loitered about in the churchyard to play

[1] *Poems of the Past and the Present* (1902), p. 227.

at ball. It was just about noon. After a short space four of the lads returned into the school to search for old pens, and were startled by hearing in the church a noise which they described as that produced by striking a brass pan. They immediately ran to their playfellows in the churchyard and told them of it. They came to the conclusion that some one was in hiding in order to frighten them, and they all went back in the school together to discover who it was, but could not find anyone. As they were returning to their sport, on the stairs that lead in to the churchyard they heard in the school a second noise. Terrified at that, they ran round the church, and when at the belfry, or west door, they heard what seemed to them the sound of some one preaching, which was succeeded by another sound as of a congregation singing psalms. Both of these noises lasted but a short time.

"With the thoughtlessness of youth the lads soon resumed their sport, and after a short time one of them went into the school for his book, when he saw a coffin lying on one of the benches, only about six feet away. Surprised at this, he ran off and told his playfellows what he had seen, on which they all thronged to the school-door, whence *five* of the twelve saw the apparition of John Daniel, who had been dead more than seven weeks, sitting at some distance from the coffin, further in the school. *All* of them saw the coffin, and it was conjectured why all did not see the apparition was because the door was so narrow they could not all approach it together. The first who knew it to be the apparition of their deceased schoolfellow was Daniel's half-brother; and he, on seeing it, cried out 'There sits our John, with such a coat on as I have' (in the lifetime of the deceased boy the half-brothers were usually clothed alike) 'with a pen in his hand and a book before him, and a coffin by him. I'll throw a stone at him.' The other boys tried to stop him, but he threw the stone—as he did so, saying, 'Take it'—upon which the apparition immediately disappeared.

"The immense excitement this created in the place may be imagined. The lads, whose ages ranged between nine and twelve, were all magisterially examined by Colonel Broadrepp, and all agreed in their relation of the circumstance, even to the hinges of the coffin; whilst their description of the coffin tallied exactly with that the deceased lad had been buried in. One of the lads who saw the apparition was quite twelve years of age; he entered the school after the deceased boy had left it (on account of illness about a fortnight before his death,) and had never seen Daniel in his lifetime. This lad, on examination, gave an exact description of the person of the deceased, and took especial notice of one thing about the apparition which the other boys had not observed, and that was, it had a white cloth or rag bound round one of its hands. The woman who laid out the corpse of John Daniel for interment deposed on oath that she took such a white cloth from its hand, it having been put on the boy's hand (he being lame of it) about four days or so before his death. Daniel's body had been found in an obscure place in a field, at about a furlong distant from his mother's house, and had been buried without an inquest in consequence of his mother alleging that the lad had been subject to fits. After the appearance of the apparition the body was disinterred, a coroner's inquest was held, and a verdict returned to the effect that the body had been ' strangled '. This verdict appears to have been mainly arrived at in consequence of the depositions of two women ' of good repute ' that two days after the corpse was found they saw it, and discovered a ' black list ' round its neck; and likewise of the joiner who put the body in the coffin, and who had an opportunity of observing it, as the shroud was not put on in the usual way, but was in two pieces, one laid under and the other over the body. A ' chirurgeon ' who gave evidence could not, or would not, positively affirm to the jury that there was any dislocation of the neck. So far as can be learnt, no steps were taken to bring anyone to justice on account of the suggested death by violence of the lad."

Bettiscombe.

Skull Superstition.—Although the legend or tradition attaching to " The Bettiscombe Skull " is now, perhaps, as widely known as any piece of West Dorset folk-lore, and has from time to time excited considerable interest among folk-lorists and others, yet so unobtrusive was its first introduction to public notice that no mention at all was made in it of its local *habitat.* I think I may say that I was the first person who put the matter forward in the Press, and that as an interesting bit of folk-lore merely, and in very simple terms.

In 1872 I stated in *Notes and Queries* (Ser. IV, x, 183):

" At a farmhouse in Dorsetshire at the present time is carefully preserved a human skull, which has been there for a period long antecedent to the present tenancy. The peculiar superstition attaching to it is that if it be brought out of the house the house itself would rock to its foundations, whilst the person by whom such an act of desecration was committed would certainly die within the year. It is strangely suggestive of the power of this superstition that through many changes of tenancy and furniture the skull still holds its accustomed place 'unmoved and unremoved.'"

Upon this the late Dr. Goodford, Provost of Eton, wrote to *Notes and Queries* (p. 436) inquiring whether I had not made a mistake as to the county, and stating that there was a similar superstition attaching to a house at Chilton Cantelo, in the adjoining county of Somerset.

I accordingly replied to Dr. Goodford (p. 509) giving him further particulars, both as to the locality and what I had heard of and about the skull, as follows :—

"The farm-house (formerly, I believe, an old manor-house), now called Bettiscombe House, in which the skull remained, or still remains for ought I know to the contrary, lies in the parish of Bettiscombe, about six miles from Bridport, in Dorsetshire. I cannot ascertain the time when the 'ghostly tenant' first took up its abode in the place, but it is tolerably certain that it was some considerable time ago. It has, I understand, been pronounced to be that of a negro; and the legend runs that it belonged to a faithful black servant of an early possessor of the property, a Pinney, who, having resided abroad some years, brought home this memento of a faithful follower. It is reported that a member of the above family, in recent years, has visited the house, but was unable to give any clue that might assist in clearing up the identity of the skull."

Since the time when publicity was thus given to the story of the skull the legend has gained both in volume and romance. It has now, I understand—and this without any justification from local sources—gained the reputation of being a "Screaming Skull"; and has attained other proportions so foreign to its simple origin that I almost regret ever having called attention to it.[1] My information had been mainly derived from a lady in West Dorset (still living and an octogenarian) who in her youthful days had often visited and stayed at the old manor-house at Bettis-

[1] See the somewhat fantastic account of a visit to Bettiscombe by a party from Charmouth in charge of Dr. Garnett, of the British Museum, for the purpose of seeing the skull, which would appear to have been sent by Miss Garnett to Ingram's *Haunted Homes* (Ser. II, 1884). Dr. Ingram gives as the basis of authority for the legend the late Mr. William Andrews's *Essay on Skull Superstitions*, which the author of that work would seem to have taken, without any acknowledgment, directly from my article already mentioned in *Notes and Queries*.

combe, and who had learnt and treasured up the legend as she had first heard it before time and publicity had lent a heightened and conjectural aspect to the tradition. Doubtless these embellishments have largely been derived from the fact that the superstition attaching to the skull, or to variants of it, is not by any means peculiar to Dorsetshire, or even to the West of England.

I will now give an account of a visit that I myself had paid to Bettiscombe, for the purpose of seeing the skull—a little later in time, perhaps, than that of the party from Charmouth—which I sent to the *Somerset and Dorset Notes and Queries* (vol. ii, pp. 252–5) from far distant Fiji in 1891. It was as follows :—

" I happened to be in the neighbourhood, and not having at that time seen the abiding-place of the 'famous skull', about which I had written some years previously, I determined to make an effort to do so ; and lest I should, by my visit, invoke the spell of any 'malign influence' I took with me the rector of the parish and a neighbouring clergyman who happened to be with him at the time. Thus accompanied and protected I arrived at the Manor-house (situated in the Vale of Marshwood—that vale as to which Hutchins quaintly observed upwards of a century ago, 'few gentry ever resided in this tract'—and nestling at the foot of a picturesque combe not far from Dorset's highest point—the famous Pilsdon Pen—evidently an early Georgian restoration of a much earlier building, as the oak beams in the hall, of considerable age, abundantly testified. The house boasted of a handsome oak staircase, but, if I remember rightly, the painted panelling was, apparently, of no older date than such restoration. Up this staircase we were courteously conducted, and, on arriving at a small door on the top landing opening on to the attic stairs, a candle was lighted and we prepared to make the ascent to the darker regions above, where the skull was supposed to dwell. To my surprise I found, on the door being opened, from one of the steps 'the skull sat grinning at us', as related by Miss Garnett. On inquiry, I learnt that the skull had been placed there in order to save going up to the attic where it formerly rested, which, owing to the ruinous condition of the timbers, was a journey of no inconsiderable danger. However, the present situation not being at all in character with the *genius loci*, and the 'good woman of the house' being besides somewhat fearful of its being carried off by one of the dogs from where it stood, I had little difficulty in obtaining her permission to reinstate the skull in its former place. So, taking it in my hands, I carefully picked my way by the aid of a lighted candle, followed by my companions, over the crazy and broken floor to where, on a niche by the side of the huge chimney-breast, lay a brick—the old shrine of the skull—upon which I reverently placed it; and there I had the satisfaction of seeing it on more than one visit in later years.

"Upon one of these subsequent visits I, with others, made a careful examination of the skull; and although none of *us* were doctors, we came to the respectful conclusion that it was *not* that of a negro, but rather that of a woman, being small, but by no means of a bad shape, ethnologically speaking, and affording no trace of the 'facial angle' which marks the full-blooded negro. The forehead certainly was low, but not receding. The upper half of the *cranium* only was preserved, the lower jaw being missing; its length was seven and a half inches, and in depth to roof of mouth five inches (full). From a phrenological point of view the 'bumps' at the base were highly developed. If I remember rightly, there were no teeth left in the jaw. So much for the skull itself. Its surroundings were certainly of a character to add to the mystery of its existence there. The dark attic extended over the entire extent of the house, the floor in a very unsound and unsafe condition, and evidently from its appearance had long been the home of bats, owls, and other 'fearful fowl', for which easy access was afforded by the many openings in the ancient, massive, and dilapidated stone-tiled roof, to say nothing of a nest of young birds I myself discovered close to the skull's resting-place. Close to the chimney-breast above mentioned is a rectangular hole or shaft in the floor, of about 3 ft. by 4 ft. 6 in., and of considerable depth extending to the bottom of the floor below, where the back of a bedroom cupboard touches. At first I thought that this cupboard was an old-fashioned 'powder-closet'; but after careful examination I was inclined to think that it might have had some connection with the aforesaid shaft, which may well have been intended for, and used as, a 'priest's hole' or hiding-place in the earlier and more troublous times that might have fallen upon Bettiscombe as upon so many other places in the West of England. This conjecture is borne out by the fact that one end of the vast attic is divided off by a lath-and-plaster partition, in which was inserted a small doorway, constituting a chamber of about 15 ft. by 12 ft. immediately under the tiles, containing a small, round, brick fire-place, with two window apertures at the end which were stopped up. This would have formed a secure retreat from any sudden surprise; when, if danger became more imminent by a threatened search of the house, it might be averted by a timely resort to the 'hole'. Of course it may have had other uses, but a better place of concealment or confinement can hardly be imagined.

" From time to time I have heard other rumours as to the ownership of the skull ; one amongst them, that it belonged to a young lady who had died, or had been made away with, after a long period of confinement in the house. To this story, if the skull be that of a woman—which I believe it is—the existence of this partitioned-off chamber lends a certain amount of corroboration ; but of the negro variant as related by Miss Garnett I do not remember ever to have heard.

" Whatever may be its origin, the superstition is still—I will not say believed in, but sufficiently established to afford protection to the skull around which it clings—an amusing instance of which I can relate.

" A former tenant of the farm once, in incredulity or in anger, threw the skull into a duck-pond opposite the house. A few mornings afterwards he was observed stealthily raking out the pond until he had fished up the skull, when it was restored to its old place in the house. It was said that Farmer G. had had a bad time of it during the interval, and had been much disturbed by all kinds of noises ! Whether these noises were caused by any other agency than that of the bats, owls, etc. before mentioned, operating upon a conscience rendered unusually susceptible by such a terrible ' act of desecration ' this deponent knoweth not. Suffice it to say that there the skull rests ' in its accustomed place ',—there, in the words of Macaulay—

' To witness if I lie.'

" And there may it long remain to attract and awe those visitors and lovers of folk-lore whose reverent feelings may lead them to make a pious pilgrimage to its shrine, but not, let us hope, to the annoyance of the ' good woman of the house , who must find it hard sometimes to retain her good-nature under the many inquisitive and often irreverent remarks of her visitors."

The " Legend of the Bettiscombe Skull ", however, unlike most such traditions, has developed a sequel of a very interesting and romantic nature, connected as it is with the Monmouth Rebellion—an event which never fails to stir the hearts of West Dorset folk—namely, an inquiry into the history or story of the skull itself ; an inquiry which, in the course of my judicial duties in the West Indies, I was able to investigate with a considerable measure, if I may say so, of success, both as to the verification of the origin of the tradition and, if it be in reality a negro's skull, as is generally believed, possibly also as to the identity of the skull.

But as this now passes somewhat beyond a mere local Dorset legend I would only here refer those of my readers who may be desirous of pursuing this subject further to what I have since written upon it in the *Somerset and Dorset Notes and Queries*, vol. viii, p. 308, and vol. ix, p. 315 (1903–5), and also to a paper of mine in the Dorset Field Club's *Proceedings* for 1910 (vol. xxxi, p. 176), in which the whole subject is reviewed at considerable length, and which contains some interesting photographs of the skull itself and of its surroundings, both at Bettiscombe and at the island of Nevis in the West Indies.

Bincombe.

Music Barrow.—The late Mr. Charles Warne, F.S.A., in his *Celtic Tumuli of Dorset* (1866) states that " on Bincombe Down there is a ' Music Barrow ' of which the rustics say that if the ear be laid close to the apex at midday the sweetest melody will be heard within ".

Bindon.

Bindon Abbey Bells.—Hutchins (vol. i, p. 354) states :

" There is a tradition respecting the bells of Bindon Abbey. It is said that they were twelve in number, and that they are now in the churches of Wool, Combe, and Fordington, viz. in Wool four, in Combe three, and Fordington six, but formerly five, the largest having been recast and made into two. The tradition may possibly be correct as to the bells in these churches shortly after the Dissolution ; but two of those at Combe, and the whole of those at Wool, are of a more modern date. They may, however, have been recast.

" There is a story that the bells were stolen by night, and hid away near the road above the church ; and that road still goes by the name of ' Bell Drong '." [1]

" The following doggerel rhyme is also current in the village :

' Wool streams and Combe wells,
Fordington cuckolds stole Bindon Bells.' "

Biggs, in his *Isle of Purbeck* (1877), p. 46, gives a similar version of this tradition, in which the lines take this form :

" Wool streams and Combe Keynes wells,
Fordington rogues stole Bindon Bells."

[1] A narrow way between two hedges or walls.

This legend is also set out in an interesting letter from the late Mr. H. J. Moule to Rev. Canon Raven, D.D., which is printed in the latter's account of the " Church Bells of Dorset " in the Dorset Field Club's *Proceedings*, vol. xxiv, p. 126 (1903).

Hutchins, in a note at p. 348 of the same volume, speaks of a MS. history of Wool and Bindon by the late Rev. W. Kendall, formerly incumbent of Bindon and vicar of East Lulworth, to which the editors of the last edition were indebted for many interesting particulars. And he added further, in another note at p. 352, that a parishioner once had told Mr. Kendall that " he had heard that in the abbey times a bell was rung at one o'clock every day, when any one might go and have a dinner and no one asked their business ", and that men at work in the field used to " unhitch their horses from the plough and go down there for refreshments ".

It would be interesting to know if this MS. history is still in existence.

Bishop's Caundle (near Sherbone).

Bell Tolling.—As to this custom see Chapter V, p. 182.

Blackdown (near Weymouth).

Dolmen Superstition.—The late Mr. H. J. Moule, in the *Folk-Lore Journal* (vol. vi, p. 117), says : " The Dolmen on Blackdown is called the Hell-stone, and folks say that the devil chucked it across from Portland—nine miles or so."

To this Mr. J. J. Foster, F.S.A., honorary secretary to the Folk-Lore Society in its early days, adds :

" It may not be out of place to observe that this interesting *megalithic* monument has been lately ' restored ' by Mr. Manfield, assisted by Mr. M. Tupper of ' Proverbial ' celebrity, who have rearranged the stones (for there are seven in all, the largest being about eight feet square, of very hard conglomerate) according to their own sweet will ! "

Blackmore Vale.

White Hart Silver.—Coker, in his *Survey of Dorsetshire* (1732), p. 98, gives the well-known legend as to the payment of " White Hart Silver " by the de la Lynde family as follows :

" From *Mapowder* the Brooke passeth through deepe and dirty soyle under *Kinges Stagge Bridge*, which got that Name upon this

Occasion : King Henry the Third, having disported himselfe in the Forest of *Blackmore,* hee spared one beautifull and goodlie white Harte, which afterwards *T. De la Linde,* a neighbour Gentleman of ancient Descent and especiall Note, with his Companions pursueing, killed at this Place ; but he soone founde howe dangerous it was to bee twitching a Lion by the Eares : For the King tooke soe great Indignation against him, that he not onlie punished them with Imprisonment and a grievous Fine of Money, but for this Fact hee taxed their Lands ; the Owners of which ever sithence yearly untill this Daye paye a rounde Summe of Money by way of Amercement unto the Exchequer, called *White Harte Silver* ; in Memorie of which this C(ountie) needeth no better Remembrance than the annuall Payment."

On this, after setting out the story from Coker, Hutchins (vol. iii, p. 738, *s.v.* " Pulham "), in referring to King Stagg Bridge, makes the following remarks :

" The story rests wholly on tradition, which probably owes its origin to many trespasses committed in this and neighbouring forests during the reign of Henry III, and no contemporary or documentary evidence relating to it has been met with."

And he goes on to say :

" Near this place, on the road to Sturminster Newton, is a small inn called ' King's Stag ', its sign displaying a stag with a gold collar round its neck, and underneath the following lines :

' When Julius Cæsar landed here
I was then a little deer ;
When Julius Cæsar reigned King
Round my neck he put this ring.
Whoever shall me overtake
Save my life for Cæsar's sake.' "

And again in vol. i, p. 188 (*s.v.* Winterborne Clenston), he makes the following pertinent observations :

" The tradition still lingers in the vale of Blackmore, but we have been unable to meet with any original evidence in support of it. If De la Lynde and his companions were punished by imprisonment and a grievous fine we should meet with some trace of it in the Pipe Rolls, or other contemporary records ; and, as regards the payment of ' White Hart Silver ', no notice of which is met with in the Pipe Rolls of Henry III., it is remarkable that it was payable in the time of Henry VIII. out of some lands in Winfrith, far distant from the vale of Blackmore, and which certainly never belonged to the De la Lynde family. And to this, the imposition of such a tax, in perpetuity, was beyond the power of our monarchs, even in the most arbitrary period of their history."

Recently, in answer to a question by a correspondent in *Notes and Queries* (Ser. XII, iii, 30), asking whether this pay was still made into the Exchequer, I reviewed (Ser. XII, iii, 97) the story as given by Hutchins and others, and later (Ser. XII, iv, 20) (1918), having in the meantime obtained some valuable information upon the subject from the Rev. Canon J. C. M. Mansel-Pleydell, a son of a late owner of the estate from which this payment was alleged to proceed, I stated that I thought that it may now be accepted that this fine had been commuted by the canon's father for a lump sum, an offer having been made to him by the revenue authorities to ' commute the annual payment by a final sum ". Canon Mansel-Pleydell was not, however, able to obtain any verification of this from the family papers, and was only able to speak from the information given him by his father some years back, as to the nature of which he had no possible doubt ; but, acting upon his suggestion, I ventured to make further inquiries from the Public Record Office and other Government offices. Owing, however, to the somewhat scanty particulars I was able to furnish them with as to the date of the alleged commutation and other details I was unable to carry the matter any further. So there it must remain for the present. I think, however, that it may now be taken that the story as to the origin of the fine is not so apocryphal as has been supposed in some quarters, though it may be a matter for great regret that such a very interesting and ancient customary payment should now have been brought to an end.

Cerne Abbas.

(i) *The Cerne Giant.*—The story of the Cerne Giant partakes largely both of myth and custom, and has been treated of in both respects by more than one writer of eminence. Our county historian, Hutchins, in a very interesting account of the Giant in vol. iv, p. 35, gives an extract from Dr. Maton's *Observations on the Western Counties*, vol. ii, p. 17, as follows :

" We descended into the town (*i.e.* Cerne Abbas) from an immense chalk hill, terminating towards it in a mountainous prominence, crowned with a very long oblong entrenchment. On the (southern) declivity of the very steep hill, generally known by the name of Trendle Hill (a little north-west of the town) may be traced a gigantic figure cut in the chalk, in the manner of the horse on White Horse Hill in Berkshire, and probably of great antiquity. It represents a man holding a club in his right hand, and extending the other, and appears to be almost 200 feet in height. There is a tradition among the vulgar that this was to commemorate the destruction of a giant, who, having feasted on some sheep at Blackmore and laid himself down to sleep after his meal on this hill, was bound and killed by the enraged peasants on the spot. Without recurring to any ridiculous story, or to any conceit of antiquaries for the origin of the figure, one may conclude that most works of this sort, especially when contiguous to encampments, were the amusement merely of idle people, and cut with as little meaning perhaps as shepherd boys strip off the turf on the Wiltshire plains."

Hutchins then continues:

"This figure has been reported to have been made by Lord Holles's servants, during his residence here, but it is more likely that he only caused it to be repaired; for some people who died not long before 1772, 80 or 90 years old, when young knew some of the same age that averred it was there before the memory of man. Fabulous as the story is of the country people killing the giant, and then tracing out the dimensions of his body to perpetuate his memory, it is perhaps a proof of the great antiquity of this figure. It extends over near an acre of ground, as does the White Horse in Berkshire, which is 150 feet from the head to the withers. It seems to have been executed by persons quite unacquainted with the rules of proportion observed by statuaries and painters, who anciently allowed seven or eight heads to the length of a human body. It is repaired about once in seven years, by the people of the town cleansing the furrows and filling them with fresh chalk. Scouring the White Horse is a custom and festival solemnized from time immemorial by a numerous concourse of people from the adjacent villages. If there was any particular day in the year for this purpose here, the memory of it now is lost, and the operation performed just when the town's-people think fit. Most antiquaries agree that it is a monument of high antiquity, and make little doubt but that it was a representation of the Saxon god Heil; so that it must be more ancient at least than A.D. 600, soon after which time the Saxons were converted to Christianity. Dr. Stukely was of a singular opinion that it was the figure of Hercules, and that the Saxon god Heil was no other than the Phoenician Hercules, or

Melicartus, who brought hither the first colony, and that this figure was not so much an object of religious worship as a memorial. The club in our giant's hand seems to have led him to imagine this."

Hutchins then refers to an account of the giant of Cerne which Dr. Stukely read at a meeting of the Society of Antiquaries on 16th February, 1764, together with a drawing of it, containing measured dimensions—which Hutchins reproduces at p. 36—and from which he gives the following extract :—

" This is an immense figure of Hercules with his club, cut out of the turf of a sloping chalk hill ; it is 180 feet in height. The proper view of it is from the opposite hill ; and it required a good deal of skill in optics to make it appear with any degree of symmetry in that situation. The inhabitants know nothing more of it, than that they fancy it to be a deity of the ancient Britons. Unquestionably it means to represent the famous and first Hercules, the Phoenician leader of the first colony to Britain, when they came hither for the Cornish tin. It is not supposed to be made in his time, but afterwards, and in memory of him, when the Britons had a notion of the latter Theban Hercules, the tamer of wild men and of wild beasts."

Dr. Stukely conjectures that " this enormous figure might be cut by the Britons in compliment to King Eli, on his expelling the Belgæ from that country and driving them into Ireland ".

Hutchins concludes his account of the giant by calling attention to the " very interesting little treatise " written by the late Dr. John Sydenham, author of the *History of the town and County of Poole,* entitled " Baal Durotrigensis : a Dissertation on the Ancient Colossal Figure at Cerne, Dorsetshire ", in which, whilst showing " the almost universal prevalence of serpent-worship and the worship of the sun he endeavours to prove, by etymology, tradition, and attributes, that this curious effigy was constructed by the Celto-Belgæ, the invading sun-worshippers, in commemoration of a victory over the aboriginal Celtæ, whom he supposes to have been devoted to the rites of the serpent ".

As I read Dr. Sydenham's erudite treatise he certainly seemed to attribute the origin of the giant to be of phallic significance ; and in this opinion he is confirmed by the late Dr. Colley March, F.S.A., who, in a very interesting paper on the " Giant and Maypole of Cerne ", which appeared in the Dorset Field Club's

Proceedings in 1901 (vol. xxxi, p. 101), remarks that one of the giant's characteristics is that it is ithyphallic, as it most unmistakably is.

If the character of the traditions or customs which have attached themselves to the Cerne giant can be taken as any indication of its origin I think it may be said that they do in a very significant manner confirm these opinions. For instance, it is said to be a certain cure for barrenness in women if they sit on the actual figure of the giant as cut in the turf; but some say that the man and woman desiring issue must actually have sexual connection on the spot in order to give full effect to the charm. Presumably this is the superstitition to which Mr. J. J. Foster alludes in a note to p. 118 of vol. vi of the *Folk-Lore Journal*, when he says:

"As Mr. Moule has alluded to Cerne Abbas I wish he had told us something of the remarkable phallic superstition which attaches to the Cerne Giant, counterparts of which are to be found in Brittany and all over India to this day."

The giant has, I believe, in recent times been subjected to various "scourings" or re-cuttings of the turf from time to time in order to effectively preserve the outlines of the figure. These outlines are said to be about two feet broad and one foot deep. On such occasions the village would naturally be the scene of considerable festivity; so much so that, as I was informed, a former vicar had put a stop to these "scourings" as they tended to practical illustrations of the above superstitions, which did not conduce, it was thought, to the morality of his parishioners.

I understand that of recent years the late General Pitt Rivers, at one time the Director of Public Monuments and owner of the property upon which the giant reclines, had—presumably in order to prevent the recurrence of such scenes—taken this interesting monument of antiquity under his own special care and protection and had taken steps to enclose it. I am sure my readers will learn with satisfaction that, according to the Report of the Earthworks Committee of the Congress of Archæological Societies presented on 29th November, 1921, the "Cerne Giant" has now been taken under the protection of the National Trust.

I have already alluded (Chapter I, p. 39) to the "festival

of the maypole " at Cerne Abbas, where the pole was set up, not on the village green as was usually the case, but in a ring just above the giant.[1] I think that much of the irregularities that are there suggested as appertaining to that custom may be attributed to the associations entailed by its close proximity to the figure of the giant.

The late Mr. Charles Warne, F.S.A., the well-known Dorset antiquary, in his *Ancient Dorset* (1872), p. 319, also refers to the Cerne Giant.

Mr. H. F. Napper, a Sussex correspondent of the *Somerset and Dorset Notes and Queries*, vol. i, p. 140 (1889), in an interesting article suggests that the Cerne Giant was, in all probability, a memorial of Corinæus and Goetmagot, the latter being a giant slain by Corinæus, the companion of Brutus, a Trojan prince, who, with their followers, had settled in this part of Britain. He considers that the local tradition of the destruction of the giant is confirmatory of this story, and that in it may also be found the origin of the figures of Gog and Magog at the London Guildhall.

It is left for our Dorset novelist and poet, Mr. Thomas Hardy, to give utterance to a tradition which I was not previously aware was attributable to the Cerne Giant. It is contained in his great work, *The Dynasts*, part i, p. 84, in a very characteristic bucolic dialogue having reference to " Boney ".

" They say that He lives upon human flesh, and has rashers of baby every morning for breakfast—for all the world like the Cernel Giant in old ancient times."

(ii) *St. Austin's Well.*—The late Mr. H. J. Moule, in vol. vi, of the *Folk-Lore Journal*, p. 118, says :

" Folks hold to the belief that St. Austin's Well, hard by Cerne Abbas, still works wondrous cures.
" I have had a case told in all detail while sketching the lovely spring."

This is, no doubt, the same well or spring at Cerne at which it is considered a very wholesome thing to dip new-born infants at the time when the sun is first shining on the water. The

[1] Dr. March, in his paper, gives a sketch showing, *inter alia*, the relative positions of the " ring " and of the enclosure of the giant.

spring itself directly faces the rising sun.[1] St. Austin's is, in all probability, the same as what is known as " the wishing well " at Cerne.

Mr. Wilkinson Sherren, in his *Wessex of Romance* (1908), p. 264, gives the following account of St. Augustine's connection with Cerne Abbas :

" There is a legend about St. Augustine's connection with Cerne Abbas, however, which wears an air of probability in its account of the horseplay of some early Wessexmen, and but for the indignity offered to a holy man, it would verge on the realm of comedy. According to William of Malmesbury, the great prelate having converted Kent to the Christian faith, travelled over the rest of the English provinces as far as Ethelbert's dominions extended, and then visited Cerne Abbas. As a token of their mission, St. Augustine destroyed the idol, Heil, and thereby dismayed and incensed its worshippers, who retired to plot their revenge. Meanwhile the company felt weary and thirsty, and St. Augustine struck his staff into the ground and ' fetched out a crystal fountain '. Before the apostolic band could refresh themselves the inhabitants advanced, and with quite a modern appreciation of the power of ridicule, fastened the tails of cows to the garments of St. Augustine and his companions, and drove them from the place. Wherefore, in punishment of this persecution, ' all that generation had that given them which they in contempt had fastened on these holy men.'

" General credence was given to this legend till 1774, and until that period the people of Cerne imagined the posterity of those who abused St. Augustine still remained, and were distinguished by caudal appendages of moderate length."

Among the items mentioned in the *Catalogue of Brand Material*, printed in *Folk-Lore*, vol. xxvii, p. 79 (1916), is one relating to apparitions to be seen in the water of St. Austin's Well at Cerne on Easter Day. Further details with regard to this superstition may confidently be expected when the Brand Committee of the Folk-Lore Society has concluded and issued its important and exhaustive work.

(iii) *Cerne Mill Stream.*—Mr. Moule also says that on the bank of the mill stream at Cerne Abbas are two bare spots in the grass, like footsteps. They are said to be the last footsteps of a man who drowned himself there, and the grass will not grow on the two spots pressed by his feet.

[1] See Chapter V, p. 179.

Chantmarle (Cattistock).

Ghost Story.—The following legendary story is taken from the late Mr. H. Nobbs Cox's serial " History of Cattistock ", issued in the *Dorset County Chronicle*, Nov., 1886.

" The original house at Chantmarle was built in the form of the letter E. and the inmates complained of various supernatural noises and appearances they alleged to have heard in one of the wings. The old servants in the last century declared they had again and again seen ' the Lady Ann ' pass through the room; but we heard from a person who long resided there with the family of Mr. Petty at the close of the eighteenth century, that although she had heard many noises for which she could by no means account yet she had never seen anything to alarm her; but the domestics would always endeavour to retire early or they said they should soon see ' the Lady Ann '. But we were assured of the truth of the following, which our informant, who was born in 1777 and died in 1849, heard from those who remember the occurrence. Our readers must know that fifty years ago almost every old place had its ghost story, and a fine old building like Chantmarle could not be an exception. . . . Now we were assured by our informant that for some years, at about the same date, a shrill piercing sound was heard in the hall at Chantmarle House, crying, ' Search for the bones of Wat Perkins.' The words were repeated three times. The terrified hearers were powerless. . . . Alarm spread through the house. Some dreadful calamity had happened at a distant period, and it was only right to take some action, but where? Accident, however, solved the mystery. Some labourers were engaged in removing a hedge near Kit Whistle, a cottage some little distance from Chantmarle, when they discovered a human skeleton, *minus* the head. They proceeded to the house Kit Whistle, where it appears that refreshments were then sold, and told the widow who occupied the house of the discovery they had made, when she replied ' Don't say a word about it and I will give you the best cow I have '. These words of the woman were soon told to the public authorities, and naturally aroused suspicion. Interrogated why she made the offer, she made further statements, and at length, when asked where the head was, said ' If I must tell 'ee, the head is under the yeath-stone ', meaning the hearthstone. The woman afterwards confessed that a Scotchman, who travelled with a pack of drapery 22 years previously, had come to her house and had fallen asleep, resting his head on the arm of the settle. She had chopped across his throat with a keen hook, and had thus murdered him in order to be possessed of his pack. She had repeatedly said, when people were speaking of their clothing, that she 'had burned better things than those'. After this discovery our informant was assured the voice was no more heard at Chantmarle House, and the old widow was tried and executed.

" Of course this is a legendary story, although we were assured that there actually was a murder as stated, whatever might be the truth about the utterances of the words. But if the house was freed from the shrill voice, it was still 'troubled' with the noises. Probably some formation of the building caused peculiar noises from the action of the wind, which superstitious people deemed supernatural. . . . The demolition of the wing(s), however, removed all these sounds. It is not exactly certain whether Chantmarle House is on the site of the old manorial residence, but it seems highly probable."

Cheselborne.

Giant's Grave.—The late Canon C. W. Bingham in *Notes and Queries*, Ser. III, ix, 10 (1866), writes as follows with reference to the tradition existing in connection with what is generally known as the " Giant's Grave ", in the parish of Melcombe Horsey, near Cheselborne:

" There is a long mound in a part of my parish which is popularly called the 'Giant's Grave', and very near two large stones which have probably rolled down from the beds of chert-like rock on the side or the chalk hill above. I discovered lately that there is a popular tradition existing—though my informant somewhat doubts its correctness—that these stones move whenever they hear the cocks crowing in Chesilborne, a neighbouring village."

To this another correspondent in *Notes and Queries* (p. 187) " C. W."—under which initials it is not difficult, I think, to recognize the well-known Dorset antiquary, the late Charles Warne, F.S.A.—replies:

" Your correspondent 'C. W. B.' has not alluded to a mythological tradition connected with the 'Giant's Grave' and the stones adjoining it, which is popular in the neighbourhood. It is to the following effect. Two giants standing on *Norden* (an adjacent hill) were once contending for the mastery as to which of them would hurl the farther, the direction being across the valley to *Hanging Hill.* He whose stone fell short was so mortified at the failure, that he died of vexation and was buried beneath the mound which has since been known as the 'Giant's

Grave'. Myths of a similar kind are often found attached to blocks of erratic stone."

Mr. Warne later gives a somewhat similar version of the origin of this superstition in his *Ancient Dorset*, p. 83, *s.v.* Nor-dun (near Nettlecombe Toot).

Corfe Castle.

King Edward the Martyr.—Mr. Wilkinson Sherren, in his book, *The Wessex of Romance* (1908), p. 267, after giving an account of the murder of the Wessex king, Edward the Martyr, by his step-mother, Elfrida, at Corfe Castle, goes on to say:

"Some of Elfrida's men discovered him mangled and bruised and dead, and conveyed him to a mean house, where lived a blind woman, who, it is said, awakened at midnight with restored eyesight, the house being radiant with light. Hearing of this marvel, Elfrida had the body removed and concealed in a well in a marshy place, where the year following it was found by some devout person, the spot being discovered to them by the illumination of a pillar of fire. Ever after the well yielded pure and sweet water, good for the healing of the infirm, being known as St. Edward's fountain. The corpse was removed to the church of St. Mary, Wareham; three years afterwards it was found to be in an uncorrupted condition, when it was removed to Shaftesbury.

. . . .

"Thus it came about that the tragedy of an old Wessex king formed the nucleus of a marvellous legend, and gave him an entrance into the ranks of the martyrs."

Culliford Tree.

Music Barrow.—Mr. Warne in his *Celtic Tumuli* (p. 1 of last Part) speaks of a similar superstition attaching to a certain tumulus at Culliford Tree as he has attributed to the "Music Barrow" on the neighbouring Bincombe Down,[1] namely, that if the ear be laid close to the apex at midday the sweetest melody will be heard within.

Evershot.

Dumb Maids' Plot.—Amongst my notes I find a reference to a tradition attaching to a field called the "Dumb Maids' Plot"

[1] See *ante*, *s.v.* Bincombe.

in the parish of Evershot, not far from Stutcombe Bottom (the fine weather musketry range of the old Evershot Volunteers), according to which three dumb sisters used to meet to while away the time by dancing on the green. This tradition was mentioned by the late Mr. S. R. Baskett, who acted as *cicerone* at a meeting of the Dorset Field Club in that neighbourhood in August 1895; but no further particulars appear to have been given, nor can I find any reference to it in the published accounts of that meeting either in the *Dorset County Chronicle* or in the annual volume of the *Proceedings* of the Society.

Folke (near Sherborne).

Church Legend.—The curious tradition is attached to the church at Folke, near Sherborne, that it was begun to be built in a wood named Broke—now called Broke Wood—and that what was built during the day was carried to its present position during the night.

Frampton.

Monastic Legends.—The *Dorset County Chronicle* of 24th January, 1918, gives the following extract from a recent issue of the *Westminster Gazette*:

"There is a legend connected with Frampton Court that a monastery stood on the site of the present house, and when King Henry VIII sequestrated its lands and dwelling the Abbott pronounced a curse upon it that the eldest son of its possessor should never live to inherit its domains. So far (the writer adds) no first born son has lived to succeed his father."

Similar things are said of many of the old houses in the West of England that once formed monastic or conventual establishments, of which Forde Abbey may be instanced as another from a Dorset source.

Hampreston (Wimborne).

Haunted Churches.—Miss M. F. Billington, in her before-mentioned paper on "Dorsetshire Ghosts" in the *Dorset County Chronicle*, says that occasionally a belief arises that a church or chapel is haunted, and mentions the church at Hampreston, near Wimborne, as being regarded with some superstitious dread because on certain nights of the year it is illuminated inside by a "brilliant white light". She thinks that probably the origin of this weird reputation may be traced to some peculiar reflection of the moon or the not unfrequent escape, under certain conditions of soil and atmosphere, of a luminous gas from a buried body. This is the phenomenon known either as " grave lights " or " corpse candles ".

Hutchins (vol. iii, p. 433) publishes a small engraving of the church of Hampreston, and although he gives a fairly full description of it he makes no allusion to the above legend.

Haythorne.

Haunted Chapel.—Miss Billington also mentions that during the recent erection of a chapel at Haythorne the idea was suddenly started that the evil one had entered and taken possession of the building. For some two or three weeks he could not be dislodged. But this was at length accomplished by a number of persons who collected outside and sang and hooted at the top of their voices. She adds that noise is generally considered a powerful element in subduing such unwelcome visitors from a worse world.

Holnest.

Church Legend.—A similar legend to that of Folke (*q.v.*) was also said of Holnest Church in the same neighbourhood.

Miss Billington is also responsible for this and the two following legends :

Holt.

Ghostly Apparition.—At a farm in this parish there is a room situated over the dairy, and appropriated to the use of one or two of the farm lads as a sleeping apartment. In this room heavy footsteps are heard ascending the stairs ; the bedclothes are turned back, and the terror-struck occupant sees himself the cynosure of a pair of huge glistening eyes—" as big as basins." He then loses sight of them, and hears the footsteps descend. If he has the courage to go and look down the stairs he may be rewarded by another terrible stare from the eyes, which then vanish into silence and darkness. A barn about a quarter of a mile from this spot, in the same parish, is also vaguely spoken of as haunted.

Kinson.

Haunted Gate.—There is a gate at Kinson, near Bournemouth, which is carefully avoided after dark, as a figure, holding its head under its arm, is believed to be its nightly occupant.

Kingston Russell (Bridport).

Spectral Coach.—At Kingston Russell House, near Bridport, a coach drawn by four headless horses, driven by a headless coachman and footman, and containing inside four headless passengers, is supposed, on certain nights in the year, to drive up to the door, stay a moment, and drive back again. But no solution is attempted to be given of the mystery.

Knowlton.

Bell Legend.—Hutchins (vol. iii, p. 362 (n.)), *s.v.* Sturminster Marshall—states that a tradition exists in the neighbourhood that one of the Sturminster bells came from the chapel at Knolton, and that when it was brought hitherto the horses' shoes were reversed so that the track might not be followed in the snow. The following doggerel is current :

" Knolton bell is stole,
And thrown into White Mill hole."

This legend regarding the lost bell is much amplified in an account given in Rev. Canon Raven's " Church Bells of Dorset ", in the Dorset Field Club's *Proceedings,* vol. xxvii, pp. 94–5 (1906), furnished by Mr. A. Reeve, in respect of a journey he had paid to the neighbourhood of Horton in 1852. He states :

" Whilst waiting I saw a small ruined tower at the distance of half a mile or so, and, on asking a man, found it was the ruin of Knowlton church. He also told me that at a very distant period there was a very valuable bell in that tower, so much so that it excited the cupidity of some fellows who planned to steal it, take it to the coast, and, having crossed the Channel, sell it in France. This, considering the loneliness of the church, could be no very difficult matter ; but somehow, after they had got the bell out of the tower, they were discovered, pursued, and overtaken at the bridge of Sturminster Marshall, and, being unable to proceed further with it, they threw it into the Stour and made off. The Knowlton people let down ropes and pulled it up nearly within reach of land, when down it went, without there being any apparent reason for the ropes breaking. A second and a third attempt were attended with the same result till, weary and dispirited, they gave it up. The old man said that there was a verse to the effect that:

" 'All the devils in hell
Could never pull up Knowlton bell.' "

Canon Raven also gives (p. 95) a fuller version of the tradition as recorded in Hutchins. He adds:

"What became of the bell subsequently it is difficult to say. Some say it was left in the river, and others that it was got out and put in Shapwick Church; and some think it was put in this church (*i.e.* Sturminster Marshall); but in Hutchins' *History of Dorset* it states that it was recovered, and was for some years in the possession of a Mr. Compton at Horton."

Leigh (near Yetminster).

Witches' Corner.—The late William Barnes, in a short paper on "The Maze, or Mizmaze, at Leigh, Dorset", in the Dorset Field Club's *Proceedings*, vol. iv, p. 156 (1879), says:

"Many years ago I was told by a man of this neighbourhood that a corner of Leigh Common was called 'Witches' Corner'; and long again after that a friend gave me some old depositions on witchcraft taken before Somerset magistrates from about the years 1650 to 1664. The cases were of Somerset, and touched in some points Dorsetshire; and one of the witches' sisterhood said that they sometimes met in Leigh Common. This proof of the meeting of witches in Leigh Common as the ground of the traditional name of 'witches' corner' is interesting as a token of truth in tradition."

Long Burton (near Sherborne).

Bell Omen.—Every Sunday morning the tenor-bell is rung by the sexton; and if it should happen to sound dull and heavy it is always said in the parish that some one is sure to die before the week is out.[1]

Lychett (Poole).

(i) *Charm connected with Objects of Antiquity.*—The late Mr. H. J. Moule wrote in the *Folk-Lore Journal*, vol. vi, p. 117:—

"Folks seem to have an odd belief in good luck coming with remnants of antiquity, judging from what a Dorchester antiquary tells me and has recorded in *Archæologia*. Some years ago

[1] See Chapter V, p. 182.

several metal objects were found in a Keltic earthwork. Among them was a curious little grotesque bull, with a quaint tail curled up, which makes it somewhat like a dog. My friend heard that these things were in the hands of a certain old woman, and offered to buy them. 'Han't got 'em—used to't—but there—'Twere loike this yer. My poor buoy, he wer turble bad, and he *pined like* a'ter they wold things. And ther—I thought myself how thick brass dog a-noül'd ouver door'd do en a power o' good.' And 'noül'd ouver door' it was found."

To which Mr. J. J. Foster added:

"This remarkable 'find', which was made in Belbury Camp, near Higher Lychett, Poole, is fully described in *Archæologia*, vol. xlviii, pp. 1–6, where the objects are figured. Mr. Franks was of opinion that the ornamentation on the bull resembled Etruscan, but that the article itself was 'late-Celtic'. Its use as recently as 1881 as a prophylactic is surely an interesting fact to students of folk-lore."

(ii) *Spectral Coffin Legend.*—Miss Billington states that one of the roads between Lychett and Poole is regarded with much horror, because a coffin carried by four headless men is reported to have been seen there many times. It is conveyed down the road some distance, and disappears through the hedge.

Lyme Regis.

Black Dog Legend.—Miss Leathes in her book, *Some Account of Lyme Regis* (1882), relates the following legend:

"Near the town of Lyme stands a farm house which once formed part of an old mansion that was demolished in the Parliamentary wars, except the small part still existing. The sitting room now used by the farmer, and also by his predecessors for a century or two, retains the large old-fashioned fireplace with a fixed seat on each side under the capacious chimney. Many years ago, when the then master of the house, as his custom was after the daily toils were over, used to settle himself on one of these snug seats in the chimney corner, a large black dog as regularly took possession of the opposite one.

"This dog, for many nights, weeks and months sitting *vis-a-vis* to the farmer, cast a gloom over his evening's enjoyment. At length, as he received no harm from the appearance, he began to look upon him as quite one of the family circle. His neighbours, however, often advised him to get rid of the fiend-like intruder, but the farmer, not relishing a contest with him, jestingly replied: 'Why should I? He costs me nothing;

he is the quietest creature in the house ; besides, he eats nothing.' One night, however, the farmer having been drinking too freely with a neighbour and excited with his taunts about the black dog, determined his courage should be no more called in question. Returning home in a rage, he no sooner saw the dog in his usual seat than, seizing a poker, he rushed with it toward his mysterious companion. The dog, perceiving his intention, sprang from his seat and ran upstairs, followed by the infuriated farmer. The dog fled into an attic, and just as the farmer entered it he saw it spring from the floor and disappear through the ceiling. Enraged at being thus foiled he struck with the poker the part where the dog had passed through and down fell a small old-fashioned box, which on being opened was found to contain a large sum in gold and silver coins of Charles I's reign.

" The dog was never more seen indoors, but to the present day continues to haunt, at midnight, a lane which leads to this house, and which has long borne the name of ' Dog Lane '. A small inn by the road side still invites the passing stranger by the ominous sign of ' The Black Dog ' portrayed in all his spectral frightfulness. The dog has been seen as recently as 1856, and may be seen at the present time by any one curious enough to watch at midnight for its appearance.

" Dogs should on no account be allowed to stray late at night in this neighbourhood, as there have been many cases of their disappearance in a mysterious manner, most likely frightened to death by the spectre ! "

Ten years later a correspondent in the *Somerset and Dorset Notes and Queries* (vol. iii, p. 112) gives as from the *Live Stock Journal* an account in almost the same words as Miss Leathes, to which I, writing from Fiji (p. 255), called attention, and mentioned that I had a hazy idea that some such legend had been attributed to the neighbourhood of the " Hunter's Lodge ", about a couple of miles or so out of Axminster, at the junction of the old turn-pike road from Axminster to Charmouth with the cross-road to Uplyme and Lyme Regis.

Netherbury.

Churchyard Legend.—The following story was given to me many years ago by an old lady member of our family, now dead ; who, in turn, had received it from her great-aunt.

" An old parish clerk and sexton living at the foot of the churchyard, the garden of whose cottage was only divided from it by a low wall, was wont to be much annoyed by a poor half-witted girl of the village repairing to the church porch night after night and disturbing his rest by singing psalms. With the intention of frightening away the intruder he, one moonlight night, wrapped himself in a sheet, and walking round the church came upon the girl as usual singing in the porch. Instead of being alarmed, however, at the unexpected apparition as had been fully counted upon, she addressed the supposed spirit as follows : ' Here's a soul coming ! Whose soul be you ? Be you my granfer's or granmer's, or —' (naming somebody who had recently been buried there). Then, after a pause, and looking round, she continued, ' H'm ! souls *be* about to-night ! For there's a black 'un, too, and he's trying to come up to the whit' 'un ; and he's coming on so fast that if the whit' un' don't take care the black 'un 'll catch en.' Upon hearing these words, the sexton, who had anticipated the flight and terror of the poor girl on his making his appearance, now felt the effects of that terror recoiling on himself ; and, looking upon it as a judgment for his cruel conduct, took to his heels with all possible speed. Upon seeing this, the girl, clapping her hands to encourage him to the utmost, exclaimed : ' Run, whit' soul ; black soul 'll catch 'ee ! Run, whit' soul ; black soul 'll catch 'ee ! ' and repeated this several times with the greatest fervency. The sexton, now becoming perfectly wild with fear on hearing these words, glanced hastily behind him, and fancying he saw a dark figure close to his heels (which was probably that of his own shadow in the moonlight) tore down the path and over the low wall into his garden, never stopping till he was safe inside his own door. From the effects of this shock a serious illness followed, and as the legend goeth, he ' peeled ' from head to foot. It is needless to add that the girl remained unmolested for the future."

Portland.

Cock Legend.—The following ancient legend is recorded in Hutchins, vol. ii, p. 829 (*s.v.* Portland), where it is attributed to Holinshed (vol. ii, 645) :

" In November, 1457, in Portland, was seen a cock coming out of the sea having a great crest on its head, a great red beard, and legs half a yard long. He stood on the water and crowed three times, and every time turned himself about and beckoned with his head, north, south, and west. He was in colour like a pheasant, and when he had crowed he vanished."

Stalbridge.

Ghost Story.—The following ghost story is taken from the Rev. W. S. Swayne's pamphlet: *History and Antiquities of Stalbridge* (1889), p. 9:

" The old manor house in the park at Stalbridge was pulled down in 1822. It was of the Jacobean style, and contained a beautiful staircase with figures of the twelve apostles about a yard high, placed at intervals between the balusters.

" In connection with the old mansion a curious story is told. It is said that for some years before the house was pulled down it was left empty in the charge only of an old housekeeper.

" The owner, however, on one occasion lent the house for the Christmas season to a lady friend of hers who had a large family of young children, making the stipulation that she should do whatever the old housekeeper required of her.

" On arriving at the house the lady and her family were met by the housekeeper, who requested all of them to make a point of not being in the hall of the house at five o'clock of an evening. This request was agreed to, and for some time observed; but on one occasion the lady had had some children in to play during the afternoon with her own children, and having said goodbye to them, was standing in the hall of the house just on stroke of five. Hardly had the hour passed when her notice was attracted by a figure issuing from the door of one of the bedrooms on the first floor, which could be seen from the hall. The figure was that of a woman enveloped in flames, who repeated to herself in an agonized voice: 'I have done it. I have done it.' The figure disappeared almost immediately into the door of another room.

" The lady ascended the stairs, and found that the doors both of the room from which the figure had emerged and that into which it had entered were locked.

" Startled by so strange an occurrence, she determined to be in the hall on another evening at the same hour. Once more she witnessed the same strange events. Now thoroughly convinced that it was something more than a mere freak of her imagination she returned at once with her children to London, and took an early opportunity of calling upon the owner. She mentioned what she had seen, and begged to know what was the meaning of it.

" The following story was then related to her.

" Some years ago the house was inhabited by a widowed mother and her only son, who was not yet of age. One day the boy came to his mother and told her that he had fallen in love with the gamekeeper's daughter. The mother reproved him for his indiscretion, and forbade him to mention the subject again. Not long after the boy returned to the subject and announced his intention of marrying the girl. Once more his mother refused to listen to him.

"Some weeks afterwards the son once more spoke to his mother on the same subject and told her that it would be far better for her to make up her mind to accept the inevitable as the girl had now been his wife for some months. The mother was so indignant that she turned her son out of the house and forbade him ever to enter it again. Some months passed away, and the mother apparently repented of her harshness, for she went to her son and told him that she would receive both him and his wife and condone his disobedience. They returned to Stalbridge House, and at first all went well, for the girl was beautiful and amiable and did her best to please her mother-in-law. One day, however, the young man returned late in the evening after a long day's hunting, and was met by the sad news that his young wife had been burnt to death. The accident had occurred in this way. His wife had entered her mother-in-law's dressing-room about five o'clock in the evening, ready dressed for dinner. The mother-in-law was sitting in a distant part of the room before her looking-glass, and the girl stood before the fire. Suddenly the elder lady heard a scream, and turning, saw her daughter-in-law enveloped in flames, having accidentally caught her dress on fire from the hearth. This story was accepted without question; and it was not until the wretched woman lay on her death-bed that she confessed to her son that she had murdered his young wife, having pushed her into the fire. After the death of the murderess the old house was haunted by her figure enveloped in flames, and exclaiming at her own crime."

Stanton St. Gabriel (Whitechurch Canonicorum).

For the *Legend of St. Gabriel's*, see Chapter XI, p. 318.

Stoke Abbott.

Phantom Coach.—The late Major Groves, of Bowood, Netherbury, many years ago, when walking with me across the fields from there to the neighbouring village of Stoke Abbott, pointed out to me a spot where a phantom coach-and-four was alleged to have appeared from time to time; but whether this apparition was in the form of the headless one of Kingston Russell [1] or the less sensational one of the Turberville type,[2] or whether any solution of the mystery was ever offered I cannot now remember.

[1] *Ante, s.v.* Kingston Russell. [2] *Post, s.v.* Wool.

Studland.

(i) *The Agglestone.*—In *Notes and Queries*, Ser. III, ix, 187, the late Mr. Charles Warne, F.S.A.,—under the initials " C. W.",—in speaking of " The Agglestone ", a remarkable mass of ferruginous sandstone, situated in the parish of Studland in the Isle of Purbeck, wrote :

" The country people say of it that his Satanic majesty (who is often a very important personage in these capricious freaks) was one day sitting on the Needles Rock, Isle of Wight, whence, espying Corfe Castle in the distance, he took the cap from his head and threw it across the sea, with the intent of demolishing that structure. But it would appear that he had over-estimated his powers of jactation, for the missle fell short of its mark ; and there it stands to this day on Studland Heath, a monument of disappointed malice, a wonder to the peasantry, and a theme of antiquarian conjecture."

Mr. J. J. Foster, F.S.A., in the *Folk-Lore Journal* (vol. vi, 117), speaks of the Agglestone as the " Devil's Night-cap " (Saxon *Haligstan*=Holy stone)—a name probably derived from its shape, an inverted cone—and states that it is nearly 17 feet in height, 35 feet in diameter, and computed to weigh some 400 tons. He confirms the legend as given by Mr. Warne, with the exception that it was the stone itself that his Satanic majesty threw, not his cap.

This same legend is also mentioned in a note to a short paper on " The Agglestone " by the Rev. J. H. Austen, in the *Purbeck Papers*, p. 79, to which is added an excellent drawing of the stone.[1].

(ii) *Haunted Cottage.*—Many years ago the late Mr. Albert Bankes, of Wolfeton, sent me the following legend :

" At Studland, near Corfe Castle, there is still living an old woman who most graphically describes a ghost story as having happened in a cottage at the bottom of our garden at Studland. A smuggler with bales of silk is supposed to have been murdered in this cottage, and from a distance at sea from on board ship the cottage appeared to be always in flames until the rector of the parish was summoned to exorcise the evil spirit."

[1] See also *Notes and Queries*, Ser. v, viii, 501.

Symondsbury (near Bridport).

Spring Superstition.—There is a spring rising in one of the fields of Symondsbury Farm, near Bridport, the water of which is considered to be very good for sore eyes. People have been known to come from some distance to obtain it.

This efficacy is said to accrue from the fact that the water, as it issues from the spring, directly faces the east; and it is believed that in order to obtain the full benefit of the cure the water should be taken at the moment that the sun's rays first light upon it.

Colour may be given to this superstition from the fact that the water is no doubt, from the appearance of the earth immediately surrounding it, impregnated with iron; and it is very likely that from this cause alone the water may be of some benefit to the patient, whether applied externally or internally.

I visited the place again in 1913 and found that the water from this spring had been diverted to a trough, or tank, lower down in the field, and no longer flows out facing the east. I have no doubt that the superstition will die out in consequence of this innovation or concession to the exigencies of modern farming.

Walditch (near Bridport).

Spring Superstition.—There is also a similar superstition attaching to a similarly situated spring in the parish of Walditch, on the eastern side of Bridport, from which, I am told, people fetch water in bottles for their eyes.[1]

Wimborne.

Haunted Barns.—Miss Billington, in her before-mentioned paper on "Dorsetshire Ghosts", speaks of the apparent facility that barns have for becoming haunted, and mentions one "about a mile out of Wimborne on the Cranbourne Road, called 'Sunday's Barn', where a man once committed suicide by hanging himself. Ever since there has been talk of the apparition of a coffin lying across the road opposite the building."

At Hill-Butts and Stanbridge, also near Wimborne, she says, are two barns, to both of which this unenviable notoriety belongs. No cattle can or will stay there on account of the horrible noises they hear.

[1] *Conf.* St. Austin's Well at Cerne Abbas, *ante*, p. 158.

Wimborne St. Giles.

Miss Billington, in the same paper, says:

"*Ghost Story*.—The high road from Wimborne to Cranbourne passes through one of the woods on the St. Giles estate. By the roadside are four or five magnificent fir trees, which give the spot a gloomy, shadowy appearance, making it in all respects a fit resort for ghosts. There is a form which haunts this place. They say it is that of a female figure dressed in white, and wearing a hood which covers her face. She paces to and fro, but as soon as one succeeds in coming near her she makes a wild rush through the hedge. After this there is a crashing sound like a waggon and horses going fast through a wood, which continues for some minutes. The popular belief is that a murder was committed there in bygone years."

Winterborne Abbas.

Stream Superstition.—According to what the late Mr. H. J. Moule states in the *Folk-Lore Journal* (vol. vi, p. 117) no man ever saw a "winter-borne break". It is dry one day and running the next; but its first downpour was never beheld. And he relates the story that years ago a watch was kept day and night for a fortnight for the breaking of Winterborne Abbas Stream. One night the watchman on duty found that his pipe had gone out. "Bridehead lodge—he beänt 'bove hundred or two yard—can't do any harm to get light there." But in those three minutes the winter-borne "broke" unseen!

Wool.

Spectral Coach.—Biggs's *Isle of Purbeck* (1877), p. 46, contains a reference to the old manor house, called Wool-bridge House, of Jacobean date, and a seat of the Turbervilles, a very old Dorset family, whose headquarters were at Bere Regis. It is said that a spectre coach-and-four drives out from Wool-bridge House in the gloom of evening; but lest any one should wait until evening in order to fathom the mystery it should be added that none can see this ghostly coach of the Turbervilles who have not Turberville blood in their veins.

This legend is to some extent amplified by Thomas Hardy in that most pathetic of all his books, *Tess of the D'Urbervilles* (vol. ii, p. 171), where, upon Tess remarking that she seemed to have seen before the old-fashioned post-chaise in which they were about to start for their ill-fated honeymoon to " Wellbridge House ", Angel Clare inquired if she had not heard of the legend of the " D'Urberville coach ", and, upon her disavowal of any such knowledge, tells her that " a certain D'Urberville of the sixteenth or seventeenth century committed a dreadful crime in his family coach, and that since that time members of the family see or hear the coach whenever—" Here he paused, and would not proceed, which made Tess ask, " Is it when we are going to die, Angel, that members of my family see it, or is it when we have committed a crime ? " But Mr. Hardy leaves us as much in the dark upon this point as Angel Clare left Tess.

So the legend is evidently not quite complete yet !

Mr. Wilkinson Sherren, however, tells us what the result is to that person of the Turberville blood who sees the phantom coach in his account of the legend which he gives in his book *The Wessex of Romance* (1908), p. 143 :

" An anecdote is told of a gentleman who, passing across the old Elizabethan bridge on his way to dine with a friend, saw the ghostly coach. On arriving at his destination he spoke of it, and inquired about the eccentric individual who used a queer old-fashioned four in hand with outriders. Much to his astonishment he was told it was the Turberville coach. Perhaps his reflections on hearing this news were not pleasant, as the old blood ran in his veins, and the sight of the phantom is said to forebode disaster to the descendant to whom it appears."

In his story Mr. Hardy does not give the exact locality in which the spectral coach-and-four might be expected to be seen ; but I have seen a letter of his to a correspondent—evidently in answer to a question relative to this legend– in which this is clearly indicated. He says :

" The legend of the phantom coach is well known here "—(the letter was written from Dorchester in 1903)—" the scene of its wayfarings being the road between Woolbridge Manor-house and the site of the destroyed Manor-house at Bere Regis, two properties formerly owned by branches of the same family—the Turbervilles. The cause of the appearances is said to be some family murder ; but this may have been invented of recent times, such supplementary details being often added to mediæval tales, as, for instance, to the legend of ' The Lost Pyx ' (versified in ' Poems of the Past and the Present ')—a black-hoofed animal that would not kneel—is subjoined by some tellers."[1]

And Mr. Hardy adds the following interesting piece of information as to the source of the legends and folk-lore contained in his books—an assurance that is hardly necessary to Dorset folk :—

" To your other question,—if the legendary matter and folk-lore of my books is traditionary and not invented,—I can answer yes, in, I think, every case, this being a point on which I was careful not to falsify local beliefs and customs."

I have been told that the late Captain Arthur Mansel, of Dorchester—in whose veins, through the Moreton and Pleydell families ran the necessary strain of Turberville blood—affirmed that he had once seen the ghostly coach-and-four on the heath between Moreton and Wool.

[1] See *ante*, *s.v.* Batcombe.

CHAPTER V

BIRTH, DEATH, AND MARRIAGE CUSTOMS AND SUPERSTITIONS

THE subject matter of this chapter is reproduced from a paper of mine in the Dorset Field Club's *Proceedings* for 1893 (vol. xiv, pp. 182–200), together with such additions and emendations as I have been enabled to make since that time. For convenience of arrangement and reference I have divided it into three parts or sections, viz. (1) those customs and superstitions appertaining to births, in which I include christenings ; (ii) deaths, in which I include funerals ; and (iii) marriages, in which I include courtship. Amongst the following items there doubtless appear several that are not peculiar to the county of Dorset, but, for obvious reasons, that is no ground for excluding them here.

I. BIRTHS

Before dealing with births themselves, however, it would be as well, perhaps, to notice any customs or superstitions that belong more to the preparation for, or the foretelling of, these interesting events.

(i) *Groaning Drink.*—That excellent West Dorset historian and antiquary, the late Mr. George Roberts, in his *History of Lyme Regis*, p. 255 (1834), tells us that it was formerly a custom for a woman to brew a barrel of beer—called " groaning drink "—for the use of the family and the gossips during her confinement. He relates an anecdote that was told him of a woman who, during the siege of Lyme Regis in the Civil War, was nearly killed in her bed by a ball at the storming of the town. Her enthusiasm was such that instead of praying to be removed, she called out to those about her to carry the barrel of " groaning drink " to inspire the town soldiers with courage.

(ii) *Magpie Omens.*—The presence of magpies (who are not gregarious birds) to the number of four, is commonly believed to foretell a birth, as the following well-known lines in the form I best know them in West Dorset testify :—

"*One*, sign of anger;
Two, sign of mirth;
Three, sign of wedding;
Four, sign of birth." [1]

(iii) *Days of the Week Omen.*—It is believed that a child's fortunes vary according to which day of the week it is born. The following lines were given by Miss Summers, of Hazelbury Bryan, in the *Dorset County Chronicle*, some thirty years ago, in support of this—to whom I am also indebted for several other items in this chapter:—

"Monday's child is fair of face;
Tuesday's child is full of grace;
Wednesday's child is full of woe;
Thursday's child has far to go;
Friday's child is loving and giving;
And Saturday's child works hard for a living.
But a child that is born on the Sabbath day
Is blithe and bonny, good and gay."

(iv) *Unlucky Omens.*—Amongst Dorset folk it is considered unlucky to take a baby downstairs the first time it leaves its native bedroom.[2] So also to have it weighed before it is three months old; or its nails cut before it is a year old.

It is very unlucky to name a child after a brother or sister who has previously died. Though by no means an uncommon practice in Dorsetshire, it is thought, nevertheless, to a be sign that it will die early.

So also if a male child happens to be born at the time of the new moon. Hence the proverb: "No moon, no man." See Thomas Hardy's *Return of the Native*, vol. i, p. 53, in illustration of this, where Timothy Fairway, repeating the above proverb, says: "'Tis one of the truest sayings ever spit out. The boy never comes to anything that's born at new moon."

(v) *Lucky Omens.*—On the other hand, it is considered a lucky omen if the child, being a girl, should "favour" (*i.e.* resemble) its father; or, if a boy, its mother.[3]

It is considered a good sign if an infant cries at its baptism. If it remains quiet and passive it is said to be "too good to live".

[1] For variants of this see Chapter VII, p. 240, *s.v.* Magpie.
[2] See *N. & Q.*, Ser. v, x, 205, 255.
[3] See *N. & Q.*, Ser. v, x, 138.

(vi) *Hardening of Infants.*—As a means of hardening a new-born infant it is thought to be a sure preventive against chilblains for its feet to be put in the snow.

(vii) *Dipping in Spring.*—So it is considered wholesome to plunge a new-born infant in a cold spring provided that care is taken where and when it is done. There is a spring in the parish of Cerne Abbas, which, directly facing the rising sun, seems to fulfil the conditions required, the new-born infant being dipped just at the time when the sun first begins to shine on the water.[1] There is a spring similarly situated on Symondsbury Farm, near Bridport, the water of which is considered beneficial for sore eyes, and people have been known to come from some distance to obtain it. Here, as in the dipping of new-born infants, in order to obtain the full benefit of the cure, the water should be taken at the moment the sun's rays first light upon it.[2]

(viii) *Alliterative naming of Children.* — Curious customs and fads are sometimes followed by Dorset agricultural labourers with regard to the naming or christening of their children. That of giving each member of the family a name with the same initial letter of the alphabet is one of them ; and in a large family sometimes considerable difficulty is experienced in providing names suitable for the occasion. An instance of this is given by a correspondent in *Notes and Queries* (Ser. VI, ii, 476), who stated that at the village of Buckland Newton there prevailed a custom, some forty years previously, of naming all the children of a family with the same initial letter. And he instances the case of a labourer with a large family, who had chosen the letter M as the family initial, and, puzzled to meet the increasing demand upon that letter, had two of his girls christened *Mahalath* and *Mehetabel* ! However, much as we may pity the innocent and unfortunate recipients of such names, we can hardly help admiring the persistency with which this Dorset labourer must have ransacked the Book of Genesis in his search after orthodox Scriptural names (once so common a nomenclature in the West of England) before he had attained his object amongst the wives of Esau and those of his remote posterity !

[1] This spring is probably identical with that of St. Austin's Well at Cerne Abbas. See Chapter IV, p. 158.

[2] There is a similar spring on the Walditch side of Bridport from which people fetch water for their eyes. See Chapter IV, p. 173.

Sometimes these strange christenings took another form. The three sons of a family named Staples, once living at Stoke Abbott, in West Dorset, were called Shadrach, Meshach, and Abednego, and were known by these Christian names in preference to their own surnames. A woman, Mary Hallet, called " Old Mary Bednego ", was the daughter of the last-named son.

II. Deaths

Before touching upon those customs or superstitions concerning deaths I will mention some of those numerous omens or portents foreboding death, to which Dorset folk, in common with so many others, are apt to give such ready credence.

Death Omens.

The unusual or inopportune actions of certain living creatures have in all countries and in all ages, one may say, been considered to be instrumental or as having some effect in foretelling or determining the misfortunes or deaths of human beings.

(i) *Birds.*—If a bird—more particularly if a robin—comes into a house, it is looked upon as an omen of death, a sign that some one in that house will shortly die. A bird tapping at the window is also a very ominous sign, and I have also heard it said that if the " sighing " of a robin is heard near a house it foretells the illness or death of some one of its inmates.

Sometimes the note of the cuckoo is equally ill-boding ; for if you hear it after Old Midsummer Day, or when you happen to be in a churchyard, you won't live the year out.

So also the crowing of a cock at unusual times. If it crows after noon, according to some it foretells a death in the family of its owner, or, as others say, it signifies that sickness in the place will shortly follow. An old woman at Symondsbury once said : " If the cock crows after twelve o'clock noon her is doing it to bring I bad news, or John may be bad ageän. I can't a-bear to hear 'en."

Mr. Thomas Hardy, in his *Tess of the D'Urbervilles* (1891), vol. ii, p. 175, gives a most graphic description of the effect caused by this widespread superstition, which occurred just as Tess was starting on her ill-fated honeymoon, the result of which so amply justified the superstition.

So if it crows by night from its perch it is often fancied to precede or foretell the death of a person.[1]

(ii) *Dogs.*—So, too, the howling of a dog by night, or before the house door, is believed to have the same significance.

(iii) *Bees.*—If a swarm of bees takes possession of the roof of a house it portends death to the owner of it. Again, if the swarm settles on a dead branch of a tree or shrub, or pitches upon dead wood, it is looked upon as a sign of death.

(iv) *Plants.*—Certain plants or shrubs, when in flower, have an evil significance attributed to them under certain circumstances. Thus, if a sprig of box *in flower* be brought in-doors death will soon cross the threshold.

So also if fruit trees blossom out of season it is considered to be a token of death.[2]

We have the authority of Miss Summers in the following triplet for saying that to bring a bunch of yellow furze, when in bloom, into the house is a sure prognostication of death :—

> " If the yaller vuz be a-cärd in
> A-thin a year there's nar a doubt
> A coffin 'ill be a-cärd out."

Miss Summers also gives several other death omens in an article on " Dorsetshire Folklore " in the *Dorset County Chronicle* in June, 1888. She says :

" The portents of death are so numerous that it is impossible to recapitulate them. A cock crowing at midnight is considered a sure sign of death in the house ; then a bird tapping at the window, or meeting a funeral, is very ominous ; also a sudden rap at the door when no human being is visible. Then if bees pitch on dead wood when swarming, the howling of a dog before the house door, the appearance of bright lights in a circular form seen in the air when there is no candle or light of any sort near, the appearance of a wraith — which is the form of the human being whose death it foretells—are certain signs of death."

(v) *Articles of Domestic Use.*—Besides subjects of natural history—such as birds, animals, and plants—supplying the medium by which a death may be foretold, such means may be afforded by certain appearances or results in objects of every day or domestic use. Thus, if when a cloth is unfolded it discloses

[1] Conf. *The Denham Tracts*, vol. ii, p. 55.

[2] Conf. *Shropshire Folk-lore*, p. 251.

a mark or crease in the form of a diamond, it is considered a sign of death. Again, if a cake, on being cut, breaks in two it has a similar significance.[1] So also if a "winding-sheet" is observed in a candle.[2]

(vi) *Church Bells and Clocks.*—Church bells and clocks, too, under certain circumstances, may prove of equally ominous import. At Long Burton, near Sherborne, it is customary for the sexton to ring the tenor bell every Sunday morning, and if it should happen to sound dull and heavy it is said that some one in the parish is sure to die before the week is out.[3] I have also heard this said in the parish of Symondsbury.

The same result, too, is said to follow if the clock happens to strike twelve whilst singing is going on in the church.

In many parts of Dorsetshire the tenor bell is tolled an hour after the deceased has passed away, unless it should happen to be after sunset when it is deferred until the following morning at an hour after sunrise. The tolling is renewed just before and after the service on the day of the funeral. The custom varies, however, in different parishes. In Symondsbury, in West Dorset, I have noticed that there is no tolling on the day upon which the death takes place; but it is done at 8 o'clock on the morning of the funeral, in addition to the usual one before and after the service. The bell after the service is tolled rather more quickly. If, after the early morning tolling, it is desired (and no doubt paid for) the tenor bell will toll the exact age of the deceased. I have been informed, however, that there have been several instances in the parish when this has been done on the day of the death, and the age tolled. This was called the "minute bell".[4]

In the *Somerset and Dorset Notes and Queries* for 1914 (vol. xiv, p. 135) appears a note of a curious and most unusual custom obtaining in the parish of Bishop's Caundle, near Sherborne, of tolling the bell four times over for every funeral. It was there intimated that in future the bell would be tolled twice only.

[1] I believe this is also known in Devonshire.

[2] Conf. *Shropshire Folk-lore*, p. 139.

[3] See Chapter IV, p. 166.

[4] This custom is referred to in Thomas Hardy's ode "To Shakespeare"; at p. 25 of *Moments of Vision, and Miscellaneous Verses* (1917):

"Thy age was published on thy passing-bell."

If a clock in a room suddenly and without any warning falls forward on the floor it foretells a death in the family of the owner.[1]

(vii) *Shivering.*—It is a very common belief that if you happen to shiver suddenly and without any apparent cause it is a sign that some one is walking over your grave, but whether that sign is also to be taken as an indication that that grave will shortly be in requisition I don't know.

(viii) *Knockings at Night.*—So, too, any mysterious knockings or tappings by night have always been considered to presage death, or something disastrous. At the funeral repast which followed on the recent death of a dairyman's daughter in a West Dorset parish, a relative remarked: "I was sure I was going to hear of something, because I heard such knockings—knockings. Then I listened, and again the knocking; and then my bed-clothes was lifted, just like this"—(showing the action by the skirt of her dress). A week after this an old washer-woman, living in the parish in which the poor girl had died, said to my informant: "I couldn't think what I was going to hear, as the same night the poor thing died I heard two or three *such* knocks in the night; and next morn—came and said her was gone."

(ix) *Deaths at Christmas.*—In some parts of Dorsetshire it is believed that the period of the year at which a person dies is instrumental in determining the deaths of others. It is said that if one person in a village dies "A-tween the wold Christmas and the new" (*i.e.* between 25th December and 6th January) there will be a great many deaths there during the ensuing year. Miss Summers gives an instance of this in writing to the *Dorset County Chronicle* in March, 1889, when she states that she was informed that one death had occurred in the village of Hazelbury Bryan during the prescribed time and that nine funerals, principally of engaged couples, had up to the time she wrote already followed in its wake. Her informant had also told her she "had mind o' two dyen in that time, and there was a fever come on, and twenty-seven on 'en died in this here village."

Mr. R. Bosworth Smith, in his *Bird Life and Bird Lore* (1909), p. 364, gives the number of the expectant deaths as twelve, and

[1] See Thomas Hardy's *A Changed Man*, p. 72 (1913).

verifies the superstition by citing an actual instance of it which occurred in the parish of Hilton.

Death-bed Customs and Superstitions.—(i) That a mild Christmastide is generally believed to be inimical to human life is shown by the well-known proverb : " A green Christmas makes a fat churchyard." When a person lies a-dying it is believed that a great deal depends upon the accessories of his situation as to whether his death will be an easy one or not. For instance, it is considered that the death will be all the easier if all the doors and windows in the house are thrown open.

(ii) So, too, the composition or the situation of the bed itself upon which the dying person is lying may make a great difference in this respect. It is firmly believed by many that if the bed or pillow be stuffed with pigeon's feathers, or as some say, with game feathers, the person who is lying upon it cannot die peacefully. This accounts for the not uncommon occurrence in olden times of a poor lingering mortal being lifted on to a mattress or clothes on the floor, or sometimes even on to the bare floor itself, in order that he may not " die so hard ! "

(iii) I have the authority of the late Mr. J. C. Mansel-Pleydell for saying that it was sometimes the practice in his own neighbourhood of Whatcombe, near Blandford, for those in attendance on the dying person to observe which way the planks of the floor lay, and if they happened to be cross-ways with the bed they turned the person round so that he would " go with the boards ".

(iv) In West Dorset it is believed that the same difficulty will be experienced if the bed upon which a dying person is lying happens to be placed directly under a beam. So recently as the summer of 1891 an old woman lay a-dying in the parish of Symondsbury, near Bridport, and, being longer in dying than was expected, several of the neighbours noticed that her bed was under a beam, and requested that the bed should be moved, or " her'll never die so hard ". I am bound to say, though, in this instance, that although the bedstead was moved accordingly, the poor old soul lingered on for some time afterwards.

(v) Mr. Thomas Hardy, in a footnote to his poem, " Julie-Jane ", in *Time's Laughing-stocks* (1909), p. 107, says that it is, or was, a common custom in Wessex, and probably other country places, to prepare the mourning beside the death-bed, the dying person sometimes assisting; who also selects his or her "bearers" on such occasions.

Corpse Superstitions.—(i) A correspondent in *Notes and Queries* (Ser. v, vi, 364), mentions the following superstition, as obtaining amongst Dorsetshire labourers. If one of twins die and the limbs do not stiffen rigidly, the funeral is delayed in the belief that the dead one is waiting for the other; and (the correspondent adds): "The carelessness of the relatives will sometimes verify the assertion, for the dead one has not long to wait."

(ii) In some parts of Dorsetshire it is believed that if a corpse remains limp and does not stiffen it is a sign that another death in the same family will follow shortly.[1]

(iii) The late Rev. W. K. Kendall, of East Lulworth (to whom I am indebted for several interesting items of folk-lore upon the subject of this paper as well as upon others), stated that he was informed that corpses had been "laid out" in the village of Lulworth with a penny in one hand and a little wooden hammer in the other. "There may be some foundation for this" (says Mr. Kendall) "and, if so, it would point to a heathen custom adopted, as many others have been, by the Roman Church."

(iv) Sometimes a plate of salt is laid upon the breast of the corpse, either as a charm against evil spirits, or, as some say, to keep it from swelling.[2]

(v) To kiss the face of a dead person is said to have the effect of preventing any unpleasant recollections of the sight arising in the future; in other words, prevents the person being "haunted" by it. The efficacy of this was firmly impressed upon a lady friend of mine who went to see an old woman from a neighbouring village who had died in the Bridport Union some years ago.

(vi) So also, in order not to dream of a dead body you have seen you should lay your hand upon it.[3]

[1] This superstition is not uncommon. Conf. *Shropshire Folk-lore*, p. 287; *The Folk-Lore of Yorkshire* (*North Riding, etc.*) (1901), p. 301; also *The Denham Tracts*, vol. ii, p. 49.

[2] Conf. *Shropshire Folk-lore*, p. 299.

[3] Conf. *Shropshire Folk-lore*, p. 298.

(vii) To touch the corpse of a person who has been hanged has been long looked upon as a " charm " or cure for certain diseases, particularly skin complaints. Similar treatment has been enjoined as a cure for a shrunken or withered limb ; when to be thoroughly effective the limb should be laid upon the neck of the corpse as soon as possible after it has been " cut down ", and before it has had time to become cold. The contact is believed to " turn the blood and change the constitution ". (See Thomas Hardy's graphic, but somewhat gruesome story " The Withered Arm ", in vol. i of the *Wessex Tales* (1888).

(viii) To find the dead body of a person who has been drowned, but which has not been recovered from the water, the following charm or expedient is sometimes adopted. A loaf of bread is procured and a small piece is cut out of the side, forming a cavity, into which a little quicksilver is poured. The piece is then replaced and secured firmly in its original position. The loaf thus prepared is thrown into the river at the spot where the person had fallen in, and is expected to float down the stream until it comes to the place where the body has lodged, when it will begin to eddy round and round, thus indicating the sought-for spot. In *Notes and Queries* (Ser. v, ix, 111), the Rev. C. H. Mayo, of Long Burton, sends an account of this from an eye-witness as having taken place in 1872, the case being that of a boy who had fallen into the stream at Sherborne, near Darkhole Mill, and had there been drowned ; but, he adds, no satisfactory results occurred from the experiment.[1]

Funeral Preparations and Observances.—(i) However unpleasant or even injurious to the health of mourners called upon to pay with uncovered heads their last respects to the dead at the grave's side a storm or shower of rain may be, yet that to the dead itself such an occurrence is of good omen we may gather from the well-known belief which, in one form or another, is common to so many countries, and in Dorsetshire is sometimes expressed in the following quaint and simple lines :—

" Happy is the bride that the sun shines on
And blessed is the corpse that the rain rains on."

[1] From a later reference to *Notes and Queries* (Ser. vii, xi, 345, 397), we learn that a similar expedient was resorted to with better success at Brentford, and on two occasions in the south of Ireland.

(ii) That the influence of a dead body for ill does not always cease even when it is placed in the coffin is apparent from the superstition which obtains in some parts of the county that it is extremely unlucky for any one to *run* after a funeral. However late a person may happen to be in joining the cortège, he should always *walk*—never *run*—or fatal consequences will at no distant date befall the unfortunate individual.

(iii) The Rev. F. B. M. Camm, writing to the *St. James's Gazette* in April, 1902, states that it was customary, during the time that he was rector of a West Dorset country parish (Monkton Wyld) for some twenty-two years, for the mourners to attend divine service in the parish church on the Sunday after a funeral (called "Mourning Sunday") and to remain seated during the whole time, holding handkerchiefs to their eyes, and apparently unconscious of what was going on. As they all sat together in the best part of the church the effect was very strange.

This customary service also obtains in other parts of West Dorset. In some the "bearers" also attend, forming up on either side of the entrance door so as to allow the mourners to pass in between them to their pews, when they take up their places in the pews immediately behind. Though it would not appear to be obligatory that handkerchiefs should be used by all the mourners in the way described by Mr. Camm, no doubt many do so to conceal their genuine grief, whilst the men throughout maintain a devout attitude.

(iv) It used to be customary in olden days for the village "quire" also to form round the grave.[1]

(v) Sometimes those present at funerals throw sprigs of rosemary into the grave after the corpse has been deposited therein. The Rev. Canon Mayo states (*Somerset and Dorset Notes and Queries*, vol. iv, p. 106) (1895), in an editorial note upon this custom, that he has both seen it done at a funeral in Dorsetshire, and has himself complied with the custom.[2]

(vi) The late Mr. Bosworth Smith in his *Bird Life and Bird*

[1] See "The Rash Bride", a poem in Thomas Hardy's *Time's Laughing-stocks*, p. 127.

[2] See same reference as to wearing of sprigs of rosemary at funerals in Wales. And see *Hamlet*, Act iv, Scene 5, "There's rose-mary, that's for remembrance."

Lore, p. 357, when making some very interesting remarks as to the fascination and interest excited amongst the poorer classes generally, and of Dorsetshire in particular, by funerals, gives a most amusing story of the preparations made for an expected funeral, which are often made long before the death happens. "How is your husband to-day?" inquired the squire of a neighbouring village about a labouring man who had long been at death's door, and whom he hardly expected to find alive when he called. "Oh, Sir!" replied the wife, "he is ever so much better to-day. Now what do you think he did last night? You would hardly believe it. He got out of bed, came downstairs, and ate a good bit of the funeral ham, and is ever so much the stronger for it."

III. Marriages

Before coming to those customs and superstitions which properly relate to the ceremony of marriage or the married state itself, I will refer to those appertaining to courtship, and to the divining of or the endeavouring to obtain an insight into the future of that married state to which, presumably, our Dorset youth of both sexes—no less than those of other counties—aspire. These latter may not inaptly be termed "Matrimonial Oracles".

Matrimonial Oracles.—Many means are adopted by Dorsetshire maidens with the object of divining who their future husbands are to be. Our "Dorset Poet", the late Rev. William Barnes, contributed to *Hone's Year Book* (p. 587), many years ago, the following interesting description of what these matrimonial oracles sometimes consisted. He says:—

"In my childhood I recollect some of my female friends, while gathering flowers in a meadow would stop and, plucking a large daisy, pull off the petals one by one, repeating at the same time the words: 'Rich man, poor man, farmer, ploughman, thief,' fancying very seriously that the one which came to be named at plucking the last petal would be her husband. Another way of knowing the future husband (inferior only to the dark words of that high priestess of the oracles of Hymen, the cunning gipsey), is to pluck an even ash leaf and, putting it into the hand, to say:

'The even ash leaf in my hand,
The first I meet shall be my man.'

"Then, putting it in to the glove, to say:

'The even ash leaf in my glove,
The first I meet shall be my love.'

"And, lastly, into the bosom, saying:

'The even ash leaf in my bosom,
The first I meet shall be my husband.'

"Soon after which the future husband will make his appearance, and the lass may observe him as accurately as she will."[1]

The same authority states that the scattering of hemp seed was practised by Dorset maidens at Midsummer (*i.e.* on Old Midsummer's Eve, at midnight) with a like object. A girl would walk through the garden with a rake on her left shoulder, and, throwing the hemp seed over her right, would repeat these lines:

"Hemp seed I set, hemp seed I sow,
The man that is my true love come after me and mow."

when, if the spell worked properly, the future husband should appear behind her with a scythe. This is, no doubt, the custom to which Mr. Barnes alludes in his poem of "Erwin and Linda", under "Mrs. Mary's Tale", published in his *Poems in National English* in 1846, in the following lines:

"The while the slowly-clanging bell
Struck twelve o'clock, and giggling maids
Stole out to try the well-known spell
That brings their unknown husband's shades."[2]

Our Dorset novelist, Thomas Hardy, handles this seductive topic in his own inimitable way in chap. iv. of the second volume of *The Woodlanders*, published in 1887, to which I would refer all readers who are interested in this subject.

Mr. Barnes also mentions another form of divination that was adopted for the same purpose. On going to bed on Midsummer Eve the girls would sometimes place their shoes at right angles to each other in the shape of a T, and say:

"Hoping this night my true love to see
I place my shoes in the form of a T."

when it was said they would be sure to see their future husbands in a dream, and perhaps in reality, by their bedside.

[1] See Chapter VII, *s.v.* Ash tree. Conf. *The Denham Tracts*, vol. ii, pp. 70–1, for similar charms used in the north of England.

[2] Conf. *The Denham Tracts*, vol. ii, pp. 278–9, for similar means of divination practised on the Border.

I am not aware, however, whether the particular form of divination practised by the heroine in Keats's beautiful poem *The Eve of St. Agnes*, with such success in bringing about the latter alternative here suggested by Mr. Barnes, ever obtained in Dorsetshire.

This anxiety to know who one's future husband is likely to be is apparently early developed amongst Dorsetshire maidens, for it is a common amusement or game amongst children to toss up a ball of cowslip blossoms, tied in a globular form called a "tisty-tossty", as a means of divining their future; when the following lines are repeated whilst they play with it:

"Tisty-tossty, tell me true
Who shall I be married to?"

The names of various boys or girls are mentioned until the ball, which is being tossed about, drops, and the name which is being uttered at that moment is taken to be the one indicated by the oracle.[1]

Miss M. G. A. Summers, in an article on "Dorsetshire Folklore" in the *Dorset County Chronicle* in June, 1888, mentions the following matrimonial oracle:—

"Another way of diving into futurity is resorted to. Take a tumbler of water that flows from a stream that runs southwards, borrow the wedding-ring of a friend and suspend it by a hair of your own head close over the water, but without touching it, holding the hair between your thumb and forefinger. If the ring slowly revolves and hits the side of the glass you will die an old maid; if it turns quickly round you will be married once, if slowly, twice. Others say as many times as the ring strikes the side of the glass so many years will pass before you are married."[2]

Wedding Omens.—(i) It is believed that if a cake of bread in baking cracks across the top or "crown" there will be a wedding in the family before long.

(ii) A similar event is foretold by the unusual presence of three magpies together, as testified by the well-known rhyme already alluded to.

(iii) To dream of a funeral portends a wedding; but to meet one either in going to or coming from a wedding is considered very unlucky.[3]

[1] See Chapter VII, p. 255, *s.v.* Cowslip.

[2] See Chapter IX, p. 279, *s.v.* Hair.

[3] *Conf.* Napier's *Folk Lore of West of Scotland*, p. 51.

(iv) Saturday is considered a very unlucky day for a wedding.

(v) Placing a piece of wedding-cake underneath your pillow in order to dream of the loved one is a very old custom, and is followed in many counties.

(vi) Equally common is the couplet:

"If you marry in Lent,
You will live to repent."

(vii) It is considered of good omen if the bees belonging to one of the wedding couple should happen to swarm on the wedding day.[1]

(viii) Fine weather, or at least sunshine, is always considered a necessary accompaniment of the wedding ceremony if the marriage is to be an auspicious one, as may be gathered from the following couplet already noticed in the second part of this chapter:

"Happy is the bride that the sun shines on
And blessed is the corpse that the rain rains on."

Wedding customs, etc.—(i) Dorset folk are not peculiar, I believe, in holding the opinion that it is more in consonance with the canons of propriety relating to matters matrimonial that the elder members of a family should marry before the younger ones; but I am not aware that in any other county there is attached any such penance or atonement on the part of the elder ones who permit a breach of this unwritten law as is indicated in the following custom as related to me by an old lady (now dead) in the parish of Symondsbury, and which I communicated to *Notes and Queries* (Ser IV, viii, 291) more than forty years ago, without eliciting any parallel or similar instance from any other county. If a younger sister or brother of a family were to marry before the elder ones, on the day of the wedding these latter were expected to dance, barefooted (I believe), over furze bushes placed on the floor. Whether this custom prevailed to any great extent may indeed be questioned, but my informant told me that not so very long before it really did take place, when the parties affected satisfactorily underwent their penance of dancing or skipping over the aforesaid "vuzzen".

[1] See Thomas Hardy's *Under the Greenwood Tree*, pt. v, chap. i, p. 258.

In some parts of Dorsetshire it is sufficient if in the case of a younger sister marrying before an elder, the latter dance at the wedding in her stockinged feet merely.[1]

(ii) It was the custom in former times not only for the bridal party to walk two and two " arm in crook ", in procession round the parish after the wedding ceremony was over, but for any " new-married folk " to attend the village " club-walking " at Whitsuntide and to join in the procession, "a-gaying round " the parish behind 'em."[2]

(iii) It would appear that the celebration of marriage was not allowed to be performed at any time of the year the parties might choose ; but no doubt the following prohibition was not confined to Dorsetshire, and, I presume, amounted to no more than the restrictions imposed by the canonical law. Some forty years ago on looking through the parish registers in the quaint old church of Horton I found the following written on one of the pages for the year 1629 : " Conjugium Aduentus tollit Hillarius(?) relaxat. Rogamen vetitat concedit Prima Potestas. 1. From ye Sounday moneth before Christmas tell ye 7 day aftr twelf day. 2. From ye Sounday fortnight before Shrowetyde tell ye Sounday aftr Estr weake. 3. From ye rogation Sounday tell 7 dayes aftr Whit Sounday, and ye 7 last daye are included in ye prohibition." If I have copied the first line correctly (it is in the usual and somewhat difficult " Secretary " handwriting of the period), it won't scan as a hexameter, for which species of verse these two Latin lines are evidently intended. I have since discovered that it is given as " Hilarique relaxat " in Chester Waters's *Parish Registers in England* (1883), p. 33, where an intermediate line is inserted.

Skimmington Riding.—No account of Dorsetshire customs connected with marriages would be complete without some reference to a " Skimmington ", or, as it is sometimes called, a " Skimmity Riding ", which is a kind of matrimonial lynch law or pillory intended for those in a lower class of life, who, in certain glaring particulars, may have transgressed their marital duties, and

[1] *Conf.* Napier's *Folk Lore of West of Scotland*, p. 52.
[2] See *Under the Greenwood Tree*, pp. 260 *et seq.*

have thus brought upon themselves this, the strongest expression of outraged public opinion that a country district is capable of conveying.[1] There is such an excellent and full description, both as to what a " Skimmington riding " is, and of the causes for which it takes place, given in Roberts's *History of Lyme Regis*, published in 1834, that I cannot do better than quote it in full here :—

" Skimmington riding still continues to hold its ground. In an account I gave of it to the late Sir Walter Scott in 1828 is the information contained in this narrative. Skimmington riding is a great moral agent, not perhaps so much in restraining the vicious as in causing them to shun public observation, thereby not holding out bad examples to the rising youth of both sexes ; in a word, it checks those instances of openly profligate and licentious conduct, which else might become too prevalent among the lower orders, who cannot, like their superiors, have recourse to legal proceedings against the person who has injured them, or divorce ; it brands with infamy all gross instances of licentiousness, and exposes to lasting ridicule those couples who by their dissensions disturb the quiet and order of the neighbourhood, and so set a bad example either by struggling for domestic ascendancy, or by their quarrelsome dispositions. A Skimmington riding makes many laugh ; but the parties for whom they ride never lose the ridicule and disgrace which it attaches. So far, it is a punishment, like the visit of Mumbo Jumbo in Africa.[2] The following are the principal causes for riding the Skimmington : (i) When a man and his wife quarrel and he gives up to her. (ii) When a woman is unfaithful to her husband, and he patiently submits without resenting her conduct. (iii) Any grossly licentious conduct on the part of married persons."

As an instance of the first cause Mr. Roberts cites from *Hudibras*, Part II, Canto ii, ll. 685 *et seq.*, and continues :

" About dusk two individuals came out of some obscure street, attended by a crowd, whose laughter, huzzas, etc., emulate the well-known *Charivari* of the French. The two performers are sometimes in a cart, at other times on a donkey, one personating the wife, the other the husband. They beat each other furiously with the culinary weapons above described, and, warmed by the applause and presence of so many spectators

[1] For instances of such mediæval lynch laws now in modern use, see *Notes and Queries*, Ser. VIII, xii, 465, and Ser. IX, i, 27.

[2] See Mungo Park's *Travels in the Interior of Africa* (1799), and *Notes and Queries*, Ser. VIII, ii, 95.

(for all turn out to see a Skimmington), their dialogue attains a freedom, except in using surnames, only comparable with their gestures. On arriving at the house of the parties represented in this moving drama animation is at its height ; the crowd usually stay at that spot some minutes and then traverse the town. The performers are remunerated by the spectators ; the parties that parade the streets with the performers sweep with besoms the doors of those who are likely to require a similar visitation. See Dr. King's *Miscellany* :

'When the young people ride the Skimmington
There is a general trembling in the town ;
Not only her for whom the party rides
Suffers, but they sweep other doors besides.
And by that hieroglyphic does appear
That the good woman is the master there.'

"Mr. Douce derives *Skimmington* from the *skimming-ladle* used in the procession. Mr. Brand says 'None of the commentators on *Hudibras* have attempted an elucidation of the ceremony. Hogarth has illustrated it.'"

Mr. Roberts's account drew from the great "Wizard of the North" a very interesting reply, and as it gives a variant of the custom as obtaining in Scotland, and, moreover, Sir Walter Scott's letter does not appear to have been otherwise published or known, I give it here :—

"We had, or perhaps I might say still have, a similar ritual of popular interference in Scotland, in case of gross scandal or nuptial transgressions and public quarrels in a household. It is called 'riding the stang', the peccant party being seated across a pole (or stang) is no very comfortable position. You will find some notice of the custom in Jamieson's *Scottish Dictionary*, *voce* Stang. I think the Doctor does not mention that men and women also were sometimes exposed to ride the stang on account of incontinence. Burns made some clever verses (not in his collected works) on a comrade of his who had been accessory to such a Saturnalian scene of punishment, in which the exposed female had suffered bodily injury, upon which account the regular police had looked after the parties who had interfered with their regular vocation. I have read in Brand's *Popular Antiquities*, or some such authority, that scholars in the English Universities were subjected to the stang when they neglect prayers. You will find a poem on the Skimmington among Prior's poems, not the folio edition where it is omitted, but in the large collection. When they ride the Skimmington, it would seem they swept the doors of those whom they threatened with similar discipline."

It will be noticed here that " Riding the Stang " approaches more nearly to the African ceremony of Mumbo Jumbo wherein the " peccant party " takes an active—or perhaps I should rather say a passive—part in the performance; whereas in a " Skimmington-riding " the punishment, in its physical effects at all events, is vicarious, and the whole ceremony is in character an effigy.

Mr. Roberts states that in 1828 " skimming-riding " still continued to hold its ground. The lapse of another half century, with its increased enlightenment and education amongst the masses, leaves us in the same position—so far, at least, as Dorsetshire is concerned—if we believe the account given in the *Bridport News* in November, 1884, of a " skimmerton-riding " (as it is there called) that had recently occurred in the parish of Whitechurch Canonicorum in West Dorset, which is interesting as showing us what changes (if any) have been wrought by that half-century in the character of the performance. The extract is as follows :—

" On Wednesday, the 5th inst., this usually quiet parish was in a state of some excitement, owing to a demonstration of a peculiar character, not immediately connected with the day, which, however, was selected for the purpose by the superior judgment of the promoters. About six o'clock in the evening, just as darkness began to reign, a strange noise was heard as of the sound of trays and kettles, and it was soon found that a " skimmerton-riding " was in progress, such a thing not having been known for years in this parish. Three grotesquely attired figures were to be seen escorted by a procession consisting of persons dressed in various queer and eccentric costumes, and who paraded the parish, also visiting Morcombelake and Ryal. The figures alluded to appeared to the villagers to represent three personages who were very well known to them, there being a male and two females, whose past conduct had caused them to be made the subject of this queer exhibition. The two female characters were conveyed about on the backs of what are described as celebrated ' Jerusalems ', which certainly seemed pretty well to enter into the joke, for one of them particularly displayed his innate agility in a surprising manner. One of the females was represented as having an extraordinary long tongue, which was tied back to the neck, whilst in one hand she held some note-paper, and in the other pen and holder. Those forming the procession were literally ' wetted ' at the various inns, and after their perambulations were concluded they repaired to a certain field where a gallows was erected, and on which the effigies were hung and afterwards burnt, having previously been well saturated with some highly inflammable liquid. Nearly two hundred people assembled in the field, and a flaming light was maintained by torches. The extraordinary proceedings terminated with a fight, in which black eyes and bloody noses were not absent. However, the Riot Act was not read, the military was not called out, and the crowd dispersed about midnight, when the village resumed its wonted quietude."

This does not appear to have been the only "Skimmington-riding" that took place in the county that year, for in the *Dorset County Chronicle* appeared an account of certain proceedings for assault taken by one woman against another at Okeford Fitzpaine. The proceedings arose out of certain circumstances which had occasioned a "Skimmington-riding" in the parish, and that not for the first time, the evidence revealing, as the Chairman said, a very discreditable state of things in the village.[1]

It is not often that the representation of a "skimmity riding" is conveyed in sculpture, but at a visit of the Dorset Field Club to Montacute House, on the Somerset borders, in September, 1908, Mr. Edward Phelips, son of Mr. W. R. Phelips, the owner of the property, read a short paper upon the many objects of interest contained in the house, in which, in speaking of the hall, he said :—

"The interest of the room centres in the plaster work at the northern end of the room representing the old custom of 'Riding the Stang', or 'Skimmity Riding'. The story represents the master of the house helping himself to beer with one hand, while with the other he nurses the baby. His wife is just about to chastise him with her shoe, while an interested neighbour is watching the proceedings from the background. The sequel is also shown, when the poor man is paraded round the village, exposed to public ridicule for his inability to keep his wife in order."

Mr. Phelips spoke of the style of the ornamentation of this room as having been introduced into England from Holland in 1580 ; so that we may gather some idea as to the length of time

[1] The same paper, about this time, contained references to similar proceedings which took place at Hope Square, Weymouth.

that " skimmity riding " has been a popular institution in the West of England.[1]

Probably few readers of the *Wessex Novels* will need to be reminded of the dramatic description of a " Skimmington-riding " given by Mr. Thomas Hardy, in chapter xvi of the second volume of *The Mayor of Casterbridge,* published in 1886, and the tragic effect which that coarsely humorous spectacle had upon the unfortunate woman whose supposed laxity of conduct had afforded the excuse for the exhibition.[2]

Wife Sale.—There can be no doubt, I think, that at one time the right of a man to dispose of his wife by sale to any purchaser—provided that the woman was a consenting party—was widely believed in by the Dorset peasantry. I have not myself been fortunate enough to discover any authentic case of such a sale, though I have some recollection of having seen an account of one as having taken place in West Dorset in comparatively recent times ; but if so I have mislaid the reference.

Mr. Thomas Hardy, however, seems to have had no doubt that such a custom had prevailed at one time, for in the opening chapter of *The Mayor of Casterbridge* he gives a most graphic picture of the sale at an improvised auction of the wife of the future mayor of the county town. A little later in the story Mr. Hardy shows that the wife in her simplicity believed that her new husband had acquired a real and binding right to her by purchase, though the exact bearings and legal limits of that right were vague. He asks were there not numerous other instances of the same belief, and adds, " She was by no means the first or last peasant woman who had religiously adhered to her purchaser, as too many rural records show." If these " records " are in any sense public ones, it might be interesting to investigate them.

Mr. Wilkinson Sherren, in his *Wessex of Romance* (1908), p. 18, in commenting on this scene, suggests that the custom

[1] See Dorset Field Club's *Proceedings* (1908), vol. xxix, p. lxxxiii.

[2] According to the Rev. C. W Whistler, in *Folk-Lore,* vol. xix, p. 90, Black Torrington, in North Devon, still keeps up the ancient custom of " Skimmington riding " when some village scandal is to be held up to public reprobation. The Rev. S. Baring-Gould's novel, *Red Spider,* is also there referred to for a very full description of such a function, the scene being laid in a village close at hand, and the ritual observed being still in use.

might have existed as a survival of Danish barter or Saxon serfdom. "In any case," he says, "the origin of it was remote, and probably had its roots in heathendom, because the instances of its observance were few, and in all likelihood were reversions to primitive paganism under stress of circumstances."

He then gives an instance of a servant girl, a native of Morecombelake (West Dorset), who explained to her mistress in 1902 that the mother of one of her "young men" had been sold to a man for £30, and that this woman still lived in 1896. This may be the instance which had slipped my memory, the locality being in my old neighbourhood.

(i) *Portland Quarrymen's Courtship and Wedding Customs.*—Hutchins, in his *History of Dorset* (third edition, vol. ii, p. 820), records a long and very interesting account given by Smeaton, the great engineer, in his *History of the Eddy-stone Light-house,* of the courtship and marriage customs prevalent amongst the native quarrymen of the Isle of Portland. From this I give the following particulars.

Owing to their having been bred up to hard labour, and possessing a very robust physique, they are very early in a condition to marry and provide for a family. They intermarry with one another, and rarely go to the mainland for a wife; and it has been the custom of the island from time immemorial that they never marry until the woman is pregnant. The mode of courtship is that a young woman never admits the serious addresses of a young man but on the basis of a thorough probation. When she becomes with child it is then considered the proper time to be married, which then almost invariably takes place. If she should not prove with child "after a competent time of courtship" they separate, concluding that they are not destined by Providence for each other, it being an established maxim strictly observed by Portland women not to allow a plurality of lovers at one time. The result is that the separation takes place, and a subsequent similar courtship may follow without any more aspersion upon the woman's honour than if she had been a widow or had remained a maid.

There was only one instance recorded in the registers of a bastard having been born within the last 150 years.

Smeaton relates that at the time of the stone being quarried for the purposes of his light-house several of the London workmen formed similar connections with Portland women, perhaps not realizing what was expected of them in certain eventualities. Upon some of them declining to assume this responsibility the Portland women arose to stone them out of the island, with the result that only one case of bastardy occurred. Since which time things have gone on according to ancient custom.[1]

So much with regard to the Portlanders. But I have heard that this custom is, or was, not altogether unknown in the western parts of Dorsetshire and in the adjoining county of Devon, where it is considered a gross breach of a man's honour to refuse to marry a woman with whom he has been " keeping company " and has caused to become *enceinte*.

The prevalence of this custom in other parts of the county, too, is clearly indicated by Mr. Thomas Hardy in his book on *Two on a Tower* (vol. i, p. 223), where one of his rustic characters delivered himself in this wise with reference to his young wife to whom he had been recently married.

" But 'tis wearing work to hold out against the custom of the country, and the woman wanting ye to stand by her and save her from unborn shame ; so since common usage would have it, I let myself be carried away by opinion, and I took her."

I think we may not unreasonably believe that those parts of the country where such a custom is a living force are not the least moral sections of our rural populations.

(ii) Mr. Wilkinson Sherren, although he makes no mention of the above courtship custom of the Portland quarrymen in his account of them in his *Wessex of Romance*, makes the following remarks upon their wedding customs (p. 85) :

" The nuptials of a quarrier used to be an affair of some pomp and circumstance, peculiarized by now obsolete customs. An anvil from the nearest blacksmith's shop was placed on the line of route, and the hollow of it charged with gunpowder and fired as the bridal party went by. The rear of the procession was

[1] This custom as obtaining amongst Portlanders is noticed by Brand (ii, 20) as a betrothing custom somewhat akin to that of " hand-fasting ", or " hand-festing ", which, he says, prevailed amongst the ancient Danes, and is still retained, I believe, in some parts of Scotland.

brought up by several quarriers carrying guns, which were discharged at intervals as a *feu de joie*. On his reappearance in the quarry the bridegroom was subjected to a curious method of extortion; the handles of a tool similar to a large pair of shears were squeezed round his neck till he cried 'Beer'; and then all the gang retired to the nearest tavern, to drink a 'randy[1] quart' at the young husband's expense."

[1] Merry-making.

CHAPTER VI

WITCHCRAFT AND CHARMS

SIMILARLY to the preceding chapter the subject matter of this one is now reproduced from a paper on " Witchcraft in Dorset ", which I contributed to the *Proceedings* of the Dorset Field Club in 1892 (vol. xiii, p. 35), together with such additional matter as I have been able to gather up since that time.

There is no part of England, I suppose, more prone to belief in the supernatural—or perhaps I might say generally more superstitious—than the West; and, of the Western counties, none more so than Dorsetshire. That this is attributable to the fact that the West of England is largely agricultural, and even pastoral, in its character, entailing in consequence a comparatively sparse population, may not be unlikely; for there is no doubt that in the more strictly agricultural and rural districts of England people were allowed—at all events until recent times—to grow up to a great degree in a state of ignorance, and were deprived of the advantages which the neighbourhood of towns usually confers by means of education and the fuller exchange of ideas and opinions, advantages hitherto practically monopolized by their fellows of the artisan class. Of all forms of superstitious belief none was more firmly impressed upon the minds of the country people than the belief of witchcraft, that is, in the existence of a malefic influence possessed by certain individuals (generally old women, though male witches, or wizards, were not uncommon) over the person and property of those with whom they might be brought in contact.

That country folk generally should be imbued with this belief is not astonishing, when it is considered that in some form or other a belief in witchcraft was indulged in in olden times by all classes, from the king on the throne and the judge on the bench to the humblest peasant who was called to give evidence. Learned treatises have been written on the subject, and witchcraft has been accorded the dignity of a State trial.[1]

[1] See the report of Hathaway's trial in the *State Trials*.

Trials for witchcraft were by no means uncommon, and if search were only made amongst the quarter sessions records of the seventeenth century in the custody of the *Custos Rotulorum* of this county, and amongst the records of judicial proceedings at the county assizes during that period, numerous presentments by juries, depositions by witnesses, and indictments upon which these trials were held would no doubt be found to exist. I would like in particular to refer to a paper relating to certain proceedings taken upon a trial for sorcery and witchcraft during the period I have mentioned from the pen of the late Mr. J. C. Mansel-Pleydell, the first President of the Dorset Natural History and Antiquarian Field Club, in vol. v (p. 1) of its *Proceedings*, and also to an account of a trial for witchcraft in this county which appears in Warne's *Ancient Dorset*, p. 158. Interesting matter upon this subject may also be found in Roberts's *History of Social Life in the Southern Counties* (1856).

Orders were sometimes made by the judges at the assizes directing the magistrates to make inquiries into suspected or notorious cases of witchcraft, and to commit the parties for trial at the assizes if necessary. For the following note of such an order I am indebted to a correspondent of the *Somerset and Dorset Notes and Queries*, vol. i, p. 225. It was an order to inquire into a case of alleged witchcraft at Sherborne in 1660, made by the judges then on the western circuit at the Dorset Summer Assizes held at Dorchester on the 10th September, 1660,[1] and was in the following terms :—

" It is ordered by this Court that Sr. John ffitz James, knight, Robert Coke Esqre., Thomas Moore Esqre., Walter ffoy Esqre., and Winston Churchill Esq., ffive of ye justices of ye peace of this county or any two of them doe take care, That the business concerninge the witchcraft and consultation with the devill and evill spiritts in Sherborne in this county bee with all speede examined, (and any) concerned in ye said business bee by them or any two of them bound to the good behaviour. And to appeare att the next Assizes and Gen^{r}all Gaole deliv^{r}y to bee holden for this county to answere ye same. And that they alsoe binde over As aforesaid such p'sons of those as by them

[1] It will be noticed from this date how unusually late the summer assizes were held in this year ; the reason being in all probability that suggested by the above correspondent, namely, the train of festivities following upon the Restoration.

are to be nowe examined as they shall thinke fitt. And alsoe such p^r^sons to p^r^secute against them as they shall alsoe thinke (fit) and certifie their said Examinations and Informations att the Assizes."

Such trials sometimes ended disastrously for the witches; and executions were not uncommon in olden times.

Sometimes, however, the courts were satisfied by the accused or suspected persons merely finding security for their future good behaviour, as the following extract from the *Somerset and Dorset Notes and Queries* (vol. ii, p. 62), relating to Gillingham Manor Court, will show:—

"2° Elizabeth, Maij 7, Lib'i Decenne. Decinnar' ibm ven't & p'sent q'd qued'm Cecilia Lambert vid' inhi'tans inf' Decenn' p'd est mulier male fame & gravit' suspect' de incantand' Et i'o p'cept Cecilie ad prox' cur' inferre duos sufficient' manucaptor' p' bona gesta ipsius Cecilie sub pen' exilij de hoc man'io."

It is interesting to find from this extract that exclusive jurisdiction in such matters was not reserved for the assize courts or the justices of the peace, but was sometimes given—at all events in Queen Elizabeth's time—to the local manor courts; though it will be observed that such jurisdiction was apparently confined to taking security for good behaviour, on pain of banishment from the manor—this alternative, however, being no slight penalty.

It has always been a marvel to me on reading the accounts of some of these old trials how many of these poor accused persons could ever have been brought, as was not infrequently the case, to plead guilty—that is, to admit having committed an offence of which, we all know, it was impossible they ever really could have been guilty. Human nature, however, I suppose, is the same all the world over (even with witches), and women were found ready to face the consequences of such an admission in an age when our penal code was a disgrace to our civilization, in return apparently for the notoriety that a confession of being a "familiar" of, or on terms of intimacy with, his Satanic Majesty would bring, and the additional fear, if not respect, inspired amongst the neighbours by such a confirmation of their powers and the consequently enhanced value of their "charms" and "spells".

Sometimes, however, such an imputation would appear to have been strenuously resisted ; and it is refreshing to find that in one case, at least, a certificate has been forthcoming from the inhabitants of the neighbourhood testifying to the innocence of the accused or suspected person. Mr. E. A. Fry, in *Somerset and Dorset Notes and Queries*, vol. v, p. 308 (1897),[1] sets out a certificate in full subscribed by numerous inhabitants of South Perrott, Stoke Abbott and other neighbouring parishes, that one Johane Guppie, of South Perrott, Dorset, was not a practitioner of " enchantments, sorcerye, or witch crafte ". The original document, which is dated in or about the year 1607, is in the Miscellanea of the Exchequer, $\frac{17}{5}$.

The above instances indeed refer to a period when the belief in, and the practice of, witchcraft were rampant ; but I think it will be seen from the material which I have gathered together in this chapter that even at the close of the nineteenth century in the county of Dorset the belief in witchcraft still eked out a flickering existence, in spite of school boards—those great enemies to folk-lore—whose chilling influence bids fair, I am afraid, to cause our children not only to lose faith in everything their fore-elders have ever taught them, but eventually to believe in nothing at all !

In the term " witchcraft " I include " charms "—which I deal with in a separate section—and which may be considered either as the means furnished by witches to bring about the object desired by their believers, or as the weapons by which the baneful influence of the witches themselves against those who fancy they are the subjects of it is sought to be avoided. Or, again, charms may be used generally as a protection against evil ; as an insurer of good luck ; as a preventive of or cure for disease or illness, in which case they might come under the head of " folk-medicine " ; or, lastly, may be unconnected with witchcraft altogether, and adopted as a means to obtain a desired end.

The general form in which expression was given to the belief that persons were subject to the evil influence of some individual who was exerting that influence to work an injury to them or

[1] Taken from the *Antiquary* of July, 1897, p. 215.

their property, was that they were "overlooked".[1] It was not only the witches proper or "wise women", or the wizards or "cunning men", who were believed capable of "overlooking" people or animals. Sometimes an unusually ill-tempered, shrewish, or for any reason particularly obnoxious old woman (whose faults would ordinarily have been expiated by the application of the "ducking stool" or the "brank"—the usual cures for a "scold") would be credited with such a power; a belief often encouraged by the poor creature as a means of protection against molestation and the petty persecution of village children, who were restrained by the fear of what might be the result of drawing her resentment directly upon themselves.

In the new *Handbook of Folk-lore*, edited by Miss C. S. Burne for the Folk-Lore Society in 1913, she impresses upon collectors of British folk-lore that the belief known as the "Evil Eye" is not a matter of art, magic, or witchcraft, but a supposed natural power inherent in certain persons, whether voluntarily or involuntarily exerted, and that they must be careful not to confuse "overlooking" and "blinking", however intentionally and maliciously done, with "ill-wishing", "cursing", "bewitching", or "putting a spell on" a person or thing, which are feats of witchcraft.

In Dorsetshire, however, it would seem that it is with this former significance that the term witchcraft is mainly used, and it is a form to which the county—and, indeed, the West of England generally—is particularly prone, as the following instances will show. The first one is taken from certain correspondence in the *Times* and *Standard* some years ago, and reproduced, if I remember rightly, in the *Dorset County Chronicle*, by which it would appear that a man of about 50 years of age applied for relief to the guardians of the Shaftesbury Union on the ground that he was unable to work. The doctor had seen him and was unable to specify any cause, though he said he was certainly incapable of labour. He himself stated the cause to be that he had been "overlooked" by his sister-in-law. His wife had been to a "wise woman" at Stalbridge, a neighbouring village, who had relieved him for a few days, but since then the spell had been

[1] For an interesting paper by Mr. Hermann Lea upon this form of witchcraft, see *Memorials of Old Dorset* (1907), pp. 292–305.

too mighty and he was as bad as ever. He declined medical aid as useless. The afflicted man was a native of Gillingham, where there was a school board and every appliance of education, yet that was not enough to eradicate this most ancient of superstitions, as firmly believed in as ever.

This story was supplemented by a correspondent living at Gillingham, who stated that in his parish the power of the "wise woman" extended over man and beast. He mentioned a case wherein an old woman with a very bad temper and tongue was supposed to be in league with the "wise woman" of Stalbridge. She was about buying some pigs from a neighbour, but there was a difference between them of a shilling a head, and when she could not get her way she said she would have nothing to do with them, and added the ominous words: "And mark my words, they will never thrive with you." Curiously enough, in about a fortnight they all died and this cross old dame had the credit of their death, and she was dreaded accordingly by her neighbours both far and near, for she was very dangerous to her own species.

The narrator of this story added that in the previous year this old woman had been very ill, but in a dream one night she saw a supposed ill-wisher of hers laughing at her through the window, and she sent to another "wise woman", who removed the illness from herself to her enemy, "which was, of course, very satisfactory for her but not for him."

Another instance is taken from the *Bridport News* in the year 1884, which further supplies the means by which the cure of the "overlooked" was effected in that case. The wife of a woodman living in one of the parishes of Dorchester had been seriously ill for a considerable time. She had been waited on by a gipsy woman, who told her she had been "overlooked". The gipsy informed her that she would never recover until the spell had been broken, which she bargained to do for a small sum of money. This was readily acceded to by the credulous invalid, whom the Romany ordered, among other things, to place certain pot-flowers out of doors, and when the flowers withered she would begin to mend. The instructions were implicitly followed, and the woman, strange to say, recovered pretty nearly as the gipsy had predicted. She stated positively that the flowers withered soon afterwards, and that coincident to this her recovery commenced.

It was generally believed that the most effectual way of neutralizing, or of removing, the baneful influence exerted by the witch, or other person who was supposed to be overlooking the sufferer, was to draw blood from the "overlooker". That this cure or remedy bears the imprint of some antiquity may be seen from Shakespeare's play of *Henry VI*, wherein (Act I, Scene V) Talbot says to Joan la Pucelle :—

"Blood will I draw on thee ; thou art a witch."

Again, later, Butler, in his *Hudibras* (Part II, canto 1), treats of the same subject.

The following account, taken from a Surrey newspaper, in which a correspondent in *Notes and Queries* (Ser. v, xi, 66) refers to what he calls a remarkable case of superstition in Dorsetshire, bears upon this point. It appeared that in a cottage in the village of East Knighton there dwelt a woman named Kerley and her daughter, a girl of about eighteen ; and the latter was supposed to be bewitched and to be the subject of the strangest manifestations. It was positively declared that articles had been thrown out of the cottage into the street, although neither window nor door was open, and these were stated to have been sent flying in all directions. An old women named Burt was set down as the cause of all the mischief, and she was declared to have assumed the form of a hare, to have been chased by the neighbours, and then to have sat up and looked defiantly at them. It was positively believed that until blood was drawn from the witch the manifestations would not cease.

It is believed that a witch often takes the form of a hare and haunts the downs and hills at night-time, being only visible at the dead of night, and that nothing will take effect upon her but a silver bullet.[1]

Mr. R. L. Bartlett, in a letter to the *Bridport News* in May, 1891, gives an instance of this from the Isle of Purbeck. He says :

[1] See *The Haunted Hare*, one of the *Songs of Dorset*, contained in a collection of poems called *The Olden and Modern Times*, by the Rev. W. Smith Marriott, published in 1855, and referred to in Chapter XI, p. 330.

" With regard to the 'silver bullet', I was born and lived the first fourteen years of my life in the Isle of Purbeck, and can well remember at Ulwell seeing my father miss a hare, though he had two shots at her. The manservant with whom I was walking immediately decided that the hare was a witch, and could not be killed unless the charge was rammed down with a *sixpence*."

The Rev. Osmond Fisher, of Cambridge, in a letter in January, 1893, sends me another story of this superstition from Purbeck. He says :—

" A labourer in the Isle of Purbeck had noticed a hare which he encountered several times at a certain stile in the evening as he was going home. A friend advised him to put a sixpence in a gun and shoot it, so he went to a shop (in Wareham ?) and borrowed a gun, and shot at the hare the next time he met it, and as it limped away he threw his sickle after it and struck it, but could not catch it. When he got home a neighbour said to him : 'Old Nanny's a-dying, and wants to see thee.' 'Shure ! do she now ?' 'Ees, and she's got a cut all across her back as if some one had cut it with a rip-hook (reaping-hook).' "

And Mr. Fisher relates a story that once upon a time the harriers in the Vale of Blackmore lost the hare. The huntsman coming to an old woman's cottage said to the man, " You just hold my horse, I want to go in there." When he came out he said : " Ah ! I knowed how it were. There she sits by the fire pantin', mud up to her knees."

Some interesting observations upon the " disappearing hare " were made by Mr. E. A. Rawlence in a paper on " Folk-lore Reminiscences " in vol. xxxvii, p. 60, of the Dorset Field Club *Proceedings* (1916).

The following instances show that Dorset folk were not slow even in the last quarter of the nineteenth century, to avail themselves of the remedy for " over-looking " here suggested when once they got the opportunity. The Rev. R. F. Meredith, rector of Halstock, writing to the *Times* in June, 1883, says :—

" There is no need to go to West Prussia for witchcraft towards the end of the nineteenth century. In a parish where the counties of Devon, Dorset, and Somerset meet, a young man, being afflicted with scrofula which caused at times contraction of the muscles of the right thigh and very considerable pain, formed the idea that a poor delicate woman living next door, wife of a labourer and mother of several children, had bewitched him, and one day in his agony rushed into her house with a large sewing needle, and before the woman had time to think, scratched her severely in the neck and in four places on her bare arm, drawing blood in each instance, then rubbed his hand on the blood, and ran off. The poor woman came to me to complain, showing the scratches, and I advised her to take out a summons before the justice, but time passed. The young man, as usual, felt relieved of his pains for a time, and his mother, a widow occupying a few acres of land with cows and pigs, tried to assure me that drawing the blood cured her son, for she considered the other woman had overlooked him."

Another case which came before the Sherborne magistrates is taken from the *Western Antiquary* (which did not, by the by, often deal with Dorset subjects) for December, 1884, p. 143, and from a similar account in the *Folk-lore Journal* for 1884, p. 349, from which it would appear that at Sherborne on the 19th September, 1884, an old woman named Sarah Smith, who lived in Cold Harbour, and was 83 years of age and in receipt of parish relief, was violently attacked by a next-door neighbour, one Tamar Humphries, a married woman, in order that the latter might draw blood from the old woman, on the ground that she had bewitched her daughter, a confirmed invalid, suffering from rheumatism. It appeared from the report that the poor old woman, who was well known as a quiet inoffensive person, was in her garden digging potatoes, when she was set upon by the defendant, who put her hands on her shoulders and said: "Oh! you Sal Smith, what's thee done to my daughter? I'll draw the blood of thee." The defendant then repeatedly stabbed her with a darning- or stocking-needle about her hands and arms, making them bleed, telling her at the same time that she was a witch and that she would draw her blood for "witching" her daughter.

The next instance is a West Dorset case, reported in the *Dorset County Chronicle* in July, 1887, in which a working man conceived the idea that certain mishaps which had recently occurred to him were the result of supernatural agency employed by his next-door neighbour, a quiet inoffensive woman, who felt the utmost indignation at the charge. Her accuser, however, was not to be pacified, but with a reap-hook in hand was about to take what he considered to be effectual means to "break the spell" when the interference of a third person prevented him from carrying out his design.

Readers of the *Wessex Novels* will scarcely need to be reminded of the vivid description of this cruel practice given in Thomas Hardy's *Return of the Native* (vol. ii, p. 95), where Susan Nunsuch attacks Eustacia Vye with the object of "drawing" her blood, and pricks or stabs her with a "long stocking-needle" under the delusion that this wayward and ill-fated young woman had bewitched her children. An additional interest is afforded in this case—unlike the others which I have mentioned—from the fact that this gross outrage took place in church, the deluded woman, no doubt, believing that a fuller success would attend her "charm" if the supposed witch could but be met with attending divine service.

It was not always, however, considered necessary to resort to such drastic treatment in order to break the witch's spell, as we may learn from a comparatively recent case of "overlooking" reported in the *Dorset County Chronicle* in December, 1913, as having occurred near Dorchester—"within a few paces of the picturesque thatched house at Higher Bockhampton (Upper Mellstock), wherein Mr. Thomas Hardy was born"—in which a man, who had complained of the illness of his two daughters from some obscure disease, was informed by a "white witch" that they and his family had been "overlooked by five evilly disposed women"; and had declared that "unless the whole family, bag and baggage, and chattels were out of the house and 'over the hills and far away' by half-past five on the following Saturday afternoon the two girls would die, and moreover the parents would catch the mysterious malady and like wise mëake a die o't." It appeared that shortly before this time some extraordinary things had also been experienced by the father, so that no delay occurred in making the required move; and, an empty cottage at Broadmayne having been requisitioned, the whole family left for their new home. They arrived before their furniture, and whilst waiting the father said to the daughter who had been taken ill first: "You must go into the next room now." And, says the report, "she was able to get up and walk into the room as well as any of the others. The spell was broken, and the girls both made a good recovery, as sudden as their ailing had been."

Another of the milder methods of counteracting a witch's evil designs comes from Purbeck, namely, by driving a nail through the centre of her foot-print on the ground—that is, if you can find it—for a witch is generally supposed to have the power of walking through any kind of soil without leaving any trace behind.

It would appear from the following account sent by a correspondent, on the authority of a Dorsetshire clergyman, to *Notes and Queries* (Ser. IV, xi, 341) that the power of the person supposed to be overlooking another did not always cease with the death of the overlooker, but that something further was required before the evil influence could be said to have entirely departed. An under-gardener in a gentleman's service did not appear one morning at his usual time; it turned out that he had been sitting up with a dying man who he believed had bewitched him, in order that the moment the man died he might set his foot on his neck, and so break the spell.

The foregoing cases are instances where the "overlooking" already existed, and where means were sought to "break the spell"; but frequently steps were taken in order to prevent the approach or advent of the evil. For this purpose the use of "charms", such as the nailing up of a horseshoe and various other means, were adopted, presumably with more or less success. There were certain physical obstacles, too, which sometimes were supposed to stand in the witch's way; for instance, a witch was always considered to be hindered in working her spell if a stream of water should happen to exist between her and her victim.

The late Mr. J. C. Mansel-Pleydell, in his above-mentioned paper on "Sorcery and Witchcraft" (*ante*, p. 202), mentions one of these means of prevention, or "supposed remedy for dispossessing a bewitched person". He says:—

"A pig's heart, stuffed as full of bright, new pins as possible, is hung up in the chimney, sufficiently high to escape the chance of being consumed summarily by the flames and to be gradually dried up; when the last pin has dropped out the witch is supposed to have no further hold on her victim."

There does not seem to be, so far as I can gather, any idea

existing amongst Dorset folk as to witches being in the habit of meeting together for the purpose of working their spells, or other evil designs in common—*e.g.* somewhat after the manner related of their fellow-witches in Scotland (*Conf.* Shakespeare's *Macbeth* and Burns's *Tam o' Shanter*). The only reference of the kind relating to Dorsetshire that I can find is a statement made by the late William Barnes[1] that many years ago he was told by a man of the neighbourhood of Leigh Common that a corner of the common was called " Witches' Corner ", and that, long again after that, a friend gave him some old depositions on witchcraft taken before Somersetshire magistrates from about the year 1650 to 1664. The cases were of Somersetshire, and touched in some points Dorsetshire, and one of the witches' sisterhood said that they sometimes met on Leigh Common. This proof of the meeting of the witches on Leigh Common as the ground of the traditional name of Witches' Corner is interesting, Mr. Barnes remarks, " as a token of truth in tradition."

I wonder if these were the depositions to which he referred in his " Fore-say " to this book, when he says: " From an old deposition on witchcraft in Dorset we find that at some meetings which the witches held at night on a common they made a waxen man-shape and christened it (christened it, forsooth!) with the name of some unhappy man who was to be bewitched—and thereafter he was bewitched—and his likeness was to be pricked with pins, which would give him the pangs of thorns in his flesh; or his waxen other self was to be holden before a fire, so that at the melting of it he himself would pine away; and we find in the answer of the witch of Horace, Canidia (*Canidiæ Responsio*, Epodon xvii) that she was wont to use the same like wicked mystery with waxen statuary."

Roberts, in his *History of Lyme Regis* (p. 261), writing nearly a century ago, says that:—

" Of superstitious belief in witches and evil spirits there still appear some traces. Our vessels and many houses have an old horse-shoe nailed up. No one now likes to own a belief in evil spirits or witches, but considers it would be a pity to receive harm from neglecting so easy a precaution. In some chimneys a piece of bacon, stuck with pins, used to be suspended to interrupt

[1] See Dorset Field Club's *Proceedings*, vol. iv, p. 156.

witches in their descent, and so prevent their visit. Toads that gained access to a cellar or house were ejected with the greatest care, and no injury was offered, because these were regarded, as being used as *familiars* by witches, with veneration or awe."

An interesting illustration of that to which Mr. Roberts alludes occurred some forty years ago in the parish of Hawkchurch, West Dorset, an account of which appeared in the *Bridport News* in March, 1884. A new tenant had recently entered into possession of a house in the village which had just been vacated, when it was necessary to displace what was thought to be a lodgment in one of the chimneys. The obstruction was got out, and was found to be neither brick nor stone, but a bullock's heart, into which was stuck a quantity of the prickles of the white thorn, some nails, pins, and other things. This bullock's heart, in exactly the same state in which it was removed from the chimney of the cottage at Hawkchurch, is now, or was, in the Literary Institute at Bridport, and was exhibited at the meeting of the Dorset Field Club at that town in July, 1889, when I myself saw it. It presented a very dry, shrivelled, and almost mummified appearance, evidently having been in the smoke for many years. A correspondent suggested that as the late occupant was a bachelor, possibly he might have used the "charm" to ward off the attacks of the ladies and to prevent "witches" from getting access to the house by means of the chimney! This correspondent is undoubtedly right in conjecturing that the obstacle in the chimney was intended to act as a charm, for a bullock's heart so placed was always considered by superstitious Dorset folk to be the most effective way of keeping witches or fairies out of a house, as it was by the chimney they were generally supposed to effect an entrance. More especially is the charm to be depended upon if the animal's heart (as in this case) be previously studded with prickles of thorns, nails, or pins, in the same way as Mr. Roberts mentioned with regard to pieces of bacon used for the similar purpose. In order to make the charm more efficacious, "maiden" thorns should be used; that is, thorns that have been grown the same year in which they were picked.

The same paper in April, 1901, mentions a similar case as occurring at Shipton Gorge, which carries the belief in such practices in West Dorset up to the beginning of the present century. It says:—

"A week or two ago the son of Mr. Fowler, sweep, of Bridport, while sweeping a chimney in one of the cottages in Shipton came upon a curious relic of past days. He had reason to go up the chimney, and about eight or ten feet from the ground he found an old canvas bag, hanging or fixed in a cranny of the wall, and inside this was discovered, wrapped in paper, a hard and dried bullock's heart, stuck through and through with thorns and pins. This is the fourth heart of the kind found in chimneys in the neighbourhood within the last few years. This was one of the charms against the witch's spell in days gone by, and was hung in the chimney with the idea that the pins and thorns added torment to the witch and broke her spell."

The late Mr. Bosworth Smith, in his *Bird Life and Bird Lore* (1909), p. 366, spoke of the belief in the "evil eye", and in the bewitching of cattle and persons, as still lingering on in Bingham's Melcombe and the surrounding villages. And he mentioned the practice of sticking pins into a bullock's or other animal's heart as still followed in that neighbourhood. But in the instance he there gave of this having been carried out only a year or two before, the "charm" would seem to have been used rather as a remedy or cure for the bewitching or overlooking than as a preventive against the spell being cast. In this case the heart, "bestuck with pins till it bristled all over with them", was set before a fire; and then "as it begins to glow and frizzle the power of the witch or wizard gradually diminishes, and when at last it burst with the heat the spell is broken and the witchcraft over."

Much in the same way, and for the same reasons, that the South African native tribesman, the supposed victim of sorcery, would set in motion the "witch-doctor" of his villages; or of the West African negro, either at home or in those more civilized countries (*e.g.* the West Indies) to which slavery has consigned him, would invoke the assistance of the "obeah-man"[1] for the protection of himself, his cattle, or his crops, so the Dorsetshire

[1] I do not include in this the darker forms of so-called witchcraft which culminated in the hideous orgies of the cult of "Voodooism", as it existed in Hayti and other places. See my paper on "Obeah in the West Indies", in *Folk-Lore*, vol. xxvi, p. 255 (1915).

peasant—and sometimes his master—stealthily consults the "wise-woman" or "cunning-man" of the neighbourhood whenever he imagines either himself or his property to be under the malefic influence of the "evil eye".

These "wise women" and "cunning men"[1] have at times attained considerable notoriety for their imaginary powers and the supposed efficacy of their spells or charms; and superstitious persons from far and near were drawn to them for the purchase of their charms or the benefit of their advice; often to the no small hurt, I am afraid, of His Majesty's liege subjects, and to the no small gain of these unscrupulous charlatans. Mr. Rawlence refers to a "wise woman" he had heard of, always picking her herbs at midnight on a full moon as they were more potent then. He also speaks of this woman as standing in front of a trap with a sick patient in it, and making great flourishes in the air with a willow wand, probably exorcizing some demon. "But," he adds, "after all it will be seen that the real cures come from the herb remedies, and that suggestions about an evil eye and flourishing the wand are only adjuncts to play on the ignorance of her patients."[2]

The spells by which the "overlooking" was attempted to be carried out took various forms. Mr. Rawlence, in a later volume the of same *Proceedings*, xxxvii, p. 59 (1916), gives a long account of one that was "worked" upon a farmer in a village near Sherborne by means of a bottle filled with evil-smelling contents that was discovered buried underneath a dead apple tree on the farm, and he relates the steps that were taken, on the advice of a "wise woman", to successfully counteract its ill effects.

Men of this class were often called "white witches". From the correspondence in connection with the case that came before the Guardians of the Shaftesbury Union already alluded to. it appeared that not long since a "cunning man" used to hold an annual levée in the neighbourhood of Stalbridge, when he sold out to crowds that thronged round him the legs torn from the bodies of living toads and placed in a bag which was worn round

[1] "Cunnèn man: (A–S. *cunnan*, to know) A cunning man, or wizard. A man to whom is imputed supernatural knowledge, and of whom folk inquire after lost goods." (Barnes's *Glossary*, 1863.)

[2] Dorset Field Club *Proceedings*, vol. xxxv, p. 87 (1914).

the neck of a patient, and counted a sovereign remedy for scrofula and the " overlooked ". It was called " Toad Fair ". Mr. Rawlence, at p. 85 of his earlier paper, speaks of one John Buckland, who lived about fifty years ago at a house in King Stag, just north of the Blackmore Vale Dairy. He was known as " Dr. Buckland ", and he held what was known as a " twoad vair ", which took place at the change of the moon in the month of May, and was for the cure of persons affected with the king's evil, running or tubercular wounds. He says :—

" Dr. Buckland collected a large number of toads, and the affected person had to open his or her clothing on to their bare chest. The doctor then seized a toad, cut off its head, and popped the writhing body into a muslin bag, which was dropped down the chest of the patient and suspended round his neck. If the patient endured the shock of the cold toad and the ' scrablen ' of its legs in its death throes, he would be healed ; but if he ' turned '—i.e. became faint or nauseated under the experience, he would die."

For an account of a similar individual who lived at Lydlinch and had a great reputation, see the *Life of William Barnes* (p. 155), by his daughter, Mrs. Baxter, published in 1887.

Roberts, in his *History of Lyme Regis*, speaks of one who lived at West Leigh, on the Tiverton and Wellington Canal, to whom persons who either had lost property, had been charged with theft, or had had very ill luck would go from Lyme Regis, a distance of 30 miles, for the purpose of consulting this famous " white witch ".

It was hardly to be supposed that William Barnes in those charming pictures he has given us of Dorset rustic life would omit all reference to witchcraft ; so we find that in one of his dialect poems he treats in a delightfully humorous way of a dozen different forms of bewitching or overlooking which may befall, in person or estate, any peasant or his employer who may have been so unfortunate as to incur the displeasure of such a " sly wold witch " as he there depicts. At the same time he mentions two of the most widely recognized " charms " for the prevention or cure of the spell.

I take the following lines from " A Witch " (p. 173) of the complete edition :—

'An' zoo, they soon began to vind
That she'd agone an' left behind
Her evil wish that had such pow'r,
That she did meäke their milk an' eäle turn zour,
An' addle all the aggs their vowls did lay;
They coulden vetch the butter in the churn,
An' all the cheese begun to turn
All back ageän to curds an' whey;
The little pigs, a-runnèn wi' the zow,
Did zicken, zomehow, nobody know'd how,
An' vall, an' turn their snouts toward the sky,
An' only gie woone little grunt, an' die.
An' all the little ducks an' chicken
Wer death-struck out in yard a-pickèn
Their bits o' food, an' vell upon their head,
An' flapp'd their little wings an' drapp'd down dead.
They coulden fat the calves, they woulden thrive;
They coulden seäve their lambs alive;
Their sheep were all a-coath'd,[1] or gied noo wool;
The horses vell away to skin an' bwones,
An' got so weak they coulden pull
A half a peck o' stwones.
The dog got dead-alive and drowsy,
The cat vell zick an' woulden mousy;
An' every time the vo'k went up to bed,
They wer a-hag-rod till they wer half dead.
They us'd to keep her out o' house, 'tis true,
A-naïlen up at door a hosses shoe;
An' I've a-heärd the farmer's wife did try
To dawk [2] a needle or a pin
In drough her wold, hard, wither'd skin,
An' draw her blood, a-comèn by;
But she could never vetch a drap,
For pins would ply [3] an' needless snap
Ageän her skin; an' that in coo'se
Did meäke the hag bewitch em woo'se."

It will be seen that I have not included the art or practice of fortune-telling—common in Dorsetshire as in other counties—as one coming within the purview of witchcraft, though, doubtless, many so-called "witches" derived no inconsiderable portion of their unholy gains from such a source. This source was mostly restricted to the more ignorant girls of the servant or peasant class, though sometimes their more educated sisters were not averse from their palms being "crossed with silver" by some wandering gipsy. The firmer application of the wholesome laws relating to "rogues and vagabonds" has had a salutary effect,

[1] A disease of the liver to which sheep are particularly subject in wet seasons or in ill-drained pastures.

[2] Prick.

[3] Bend.

and practically the Romany forms the only professional class of fortune-teller now existing.

More recently, however, there would seem to have been a revival of this practice amongst persons of a higher social sphere, who think, and apparently with some reason, that so long as they cross their foolish victims' palms with *gold* they are absolved from the penalties of the law!

In the various instances of this practice which have reached me from a Dorset source—all alike sordid in the desire to obtain gain from the ignorant and the credulous—I have failed to find any trace of that more wholesome, if equally superstitious, form of "fortune-telling rhymes", which at one time obtained amongst their northern ancestors. This form partook more of an amusement or a game, where the sybil was selected from the company present or provided from elsewhere; and whose duties were carried out duly screened from observation within some enclosed portion of the room whence the oracle could only hear, not see, the proposer of the question that was put to her. Both question and answer had to be made in verse—based on the old Scandinavian Runic rhymes—and the question might be made personally, or vicariously by any one else holding the hand of the person desiring it to be put. This survival has been most graphically described in Sir Walter Scott's novel of *The Pirate* (vol. ii, chapter i, of the "Border Edition"), where in the old Udaller's hospitable home in Zetland "Norna of the Fitful Head" gave such startling answers to her questioners.

Charms

I now come to that branch of my subject which though at times strongly savouring of witchcraft cannot be said to be necessarily a part of or connected with it, viz. "charms". Those charms which are more particularly connected with witchcraft, and which may be distinguished as "spells", I have already dealt with. The remaining ones may be divided into two broad classes: (i) those which relate to the prevention of, or cure, for disease or illness, which may be considered as appertaining to "folk-medicine"; (ii) those miscellaneous and various charms which are adopted for the purpose of realizing a particular object, or bringing about a particular event.

The late William Barnes in his " Fore-say " to this book, says : " Charms or spells have seemingly always been a share of the folklore of Dorset, as of all England. A charm (Saxon : ' cyrm ') is by its first meaning a mingled sound of voices of men or birds, and in folklore it seems to mean a form of muttered words ; and a spell was a form of words and then also a message,—whence Godspel—Go'spel, the good message. A telegram is indeed a wire spell, and a telegraph a spellwire."

The following charms I have noted down from time to time as appertaining to Dorsetshire, though doubtless in several cases not to Dorsetshire alone.[1]

Toothache (i) Go to a young oak tree ; cut a slip (slit) in the tree ; cut off a bit of your hair and put it under the rind ; put your hand to the tree, and say to the tree : " This I bequeath to the oak tree. In the name of the Father, and of the Son, and of the Holy Ghost. Amen."[2]

Another way of executing this charm is given by Mr. Rawlence at p. 83 of vol. xxxv of *Proceedings* of the Dorset Field Club (1914).

(ii) The following somewhat cynical " sort of negative cure ", Mr. Rawlence obtained from North Dorset (*ibid*., p. 84) :—

" Get an honest lawyer's pocket handkerchief ;
Wash it in an honest miller's millpond ;
Dry and iron it with an honest tailor's goose.
If you can do that you will never have the toothache again."

(iii) Peter and Paul sat on a marble stone ;
Jesus came to them alone.
" Peter," said he, " what makes you so quake ? "
" Why, Lord and Master, it is the toothache."
" Whoever will carry these words for my sake
Shall never be troubled with the toothache."[3]

(iv) As Peter sat on a stone weeping, our Saviour came to the Mount of Olives and said : " How is it here, Peter ? " Peter answered and said : " My Lord and my God, grievously tormented with the pain of the tooth." Our Saviour said unto Peter : " Arise, Peter, and be made whole. Whosoever believeth

[1] *Conf.* Napier's *Folk Lore of West o Scotland* (1879), chap. vi (" Charms and Counter Charms "), wherein several of those common to Dorsetshire are mentioned.

[2] Conf. *Notes and Queries*, Ser. v, viii, 143, 275.

[3] For a similar one at Crewkerne, co. Somerset, see *N. & Q.*, Ser. v, viii, 275. Conf. *Denham Tracts*, vol. ii, p. 10.

on me and keepeth these words in memory or in writing shall never be troubled with the pain of the tooth. In the name of the Father, and of the Son, and of the Holy Ghost. Amen."

A rather shorter and somewhat varied form of this charm is given by Mr. Rawlence (*ibid.*, p. 84), wherein he states that in order to make the charm effectual a lady must write it for a gentleman, and a gentleman for a lady, and the party receiving it must not say " Thank you " for it.

(v) Double or twin nuts are sometimes carried in the pocket as a specific against toothache.

Nose-bleeding.—Mr. Rawlence (*ibid.*, p. 82) gives the following charm to be said in order to stop bleeding at the nose :—

" Let the blood stand still as the waters did in the river Jordan. In the name of the Father, and of the Son, and of the Holy Ghost. Amen."

Shingles.—" Verdigrease from the pump is an excellent cure for shingles " (*ibid.*, p. 83).

To stop a Snake.—Repeat the words : " Let God arise, and let his enemies be scattered."

The same effect is also produced by repeating the following verse from the Psalms : " They are as venomous as the poison of a serpent ; even as a deaf adder that stoppeth her ears, and refuseth to hear the voice of the charmer, charm he never so wisely."

Snake bite.—In the case of a bite from an adder (or presumably any other poisonous snake), the fat taken from the one that has caused the injury is considered the best cure for it.

Boils.—Creep under a bramble three mornings following against the sun at sunrise.[1]

Warts.—Barnes, in his " Fore-say " says : " A very common work of charming in Dorset is that of charming away of warts, which we must believe is an easy one for so mighty a form of magical might ; but it is sometimes tried on very bad, if not deadly, ailings in cattle."

(i) Steal a piece of beef, rub the wart with it, and throw it over your shoulder, or bury it ; and as the meat rots, so will the wart disappear.

[1] See Chapter VII, p. 255, *s.v.* Bramble.

Of this Mr. Rawlence (*ibid.*, p. 84) gives a variant of this from a South Dorset source: "Steal something (*e.g.* a pea, a bean, or piece of meat) and rub it on the wart, then throw it over the left shoulder and bury it, and tell no one."

(ii) Go to a sloe-bush unseen, bite off part of a growing sloe, leaving the portion with the stone in it still on the bush; rub the wart with the part bitten off, and throw it over your head or shoulder.

Another, also from North Dorset, is given by Mr. Rawlence, (*ibid.*, p. 84).

(iii) Take a small stick and cut on it as many notches as you have warts, then put it in the ground, and as it rots the warts will disappear.

(iv) The following charm for warts was given by Mr. Edmund Gosse in *Longman's Magazine* for March, 1889, having been found amongst some unpublished papers of his father, the late Philip H. Gosse, F.R.S., depicting the latter's childhood at school in Poole in the early part of the nineteenth century:—

"I was told to rub the wart with a bit of cheese, which was then to be buried secretly, and I was then assured that as the cheese decayed so would the wart. I followed the directions implicitly, and the wart did disappear totally within a few days, with no further process; but how much of the result was owing to the magic I dare not say."

Worms.—Barnes, in his "Fore-say" (*ante*), gives the translation of what he calls a very old charm of our race—a charm against a worm—from the old Saxon, and which may well have been at one time known to Wessex folk:—

"Go out, worm,
With bad little worms;
Out from the marrow
To the bone;
From the bone
To the flesh;
Out from the flesh
To the hide;
Out from the hide (or skin)
To this arrow.
O Lord, be it so."

A Stye.—Cross the "stye" three times with a wedding-ring, which must be of gold to be efficacious."[1]

[1] Conf. *Notes and Queries*, Ser. v, viii, 181. Also Jones's *Finger-Ring Lore*.

Sore eyes.—Water from a spring which rises facing due east is said to be a cure for sore eyes, especially if the water be taken at the moment the sun's rays first light upon it. A spring rising in a field at Symondsbury Farm, near Bridport, has this reputation. It certainly is most delicious water to drink, and is possibly impregnated with iron, which may account for its real or supposed efficacy.[1]

Jaundice.—The late Canon Bingham wrote (under the initials C. W. B.) as follows to *Notes and Queries* in 1854 (Ser. I, x, 321) :—

" I scarcely know whether ears polite will tolerate the record of a sovereign remedy for jaundice which fell under my notice in a parish in Dorsetshire a few weeks since, but which I find upon inquiry to be generally known and practised in the neighbourhood. The patient is made to eat nine lice upon a piece of bread and butter. In the case referred to, I am bound to state for the credit of the parish, that the animalcules were somewhat difficult of attainment ; but that, after having been duly collected by the indefatigable labours of the village doctress, they were administered with the most perfect success."

Quinsy.—A band of silk worn round the neck was said by a correspondent in *Folk-Lore,* vol. viii, p. 387 (1897), to have been used by a gentleman in Dorsetshire as a preventive against quinsy, who also mentioned that it had been similarly used by another gentleman in Shropshire.

Rupture.—" It was believed that if a young maiden ash (*i.e.* not polled) were split and a ruptured child drawn through it he would become healed." [2] The proper process is for the patient to be passed nine times through the cleft, and the cleft should be bound up again in order that the divided parts may grow.[3]

It is stated in *Folk-Lore,* vol. xix, p. 88—wherein illustrations of this are given—that in the Taunton Museum are preserved two specimens of young ash trees (which I have myself seen) split for the purpose of passing children suffering from congenital hernia through, one having been used within the last twenty years.

[1] See Chapter IV, *s.v.* Symondsbury.

[2] Barnes's *Glossary* (1863), *s.v.* " Maïden-tree ", wherein the author states that he has known of two such trees through which children have been so drawn. See Chapter VII, p. 252, *s.v.* " Ash tree ".

[3] Conf. *Shropshire Folk-lore,* p. 196.

Epilepsy.—Roberts, in his *History of Lyme Regis*, p. 261, states that in April, 1826, a respectable looking woman was engaged in collecting a penny from each of thirty young women, unmarried, the money to be laid out in purchasing a silver ring, to cure her son of epileptic fits. The money was to be freely given, without any consideration, or else the charm would have been destroyed.

Mr. G. W. Floyer, writing to the *Dorset County Chronicle* (*c.* 1882), gives the following version of the same charm as prevailing in the Isle of Purbeck. He says it is customary for a young man to collect thirty pennies from the maidens of his acquaintance, or in the case of a maiden from the bachelors of her acquaintance, to change them for half-a-crown out of the money presented in the offertory, then to have the coin beaten out and made into a ring. The ring is then worn as a trustworthy charm against epilepsy.[1]

To prevent forgetfulness of deceased's husband or lover.—For this I am indebted to Mr. T. Hardy's collection of short stories in *A Changed Man* (1913), in one of which a young and buxom widow thus expresses herself (p. 392) :—

"I've pulled grass from my husband's grave to cure it—wove the blades into true lovers' knots ; took off my shoes upon the sod—"

"Upon the sod—why ? "

"To feel the damp earth he's in, and make the sense of it enter my soul—"

To recover lost memory.—From the evidence in a case of assault before the county bench at Dorchester involving suggestions of witchcraft, and reported in the *Dorset County Chronicle* in January, 1918, it appeared that one of the parties had been in the habit of wearing a piece of black worsted round her thumb as a charm with a view to the recovery of her lost memory.

Fits.—Mr. Floyer also states that at a certain village in Purbeck a mother came to the clergyman to ask if he would have any objection to her daughter's stealing a cup from him ! She had been told that pounded crockery, which had been taken

[1] Conf. *Shropshire Folk-lore*, p. 192, where twelve such pennies are exchanged for a shilling from the offertory alms.

unawares from a minister and taken internally, was a sure cure for fits.

The late Rev. O. Pickard-Cambridge, F.R.S., of Bloxham Rectory, near Wareham, informed me that a woman once begged him to let her have a little drop of consecrated wine to be administered to her ailing baby. She seemed to think it quite a natural request to make.

Consumption.—The sufferer must go to a sheepfold sufficiently early in the morning to see the sun rise and the sheep leave the fold. An old lady in West Dorset told me of the case of a young lady of Beaminster, who, nearly a century ago, had to walk a mile and a half in order to do this. Whether the task was rendered any easier by the circumstance that the shepherd attending the sheep was a young man—the farmer's son—can only be conjectured; but the fact remains that the young lady eventually recovered her health, though the shepherd died a young man.

Cramp.—It is considered a preventive against cramp to put your shoes in the form of a T on going to bed.[1]

Headache.—It is believed that a snake skin worn in the hat or bonnet is a remedy for headache.

Bronchitis or Whooping-cough.—(1) Take nine hairs from the "cross" or back or a white she-ass; sew them in a silken case or bag, and wear them round the neck. A correspondent tells me that this remedy was tried some forty years ago in a Dorset town, when a journey of more than a dozen miles had to be taken to find the desired kind of animal.

(ii) When the patient is a child the following alternative was sometimes used. Pass the sufferer under the body of a donkey, and then over its back, three times. In order to avoid taking cold these rites were generally performed indoors, the animal having been brought into the house for the purpose.

Mr. R. Bosworth Smith, in *Bird Life and Bird Lore* (1909), p. 367, says that "whooping-cough in a child is best cured by putting the sufferer on a donkey with the face towards the tail, and the figure of the Cross does the rest".

Mr. Rawlence also gives several instances of the observance of

[1] Conf. *Shropshire Folk-lore*, p. 191.

this superstition in the Dorset Field Club *Proceedings* for 1916 (vol. xxxvii, p. 58).

(iii) Sometimes the child would be passed nine times under and over an arched or double-rooted briar.[1]

Troublesome Infants.—A correspondent of *Notes and Queries* (Ser. IV, 406, 457), says that in the centre of Dorsetshire it appears to be commonly believed that a dose of hare's brains is an excellent soporific for troublesome infants. And he gives an instance of this in which a woman, having recently had the misfortune to become the mother of twins, had consulted his wife as to the desirability of a dose of hare's brains. On the lady's husband mentioning this circumstance to his keeper in the hope of soliciting some information as to the prevalence of the belief, he was informed that shortly before the wife of the keeper on the adjoining manor, who had been recently confined, had called at his house and had told his wife that she had been down to the squire's house to beg a hare's head from the cook, in order to give the brains to her baby as a sedative.

This superstition is said to be equally common in Devonshire, where sometimes calves' brains are given instead, or even a bit of the flesh beneath the lobe of the ear of a sucking-pig.

From another correspondent in the same periodical,[2] it would appear that sometimes a dose of *rabbits'* brains was used for the same purpose. He states that a poor woman of Lyme Regis, whose child was very restless and fractious, had consulted an old woman of the town as to what she ought to do. The old woman assured her that the child would never be well until he had eaten the brains of a rabbit; whereupon a rabbit was purchased and the brains were gravely stuffed down the child's throat.

It is often supposed that in these cases the fractiousness of the child is owing to the mother, who has longed for something she could not have before the child's birth, which longing is indicated by these symptoms. As a lady correspondent put it: "Some wee infants are seen almost continually moving their mouths or tongues as if wanting *something*; it is usually something the

[1] Conf. *Shropshire Folk-lore*, p. 195. Also see Chapter VII, p. 255, *s.v.* Bramble.

[2] *Notes and Queries*, Ser. VI, xi, 306.

mother was very fond of, or wished for, and could not get (and she gave an instance of it within her own experience). If no one could guess *what* the child was longing for the nurses said that the *next* best thing was ' hare's brains '." [1]

Quarter-evil in calves.—In order to prevent this disease you must be sure to commence rearing the calves by hand on the same day of the week as Old Christmas Day falls upon.[2]

" Good Friday Bread," properly made and " stood " for a year, was a great specific for this disease. A portion of the bread was crumbled, mixed with cider, and given as a drench.[3]

Loo, or looer in cows.—A disease that breaks out just above the hoof. Mr. Rawlence, in the Dorset Field Club's *Proceedings* for 1916 (vol. xxxvii, p. 64) gives a cure for this which he obtained from Pulham in 1905. He says :—

" Find the cow where she is resting early on a dewy morning. Turn her up, and mark carefully the spot where she places the diseased foot at the third step. Then cut out the sod and place it upside down in a white thorn bush, and as the sod dries up and dies so the ' looer ' will dry up and heal."

Abortion in cows.—In the same volume, p. 62, Mr. Rawlence mentions the use of a " maiden " ash tree as a charm against abortion in cows. He says :—

" Some years since, in going over a farm—I think it was at Holwell—I observed a calf that had been prematurely born placed high up in the fork of an ash bush in the hedge. I asked the farmer what led him to place it there, and elicited the information that if the dead calf was placed in the fork of a " maiden " ash (i.e. an ash tree grown direct from the seed) and with its head towards the east, that it would prevent other cows in the herd from casting their calves. On further inquiry I gather from the late Mr. J. J. Young, of Pinford, that when he was a boy the custom was quite common in the neighbourhood of Glanvilles Wootton. Also I heard of a farmer in the neighbourhood of Wincanton who was a great believer in this specific ; and if a cow was observed to have been afflicted in this way all his men had to turn out and walk the farm until the *fœtus* had been discovered and duly placed in the ash tree."

[1] See Chapter VII, p. 234, *s.v.* Hare.

[2] See Chapter VII, p. 233.

[3] See *Somerset and Dorset Notes and Queries*, vol. ix, p. 113.

Mr. Rawlence added some further interesting observations on the subject from a more general point of view.

The above charms against diseases in cattle came more especially from the Blackmore Vale country.

Apropos of the same subject, Mr. J. J. Foster sends to *Folk-Lore*, vol. xxviii, p. 451 (1917), the following note :—

" I have often read and heard of the old superstition that a goat turned in with the cows that are in calf would prevent them from slipping the calf ; and I actually saw this in a field—a goat running with a lot of calves—and was told this was the usual practice to ward off the evil eye."

Rheumatism in pigs.—Mr. Rawlence (p. 64) also mentions the following cure for rheumatism and lung trouble in pigs. He says :

" — is a great pig-breeder, and at times some of his pigs got crippled with rheumatism. He told me that the way to cure this was to cut off the tips of their tails. He said that ' it made a tar'ble mess as they bled zo '. I suggested cauterizing the tips to stop bleeding, but he replied, ' Bless 'ee, 'tis the bleedin' that does the good, as it dräas the blood away from their heads.'

" He also told me that when a pig had anything the matter with its lungs the best way to cure it was to open its mouth and make four gashes in its throat. ' A pig al'as zwallers everything and never allows it to come out of its mouth ag'in, so that the blood gets down into its lungs and cures 'em.' He could not tell me why four gashes were necessary, but was very firm that it must be four."

King's evil.—It is believed that a seventh son can cure diseases, but that a seventh son of a seventh son can cure the "king's evil".

The power of a seventh son in such matters was generally recognized by superstitious folk. Roberts, in his *History of Lyme Regis* (p. 261), speaking of this subject, states that once when at a farmhouse near Lyme Regis in 1828 engaged in taking a view, though the other children about him were made to stand off, one little urchin was allowed to lay hold of his pencils, etc. On his remarking to his mother upon this deference shown to the child, she replied, " He's a seventh son, sir," and added that " she did think, to cure all diseases, should be the seventh son of a seventh son, but many folks do come to touch my son."

" Touching for the king's evil " was a very prevalent practice in bygone days.

Bed charm. "Matthew, Mark, Luke, an' John,
Be blest the bed that I lie on.
Vow'r corners to my bed,
Vow'r angels all a-spread,
Woone at head, an' woone at veet,
An' two to keep my soul asleep." [1]

Butter-making.—If you want always to have a cool hand for making butter, have a young puppy, cut it open, and put your hand and arm in whilst the animal is still warm.

To find a drowned corpse.—The following account was sent to *Notes and Queries* (Ser. v, ix, 111) by the Rev. Canon Mayo :—

"On January 24th, 1872, a boy named Harris fell into the stream at Sherborne, Dorsetshire, near Darkhole Mill, and was drowned. The body not having been found for some days the following expedient was adopted to discover its whereabouts. On January 30th a four-pound loaf of best flour was procured, and a small piece cut out of the side of it, forming a cavity, into which a little quicksilver was poured. The piece was then replaced and tied firmly in its original position. The loaf thus prepared was then thrown into the river at the spot where the body fell in, and was expected to float down the stream until it came to the place where the body had lodged, when it would begin to eddy round and round, thus indicating the sought-for spot. An eye-witness of this experiment, from whom I received this account a few days after it happened, told me that no satisfactory result occurred on this occasion.[2]

To test love and friendship.—If two persons be desirous of testing their love or friendship for one another, a key is secured between the pages of a Bible, being carefully placed at the passage in the first chapter of the Book of Ruth, v. 16, commencing "Whither thou goest", etc. The book is then held up by the bow of the key on the fore-finger of their right hands, and the person whose love or friendship is the subject of the test repeats the above verse. If the Bible turns (as it generally does) it is considered a favourable augury for the continuation of the affection or friendship.

Sometimes this species of divination is carried out in the absence of the subject of the test, when the inquirer obtains the

[1] There are many variants of this rhyme. The above is from Barnes's *Glossary*, 1863, *s.v.* Charm.

[2] For a very recent account of a successful experiment carried out on these lines at Wheelock Brook, Sandback, Cheshire, see the *Evening Standard of* 7th January, 1921

assistance of some third person to hold the book. The turning over then takes place, when the name of the person inquired about is mentioned.[1]

The charms, or means of divination, practised by rustic maidens in order to test the sincerity of their sweethearts, such as throwing apple pips into the fire, scattering hemp seed, and placing their shoes in the form of a T on Midsummer and Christmas Eve are well known and are referred to elsewhere.

To treble money.—The following account, taken from a London paper, appeared in the *Dorset County Chronicle* in 1882 :—[2]

" On the 23rd December a dairyman left home for a market held in the neighbourhood of Bridport, his wife remaining in charge of the dairy. On returning home he found his wife agitated and apparently unwell. She simply complained of slight indisposition, which continued till the following Saturday. During the morning the dairyman went to his cash box, which was kept in a bedroom, and at once missed between £3 and £4. The wife was at first reticent on the matter, but ultimately confessed that a couple of women (strangers) had promised her, during his absence on the previous Saturday, that for a few shillings they would convert any amount of gold to treble its value by Easter Sunday next, provided they were allowed to trace the planets upon the coins and then secrete them about the premises ; but on no account were they to be touched before Easter Sunday, or the planets would be unpropitious and visit the house with affliction. The dairyman, in spite of these protestations, forced from his wife the knowledge that the money was hanging in the chimney. He there found a semi-smoked heart, evidently that of a pig or sheep. It was tightly encased in wrappings of scarlet and black material. A number of crosses and other emblems formed of projecting pins covered it completely on one side. On opening it, the cavity of the heart was found to contain several farthings, which had been brightened by some rough substance. It is believed the strangers were travelling gypsies, but at any rate they have absconded the richer by several pounds."

To keep witches out of a house.—The charm of a bullock's heart studded with thorns and pins is described *ante*, p. 213. Also in order to prevent them from dancing over dough whilst

[1] Conf. *Shropshire Folk-lore*, p. 174. Also Napier's *Folk Lore of West of Scotland* (1879), p. 106.

[2] See also a similar account in *Folk-Lore Journal* for October, 1883.

left overnight to ferment, it was customary to mark a cross on it.[1]

So a cross drawn on the malt before mashing up for brewing kept it from being bewitched.

Scriptural riddle or charm.—In *Folk-Lore* (vol. xvi, p. 98) (1905), a correspondent at Leweston, near Lyme Regis, gives the following lines, which appear as a riddle in Miss Salmon's *Folklore of the Kennet Valley*, as told to him as a charm by an old Dorset woman now dead. She did not know why it was supposed to be called a charm.

(*Judas Iscariot*) " *J. I.* and *P. P.* (*Pontius Pilate*)
They both did agree
To put to death J. C. (*Jesus Christ*)
Which they could not do without the will of G. (*God*).

(*Mother Mary*) " M. M. and M. V. (*Mary the Virgin*)
Wept with horror and grief to see
The malice and wickedness of P. P." (*Pontius Pilate*).

To prevent fishing-boats from being bewitched. — I think I cannot conclude this chapter better than by giving an extract from a very interesting article by the late Dr. H. Colley March, F.S.A., on " Witched Fishing Boats in Dorset " in *Somerset and Dorset Notes and Queries*, vol. x, pp. 49–50 (1906). He said :—

" In considering cases of witchcraft it is necessary to bear in mind certain fundamental distinctions that, in these days, are apt to be confused. Disease, such as epilepsy or fever, results from the sick person being possessed by an evil spirit. Evil spirits also produce storms, mishaps, and bad luck. Witches or wizards are able, to some extent, to direct the action of evil spirits, so as to injure this or that person. Wise men and wise women know methods of counteracting this maleficence. The witch can be discovered and destroyed. The unclean spirit can be exorcised, or his course hindered or arrested. Hudibras speaks of those who

'Chase evil spirits away by dint
Of cickle, horse-shoe, hollow flint.'—II, iii, 291–2.

" The sickle is a sharp cutting implement, which like the open knife fastened in a bible, was avoided by evil spirits. The earliest horse-shoe was a closed circle, and, like other ringed enclosures, offered a resistance to the passage of evil spirits.

" The practice which I am about to relate was followed by

[1] *Somerset and Dorset Notes and Queries* (1904), vol. ix, 113.

the Abbotsbury fishermen, of whom my gardener's father, still living, was one. I mentioned it to the late H. J. Moule, Curator of the Dorset County Museum, and he told me what at my request he reduced to writing, thus :—

" 'Well within my remembrance—I think in the forties, certainly in the late thirties—it was not uncommon for row-boats at Weymouth to have ' holy stones ' tied to nails or staples in the bows, close beneath the gunwale. I once saw a man in the act of doing this at the quayside. Holy stones were beach-pebbles with a natural hole through them, such as are not uncommon among the shingle. Whether holy from having a hole through them, or from being sacred, or both, I know not.'

" At Abbotsbury the fishing boats do not carry a sail. The bows differ from the stern only in being a little sharper. The boat is drawn up on the beach stern first by a rope called the start-rope, which is fastened into the lower part of the stern-post, and then the end of this rope used to be threaded through a beach-holed-stone to keep away the witches, that is, to keep any evil spirit, whether under the direction of a witch or not, from getting aboard the boat. The net, when dry, is folded up and placed in the stern-hatch, a compartment open above but closed from the rest of the boat at the stern thwart.

(Dr. March also contributes a sketch of such a boat.)

" Sometimes a boat, manned by its owners, is unable to catch fish. There may be fish about in plenty, and neighbouring boats may get hundreds, but this particular boat gets none. Then it was known that this boat was ' witched ', that is, that an evil spirit had got on board, because the holed beach-pebble had not been placed, or not properly placed, or not placed soon enough, on the start-rope. Then, to dispel the bewitchment, a mackerel stuck with pins was placed in the stern-hatch. The sharp points, like the ' cickle ', or the open knife, oppose a resistance to the evil one.

" It is customary, in the same neighbourhood, to attach to the key of a house a holed beach-stone, for luck. I have heard no story connecting this practice with witches, but the association is obvious. And it is impossible not to see a like motive for the ancient practice of dragging a sick or epileptic child through a hole in a large ' druidical ' stone, or through a prickly bramble, gorse, or goose-berry bush. The child would be pulled through, but the evil spirit could not follow; it would be filtered out and left behind . . . ."

CHAPTER VII

SUPERSTITIONS RELATING TO NATURAL HISTORY

In a paper which I contributed to the Dorset Field Club's *Proceedings* in 1889 (vol. x, pp. 19–46) I gave a list or glossary of the local or dialect names of the common objects of natural history that we see around us, such as animals, birds, insects, plants, etc., to which I added an account of any superstitions from a Dorset source that might be known to bear reference to them.

For the purposes of this chapter I propose to take those superstitions from their setting, together with such additions as I have made since that time, and to deal with them as merely local superstitions attaching to natural history objects, summarized under these four sub-divisions: (i) animal-lore; (ii) bird-lore; (iii) insect and reptile-lore; (iv) plant-lore.

I. Animal-lore

(i) *Ass* (*Nirrup*).—The domestic ass or donkey is usually ashen colour, with a black cross over the shoulders, formed by a longitudinal and a transverse dark streak. These three stripes are said to denote the three strokes given by Balaam to his ass. Others as devoutly believe that these marks have reference to our Saviour having ridden into Jerusalem upon an ass.

Nine hairs from the "cross" or back of a white she-ass, sewn in a silken case or bag and worn round the neck, are said to be a specific for bronchitis or for whooping-cough. The sufferer should, further, be passed under the body of the animal, and then over its back, three times.[1]

(ii) *Bullock.*—A bullock's heart placed in a chimney is considered to be the most effectual way of keeping witches, or fairies, out of a house, as it is by the chimney that they are generally supposed to effect an entrance. More especially is the charm to be depended upon if the animal's heart be previously studded with prickles of thorn, nails, or pins. "Maiden" thorns

[1] See article on "Wessex Witches" in *Nineteenth Century Review* for June, 1903, by Herman Lea.

(*i.e.* those which have grown the same year in which they are picked) are generally sought after for this purpose.

Some years ago upon a house at Hawkchurch, in West Dorset, being vacated by its tenant an obstruction was found in one of the chimneys, which, on being removed, was found to consist of a bullock's heart, into which was stuck a quantity of the prickles of the white-thorn, some nails, pins, and other things. The object of the obstruction was considered to have been to prevent the access of witches to the house by means of the chimney.[1]

(iii) *Calf.*—If you wish to prevent quarter-evil in calves you must be sure to begin the rearing of them by hand on the same day of the week as Old Christmas Day falls upon.

Their ears should also be slit at Eastertide in order to prevent them falling into ditches.

The female calf of a twin, of which the other is a bull (billy), is called a "freemartèn". It is always said to be barren. (See note in Barnes's *Glossary* (1863), *s.v.* "Freemartèn" as to this.)

(iv) *Cat.*—A cat that is born in May is said to bring snakes into the house.

If you want your cat to be a good "mouser" you should get some one to *give* you one; a cat that is *bought* is never good for much.

A cat should never be allowed to sleep in or on a child's bed, as it is believed that it will kill it by sucking its breath. In some parts it is said that the baby will suck the cat's hairs, and so be choked.

It is generally believed that a young woman who nurses a cat on her knee will never be married, and that the girls who are fond of cats will die old maids.[2]

(v) *Cattle.*—If cattle during wet and miserable weather are seen feeding at the top of a hill it is considered a sign that the weather will soon clear up. This I have not infrequently verified myself.

(vi) *Colt.*—It is generally believed that colts born in May have

[1] See Chapter VI, p. 213.

[2] Conf. *Shropshire Folk-lore*, p. 212.

an awkward trick of lying down in water as you ride through upon them.

(vii) *Cow.*—In the dairy districts the presence of a new-comer amongst the milkers is generally believed to account for a cow " keeping back " her usual yield of milk. It is commonly said to have gone up into its horns ; when the only cure is for the milkers to break out into a song by way of inducement to the animal to resume its normal career of usefulness.[1]

(viii) *Dog.*—The howling of a dog by night, or before the house door, is looked upon as an omen or sign of death.

Dorsetshire being an agricultural, and particularly a dairy-farming county, perhaps the following somewhat repulsive recipe or charm for a cool hand in butter-making may be of special interest to some : Take a young dog or puppy, cut it open, and put your hand and arm inside whilst the animal is still warm.[2]

(ix) *Donkey* (*Nirrup*), see *Ass.*

(x) *Hare.*—Two correspondents of *Notes and Queries* (Ser. VI, iv, 406, 457) give evidence from a Dorset source of the belief in the efficacy of a dose of hares' brains as a means of soothing troublesome infants, or to satisfy their " longings " when the special thing for which they crave cannot be guessed.[3]

It is a common belief that an old witch often takes the form of a hare, and haunts the downs and hills at night, being only visible at the dead of night, and that nothing will take effect against her but a silver bullet.[4]

The Rev. Canon Fletcher, in *Notes and Queries* (Ser XI, viii, 346) (1913), speaks of the old prejudice—widely spread, too, he says, throughout the county at the present day—against the use of the flesh of a hare for human food. It arises, apparently, from the well-known superstition that witches change themselves into the form of hares.

[1] See Hardy's *Tess of the D'Urbervilles*, vol. i, p. 217.

[2] See Chapter VI, p. 228.

[3] See Chapter VI, p. 225.

[4] See " The Haunted Hare "—one of the " Songs of Dorset "—contained in a collection of poems called *The Olden and Modern Times*, by the Rev. W. Smith Marriott, published in 1855. See also Chapter XI, p. 330.

(xi) *Horse.*—The belief that the character and quality of a horse can be gauged by the number of white legs, or " stockings ", he possesses is too widely spread for me ever to imagine that the following is even confined to Dorsetshire.

" If you have a horse with *four* white legs,
Keep him not a day ;
If you have a horse with *three* white legs,
Send him far away ;
If you have a horse with *two* white legs,
Sell him to a friend ;
If you have a horse with *one* white leg,
Keep him to the end."

The efficacy of a horse's shoe nailed on to or over the door of a stable or dwelling-house, or even a vessel in affording protection against evil (*e.g.* witchcraft) or in insuring good luck is very commonly believed in by Dorset as by most other folk.

To pick up a " cast " horseshoe is considered an omen of good luck in most counties ; but some Dorset folk require more than this, for, as an old gardener once said, " 'Tisn't every shoe that is lucky ; 'tis only the vu'st (first) shoe that the colt or hoss do drow (throw) after his vu'st shoeing that be the lucky one."

(xii) *Mouse* (*Mouel*).—See *Shrew-mouse.*

(xiii) *Pig* (*Mallock*).—You should never eat pigs' brains or, as some say, pigs' marrow, as it makes you tell all you know.

Some people are very particular as to the time or phase of the moon when their pigs are slaughtered for market, as it is believed that if they are killed during the waxing of the moon the carcases will gain in weight, but that the reverse will be the case if it be done when the moon is waning.[1]

In *Somerset and Dorset Notes and Queries* (vol. iii, p. 29) (1892), in referring to a statement in the Rev. W. D. Parish's *Dictionary of Sussex Dialect,* p. 57, that the six little holes on the inside of each of the knuckles of a pig's foreleg represent the marks of the devil's fingers (or claws) when these animals entered into the herd of swine as told in the Gospel narrative, Canon Mayo says that the same superstition with respect to them is current in Long Burton, near Sherborne.

(xiv) *Rabbit.*—The same efficacy attributed to a dose of hares' brains in soothing a troublesome infant is, we learn from a

[1] Conf. *Shropshire Folk-lore,* p. 258.

correspondent in *Notes and Queries* (Ser VI, xi, 306) (1885), to be derived from those of a rabbit. He mentions the case of a poor woman of Lyme Regis, whose child was very restless and fractious, who had consulted an old woman of the town as to what she ought to do. The old woman assured her that the child would never be well until it had eaten the brains of a rabbit; whereupon a rabbit was purchased, and the brains were gravely stuffed down the child's throat.[1]

(xv) *Shrew-mouse* (*Shrow-crop*).—Barnes, in speaking of this little animal, has the following note in his *Glossary* (1863), p. 38: "The folklore of Dorset is that if it run over a man's foot, it will make him lame. Thence, in Hampshire, it is called the 'Overrunner'."[2] Again, in the later edition of the *Glossary*, published in 1886, p. 99, *s.v.* "Shrocrop" (*sic*), he says: "It may not seem clear what a shrew-mouse has in common with a woman shrew. The shrew-mouse gives a shrill shreaking (*sic*) sound, and I believe the shrew is so-called from her shrill shreaking (*sic*) voice in scolding."

This superstition is further alluded to in one of Barnes's dialect poems called *A lot o' maïdens a-runnèn the vields* (p. 458):

"What's that, a mouse?"
"O no,
Teäke ceäre, why 'tis a shrow!
Be sure don't let en come
An' run athirt your shoe;
He'll meäke your voot so numb
That you won't veel a tooe."

It is commonly believed that field-mice (*mouels*) occasionally possess a fine voice, and warble during their nightly visits to the house. This is, however, of rare occurrence, and is considered a lucky omen.

(xvi) *Weasel*.—The smallest of the weasel kind, says Barnes in his *Glossary* (1863), p. 96, is called a "veäre". This, I take to be the same as the old Norman-French word "vair"—the name of one of the heraldic "furs"—the word there representing the fur of a species of squirrel, much used for lining cloaks and mantles according to the sumptuary laws of olden times.[3]

[1] See Chapter VI, p. 225.

[2] See *Folk-Lore*, vol. xix, p. 88.

[3] See Woodward's *Heraldry: British and Foreign*, 1896, vol. i, p. 70.

In West Dorset, however, it would seem that the origin of the dialect word has been misunderstood, for there it is called "veäry"; and it is believed that you can never succeed in catching or shooting a weasel, because it at once changes into a fairy and becomes invisible. But that, apparently, does not prevent it from being *trapped*, as so many barn and stable-doors in that part of the county amply testify.

II. Bird-lore

Mr. Bosworth Smith, in his *Bird Life and Bird Lore* (1909), p. 29, is of opinion that "folk-lore connected with four-footed animals is, unfortunately, fast dying out in civilized and Christianized countries; but it is otherwise, for pretty obvious reasons, with birds, in whose case, in out of the way districts at least, it is still hale and vigorous. Legends still cluster round all the favourite or remarkable birds; the cuckoo, the woodpecker, the magpie, the raven, the nightingale, the robin, the wren. And folk-lore has, of course, not least to say about the owl".

It is not surprising, therefore, that in Dorsetshire where there are so many "out of the way districts" still permitted to remain as such, I have been able with the exception of the nightingale—a bird, I believe, unknown to the county—to collect something with reference to each of the birds mentioned by Mr. Bosworth Smith, and many besides.

(i) *Bird.*—With reference to birds generally it may be said that if any bird, more particularly a robin, should come into a house it is looked upon as on omen of death, a sign that some one in that house will shortly die.

A bird tapping at the window is also a very ominous sign.

It is commonly noticed that immediately before a thunderstorm birds will cease their singing and seek shelter.[1]

(ii) *Cock.*—A cock crowing at the door is a sign of a coming visitor.

If a cock crows in the afternoon, according to some it foretells a death in the family; or, as others say, it signifies that sickness in the place will shortly follow. An old Dorset woman once said: "If the cock crows after twelve o'clock noon her is

[1] See Chapter VIII, p. 270.

doing it to bring I bad news, or John may be bad agëan. I can't a-bear to hear en."

The crowing of a cock by night is often fancied to precede, or foretell, the death of a person. On the recent death of a dairyman's daughter in a country parish in West Dorset, at the funeral repast which followed an elderly relative remarked: "There, I could tell I was going to hear of something 'cause our cocks crowed so in the night."

The late crowing of a cock (*e.g.* on his perch) also portends wet weather, as the following distich shows:—

"If a cock goes a-crowèn to bed,
He'll certainly rise wi' a watery head." [1]

As to the ill omen attaching to an "afternoon crow" see Thomas Hardy's *Tess of the D'Urbervilles*, vol. ii. pp. 174–5.

(iii) *Cuckoo*: pr. *Goo-koo* (*Gawky*).—It is commonly believed that whatever you happen to be doing when you first hear the cuckoo you will be mostly doing during the year. It is also important when and where you hear it; for if it is heard after Old Midsummer Day, or you happen to be in a churchyard, you won't live the year out.

That Midsummer is an unusually late period to hear the cuckoo we may gather from the following lines which were repeated by an old woman who has recently died in the village of Symondsbury in West Dorset, aged nearly 90:—

"Cuckoo is here (heard ?) in April,
Cuckoo is here (?) in May,
Cuckoo here (?) on Midsummer's Eve
But not on Midsummer's Day."

With this we may compare a local variant of the better-known rhyme:—

"In April
He comes;
In May
He sings all day;
In June
He changes his tune;
In July
He prepares to fly;
In August
Go he must."

It is firmly believed by old country people that cuckoos do not migrate but change into hawks, and so pass the winter here.

[1] See Chapter VIII, p. 271.

(iv) *Duck* (*Homble*).—It is a subject of common belief that ducks hatched out in May are more liable to sprawl than those hatched at any other time of the year.

(v) *Goose.*—It is generally believed that if geese are seen to fly uphill it forecasts fine weather. If they fly down hill the reverse may be expected.[1]

(vi) *Hen.*—It is considered unlucky to set a hen upon an *even* number of eggs. I have been told that it used to be considered in Dorsetshire that the proper way of " setting a hen " was to put its head under its right wing and swing it round till it fell asleep before putting it on the eggs.

Upon this subject I some time ago received the following note from the late Rev. W. K. Kendall, Vicar of East Lulworth, to whom I am indebted for several interesting items of folk-lore :—

" In setting eggs under a broody hen the country people believe it best to set it under an uneven number, as 9, 11, 15 etc., and many also are careful to set them during the increase of the moon. These fancies are as old as Columella, who says (viii, 5) : '*Numerus ovorum quæ subjiciuntur impar observatur nec semper idem . . . Semper autem cum supponuntur ova considerari debet, ut lunâ crescente a decimâ usque ad quintam decimam id fiat.*' "

It is to be observed that in Columella's time (early part of first century of Christian era) it was not sufficient that the moon should be merely waxing ; it must have been nearly full. I am not aware that that restriction obtains in Dorsetshire, either in the setting of hens or with regard to the similar superstition attaching to the slaughter of pigs (*q.v. ante*, p. 235).

A hen that crows is not considered to be of much value. The following couplet is common :—

" A whistling woman and a crowing hen
Are neither good for God nor men."

(vii) *Magpie.*—The belief that the appearance of the magpie, according as it is seen alone or accompanied by others of its species, has an influence on the course of human events is common to many counties or countries. The form of the jingle expressing that belief best known to me in Dorsetshire is the following :—

[1] See Chapter VIII, p. 271.

"*One*, sign of anger;
Two, sign of mirth;
Three, sign of wedding;
Four, sign of birth" (or, sometimes, "death").

And some will add:

"*Five*, heaven; *six*, hell;
Seven, the de'il's ain sell."

The last line savours too strongly, I fancy, of a Scottish accent to please Wessex ears.

A very close variant of this, but excluding "death", is adopted by Mr. R. Bosworth Smith in his before mentioned book (p. 316), and in speaking of it he says: "Happily, a magpie is seldom seen by himself; . . . The parent birds are never, except by the merest accident, out of sight of each other. It you wait a minute or two, therefore, it is generally easy to turn your sorrow into mirth; and if not you can at least do something to avert or mitigate the evil consequences." What these remedies are varies in most counties. In Dorsetshire some persons will spit on seeing a single magpie; whilst an old-fashioned labourer would respectfully raise his hat. Others, again, will return home after commencing a journey at the untoward appearance.

Another variant, which I have received from West Dorset runs:

"One for sorrow;
Two for mirth; (or joy)
Three for a wedding;
Four for a birth; (or boy)
Five for silver;
Six for gold;
Seven for secrets
Never to be told.'

It is believed in some parts of Dorsetshire that if a magpie should happen to remain all day over, or about, a man at work in a ploughed field, the man will be sure to die.

The magpie's power to imitate the human voice is strongly believed in; and though not as capable in this respect as the parrot, yet many can pick up words or even sentences. It was always believed that a magpie, or a jackdaw, would do this more easily if his tongue were slit; but Mr. Bosworth Smith tells us (p. 328) that "the old superstition that she will only talk, or talk well, if her tongue is slit with a thin and sharp silver sixpence died a natural death about the time that the coins of the realm had to be 'milled', and thus were rendered unsuitable for so stupidly cruel an operation".

(viii) *Martin.*—It is considered very lucky if martins, or swallows, should build under the eaves of your house. But it is equally unlucky to take their eggs or destroy their nests.[1]

(ix) *Owl.*—As with the magpie, so with the various types of owl, Mr. Bosworth Smith has many interesting remarks to make,[2] remarks which are as applicable to Dorsetshire—a county in which he had derived his earliest experiences of these birds—as to the numerous other parts of England in which the owl is happily still be be found. He says (p. 52):—

"The cries of the different species of owls differ much from each other, but they are always weird, sonorous, solemn; and they have always been regarded by the most diverse races and from the earliest times as the harbingers of disaster or death."

In speaking of the commonest species of owl—the white or barn owl—he says (p. 16) that he

"Screeches, snaps, snorts, snores, squawks, hisses; but it is now, I think, established that he never hoots . . . Little wonder is it that country folk, hearing in the dusk this uncanny medley of strange noises proceeding from an ivied tower or a primeval oak or beech, should hear them with something akin to awe, and should regard the appearance and the cry of the bird from which it comes—as it has more or less, at all times and places, and in every species of literature, been regarded—as the harbinger of calamity, disease, and of death."

And he goes on to say, p. 21:—

"Perhaps the peculiar shape of the white owl's face—heart-shaped when he is awake, elongated and thinner when he is asleep, and only becoming round, like other owls, after he is dead—marked him out for special suspicion and dislike. He perished almost as much for his supposed virtues as for his supposed vices. Different parts of his body were believed to possess magical powers; and, strangely enough, the very same organ was supposed to possess different powers at different times. His heart, if carried into battle, acted as a charm inspiring valour and averting danger; while, if laid on the left breast of a sleeping woman it caused her to divulge her secrets. To this day it is probable that the white owl owes its safety,

[1] Conf. *Shropshire Folk-lore*, p. 217.

[2] *Bird Life and Bird Lore*, pp. 1–74.

in some parts of England, to the belief that it has something supernatural about it."

This protection is, apparently, not accorded to other owls—*e.g.* the brown owl—for the same writer, at p. 69, says :

" The belief, still prevalent in country districts, that an owl perching on the windows of a house or hooting near it [1] presages the death of an inmate, marked him out for special persecution at the time of family gatherings, and the so-called 'duck-hunt' was a common accompaniment of Christmastide."

Mr. Bosworth Smith then gives a vivid description of this cruel pastime, in which the owl was lashed to the back of a duck, when the duck and rider were launched upon a pond. The duck, of course, made continuous efforts by diving to get rid of its rider, which only made the latter grip the harder. " Each time the duck rises to the surface the owl looks more pitiable, and is welcomed only by the pitiless laughter of the onlookers till death by drowning puts an end to his sufferings."

The contest sometimes ends in the death of both birds according to a writer in Hone's *Every-Day Book*, vol. ii, p. 702, who, in a description of the rustic sports indulged in at the annual " revel " at Hungerford, in the county of Wilts, tells us that in this sport of " duck-hunting ", which generally concluded the whole, the owl often commenced an attack upon the head of the duck, who naturally takes to the water as a means of defence. This attack is renewed as the duck emerges from its dive, " until the poor animals generally destroy each other, unless some humane persons rescues them."

I am glad that Mr. Bosworth Smith cites his instance of " duck-hunting " from one of the late Rev. J. G. Wood's books [2] and not from his own personal observation in Dorsetshire, but, inasmuch as Wilts is a county adjoining Dorsetshire, it cannot be supposed that such brutal sports were unknown to our own county, though, happily, I have not been able to trace any instance of it within its confines.

With regard to the "short-eared" owl, Mr. Bosworth Smith says (p. 46) : " Folk-lore, which has so much to say about other species of the owl, is silent, or almost silent, about her. No poet has sung of her."

[1] Or flying over it (West Dorset).

[2] *My Feathered Friends*, p. 143.

(x) *Peacock.*—It is considered unlucky to keep peacock's feathers in the house.

(xi) *Raven.*—According to Mr. Bosworth Smith—who has devoted more than one hundred pages of his book to the subject of the raven—though that bird is gradually disappearing from the interior districts of England " he seems to cling most fondly to the coasts of Cornwall, of Devon and of Dorset " (p. 84). This is only as it should be ; for, placed by the ancient Romans at the head of all the birds of omen, the raven, " the bird of Odin," was again " the sacred bird of the supreme Divinity of all the Teutonic and Scandinavian races," the direct ancestors, of course, of our own Wessex—whose most fitting representative, perhaps, is now the county of Dorset—a name only recently made popular through the genius of Mr. Thomas Hardy.

As a bird of ill omen, then, the raven is considered in Dorsetshire as in most places ; but I am not aware what particular evil it portends to the person who happens to meet it. Even Mr. Bosworth Smith, with his great knowledge of Dorset bird life and lore, can say no more from the point of local folk-lore than that " the raven has been almost universally regarded as a prophet of evil " (p. 108). It is nearly always met with alone; herein he compares unfavourably with rooks and magpies. Possibly it is from this habit of segregation that the raven has acquired his ill-omened reputation. I have myself been informed that if a raven croaks as it flies over or near you it is a sure sign of death.

(xii) *Robin* (*Reddick, Ruddock*).—The robin, no less than the wren, has always been looked upon by country folk with affection and regard. The sweet and pretty legend that the red plumage of his breast is owing to the fact that it was a robin that wounded itself by pressing against the thorns that composed our Saviour's crown made it an object of veneration to many, so that we cannot wonder that it forms a conspicuous subject for augury.

If a robin comes into the house it is looked upon as an omen of death ; and I have heard it said that if the " sighing " of a robin is noticed near a house it foretells illness or death to some one of its inmates. It is extremely unlucky for any one to kill a robin, and it used to be said as a warning to children that if they ever took a robin's egg from a nest their little fingers would be sure to grow crooked.

For the connexion of the robin with the wren see *Wren* (*post*).

(xiii) *Rook.*—When rooks are observed to dart suddenly down whilst in the air, or play "breakneck" as it is sometimes called, it is commonly believed to portend stormy weather.[1]

(xiv) *Swallow.*—The same omen of good luck is attached to swallows building about your house as in the case of martins (*q.v. ante*).

The two birds have also a similar degree of reverence attached to them as the robin and the wren, as may be seen in the lines of the old doggrel:

"The martin and the swallow
Are God Almighty's bow and arrow."

(xv) *Wood-pecker* (*Yaffle*).—If the green wood-pecker (*picus viridis*), whilst flying from tree to tree or wood, frequently utters its discordant or, as some people would have it, laughing cry, it is a sign of rain.[1]

(xvi) *Wood-pigeon or Ring-dove* (*Culver, Wood-quest*).—In connection with pigeons may be mentioned the common superstition—by no means confined to Dorsetshire—that pigeons' feathers should always be thrown away, and never on any account used for stuffing beds or pillows; for it is believed that persons cannot die peacefully if lying upon them.

This accounts for the not uncommon occurrence in olden times of a poor lingering mortal being lifted on to the floor in order that he may not "die so hard".[2]

(xvii) *Wren* or *Kitty-wren* (*Cut, Cutty*).—It is a sign of good luck if a "cutty", or "cuddy", builds in your hayrick, though if it is heard to sing or cry it is a sign of rain.

In conjunction with the robin the wren is always regarded with affection and treated as a friend by the poor, who often repeat the following verse:—

[1] See *Somerset and Dorset Notes and Queries*, vol. i, p. 182. Also Chapter VIII, p. 270.

[2] I believe it is a Hindoo and Mahomedan custom to lay a dying man on the floor. *Conf.* Henderson's *Folk-lore of the Northern Counties*, p. 60, and Gregor's *Folk-lore of North-East of Scotland*, p. 205. See also Chapter V, p. 184.

"If 'twere not for the robin and the wran
A spider would overcome a man."

Again, the particular providence which is supposed to watch over them is testified to by the lines often heard:

"The robin and the wren
Are God Almighty's cock and hen."

I trust—for of this I am not certain—that the barbarous custom of "hunting the wren" at Christmastide was never popular in Dorsetshire.

The wider spread of education amongst our country folk and the institution of such societies as those for the "Prevention of Cruelty to Animals" and for the "Protection of Birds" have done much of recent years to check this instinct for such brutal pastimes, and to soften the manners of the people and their conduct towards the lower animals.

III. Insect and Reptile Lore

(i) *Adder.*—It is said that if a man or an animal has been bitten by an adder the best remedy that can be used is the fat taken from the adder that has inflicted the injury. There seems to be an idea that the pest that has caused the injury contains in itself also the antidote or remedy.

If you dream of adders—or sometimes, it is said, of snakes generally—it is a sign that you have enemies who are trying to do you some secret mischief.[1]

It is believed that an adder can only die at sunset; a belief that would seem to extend also to slow-worms and snakes in general, and not by any means to be confined to Dorsetshire.[2]

A correspondent in *Folk-Lore*, vol. xix, p. 473, speaks of having witnessed in 1869 an adder swallow her young on his approach in an orchard near Tyneham House, in Purbeck. I was hitherto rather inclined to believe that this interesting occurrence was only superstition.

(ii) *Bee.*—In most counties the bee is considered as a peculiarly apt subject of augury for good or ill.

In Dorsetshire it is believed that if a young humble-bee (*dumble-dore*) comes inside the house it denotes the arrival of a

[1] See *Wasp, post.*

[2] Conf. *Shropshire Folk-lore*, p. 239. Also *Notes and Queries*, Ser. x, i, 168, 253, and *Somerset and Dorset Notes and Queries*, vol. ix, pp. 70, 113.

stranger during the day. You must not, however, drive it out or it will bring you ill luck, for such an act is looked upon as driving out a friend.

But it is at the time of swarming that bees become particular objects of veneration and often of alarm. For instance, if a swarm of bees takes possession of a roof of a house it portends death to the owner of it.

Again, if the swarm settles on the dead branch of a tree or shrub, or pitches upon dead wood, it is looked upon as a sign of death.

It is, moreover, considered very unlucky to "pot" a swarm of bees after nightfall.

The time of the year at which the swarming should take place in order to be of value to the owner is shown by the following lines :—

"A swarm of bees in May
Is worth a load of hay.
A swarm of bees in June
Is worth a silver spoon.
A swarm of bees in July
Is not worth a fly."

It is considered an excellent sign for the future welfare of a newly married couple if a swarm of bees belonging to one of the parties should happen to take place on the wedding day.[1]

To dream of bees is looked upon as a sign that you have enemies who are trying to do you some mischief.

Informing bees of the death of their master or mistress by tapping upon their hives and announcing it in order to prevent their forsaking the place is a common superstition in Dorsetshire as in other counties.

A lady correspondent in *Notes and Queries* (Ser. XI, ix, 236) (1914) speaks of having seen the old gardener of an English lady walk into the garden at night and, tapping on each beehive with the door-key, say distinctly at each hive : "The mistress is dead." Had he not done so he believed that the bees would have left the garden. This, she adds, was in 1886, and the man was from Dorsetshire.

(iii) *Beetle* (*Biddle*).—It is commonly supposed that if you kill a black-beetle twenty of them will come to the funeral.

[1] See Thomas Hardy's *Under the Greenwood Tree*, pt. v, ch. i, p. 258. Also for a vivid description of a Dorset "honey-taking".

No doubt this belief may be attributed to the fact that no matter how many of them you may destroy there is apparently no diminution whatever in their numbers.

(iv) *Fly.*—A similar superstition obtains with regard to this insect.

(v) *Lady-bird* (*God Almighty's Cow*).—The number of spots on the wing of a lady-bird (*cocinella septem punctata*) is sometimes taken to foretell the price of wheat, each spot representing a shilling per bushel.

Barnes, in his *Glossary* (1863), p. 58, says: "Children will often catch this insect, and—as Howitt says children do in Germany—put it on the tip of a finger, repeating:

"Leädy-bird! leädy-bird! vlee away hwome;
Your house is a-vire, your childern wull burn."

He also speaks of a similar practice from a Spanish source.

(vi) *Louse* (*Loup*).—A "loup" is a kind of sea-louse, somewhat like a wood-louse, which in warm summer weather eats the bait which fishermen set in their lobster pots.

The late Canon Bingham is my authority—under the initials C. W. B. in *Notes and Queries* (Ser. I, x, 321, 1854)—for an alleged sovereign remedy for jaundice which came under his notice in a certain parish in Dorsetshire, and which he found upon inquiry was generally known and practised in the neighbourhood. The patient was made to eat nine lice on a piece of bread and butter. These animalcules were not, however, sea or wood lice, but the ordinary or domestic kind, which, he added, "were somewhat difficult of attainment; but that after having been duly collected by the indefatigable labours of the village doctress they were administered with the most perfect success."[1]

(vii) *Moth.*—A large white moth, such as the puss-moth (*phalæna vinula*) and the pale tussock-moth (*phalæna pudibunda*) are called "millers", or "millards", by children in Dorsetshire, who, according to Barnes (*Glossary*, 1863, p. 70), catch them, and, having interrogated them on their taking of toll, make them plead guilty, and condemn them in these lines:

"Millery, millery, dousty poll!
How many zacks hast thee a-stole?
Vour an' twenty an' a peck.
Hang the miller up by's neck."

[1] See Chapter VI, p. 222.

A variant of this verse is given by a correspondent—Σ—in *Somerset and Dorset Notes and Queries*, vol. i, p. 269 (1889), as follows :—

" Melleree, Melleree, dousty pwoll !
How many zacks 'st thee astwole ?
Dree o' whit', an' dree o' black ;
Thou sh't be hangèd by the neck."

" This suggestion," he says, " of summary condign punishment was doubtless an outcome of the fact that, in the west country at least, from time immemorial until within the writer's own experience, it was the universal custom for the labouring man's wages (in some places only a shilling a day) to be largely paid in corn, too often ' seconds ', little better than ' tail '-corn, which was as regularly carried to one of the grist mills to be found in well-nigh every village, where the cost of grinding was defrayed by a dip, larger or smaller, of the miller's toll-dish.

' Well colde he stealë corn and tollë thrice.'
Chaucer, *Prologue*."

(viii) *Slow-worm.*—Mr. R. Bosworth Smith (p. 367) speaks of a Dorset labourer who gave as his reason for having killed a slow-worm that " if it do sting 'ee you are sure to die within seven year ". And this regardless of the fact that a slow-worm has no sting !

As to the belief that a slow-worm can only die at sunset, see *ante, s.v. Adder*.

(ix) *Snail.*—When snails in any unusual quantity are seen about, especially black ones, they are said to portend rain, hence the saying :—

" When black snails cross your path
Black clouds much moisture hath." [1]

The value of the snail for medicinal purposes is well known. Richard Jefferies in his book *Round about a Great Estate*, p. 189, states (*Notes*, p. 204) that in Dorsetshire an extract of snails is still sometimes prepared, and, mixed with rum, is rubbed into weak backs, or legs, especially of children.

I myself have known of the use both internally and externally, of the " liquor " of snails in West Dorset. I think this was used as a cure, or palliative, for " sore legs ".

[1] See Chapter VIII, p. 271.

The following lines are often used by children in the endeavour to charm snails out of their holes :—

> " Snail, snail, come out of your hole,
> Or else I'll beat you as black as a coal."

(x) *Snake.*—It is believed that a snake can always be stopped, or diverted from your path, if you repeat the following verse : " Let God arise, and let His enemies be scattered." Or this one : " They were as venomous as the poison of a serpent ; even as a deaf adder that stoppeth her ears and refuseth to hear the voice of the charmer, charm he never so wisely." [1]

Some people believe that a snake-skin worn in the hat, or bonnet, is a remedy for headache.

If you dream of snakes it is a sign that you have some enemies who are secretly trying to do you mischief.

(xi) *Spider.*—If you take a money-spider (*arauna scenica*) by the thread that it hangs from and swing it three times round your head without throwing it off, and then put it in your pocket, it is believed that it will soon bring you money.

That the spider is considered capable of exercising a very baneful influence over human beings is shown by the distich :—

> " If 'twere not for the robin and the wran
> A spider would overcome a man." [2]

(xii) *Toad.*—The idea that the toad is capable of exercising the most malign influence over persons is firmly rooted amongst the superstitious of most countries. In Dorsetshire it is believed that if a toad should once seize a person, nothing will make it loosen its hold unless boiling water be poured upon it.

It is considered very unlucky if a toad goes over your foot.

Whenever you see a toad you should always spit or throw a stone at it, in order to ward off any evil effects which the sight of it might otherwise cause you. The idea here of spitting as a preventive of ill may have something to do with the power the toad is said to possess of spitting its " swelter'd venom " at those who happen to annoy it. I have heard more than one curious story of the baneful effects which this " spitting " is supposed to have caused.

[1] See Chapter VI, p. 220.

[2] See *ante, s.v. Wren.*

The belief that a toad, or portions of a toad, tied up in a bag and worn as a charm is of great efficacy as a preventive against evil is prevalent in many parts of Dorsetshire. Not long ago a " cunning man ", or witch-doctor, used to hold an annual levée in the neighbourhood of Stalbridge, where he sold out to crowds that thronged round him the legs torn from a living toad and placed in a bag, which were to be worn round the neck of the patient, and were counted a sovereign remedy for scrofula and the " overlooked ". It was called " Toad Fair ".

In the *Life of William Barnes*, by his daughter, the late Mrs. Baxter (" Leader Scott ") (1887), p. 155, is an account of a quack who lived at Lydlinch, and who professed to cure the king's evil or scrofula by means of a charm consisting of a toad sewn up in a small bag, which was to be worn round the neck. It was, however, only beneficial in the beginning of May at a particular phase of the moon.

In Roberts's *History of Lyme Regis* (1834), p. 261, the author states that toads that had gained access to a cellar or house were ejected with the greatest care and no injury was offered, because they were regarded, as being used as *familiars* by witches, with veneration and awe.[1]

(xiii) *Wasp.*—The same superstition is attached to dreaming about wasps as it is in the case of bees or snakes (*q.v.*), namely, that it is a sign that some one is secretly trying to work you some mischief.

IV. Plant-lore

(i) *Apple tree.*—If an apple tree blossoms out of season—*e.g.* in the autumn—it is regarded as a sign that one of the owner's family will die before very long. Upon this subject the late Canon Bingham made the following communication to *Notes and Queries* (Ser. IV, x, 408) (1872) :—

" Remarking an apple blossom a few days ago " (month of November) " on one of my trees I pointed it out as a curiosity to a Dorset labourer. ' Ah ! Sir,' he said, ' 'tis lucky no women folk be here to see that ' ; and upon my asking the reason he replied, ' Because they's be sure to think that somebody were a-going to die.' "[2]

[1] See further on this subject, Chapter VI, pp. 215-16.

[2] This superstition is referred to in somewhat similar terms by Mr. Bosworth Smith in his *Bird Life and Bird Lore,* 1909, p. 365.

I have been told by an old lady in West Dorset that if the sun is seen to shine through the branches of an apple tree on Old Christmas Day (6th January) it denotes a fine " blooth " (*i.e.* collective blossom), and that a good crop of apples may be expected.

An apple pip is often used by girls as a test of their lovers' fidelity. If, on putting it in the fire, it bursts with the heat she is assured of his affection ; but if it is consumed in silence she may know that he is false. Whilst they anxiously await the effect the following couplet is usually pronounced :—

" If you love me, pop and fly ;
If you hate me lay and die."

I have not myself met with any instance in Dorsetshire of the ancient custom of " wassailing ", or drinking the health, of apple trees on the eve of Twelfth Day, similar to that which obtains in some parts of Devonshire, Herefordshire, and other cider-drinking and making counties. It may be that the apple crop in our county is not considered of sufficient importance to warrant such rites being carried out as in those counties which are more noted for the high quality of the cider made there—and of which large quantities are exported—that in Dorsetshire, I think, being reserved more for local consumption, and particularly for the sheep-shearing, hay-making, and harvesting seasons. In a recent volume, however, of *Folk-Lore* (xxix, p. 71) (1918) containing notes of the folk-lore material now being collected by the " Brand Committee " of the Folk-Lore Society, there appears some indication that similar rites have been carried out in Dorsetshire, when cakes or toast dipped in cider were put in the branches or forks of apple trees and libations of cider were poured out upon or thrown against their trunks, to the accompaniment of shouts and the firing of guns, whilst songs or rhymes were sung in their honour, to which sometimes " rough music " was added. Full particulars of these ceremonies will no doubt appear in due course when that material comes to be published. In the meantime I append a verse given there as a Dorset variant, as follows :—

" Stand fast, root ! bear well, top !
Pray God send a good howling crop !

Hats full, caps full, dree bushel bags full !
(*cresc.*) Now, *now*, NOW ! " (*Fire-arms discharged.*) [1]

At a meeting of the Dorset Field Club held at Dorchester in December, 1920, in the discussion which followed the reading of a paper by Mr. W. O. Beament on " The Apple Tree Wassail ", Mr. Stanhope Rodd stated that apple wassailing was still kept up in his own parish at Chardstock.[2]

Apropos of this custom of wassailing the apple trees may be noticed the superstition which Brand gives us in a general statement (i, 273, (n.)) : " There is an old saying that when it rains on St. Swithin's Day it is the Saint christening the Apples."

I was not aware that this superstition had any special reference to Dorsetshire until I had read Thomas Hardy's interesting collection of short stories, published in 1913, under the title of *A Changed Man*. Mr. Hardy is as surely to be depended upon for his knowledge and application of his county's folk-lore as ever Mr. Barnes was for its dialect. Here in that charming story of " The Romantic Adventures of a Milkmaid " one of the characters observed (p. 355) :

" But I hope it won't be long after the time when God A'mighty christens the little apples."
" And when's that ? "
" St. Swithin's—the middle of July."

It will be noticed that here it is the Almighty not the Saint which shows His solicitude for the welfare of the apple crop—a solicitude apparently equally shown by the Church in the olden days when the " Blessing of New Apples " (*Benedictio Pomorum in Die Sancti Jacobi*) was ordained to be observed ten days later, St. James's Day (25th July), according to the *Manuale ad Usum Sarum*.[3]

(ii) *Ash tree*.—The properties of the ash tree, whether for the purposes of charms or divinations, are well known.

In Dorsetshire the belief was wide spread that if a young

[1] *Conf.* Brand's *Popular Antiquities*, i, 2, where it seems to be considered that these ceremonies were a relic of the heathen sacrifice to the goddess Pomona.

[2] This paper subsequently appeared in vol. xlii of the *Proceedings* (1922).

[3] Brand, vol. i, p. 274.

" maiden " ash (*i.e.* not polled) were split and a ruptured child drawn through it, the latter would become cured.[1]

The late William Barnes (*Glossary*, 1863, p. 69, *s.v.* " Mäiden tree ") states that he had known of two trees through which children had been so drawn.

Mr. Sidney Hartland, F.S.A., sends an interesting letter on this subject to *Folk-Lore*, vol. vii, p. 304 (1896), in which mention is made as to the manner in which the rite was performed in the neighbourhood of Bishop's Lydeard in Somersetshire. On p. 307 appeared a photographic reproduction of a split ash sapling and model now preserved in the County Museum at Taunton.

Some people, believing the ash to be diœcious (*i.e.* that the male and female flowers were found on different trees) select what they suppose to be a female ash for a male patient, and *vice versâ*. But I have the authority of that well-known Dorset botanist, the late Mr. J. C. Mansel-Pleydell, first President of the Dorset Field Club, for saying that although some members of the ash family are diœcious it is not the case with the common ash, which is undoubtedly polygamous. Further, as the tree to be selected must be a sapling—and therefore not old enough to bear fruit—its sex, even if different, could not be ascertained.

Mr. E. A. Rawlence, in a paper in the Dorset Field Club's *Proceedings* for 1916 (vol. xxxvii, p. 62) speaks of the value of an ash tree in preventing cows from casting their calves. He says :

" Some years since in going over a farm—I think it was at Holnest—I observed a calf that had been prematurely born placed high up in the fork of an ash bush in the hedge. I asked the farmer what led him to place it there, and elicited the information that if the dead calf was placed in the fork of a maiden ash (*i.e.* an ash tree grown direct from the seed) and with its head towards the east that it would prevent other cows in the herd from casting their calves. On further enquiry I gathered from the late Mr. J. J. Young, of Pinford, that when he was a boy the custom was quite common in the neighbourhood of Glanvilles Wootton. Also, I heard of a farmer in the neighbour-

[1] *Conf.* Gilbert White's *Natural History and Antiquities of Selborne*, 1833, p. 233, as to this. Also his remarks (p. 234) on the " shrew-ash ", the existence of which I have not been able to discover in Dorsetshire. See also *Folk-Lore*, vol. xix, p. 88.

hood of Wincanton who was a great believer in this specific; and if a cow was observed to be afflicted in this way all his men had to turn out and walk the farm until the *fœtus* had been discovered and duly placed in the ash tree."[1]

The ash is also considered as throwing some light upon the probable success or otherwise of the corn crops, as the following couplet would tend to show:

"As ash do coaly
Wheat do lowly."

That is, as the bud of the ash blackens so in proportion will the wheat be light or heavy in ear.

The ash, in conjunction with the oak (*q.v. post*) is a very favourite test, according as one or the other is the first to put forth its leaves, as to what kind of weather may be expected during the ensuing season:

"If the ash is before the oak,
Then there'll be a very great smoke;
If the oak is before the ash,
Then there'll be a very great splash."

Variants of this are common, even to the extent of being exactly the opposite, as these lines would indicate:

"If the ash is before the oak,
Then there'll be a very great soak;
If the oak is before the ash,
Then there'll be a very small splash."[2]

I think that in most seasons it will be noticed that the oak leaves are out before those of the ash.

The ash leaf is frequently invoked by young girls as a matrimonial oracle in the following way: The girl who wishes to divine who her future lover or husband is to be plucks an *even* ash leaf, and holding it in her hand, says:

"The even ash leaf in my hand,
The first I meet shall be my man."

Then, putting it into her glove, adds:

"The even ash leaf in my glove,
The first I meet shall be my love."

And lastly, into her bosom, saying:—

"The even ash leaf in my bosom,
The first I meet shall be my husband."

Soon after which the future lover, or husband, will be sure to make his appearance.

[1] See Chapter VI, p. 226.

[2] See Chapter VIII, p. 272.

The use of ash twigs, in place of hazel, as "divining rods" for the purpose of finding water, is not unknown in the county.[1]

(iii) *Bergamot.*—The plant bergamot must not be kept in a house or you will never be free from sickness.[2]

(iv) *Box.*—If a sprig of box *in flower* be brought indoors death will soon cross the threshold.[3]

(v) *Bramble.*—To creep under a bramble three mornings following against the sun, just as it rises, is said to afford a complete cure for boils.

Another form in which the bramble or briar is used as a remedy for sickness is where a child suffering from whooping-cough is passed nine times under and over an arched briar; *i.e.* one that is rooted at both ends.[4]

(vi) *Comfrey.*—The late Mr. H. J. Moule wrote in the *Folk-Lore Journal* (vol. vi, p. 116) that "the plant comfrey (*symphytum officinale*) is a capital cure, but I don't know what for or in what form. A salve, I think (presumably for sores) but you must take care to use the red-flowered sort for men and the white for women."[5]

I have been told that it has great healing properties, and is most efficacious in bathing wounds or cuts. I have heard of the white blossoming comfrey being grown in the neighbourhood of Bridport for cows to eat. The outer leaves would be stripped off and given to them.

(vii) *Cowslip.*—A cowslip-ball, consisting of blossoms of cowslips tied in a globular form called "a tissty-tossty", is often used by Dorset children in their play as a means of divination.

Whilst playing with it the following lines are repeated:—

"Tissty-tossty, tell me true,
Who shall I be married to?"

The names of A, B, C, etc., are successively mentioned until the ball drops, when the answer is supplied.

And again:—

"Tissty-tossty, four-and-foarty,
How many years shall I live hearty?"

[1] Conf. *Denham Tracts*, vol. ii, pp. 70–1.

[2] *Notes and Queries*, Ser. IV, iv, 58.

[3] See *Furze* (*post*).

[4] Conf. *Shropshire Folk-lore*, p. 195.

[5] *Conf.* Black's *Folk Medicine*, pp. 108 *et seq.*

The numbers one, two, three, four, etc., are called out until the ball drops as before.[1]

(viii) *Daffodil* (*Daffodowndilly*).—You should always take care when daffodils or Lent lillies (*narcissus pseudo-narcissus*) are brought into the house for the first time in the season that they should consist of a good quantity, for otherwise something is sure to go wrong with your poultry.

(ix) *Dock*.—For the supposed efficacy of the leaves of this plant in alleviating the irritation caused by nettle stings, see *Nettle*.

(x) *Ever-green*.—See *Plant*.

(xi) *Furze* (" *Vuz* " or " *vuzzen* ").—The same superstition exists as in the case of box (*q.v.*), namely, that to bring a branch of yellow furze or gorse in bloom into the house is a sure prognostication of death.

Miss M. G. A. Summers sent the following lines on this subject to the *Dorset County Chronicle* in March, 1889 :—

" If the yaller fuz be a-cärd in,
A thin a year ther's nar a doubt
A coffin'll be a-cärd out."

There is a very pretty legend attached to the concurrent blossoming of the gorse and heather mentioned by Mr. Bosworth Smith in his *Bird Life and Bird Lore*, p. 367. He says :—

" In that large portion of Dorset . . . the heath country, where the heather and the dwarf autumn gorse are often in their full glory together . . . the inhabitants believe that, as the blossom dies down, it is taken up to heaven ; and the purple of the heather is transformed into the gates of amethyst and the yellow of the gorse into the golden pavement of the Celestial City."

As to the custom of jumping over furze bushes at a wedding, see Chapter V, p. 191.

(xii) *Heather*.—See *Furze*.

(xiii) *Hemp*.—Hemp having been so largely grown, owing to its good quality, in West Dorset, it is not surprising that any old customs or superstitions connected with that plant should be equally prevalent.

The scattering of hemp-seed was practised by many a Dorset maiden at Midsummer with a view to divine who her future husband might be. She would walk through the garden with a

[1] See Chapter V, p. 190.

rake over her left shoulder and throw the hemp-seed over her right, saying at the same time:

"Hemp-seed I set, hemp-seed I sow (or throw),
The man that is my true-love come after me and mow."

If the spell works properly the future husband will appear behind her with a scythe.[1]

(xiv) *Leek* (*Silgreen*).—The leaves of the house-leek (*semper vivum tectorum*) are thought to be cooling and are used with cream for the blood.

(xv) *Lily*.—The same value that is attached to the lady-bird (*q.v. ante*), in foretelling the price of wheat according to the number of the spots on one of its wings, accrues to the white garden-lily (*candidum*), where a similar calculation is made from the number of the blossoms as shown on the majority of its spikes, each blossom representing one shilling per bushel.

As to the danger of bringing Lent-lilies into the house, see *ante, s.v. Daffodil*.

(xvi) *Liverwort* (*Mary's Tears*).—Barnes, in his later *Glossary* (1886), speaking of the spotted liverwort (*pulmonaria*) says:

"At Osmington, and no doubt at other places in our county, there is a survival of a sweet, simple, old-world piece of folk-lore about the spotted liver-wort. The cottagers like to have it in their gardens, and call it 'Mary's Tears'. The legend is that the spots on the leaves are the marks of the tears shed by St. Mary after the crucifixion. Farther—and this to me is a quite unknown tradition—her eyes were as blue as the fully opened flowers, and by weeping the eyelids became as red as the buds."

This statement bears the initials "H. J. M."

Another form of this legend is given by the late H. J. Moule in the *Folk-Lore Journal*, vol. vi, p. 118, as follows:—

"There stood by the cross His mother. Now, there grew on Mount Calvary a green-leaved plant with flowers of deep azure blue, but the buds were red. St. Mary's eyes were as blue as the flowers, but with weeping her eyelids were as red as the buds. And, as she wept, her tears fell on the leaves and spotted them. And spotted they have been from generation to generation ever since; and the plant is grown in cottage gardens and its name is 'Mary's Tears'. But books call it *Pulmonaria*."

[1] For a fuller account of this custom and superstition see Chapter I, p. 44, *s.v.* "Midsummer Eve." And Chapter V, p. 189.

Since my paper was published, as stated at the beginning of this chapter, I received a letter from a lady ("C. H. P.") who had spent her childhood in North Dorset, and to whom I am indebted for several interesting items of plant-lore, etc., in which she says: "It is not correct to call this plant *Liverwort*, that is, *Hepatica*; it should be called *Lung-wort.* I have heard it called 'Faith, Hope and Charity'. The flowers are first red, then lilac, then blue. Probably the name 'Mary's Tears' was originally applied to the larger kind—*Pulmonaria angustifolia*—which has handsome and conspicuously spotted leaves."

(xvii) *Nettle.*—The pharmacopeia obtaining in the country lore of most districts provides for the alleviation or cure of the effects of a sting from this obnoxious plant. The efficacy of a dock-leaf has been tested in many counties. In Dorsetshire the following lines should be repeated, whilst the place stung should be rubbed with the leaves:

"Dock, dock, shall have a smock,
Nettle shall have nar a one." [1]

William Barnes in his dialect poem *Dock-Leaves* (p. 10) refers to this remedy for nettle stings when he says:

"How we,—when nettles had a-stung
Our little hands, when we wer young,—
Did rub 'em wi' a dock, an' zing
'*Out nettl', in dock. In dock, out sting*'."

The following lines show what is considered the proper time for getting rid of the plant altogether:

"Cut nettles in June,
They come again soon.
Cut them in July,
They're sure to die."

(xviii) *Nut.*—It is considered lucky to carry a double nut in the pocket.

If two kernels of a nut are found in a single nut-shell it is unlucky to eat both yourself; you should always give one away. Hence, presumably, the modern custom of "phillipina".

(xix) *Oak tree.*—The aid of the oak tree is sometimes invoked as a charm against tooth-ache. The proceeding is as follows:

[1] Conf. *Choice Notes from Notes and Queries* (*Folk-Lore*), 1859, p. 255, and *Shropshire Folk-lore*, p. 184.

Go to a young oak tree ; cut a slit in the tree ; cut off a bit of your hair ; put it under the rind ; put your hand up to the tree, and say : " This I bequeath to the oak tree in the name of the Father, and of the Son, and of the Holy Ghost. Amen." [1]

For the use of the oak, in conjunction with the ash, as an augury of the coming seasons, see *Ash tree.*

(xx) *Oats.*—Oats, which from lack of soil or food have degenerated into the wild form, are called " cheats " in Dorsetshire. Of these the bearded darnel (*lolium temulentum*), so called from its long awns, is supposed by some writers to be the " tares " to which the Saviour alluded in His parable of the tares and wheat.[2] The seeds of this species are said to have a very peculiar intoxicating effect. When malted with barley the ale produced from the mixture produces speedy drunkenness, and if they are ground up with bread corn, the bread, if eaten hot, produces a similar effect. Smith in his *Bible Plants* states that even death has been caused by eating bread containing darnel. It is also said to cause blindness. The attribution of poisonous properties to the bearded darnel is not mere folk-lore.[3]

(xxi) *Pear tree.*—In some parts of Dorsetshire the same superstitions which obtain as to the blossoming of apple trees out of season apply also to pear trees—and, indeed, to fruit trees generally—when such an unusual occurrence presages trouble or death. See *Apple tree.*

(xxii) *Pimpernel.*—The common or scarlet pimpernel (*anagallis arvensis*) called in Dorsetshire *The Poor Man's Weather-Glass* from its delicate sense of perceiving the approach of rain—when it closes its flowers—is often apostrophized by children as follows :—

" Pimpernel, pimpernel, tell me true
Whether the weather be fine or no.
No heart can think, no tongue can tell
The virtues of the pimpernel." [4]

(xxiii) *Plant.*—When a plant is " primed " or cut you must take care that the turnings or cuttings are never put in the

[1] See Chapter VI, p. 219.

[2] See Taylor's *Half-hours in the Green Lanes*, 1877, p. 275.

[3] See further upon this subject, *Notes and Queries*, Ser. VII, vii, 46, 198.

[4] See also *Notes and Queries*, Ser. XI, i, 76.

fire, but are thrown away ; otherwise the plant will never thrive. Particularly is this to be observed in the case of Christmas decorations of evergreen plants, which should never be burnt after they are taken down, on pain of the most terrible disasters following upon the infringement of the rule, death or the serious illness of some one in the house before another year is out.[1]

(xxiv) *Rose.*—It is considered injurious to your health to smell white roses, but beneficial to smell red ones.

A correspondent in *Notes and Queries* (Ser. XI, vi, 509) (1912) states that *The Academy* (lx, 355) published a poem by Thomas Hardy describing a custom of planting an onion at the foot of a rose tree, with the object of making the flowers healthy and improving their perfume. The custom, he said, seemed to be prevalent in Wessex.

(xxv) *Sloe.*—The sloe (*prunus spinosa*) is used in some parts of Dorsetshire as a charm for the cure and against the recurrence of warts ; when in order to obtain the wished for result the following process is particularly to be observed. Go to a sloe-bush unseen ; bite off part of a growing sloe, leaving the portion with the stone in it on the bush ; rub the wart with the part bitten off, and throw it over your head or shoulder.[2]

(xxvi) *Thorn.*—" Maiden " thorns (*i.e.* thorns which have grown the same year in which they are picked) are often selected for the purpose of being stuck, with pins, into a bullock's, horse's, or other animal's heart to be used as a charm, or for purposes of " overlooking ".[3]

(xxvii) *Toad-stool* (*Toad's meat*).—The rings of fungi, so often seen in the grass of our downs, are called in Dorsetshire " veäry-rings ", because they are believed to have come from the dancing of fairies.

" The belief in fairies," says William Barnes (*Glossary*, 1863, pp. 96–7, and *Glossary*, 1886, p. 115), " one of the most poetical and beautiful of superstitions, still lingers in the West." " Toad-stools " or " swams " (our forefathers' word for the Latin *fungi*)—or " pixy-stools " (fairy stools) as they are called in Devon—as they enrich the soil " and bring the fairy-ring by

[1] See Chapter I, *s.v.* Candlemas Day as to the converse of this.

[2] See Chapter VI, p. 221.

[3] See an article by Mr. Herman Lea on " Wessex Witches " in the *Nineteenth Century Review* for June, 1903.

rotting down after they have seeded outward from the centre, so that the ring of actual fungi is outside of the fairy-ring, it was natural for those who believed the ring to be brought by the dancing of fairies to guess that the fungi were stools upon which they sat when tired."

He also gives expression to this superstition in the following extract from his eclogue on " The Veäries " (p. 73 of the *Poems*):

" But zome,
Do zay do come by lightnèn when do thunder;
An' zome do zay sich rings as thik ring there is,
Do grow in dancèn tracks o' little veäries,
That in the nights o' zummer or o' spring
Do come by moonlight, when noo other veet
Do tread the dewy grass but their's, an' meet
An' dance away together in a ring."

According to the late Rev. W. K. Kendall, " fairy rings " are supposed to be made by " dancing tracks of little fairies " ; and it is believed that if you can run nine times round one of these rings without drawing breath a fairy will bring you something good.

(xxviii) *Tree.*—" If you plant a tree or trees, and you are very anxious that they should thrive, you must not go and look at them, or look out of the window at them, ' on an empty stomach.' There is a blasting influence in your eye then which will make them pine away. And the story is that a man, puzzled by the withering of his newly planted choice trees, went to a white witch to inquire who was the evil-worker. The white witch, after ascertaining the facts, told him it was *himself.*"

The above is an extract from a letter from Mr. Thomas Hardy to Mr. Edward Clodd (30th October, 1896), read at a meeting of the Folk-Lore Society in November of that year, and recorded in *Folk-Lore,* vol. viii, p. 11).

(xxix) *Wheat.*—It is said that on first eating anything made of new wheat you ought to fill your mouth quite full, and then you will not want for anything during the year.

(xxx) *Wood.*—If, when pieces of wood are placed on a hearth fire, or the sticks are pushed together, they kindle or blaze up without any persons' interference, it is looked upon as a sign that a stranger may shortly be expected.[1]

[1] See Chapter IX, *s.v. Fire.*

CHAPTER VIII

WEATHER-LORE

THIS chapter formed the subject of a paper which I read at a winter meeting of the Dorset Field Club at Dorchester in January, 1913,[1] and as that period is so recent, I am unable to do more than reproduce that article here with such additions to it as I have been enabled to make since that time.

It is only to be expected that in a county like Dorsetshire, with a population so largely addicted to agricultural and pastoral pursuits—to say nothing of that part of it employed upon its large extent of sea-board—that signs and portents in any way indicative of what the weather is likely to be are eagerly looked for and carefully treasured up, resulting in a strong belief in those superstitions to which they give rise.

It is, of course, impossible to say that many of the things that I note in this chapter are peculiar to Dorsetshire, or even to the West of England. As with plant and flower-lore, so it is obviously impossible that the study of weather-lore, if it be at all exhaustive, can be confined within the narrow geographical limits of a county.

It is difficult for me here to deal with the subject in a scientific or orderly method that would satisfy the student of comparative folk-lore ; so I shall be content to adopt some simple method of classification or arrangement that will make it easy for any such student to select the material he may desire for the purposes of comparison or generalization. The older chroniclers of the domestic customs and superstitions of the people were by no means scientific or orderly in the treatment of their subject matter, but one was nevertheless always able to find what one wanted. One of the most usual methods was that of taking the particular days of the calendar or periods of the year and adjusting and assigning to them the subject matter suitable to each. It is this method that I will now begin with, dealing with it in chronological order.

[1] See vol. xxxiv, p. 137, of the *Proceedings.*

Some forty years or so ago the *Dorset County Chronicle* (I think at my suggestion, for I was anxious at that time to collect and preserve all the items I could of what may be termed Dorset folk-lore) instituted in its pages a " Folk-lore Column " for the collection of such items, and which I from time to time helped to supply with material. From that source, under date 17th December, 1891, I now give my first item.

New Year's Day.

It reads somewhat in the form of a prophecy from *Old Moore's Almanac*, and there is an old-world savour about it, but my note-book does not give the actual source whence it was taken. It treats of what we may expect should New Year's Day chance to fall upon a Thursday.

" Winter and summer windie. A rainie harvest. Therefore we shall have overflowings ; much fruit ; plentie of honey ; yet flesh shall be deare, cattel in general shall die ; great troubles ; warres."

Candlemas.

If Candlemas Day (2nd February) is a fine day, winter is to come ; if it's a middling day, winter is half over ; it it's a very rough day, winter is past.

Another and rhythmical form of this belief was sent to me years ago, together with several other interesting items of Dorset folk-lore, by the late Rev. W. K. Kendall, of East Lulworth, himself an early member of the Dorset Field Club.

" If Candlemas Day be fair and fine,
Half the winter is left behin'.
If Candlemas Day do bluster and blow,
The winter is o'er, as all good people do know."

Yet another instance of mild weather at Candlemas being taken as a harbinger of something more severe later on is furnished by the old saying that " as much ground as the sun shines on on Candlemas Day will be covered with snow before Lady Day ".

The late Mr. Hugh Norris, of South Petherton, for many years Somerset editor of *The Somerset and Dorset Notes and Queries* (vol. i, pp. 160–2), gives a list of some West Country weather proverbs, from which I extract his version of the above saying, clothed in a rich vernacular—perhaps a little more Somerset than Dorset—" Za much groun' as ez cove'd wi' zun pon Cannelmas Day 'll be cove'd wi' znaw avore Lāādy Day."

In the following instance relating to Candlemas, furnished to *Notes and Queries* in 1872 (Ser. IV, x, 82) by F. C. H. (the well known Roman Catholic ecclesiastical authority, the late Dr. F. C. Husenbeth), attention is called to the alteration in these old dates—a fact, I am afraid, generally ignored—caused by the introduction of the New Style. He says:

"In Dorsetshire people anxiously look for the dew-drops hanging thickly on the thorn-bushes on Candlemas morning. When they do, it forebodes a good year for peas. But these weatherwise seers are apt to forget that all these old saws were adapted to the Old Style, according to which what used to be Candlemas is now St. Valentine. *N'importe*, the weather prophet coolly moves on his peg and goes on predicting with equal confidence."

The following forecasts as to the kind of weather to be expected are based upon what has already obtained in particular months of the year.

January.

"A January Spring
Isn't worth a pin."
(or, in West Dorset, "is good for nothing.")

Mr. Norris renders this latter version in the vernacular as follows: "A January spring edd'n good vur noo-thing"; because crops then become too forward—"winter proud," as it is called—and are liable to be damaged by later cold weather.

Another version has:

"January Spring
February wring."

And a West Dorset variant of this last runs:

"A January Spring
Makes a February ring."
(*i.e.* a ringing frost—the reverberation on the hard, frosty surface).

February.

If a mild January was considered unseasonable and undesirable, similar weather during the following month of February seemed even less to the taste of the Dorset agriculturist, if we may judge from a couplet sent in 1889 to the *Somerset and Dorset Notes and Queries* (vol. i, p. 269) by G. W. F., under which initials it is not difficult to recognize Mr. G. W. Floyer, another old member of the Club:

"Of all the months that are in the year
Curse a fair Februeer."

According to Mr. Norris, this month shares, in slightly different terms, the epithet given to it by many other counties of "Veb'uary vell-ditch".

March.

The following proverb is no doubt common to many counties besides Dorsetshire: "If March comes in like a lion it will go out like a lamb," and *vice versâ.*

It is widely believed that March and the two following months afford the greatest trial to a weakly constitution, owing to their often rapid changes of temperature. It is thus expressed in Dorsetshire:

"March wull sarch,
Eäpril wull try,
May'ull tell
If you'll live or die."

This may be written in two lines, as in Barnes's *Grammar and Glossary* (1863), p. 38.

Another common one is:

"March winds and April showers
Will bring forth May flowers."

Or in a rather more amplified form from West Dorset:

"January's could,
February's vill-dyke,
March winds,
April showers
Will sure to bring
Many [May] flowers."

The value to agriculturists of a dry March is well recognized in the proverbial sayings of many counties. In West Dorset I find the somewhat unusual form of "A bushel of March dust is worth a King's ransom when do vall on thornèn leaves," given by a correspondent in *Notes and Queries* (Ser. v, i, 505), who suggests that the March dust is valuable at the close of the month when the thorn begins to unfold its leaves rather than at an earlier period.

Mr. Norris is responsible for the following:—"Zoo many vogs en Maärch, zoo many vrausts (or, *var.* "vloods") en May."

Also for the statement that when in spring snow lies for some time on the hill-sides and under hedges the popular belief is that " 'Tes awaitin' vur mōōa."

Easter.

The following quatrain speaks for itself :—

" Sun Easter Day,
Little grass, but good hay.
Rain Easter Day,
Good deal of grass, but bad hay."

The late Mr. Bosworth Smith in his *Bird Life and Bird Lore* (1909), p. 364, includes the state of the weather on Good Friday as being an equally important factor in this matter as that upon Easter Day. His version reads :

" Rain Good Friday or Easter Day,
Much good grass, but little hay."

May.

The changeable weather usually experienced in the month of May is neatly expressed in one of Mr. Norris's contributions : " May's ha'f zumma 'n ha'f wenta."

" A Zunny May 'n a drepping June
'll pŭt all things en good tune."

A comfortable thought, as Mr. Norris says, for a late spring.

Midsummer.

" A dry Summer never goes begging."

Or, a West Dorset variant :

" A dry Summer never begs its bread."

Meaning thereby that fine dry weather in summer time is good for corn crops, particularly wheat.

Michaelmas.

The unseasonable effects of early frosts are shown by the following lines :—

" A frost before Michaelmas Day
Hard enough to bear a duck,
All the winter after
Nothing but muck."

Christmas.

Similar to the last is one referable to Christmas : " If the ice will bear a horse before Christmas it won't bear a duck after."

" A light Christmas, light harvest."

" Light " here presumably refers to a mild Christmas.

The same result of unseasonably mild weather, as already expressed as prevailing at Candlemas, is, with regard to Christmas, shown by the following: " If the sun shines on Christmas Day it will snow on Candlemas Day."

The same idea is more graphically expressed, perhaps, in this variant of the aphorism: " How far the sun is within the stall on Christmas Day, so far the snow will be on Candlemas Day."

As a West Country variant of the common saying that " A green Christmas makes a fat churchyard " Mr. Norris gives the following as indicating the fatal effects of a trying spring on the constitutions of the sick and aged who have survived a mild winter: " Ev a chich'ard da look lik' a pastur' vēēl 'pon C'ursmas Day 'll look lik' a plow'd vēēl avoa Medzumma Day."

He also gives the following: " Dree whit' vrauses (frosts) vollerin' avore C'ursmas 'll bring rain," a saying not by any means peculiar to Dorsetshire or even the West Country.

It is often said that if the sun shines through the branches of an apple tree on old Christmas Day it is a sure sign of a good crop to follow.

Particular Days of the Week.

The weather obtaining on particular days of the week has been made the subject of note or observation. In Dorsetshire it is said that " Friday and the rest of the week are never alike ", referring to the exceptionable weather usually met with on a Friday.

And sometimes it takes the form, in other counties, of " Like Friday, like Sunday ".

The former expression would appear to be at least as old as Chaucer. See the *Knighte's Tale*, 681 (Skeat's edition), " Selde is the Friday al the wyke i-lyke."

Moon Weather-lore

The various phases of the moon bear a large part in the weather-lore of most counties, and amongst these phases the time of the new moon is predominant.

In 1874 I sent to *Notes and Queries* (Ser. v, i, 48) an illustration of this from a Dorset source, wherein I stated that I had been

[1] Conf. *Shropshire Folk-lore*, p. 261 (n.).

informed by an old Dorset shepherd that " a Saturday's new moon once in seven years was once too often for sailors "—meaning thereby that sailors have a special dread of a new moon falling upon that day of the week. And I mentioned in illustration of this that the new moon for the previous August had fallen upon a Saturday, and that both the weather and sea had been unusually rough for that time of year.

Hence the proverb :

" A Saturday's moon is the sailor's dread."

This is intensified should the full moon also fall on a Sunday, as is shown by the following couplet :—

" A Saturday's moon and [a] Sunday's full
Never did good and never wull."

A variant of this from West Dorset was sent in 1856 to *Notes and Queries* (Ser. II, ii, 516) by " Clericus Rusticus " (Rev. H. Rawlinson, Rector of Symondsbury) :

" A Saturday's change and a Sunday's full
Comes too soon whenever it wool."

When the moon is " cupped " (*i.e.* has her horns turned directly upwards) it is popularly supposed to forebode a wet month. This position of the moon is sometimes spoken of as " lying on her back ".

" As many days as the moon is old at Middlemas (*i.e.* Michaelmas), so many floods before Christmas."

I now come to what I may term miscellaneous weather forecasts, or circumstances and incidents portending wet or fine weather.

Predictions of Rain.

" Predictions of rain," says " M. G. A. S." (Miss Summers, of Hazelbury Bryan) in the *Dorset County Chronicle* (Folk-lore column), in March, 1889, " are manifold. Painful rheumatism, shooting corns, spiders leaving their cobwebs and creeping about the rooms, soot falling down the chimney, stones drying quickly, cats washing over their ears with their paws. I was astonished by an exclamation I heard yesterday denoting the belief in ' weather prophets ', which still clings to Dorset. ' Dear-a-me,' says an old woman, ' a weät zummer is a'-fore us.' ' Bad job this year,' says her companion. ' I didn't mind you 'twere a' tween the 18th and 20th.' " " Thus," adds Miss Summers, "rain between these dates denotes a wet summer." I presume this would mean such a period in any month before summer commences.

Another prediction of rain is that when Hardy's Monument is plainly visible from Dorchester, it is a sign of bad weather; or, as another contributor to the *Dorset County Chronicle* in March, 1898, rhythmically puts it:—

> "When Hardy's Monument is plainly seen,
> There'll soon be heavy rain, I ween."

From an illustration that has such an interesting naval connection with the county I will pass on to one of a more military character, namely, that the playing of a German band usually brings rain. A correspondent in *Notes and Queries* in 1887 (Ser. VII, iii, 306) states that during the haymaking season in Dorsetshire in the previous year a man was heard to say: "I thought it would rain, the Germingham (German) band was in the village." It appears to be a firmly rooted idea in the rural districts of Dorsetshire—and also of Somersetshire (*ibid.*, p. 432) that the arrival of these foreign musicians changes the weather for the worse. It is stated in *Folk-Lore,* vol. xx, p. 348 (1909), that a candidate in a recent Civil Service examination gave as a reason for the decreasing number of German bands in this country that people will not give them money because they bring rain!

The direction of the wind as indicating wet weather will, I think, to most minds afford something more than a merely superstitious belief in the correctness of the following lines, which are not, I take it, peculiar to this county.

> "The south wind always brings wet weather;
> The north wind wet and cold together;
> The west wind always brings in rain;
> The east wind blows it back again."

The face of the sky is eagerly scanned by the weather-wise as indicative of bad or fine weather; and the following lines represent, I think, the form in which this old adage is generally known to Dorset folk:—

> "Red in the morning,
> Shepherds' fore-warning;
> Red at night,
> Shepherds' delight."

Or, a shorter version :—

"Red in the morning,
All day storming."

Mr. Norris gives a combination of these two :

"Urds (red clouds) en tha marnin',
All tha day starmin' ;
Urds en tha night,
'Z tha shephe'ds' delight"
(or, "All the day bright").

The general distrust of "mackerel" sky from a weather point of view is shown from two rhymes given by Mr. Norris in his list of weather-lore items above mentioned.

"Mack'el sky en māā's (mare's) tails,
Da māāke zailas (sailors) lowa zails."

And :

"Mack'el sky,
Wun't be vaour 'n twenty hours dry."

The old Dorset proverb that

"A fog on the hill
Brings water to the mill,"

is, of course, a clear indication of rain.

The ancients were not the only people to practise divination from observations of the flight of birds or the actions of animals. In Dorsetshire it is commonly believed that if rooks are seen to be flying round and round, cawing loudly or in a "charm", as the rustics would say, and frequently dropping in their flight and recovering themselves, it is a sign of imminent and very stormy weather. This is more than a mere superstition, and is easily verified. (See also *Somerset and Dorset Notes and Queries*, vol. i, p. 182, where this action of the rooks is spoken of as "playing breakneck".)

It is commonly noticed that immediately before a thunder-storm birds will cease their singing and seek shelter.

If the green wood-pecker (*picus viridis*)—called in Dorsetshire the "yaffle" (from his joyous laugh of "yaffala, yaffala, yaffala"), the "wood-wall," and sometimes the "rain bird" (see R. Bosworth Smith's *Bird Life and Bird Lore*, p. 405 (1909)—whilst flying from tree to tree or wood frequently utters its discordant, or, as some people would have it, laughing cry, it is a sign of rain.

Again, if a wren ("cutty") is heard to cry or sing much it is said to be a sign of rain.

So, also, if geese fly, or flutter, down hill.

Or if a cock crows upon his perch. Hence the rhyme—

> " If a cock goes a-crowèn to bed,
> He'll cëartainly rise wi' a watery head."

The same significance is attached whenever snails, especially black ones, are seen crawling about to any extent. Thus an old saying:

> " When black snails cross your path,
> Black clouds much moisture hath."

Mr. Hardy—no mean authority upon matters of natural history folk-lore—in *Far from the Madding Crowd* (chapter xxxvi) wherein he gives a most vivid picture of the thunderstorm at Weatherbury, describes the varying action of animals under such circumstances. He speaks of the sheep " trailing homeward head to tail," and, later, when in the field, of the flock crowded together around some furze bushes and grouped in such a way that their tails, without an exception, were turned towards that half of the horizon from which the storm threatened; the confused behaviour of the rooks; the horses moving with timidity and caution, the unusual shifting about after dark of toads and slugs, and the dropping of spiders from the ceiling to the floor as all indicating the imminent approach of a storm.

Portents of fine weather.

If cattle during wet and miserable weather are seen feeding at the top of a hill it is considered a sign that the weather will soon clear up. This I have not infrequently verified myself.

As we have heard that if geese fly, or flutter, down hill it denotes rain, so, if they do so uphill, it foretells fine weather.

The adage is common to most counties, I think, that

> " If it rains before seven
> It will be fine before eleven."

The common, or scarlet, pimpernel (*anagallis arvensis*) called in Dorsetshire " the poor man's weather-glass " from its delicate sense of perceiving the approach of rain—when it closes its flowers—is often apostrophized by children in their games in the following lines:—

> " Pimpernel, pimpernel, tell me true,
> Whether the weather be fine or no.
> No heart can think, no tongue can tell
> The virtues of the pimpernel." [1]

The ash, in conjunction with the oak, is a very favourite test,

[1] See Chapter VII, p. 259.

according as one or the other is the first to put forth its leaves, as to what kind of weather may be expected during the ensuing season.

"If the ash is before the oak,
Then there'll be a very great smoke;
If the oak is before the ash,
Then there'll be a very great splash."

But, as I have said in a former paper in the Dorset Field Club's *Proceedings* in 1899, dealing with superstitions applicable to the ash tree, the variants of this weather forecast are many. Some that I have heard, even in this county, are exactly the opposite to what I have given above, as in the following lines:—

"If the ash is before the oak,
Then there'll be a very great soak;
If the oak is before the ash,
Then there'll be a very small splash."[1]

I think it will be noticed that in the large majority of seasons the oak leaves are out before those of the ash. But I will leave it to observers themselves to say which of the two versions given above they consider the more correct one.

I will conclude this chapter with a reference to the rainbow, which, somewhat curiously, seems to have been made but little use of as a weather portent, at least, so far as it has come to my notice.

A correspondent in *Notes and Queries* (Ser. VII, xi, 17) (1891) states that in Dorsetshire half a century before, the secondary rainbow was called the "water-gull", and was supposed to be necessary to make the weather sign a satisfactory one. If one was seen alone, or with only an imperfect "water-gull", it was deemed unlucky. In other parts of England (*e.g.* Yorkshire) it would seem that attempts were made to "cross out", or get rid of, the bow, by making a cross on the ground. Sometimes this was done by the foot, or by taking two pieces of stick and laying them on the ground and placing a small stone at the end of each stick. Sometimes straws were similarly used, or even the crossing of the forefingers of each hand was considered quite as effectual. This charm was supposed to cause the rainbow to disappear; but one may well believe that by the time some of these charms were got ready the rainbow had disappeared of its own accord. (*Ibid.*, x, 366, 471.)

[1] See Chapter VII, p. 254.

CHAPTER IX

MISCELLANEOUS CUSTOMS AND SUPERSTITIONS

I

SUPERSTITIONS RELATING TO OBJECTS OF DOMESTIC USE OR TO MINOR EVENTS

IN this division I propose to deal with superstitions relating to objects of domestic use, and with those arising out of the minor events of common occurrence in daily life not elsewhere dealt with. These are now brought together and arranged in alphabetical order.

(i) *Bed.*—It is unlucky to " turn " your bed when bed-making on a Sunday or on a Friday.

(ii) *Bell.*—A correspondent (" R. T. ") in Hone's *Every-Day Book* (vol. ii, p. 373) gives an interesting account of bell-ringing in churches about the end of the first quarter of the last century; and as he indicates more than one Dorset town where this practice obtained, I will reproduce that part of his letter here.

" In most of the towns of the West of England they have a custom of ringing one of the church bells (generally the treble bell) in the mornings and evenings. Among other towns I noticed at Dorchester, Dorset, the practice of ringing a bell at six in the morning in the summer, and seven in the winter, and at eight in the evening, concluding after ringing at eight o'clock with striking as many strokes as the month is days old; and this practice, I was informed, was for calling people to work in the morning, the time for dinner, and for leaving work in the evening.

" At another town in Dorsetshire, Sherborne, they have an almost endless ' ding-dong ', ' twing-twang ', ' bim-bome ', throughout the day. Happening to be there lately on a market day (Saturday), I was awakened in the morning at *four* o'clock by the ringing of the ' church treble bell '; at *six* o'clock the church ' chimes ' were in play; at a quarter before *seven* the ' almshouse bell ' began and continued to ring till *seven*, which is said to be for the purpose of calling the scholars of King Edward the Sixth's Grammar-school to their studies, who were no sooner assembled than the ' school bell ' announced the master's approach. At *half-past eight* the ' almshouse bell ' summoned the almsmen and women to prayers; at *nine* the 'chimes'; at *eleven* the 'wholesale market bell'; at *twelve* the 'chimes'; at *one* the 'school bell' for dinner; at *half-past one* the 'retail market bell'; at *three* the 'chimes', and the church 'great bell'[1] tolled twice at a short interval, when, what is appositely enough called the 'tanging bell' rang until the minister and religiously inclined had assembled for prayer; at *four* the 'almshouse bell'; at *six* the 'chimes'; at *seven* the 'school bell' for supper; at *eight* the 'church bell', which rang a quarter of an hour, and concluded by giving eight strokes; at *nine* the 'chimes', and the 'school bell' for bed.

"So much bell ringing and tolling naturally led to an inquiry of the several causes that gave rise to it. By some the first morning and eight o'clock bell is called the 'curfew bell', and the practice of ringing it is said to have been continued from the time of William the Conqueror, who, by one of his laws, ordered the people to put out their fires and lights, and go to bed at the eight o'clock curfew bell; and others affirmed it to be for the purpose of summoning the people to their labours."

As to the "Curfew bell" custom at Stoke Abbott, see Chapter III, p. 134.

(iii) *Bellows.*—It is very unlucky to put a pair of bellows on a table.

(iv) *Boot.*—If boots creak as they are walked in it is a sign that they have not been paid for. So also with shoes. See *Shoe.*

(v) *Candle.*—I have heard it said that the overhanging red-hot wick, or "spark", of a candle is a sure indication of the advent of a stranger. See *Soot.*

(vi) *Christening Palm* (or *Pane*).—See *Palm.*

(vii) *Clothes.*—If by any accident you should put on any article of clothing inside out it signifies that you will receive a present; but if you change you destroy the effect.

It is considered dangerous, or prejudicial to health, to change any article of underclothing before the completion of the month of May.

[1] "This bell is said to weigh 3 *tons* 5 *cwt.*, and to be the treble of a ring of bells brought from Tournay by Cardinal Wolsey, whereof one is at St. Paul's, one at Oxford, one at Lincoln, and one at Exeter. The motto on the crown of this bell, which is called the 'great bell', is said to be:—

> 'By Woolsey's gift I measure time for all;
> For mirth, for grief, for church I serve to call.'"

Hence the well-known couplet:

"Never change a clout
Till May is out."

It must not be forgotten that this superstition probably originated in days when the month of May commenced some twelve days earlier than it does now.

Nor should they be left off except on a Sunday, as the following colloquy, reported from a Dorsetshire source by a correspondent in *Notes and Queries* (Ser. v, x, 23) (1878) shows:—

"Haymaker to her companion:
'No, you won't catch a cold, 'cause you left en off a Sunday.' 'Oh, ees; I shoulden a left en off any other day.' Stranger, listening on the other side of the hedge, to a weeding woman: 'Is that true?' 'Lor, yes, mum, everybody do know that; and when you do up for the first time after sickness should always be on a Sunday.' 'Yes, because it is a quiet day.' 'No, that bean't, if your man's whoam and children. But 'tis all the same wi' yer clothes; they do wear twice so long if you put 'em on fust time a Sunday.'"

(viii) *Cobwebs.*—If cobwebs are seen upon a ceiling it is a sign that no kissing goes on in the room, as the upturned face would notice them and they would be swept off.

I have heard of the converse of this.

(ix) *Confirmation.*—It is stated in Black's *Folk-Medicine*, published by the Folk-Lore Society in 1883, p. 187, that it is a Dorsetshire belief that the laying of the bishop's right hand upon your head at a confirmation is lucky, and the left unlucky.

Miss Summers, in the *Dorset County Chronicle* in June, 1888, mentions the case of an old woman who boasted that she had been confirmed more than once. On being expostulated with she assured her hearer that she had heard that it was "good for the rheumatics", so she thought she would try it.

(x) *Corn.*—It was formerly the custom to arrange the sheaves of corn in the harvest field in "shocks", or cones of sheaves, of ten, so that in each "shock" the last or tenth sheaf represented the tithe.[1]

(xi) *Curfew Bell.*—See *Bell.*

(xii) *Day.*—To the days of the week various superstitions are attached, such as the following:—

[1] See *Notes and Queries*, Ser. x, ii, 349.

"Monday for wealth,
Tuesday for health,
Wednesday the best day of all;
Thursday for crosses,
Friday for losses,
And Saturday no luck at all." [1]

As to the consequences of sneezing or cutting your nails on any particular day of the week, see *Sneeze* and *Nail*.

As to the fortunes of an infant according to the day of the week upon which it happens to be born see Chapter V, p. 178.

(xiii) *Dream.*—Dorset folk are great believers in dreams and their effects. Superstitions attaching to dreams concerning objects of natural history, or of ordinary domestic occurrences, are to be found related under the several heads connected with those objects or subjects.

Some dreams, however, are more to be relied upon than others. According to Miss Summers (*Dorset County Chronicle*, June, 1888), all dreams that are dreamt on a Friday night and repeated on Saturday morning are supposed to be trustworthy, for

"A Friday's dream on a Saturday told
Is sure to come true if it's ever so old."

In a review in the *Dorset County Chronicle* in August, 1883, of a paper on "Dorsetshire Ghosts" by Miss M. F. Billington in *Merry England* for that month, an amusing story is given of the prevalence of the belief in dreams. One man who had lost two children a few years previously actually found himself a local celebrity on the strength of stating that he had seen, in a dream, his two children in heaven sitting on little wooden stools! People flattered his vanity by coming miles to hear the relation of this dream; till, at last, he felt, as it were, commissioned to go into the neighbouring villages and preach his vision.

(xiv) *Ear.*—If your ear tingles it is a sign that somebody is speaking of you; if it were the right ear then the speech was favourable, if the left the reverse.[2]

(xv) *Egg-shell.*—It is believed that something serious will happen if egg-shells are thrown into the fire.

(xvi) *Fairy.*—"It is believed that fairies come down the chimney and do a deal of harm if you don't stop them. The way

[1] *Dorset County Chronicle*, June, 1888.

[2] Conf. *Napier's Folk Lore of the West of Scotland*, p. 137.

to keep them out is to hang a bullock's heart in the chimney" (Mr. H. J. Moule in *Folk-Lore Journal,* vol. vi, p. 116). See *Bullock* (Chapter VII, p. 232), where the same precaution is said to be effective in the case of witches. As to "fairy rings" see *ibid.*, p. 260, *s.v. Toadstools.*

It is firmly believed by many Dorset folk that fairies can get into a house not only down the chimney but also through the keyhole. William Barnes gives effect to this belief in his dialect eclogue on "The Veäries" (p. 74 of the *Poems*) by a most graphic description of a little fairy elf who was discovered in a house in the early morning—having effected an entrance through the key-hole by night, but was unable to get out again—as worthy a subject for Cruikshank's pen as any of those inimitable elfin scenes that he has so charmingly illustrated in the fairy tales of the brothers Grimm.

"Why, when the vo'k wer all asleep, a-bed,
The veäries us'd to come, as 'tis a-zaid,
Avore the vire wer cwold, an' dance an hour
Or two at dead o' night upon the vloor;
Var they, by only utterèn a word
Or charm, can come down chimney lik' a bird;
Or draw their bodies out so long an' narrow,
That they can vlee through keyholes lik' an arrow.
An' zoo woone midnight, when the moon did drow
His light drough window, roun' the vloor below,
An' crickets roun' the bricken he'th did zing,
They come an' danced about the hall in ring;
An' tapp'd, drough little holes noo eyes could spy,
A kag o' poor aunt's meäd a-stannèn by.
An' woone o'm drink'd so much he coulden mind
The word he wer to say to meäke en small;
He got a-dather'd [1] zoo, that after all
Out tothers went an' left en back behind
An' after he'd a-beät about his head
Ageän the keyhole till he wer half dead,
He laid down all along upon the vloor
Till gramfer, comèn down, unlocked the door:
An' then he zeed en ('twer enough to frighten en)
Bolt out o' door, an' down the road lik' lightenèn."

(xvii) *Fire.*—If a wood fire, smouldering on the hearth, suddenly bursts out into a flame without any person's inter-

[1] Bewildered.

vention it is considered a sure sign that a stranger will arrive very shortly.[1]

The extension of this belief to a coal-fire—though, perhaps, not in Dorsetshire—is indicated by the sudden leaping up of the " dying flame " in Scrooge's room on the appearance of Marley's Ghost in Charles Dickens's *Christmas Carol* (1843). But to judge from Leech's illustration of the scene the *candle* flame would here appear to be intended.

So, too, if a fire burn on one side of a grate only.

Sometimes when a log of wood, particularly if of ash, is burning on a fire a spark will fly out towards a person who is sitting near. In such a case the person should immediately spit at the fire, for, it is said, whenever the fire spits at you you should always spit at it again, in order to prevent anger on your part presumably against those whom you may subsequently meet.

Apropos of this last superstition, I was told by an old lady in West Dorset that she had heard of an old man who was sitting in the chimney corner when the fire commenced sending out its " spits ". His wife, anxious to protect him against the effect of any evil influences, called to him : " Father, come out ! Father, come out ! " He replied : " I won't come out " ; to which he presently added : " I wool come out if devil is in vire." Meaning, presumably, if the fire should direct its " spits " towards him.

In making a fire of " nicky wood " (*i.e.* faggots or bundles of small wood) you should always first burn the " bond " (*i.e.* the piece binding the faggot together) or you will never get rich.[2]

(xviii) *Fork.*—If a person is injured by the point of a " pick " (*i.e.* a hay-fork) or other agricultural fork, the point must be immediately thrust into the fire in order to prevent the wound from festering or from becoming inflamed. Some say that it should be stuck into the ground at once in order to have the desired effect. It is intended, of course, to act as a charm.

(xix) *Ghost.*—In her previously mentioned paper on " Dorsetshire Ghosts " (see *Dream*), Miss Billington shows how common is the belief in ghosts amongst Dorset folk. What they are the believers in them do not pretend to explain. One person, she

[1] See Chapter VII, p. 261, *s.v. Wood.*

[2] See a proverb to this effect, Chapter X, p. 296.

said, after telling a strange tale, remarked to her: "I never knows what they be; because if they was spirits gone to heaven they wouldn't want to come back; and if they was gone to t'other place they wouldn't be let come back."

Miss Billington mentions several "ghost stories" incident to various places in the county, which, with others, have been noticed under the names of those localities where they are alleged to have occurred.[1]

(xx) *Hair.*—"M. G. A. S." (Miss Summers), in an article on Dorsetshire Folk-lore in the *Dorset County Chronicle* in June, 1888, mentioned several superstitious customs and beliefs relating to the hair. She says:

"It is true that even around the hair on our heads a diversity of superstitions cluster. Thus Friday is considered an unlucky day for cutting the hair.

'Friday cut and Sunday shorn,
Better never have been born.'

"We also find that the superstitious are very careful to preserve the hair that falls from their heads and not throw it carelessly away, for if a magpie find it and use it for the lining of its nest the death of the person from whose head it has fallen is inevitable within the space of one short year.

"Again, from time immemorial, a lock of hair has been a much prized love token, a memento of the absent one which is always preserved with the greatest care.

"Some who wish to look into futurity and discover who is fated to be their future partner go through the following curious ceremony: Two girls sit together in a room from twelve till one o'clock in the morning unknown to any one. They then take as many hairs from their heads as they are years old and tie them up in a linen cloth. Immediately on the clock striking one they put each hair separately on the fire saying:

'I offer this my sacrifice
To him most precious in my eyes;
I charge thee now come forth to me
That I this minute may thee see.'

"Immediately she has repeated this the spirit of her future husband will appear and walk round the room; each seeing her own and not her friend's fiancé.

"Again, great care is taken that none of the hair should be thrown on the ash heap, for if a witch get only a single hair in her possession she can bewitch the person to whom it belongs.

[1] See Chapter IV.

" Another way of diving into futurity is resorted to. Take a tumbler of water that flows from a stream that runs southwards, borrow the wedding ring of a friend and suspend it by a hair of your own head close over the water, but without touching it, holding the hair between your thumb and forefinger. If the ring slowly revolves and hits the side of the glass you will die an old bachelor or old maid ; it if turns quickly round you will be married at [but ?] once ; if slowly, twice. Others say as many times as the ring strikes the side of the glass so many years will pass before you are married. One old lady assured me this was a sure token, as the ring struck the glass three times when she tried it, and she was married three years afterwards." [1]

You should always have your hair and your nails cut during the waning of the moon, as it is believed that they will not grow again so fast during that phase of the moon.

(xxi) *Hiring.*—A strong prejudice exists against a new servant entering service in the afternoon.

The system of hiring agricultural servants at the principal fairs—where they engage themselves for a twelvemonth—still obtains in many parts of the country, the men bearing the mplements of their calling, the shepherd his crook and the carter his whip. This custom, however, is not so popular as it was formerly, the farmers not caring to bind themselves for so long a time as a year to one who may not be suitable. I believe that domestic servants also are sometimes hired in this way in country districts in the north.

(xxii) *Journey.*—It is unlucky, having once started on a journey, to turn back in order to fetch something which had been forgotten.

(xxiii) *Kettle.*—A kettle that is a long time in boiling is said to have a " twöad " in it.

(xxiv) *Knife.*—If a knife should fall on the ground or floor it is a sign that a stranger, a man, will come to the house during the day ; if a small knife, a short man ; if a large knife, a tall man (*Symondsbury*).

It is very unlucky to cross knives in laying a table. But, if through any inadvertence they should happen to be crossed care should be taken that the same person should not uncross them.

[1] See Chapter V, p. 190.

You should never give a knife to any person as a present without taking something in exchange, a small sum of money, for instance. Otherwise the gift is said to " cut love ", and will bring ill-luck.

(xxv) *Ladder.*—It is considered very unlucky to pass under a ladder unless you spit immediately afterwards.

(xxvi) *Luck.*—Luck can attach itself to persons as well as to things. Hawkers, market women, and others often endeavour to induce persons who are considered to be lucky in their dealings or purchases to become their first purchasers for the day. It is thought that this will bring luck to their day's trading. Some of them set especial store upon the money so obtained, and spit upon it or set it aside.

In selling corn, cattle, or other farm produce, the seller is generally expected to return a part of the price, not so much as a discount as " for luck." [1]

With regard to the very numerous superstitions or omens indicating good or ill luck, I have thought it better to deal with them in relation to the various objects or incidents which give rise to them rather than to tabulate them here. Those which comprise matters relating to witchcraft or charms will be more generally found in the chapter dealing with those subjects—Chapter VI.

(xxvii) *Money.*—You should always be sure to turn over " for luck " any money that may happen to be in your pocket when you first see the new moon.

(xxviii) *Month.*—The following is a very simple but effective *memoria technica* for ascertaining the number of days in any month. Commence counting on your four fingers alternately with the spaces between, when the *fingers* will be found to denote the long months and the *spaces* between the fingers the short ones.

(xxix) *Moon.*—The first time that you see the new moon you must be very careful that it is not through glass or over the right shoulder.

Also be sure to turn over any money that you may happen to have in your pocket at the time " for luck ".

The various superstitions relating to weather-lore connected with the moon are more fully dealt with in Chapter VIII.

[1] Conf. *Shropshire Folk-lore*, pp. 266, 273.

(xxx) *Nail.*—A similar superstition obtains with regard to the cutting of your nails during the waning of the moon as it does to the hair. See *Hair.*

Further, it is considered unlucky to cut your nails on a Saturday. But this last does not seem to agree with what is stated in the following lines describing the consequences that are believed to ensue from cutting your nails on any particular day of the week.

> " Cut them on Monday, cut them for health ;
> Cut them on Tuesday, cut them for wealth ;
> Cut them on Wednesday, cut them for news ;
> Cut them on Thursday, a pair of new shoes ;
> Cut them on Friday, cut them for sorrow ;
> Cut them for Saturday, see your sweetheart to-morrow ;
> Be he that on Sunday cuts his horn,
> Better that he had never been born." [1]

Some say that a baby's nails should never be cut, but that the mother or nurse should bite them.

(xxxi) *Palm.*—This was a covering called a " Christening Palm ", used in West Dorset in bye-gone days for christening purposes.

In 1875, in *Notes and Queries* (Ser. v, iii, p. 288), I described one of these " palms ", now in my possession, in which several bye-gone members of our family had been christened, or at which ceremony it had been used ; not so much, perhaps, as having been worn by the infant at the actual baptismal ceremony, as that in which it was enveloped when brought down for inspection by the guests afterwards. It is some 5 feet in length, and a little less in breadth, made of a rich crimson satin, lined with pink silk now somewhat faded, with a double edging of what seems to be silver lace. And I there asked for information as to when this custom flourished and whether any traces of it still survived.

A Dorset correspondent (vol. iv, p. 138) answered my question by stating that the " palm ", or " pall ", was not in use only for the baptism of the infant, but—certainly as late as forty years previously—was used as the wrapper in which the child was brought down to see company. This correspondent mentioned

[1] *Dorset County Chronicle*, June, 1888.

amongst other christening garments of about the end of the seventeenth century which he or she had in his or her possession: "A palm, 54 in. by 48, of rich stiff silk, lined with white satin."

Another correspondent (iii, 413) spoke of having seen "a similar cloth in the possession of one of the old county families in Devonshire, used at all the christenings of the family for several generations. They called it a 'christening pane', evidently derived from the Latin word *pannus*."

This is evidently what is referred to in Hewett's *Peasant Speech of Devon* (1892), p. 110, as a "Pame": "A square of velvet or satin, used as a christening wrap."

No doubt the introduction in more modern times of christening cloaks and other robes of greater adaptability for the purposes of the actual ceremony has led to the disuse of the "palm" thereat.

This covering must not be confounded—as would seem to have been the case with some of these correspondents—with the "Chrisome cloth", which was set by the minister at baptisms on the head of the newly anointed infant.

I may say that only within the last year or two I have come across a very similar "square" to my own, almost alike in size, rich texture and colour, belonging to an old lady now resident in the London district, but of which she could give me no further account than that it had belonged to her great-grandmother, and had, she believed, been used in olden time for similar purposes. This is the only other "Christening Palm" that I have seen.

(xxxii) *Repetition of Events.*—If an unpropitious event happens three times it is considered peculiarly ominous. Hence the saying: "First and second, beware of the third."

(xxxiii) *Salt-cellar.*—It is very unlucky to upset a salt-cellar. If salt should happen to be spilt, in order to avoid evil consequences some of it must be thrown over the left shoulder.

You should never help any other person to salt; it is believed to be helping him, or her, to sorrow. Hence the distich: "Help me to salt, help me to sorrow." It is said, however, by some that the evil can be averted by giving a second helping.

(xxxiv) *Sampler.*—Sampler work formed a very customary occupation for our grandmothers and great-grandmothers in their days of early girlhood, when the use of the needle found a more important place in the domestic economy of a household than its apparently does at the present day, and this continued well into the nineteenth century. Specimens took the form of small handworked pictures or combinations of geometrical drawings with thread-worked designs of animals, birds, trees, with pious texts or verses, and posies. To these would usually be added the name or initials of the child executing the work, together with the letters of the alphabet and the date. These happily are still to be found in many old-fashioned farm houses of the country, and are highly prized.

Somewhat earlier in time samplers proper took the form of long strips of unbleached linen or fine canvas, upon which were worked conventional or geometrical patterns in woollen or silken thread—one line below the other in gradually increasing depths—with, usually, the letters of the alphabet, the initials of the worker, and the year or date.

Still earlier—and very prevalent in the Stuart period—embroidered pictures, almost miniature panels of tapestry, with raised work—known as "stump" work—were the fashion, the subject matter generally being a classical or Biblical story. These, of course, are now very scarce, and are much sought after.

I have in my possession a very good specimen of this long sampler work, of rather an early period, with the usual geometrical patterns worked in ten rows of gradually increasing depths, and on the lower part the letters of the alphabet (omitting J and U) with the initials "E. V." and the date "1678". The colours of the whole are still wonderfully preserved. This is believed to have been the work of a member of our family when a young girl.

This sampler has always been accompanied by a beautifully worked picture (also in my possession) which is known as "Fair Rosamond and Queen Eleanor". This forms a panel of some 15 in. by 10 in., and is very finely embroidered in various coloured silk threads and enriched with gold and silver thread or wire over raised or "stump" work. In later years, I regret to say, some coarser work has been added to it by less skilful hands in parts where it had evidently been left unfinished. There is no date upon it; but the period is no doubt, I should say, late Stuart.

In 1910 I sent a description of these two interesting specimens of sampler work to *Notes and Queries* (Ser. XI, ii, 303), in which, after giving a short description of the scene depicted—the Queen approaching the labyrinthine bower in which "Fair Rosamond" is seen playing on a guitar, and the royal lover, unconscious of any danger, advancing from the opposite direction—I said:—

"Tradition has it that this picture was worked by a member of the family in Dorsetshire when a girl at school (at Weymouth, I think), and was left unfinished owing to the breaking out of the Monmouth Rebellion. Inasmuch as this rebellion occurred in 1685, and as I have also one of the usual long samplers worked in geometrical designs, letters of the alphabet, followed by the initials 'E. V.' and the date '1678'—which would evidently be the earlier work of a young girl—I am disposed to think that the above tradition has been well founded, and that it was the same hand, when somewhat older, that sought to weave in fairly imperishable material (if well taken care of) the loves of one of the most powerful of the Plantagenet sovereigns and his so-called 'concubine'.

". . . But I can scarcely think that this nimble-fingered ancestress of mine evoked the idea of the drawing out of her own head. One is fain to believe that the subjects chosen or allowed to be selected by school girls were rather religious than classical, and more often portrayed the well-worn Biblical stories of Adam and Eve, Hagar and Ishmael, Joel and Sisera, or Jehu and Jezebel, than the illicit loves of heathen gods and goddesses or those of our own royal personages."

I have never myself come across this subject so illustrated before, and would like to ask if this particular story has ever formed a popular subject for tapestry or embroidered sampler work.

(xxxv) *Scissors.*—The same superstitious belief exists with regard to a pair of scissors as in the case of a knife, namely, that it should never be the subject of a gift between friends, on the ground that such an act will sever or "cut" friendship or love. See *Knife.*

(xxxvi) *Shivering.*—If you shiver suddenly or involuntarily somebody is said to be walking over your grave, or, presumably, where your grave is to be.

(xxxvii) *Shoe.*—Throwing an old shoe after a person for luck is not restricted in Dorsetshire to weddings only, but is practised in some parts whenever any important or unusual expedition or journey is to be undertaken.[1]

A similar belief exists in wearing shoes that creak as in the case of boots (*q.v.*), namely, that they have not been paid for.

(xxxviii) *Sneeze.*—The consequences of sneezing on any particular day of the week are shown in the following lines :—

"Sneeze on Monday, sneeze for danger ;
Sneeze on Tuesday, kiss a stranger ;
Sneeze on Wednesday, get a letter ;
Sneeze on Thursday, something better ;
Sneeze on Friday, sneeze for sorrow ;
Saturday, see your true love tomorrow." [2]

(xxxix) *Snow.*—Certain superstitious beliefs connected with snow are dealt with in Chapter VIII on *Weather-lore.*

(xl) *Soot.*—If a piece of soot clings to the bar of a grate it is a sign that a stranger may be expected ; and if it hangs down in a long flake you can ascertain what day the stranger will come by clapping your hands close to it until it falls off by reason of the current of air thus created, whilst repeating at each stroke a day of the week. The day last-named before the soot falls will be the day on which the stranger will arrive.[3]

I have heard that the "spark" or red-hot overhanging piece of the wick of a candle is equally efficacious in this respect. See *Candle.*

(xli) *Spade.*—It is unlucky to carry a spade into the house on your shoulder.

(xlii) *Spitting.*—Spitting on money that has been received from a purchaser as a means of bringing good luck is commonly adopted by agricultural and other sellers.

Spitting on other occasions so as to avoid the consequences of doing an act that is thought to bring ill-luck (*e.g.* passing under a ladder) has elsewhere been dealt with.

(xliii) *Stairs.*—It is unlucky for persons to pass one another on the stairs ; or to trip going downstairs. But it is considered lucky to stumble or fall when going upstairs. See *Stumbling.*

[1] Conf. *Shropshire Folk-lore*, p. 274.
[2] *Dorset County Chronicle*, June, 1888.
[3] Conf. *Shropshire Folk-lore*, p. 275.

(xliv) *Stone.*—The late Mr. Moule in *Notes and Queries* (Ser. VIII, viii, 52), writing in 1895, tells us that when he was a boy it was common enough to see perforated stones, called "holy stones" or "holy flints" in Dorset where they abound, sea-rolled flints with a natural bore, tied as charms inside the bows of Weymouth boats. He says that he had seen a boatman in the act of fastening one in his craft.

(xlv) *Stumbling.*—It is always considered an omen of good luck if you fall or stumble when going upstairs, the reverse on coming down. See *Stairs.*

(xlvi) *Towel.*—It is believed that if two persons chance to wipe their hands on the same towel a quarrel between them is sure to follow.

(xlvii) *Visitor.*—It is unlucky to watch a visitor away from the house.

(xlviii) *Washing.*—It is unlucky to wash [do any washing] on New Year's Day.

(xlix) *Work.*—It is unlucky to begin any new work on a Friday.

CHAPTER X

PROVERBS AND PROVERBIAL SAYINGS

As to the value of proverbs in any collection of folk-lore I think there can be no doubt. It has been well said of them in the *Handbook of Folk-lore,* edited by the late Sir Laurence Gomme for the Folk-lore Society in 1890, p. 159 :—

" In philology they often supply a guide to the true meaning of words. In ethnology they supply evidence as to the continuance of old races supposed to be extinct. In history they supply evidence of great popular movements unnoticed in chronicles and legal records. In archæology they refer to old monuments and give a clue to their use in prehistoric days. In every-day life they tell us much of the people's view of political and social events. In custom and belief they allude to old faiths, superstitions and laws. In meteorology and other physical phenomena they supply us with evidence as to seasons, changes in weather, changes in topographical features, and other facts which refer back to ages before these things became matters of learning and science."

And again, p. 160 :—

" Even now, in our own country much of the popular wisdom is preserved in old rhymes or in old proverbs ; and it is well ascertained that during the middle ages much of law, and not a little of medicine, was preserved amongst professions not necessarily clerkly by these two agencies."

It must not be supposed that all the proverbs and proverbial sayings that I have brought together here are peculiar to the county of Dorset. It is very probable that some of them may be heard in any of the adjoining counties or even further afield. For instance, I have come across several that are well known in Dorsetshire in Miss C. S. Burne's work on *Shropshire Folk-lore* (1883). Indeed, it is not unlikely that most of them would be found, in some form or other, in such a colossal collection as that of the late Vincent Stuckie Lean, and many doubtless even in Ray. The geographical boundaries of any particular county can no more restrict these sallies of homely wit from spreading across the border than they can impose any artificial limits on plant or weather lore, though in each case, perhaps, there may be local or dialect forms of giving them expression. But from this I have endeavoured in the very great majority of the examples that I have given to keep them free.

I have felt some difficulty in making a satisfactory arrangement or division of this part of my subject. There are many forms of what is known as a proverb, which may be defined to be in dictionary language, a sentence which briefly and forcibly expresses some practical truth, or, as I would prefer to express it, as being more applicable to my purpose here—a wise saw or saying of homely wit, prompted by the daily life and experiences of simple country folk.

In such a modest collection of proverbs as ordinarily would be found within the borders of a county no such elaborate classification is required as might be necessary for the study of the subject generally, or for the comparison of the proverbs of various peoples. Yet I do think it advisable even here to make some distinction or division, if only for purposes of easier reference—the alphabetical system adopted by Hazlitt,[1] for instance, being obviously defective for this purpose owing to the varying phraseology in which so many proverbs are couched.

Miss Burne, in dealing with this subject in *Shropshire Folk-Lore*, p. 587, seems to have experienced much the same difficulty in arriving at a satisfactory scheme of division. Later, when she edited the recent edition of the *Handbook of Folk-Lore* for the Folk-Lore Society, published in 1914, she decided that the best way of achieving this object was by making the division according to form, rather than to the material or subject matter.

Proverbs naturally fall into two groups : (i) *Proverbs proper*—that is to say, proverbs which form complete sentences for citation, as simple maxims and aphorisms ; and (ii) *Proverbial Sayings*, or expressions consisting of parts of sentences only, which may be woven into the speaker's own remarks. These latter again may be subdivided into *Metaphors* and *Similes*.

This arrangement, I think, should ordinarily be sufficient for any local, or county, collection ; but as Dorsetshire has a good number of proverbs that bear only a local significance, I will

[1] *English Proverbs and Proverbial Phrases*, by W. Carew Hazlitt, London, 1869.

add here a third division, namely *Local Proverbs and Proverbial Sayings*. I will take these first.

I. Local Proverbs and Proverbial Sayings

(i) **Batcombe**

Batcombe Boys

An alliterative expression meaning women. A term generally applied to women employed in field labour. This expression appears to have spread far afield, for in West Dorset it used to be said when a lot of women were out haymaking : " You've got a good lot of ' Batcombe boys ' out helping you." I do not know the origin of the local application of this expression.

(ii) **Beaminster**

The Beaminster woman has got hold of you

Said of a lazy person. From a comparison of this proverb with the saying : " Laurence has got hold of you " (*post*, p. 301), it would seem that Beaminster has some claim to be called the " Sleepy Hollow " of the district.

(iii) **Bradpole** (Bridport)

I'm not as bad as that if I do live at Bradpole

It is said that the Bradpole people were once asked why, when their church was first built, the sacred building was not correctly placed (*i.e.* with the chancel facing the east). " Oh," was the reply, " there was an apple tree growing in the way." In due course of time, or by accident, the church required rebuilding, and when it was completed it was ascertained that the defect of position had not been remedied. " Why did you not make the necessary alteration in the site ? " was again the query. " Because," was the answer, " a duck was sitting in the required direction."

This joke is borne in mind by the villagers, and the above phrase is still occasionally heard. Sometimes also a Bradpole man is teased by persons in the neighbourhood greeting him with " Bra'pole man ! Then you have had a pat in the poll "—a punning allusion.

(iv) **Bridport**

Stabbed with a Brydport dagger

" That is, hanged. A great quantity of hemp is grown about this town, and on account of its superior qualities, Fuller says there was an ancient statute, now disused, that the cables of the royal navy should be made thereabouts."[1] The statute was 21 Henry VIII.

(v) **Broadwinsor**

As much akin as Leuson (Lewesdon) hill to Pilsen-pen (Pilsdon)

" That is, no kin at all; though both are high hills,[2] the first wholly, the other partly in the same parish, *viz.* Broadwinsor. These hills are eminent sea-marks, known to the sailors by the names of the Cow and Calf. This is commonly spoken of persons who are near neighbours, but neither relations nor acquaintance."[1]

Another, perhaps more modern, form of this proverb is :—

As far off as Lewesdon Hill from Pillesdon Pen

denoting a distinct severance of friendly relations between near neighbours.

(vi) **Dorchester**

The Devil p . . . d piddles about Dorchester [1]

" This saying arises from the number of small streams running through different villages hereabouts, which, from that circumstance have their names terminating in puddle—pronounced piddle—as Piddle-town, Toll-piddle, Aff-piddle, etc., etc. These waters are very inaptly called puddles, being most of them clear and running."

(vii) **Eggardon**

As old as Eggardon hill

Sometimes pronounced locally " Eggan " or " Aggan ".

A West Dorset way of expressing anything particularly old.

(viii) **Houghton (near Blandford)**

Houghton Owls.

A nickname borne by the inhabitants of a small hamlet near Blandford, who are known as " Houghton Owls ".

[1] Grose's *Provincial Glossary*, 1811, p. 67; Ray's *Proverbs*, 1768, p. 239. Taken from Fuller's *Worthies of England.*

[2] The two highest hills in Dorsetshire.

Mr. Wilkinson Sherren, in his *Wessex of Romance* (1908), p. 12, gives the origin of this " whimsical appellation " :—

" Many years ago John Joyce, a native of the place, missed his way in the wood, and being both timid and benighted, he called out lustily for help. The only answer to his cries was the hoot of the owls (' Whoo-whoo-whoo ') mistaken by him for an answering human voice."

Mr. Sherren regards this as a reasonable assumption for the origin of the parallel story told by Thomas Hardy in *Far from the Madding Crowd* (chap. viii), of Joseph Poorgrass in Yalbury Wood.

(ix) **Lyme Regis**

Dorsetshire Dorsers

" Dorsers are peds or paniers, fixed on the backs of horses, in which higglers carry fish, poultry, and other provisions and wares. Probably these were invented or first generally used in Dorsetshire, as the fish-jobbers, according to Fuller, used to carry their fish from Lyme to London."[1]

An interesting correspondence took place in *Somerset and Dorset Notes and Queries*, vol. iii (1893), in which I took part, on the subject of " Dorsetshire Dorsers."

(x) **Netherbury**

That'll do for Bowood Club

Said of any exaggerated statement. Bowood is a tything in the parish of Netherbury. The origin of the saying is unknown to me.

(xi) **Poole**

(1) *If Pool was a fish-pool and the men of Pool fish,*
There'll be a Pool for the devil and fish for his dish.

" This satirical distich was written a long time ago. Pool is at present a respectable place, and has in it several rich merchants trading with Newfoundland."[1]

(2) *When do you fetch the five pounds* ?

" It is said that a rich merchant of Pool left by his will the sum of five pounds, to be given every year, to set up any poor man who had served his apprenticeship in that town, on condition that he should produce a certificate of his honesty, properly

[1] Grose's *Provincial Glossary*, 1811, p. 67

authenticated. This bequest has not, it is pretended, been yet claimed, and it is a common water joke to ask the crew of a Pool ship whether anyone has yet received that five pounds."[1]

(3) *Shoot zaftly, doey now* [1]

"Another gird at the Poolites. A privateer of that town having, it is said, loaded their guns, on their return to port wished to draw out the shot, but did not know how; nor could they think of any other method than that of firing them off and receiving the shot in a kettle; the person employed to hold the kettle, being somewhat apprehensive of danger, prayed his companion who was to discharge the gun to shoot zaftly.[2] This is told of divers other ports; and in all likelihood with equal truth."

(xii) Shaftesbury

(1) Shaftesbury was once said to be famous for three things:—

More strong beer than water.[3]
The churchyard higher than the church.
More rogues than honest men.

With regard to these sayings, a friend wrote to me from Shaftesbury in 1882: "As regards the strong beer and water question we have now plenty of water. The old churchyard of the parish of St. James is higher than the church. Let us hope as regards the third that Shaftesbury has improved!"

(2) *I won't go there to live where 'ee got to pay a penny a bucket for your water.*

Another allusion to the difficulty and expense of supplying Shaftesbury with water in the olden time.

(xiii) Shapwick

A Shapwick Monster

Said of something too extraordinary to be explained. The following story is told of its origin:—

Once upon a time certain fishermen, passing over a down or hill in the parish of Shapwick, by accident dropped a tortoise or lobster from their panniers. Some workmen coming by

[1] Grose's *Provincial Glossary*, 1811, p. 67.
[2] Softly.
[3] This, no doubt, was in allusion to the difficulty in former days of supplying Shaftesbury with water. See Chapter III, *s.v.* Shaftesbury.

discovered the curiosity but could not determine what the uncommon object might be ; so, leaving the suspicious creature, went in search of their neighbours to get, if possible, some further light on the subject. After repeated inquiries in this direction to no effect, it was suggested that the wise man of the village should be fetched ; and, being as infirm as he was gifted, he was brought to the scene in a wheelbarrow, and after due scrutiny he pronounced the unknown intruder to be a " monster ". On the circumstance becoming known it passed into a proverb to call any uncommon or inexplicable object " a Shapwick monster ". I believe I have seen somewhere some verses on this subject.

(xiv) **Stourpaine**

Going to have a flare up and pin the basket

An expression used many years ago in the neighbourhood of Stourpaine, near Blandford, in reference to the club at Stourpaine, signifying a flourishing finish or wind-up. I do not know its literal meaning.

(xv) **Stour Provost**

As old as Duncliffe Hill

A North Dorset way of expressing anything particularly old.

(xvi) **Wareham**

Wareham Cuckoo

The following story contributed to the *Dorset County Chronicle* in September, 1904, gives the origin of this expression ; a story which the correspondent remarks seems to be a Dorset rendering of a well-known continental fable.

" The inhabitants of Wareham—a town always noted for its gardens, the produce of which in olden days was conveyed by water to Portsmouth, where it had a ready sale—have for centuries past prided themselves upon the mildness of their seasons, the richness of the soil in the gardens, and the early season at which the produce is matured and fit for the market. It was at Wareham that the cuckoo was first heard in the county, and strangers frequenting Wareham Spring Fair, formerly held on April 6th, were wont to confirm this statement ; but there came an April fair day when the note of the cuckoo was not to be heard, and it also happened that this season's produce was very late in ripening. The wise men of Wareham declared that the backwardness of the season was to be attributed to the non-arrival of the cuckoo, and they devised a plan whereby the bird should be compelled to become a permanent resident. The following year the cuckoo was both seen and heard at Wareham fair, and the wise men of the town immediately erected a high fence around the field in which the bird was located. The cuckoo observed this erection with contentment, but when the work had been completed it flew away. 'Oh!' said one of the wise men of the town, 'we ought to have made our fence a little higher.'"

II. Proverbs Proper

1. *A light-heeled mother makes a heavy-heeled daughter.*

Signifying that a quick, industrious mother often fails to train her daughter to follow in her steps; or, perhaps, that she prefers to do the work herself rather than take the trouble to teach her.

2. *A man must ask his wife if he is to get on in the world.*

Meaning that a wife must co-operate with her husband if he is to be successful.

3. *A peck of worry won't pay a pound of debt.*

A hint as to the uselessness of unnecessarily worrying over troubles.

4. *A pigeon-pair* (*i.e.* *a boy and a girl*) *is as bad as a single.*

That is, for being spoilt.

5. *A sighing heart will never break.*

Implying that those who give expression to their feelings generally suffer less.

6. *A slut always carries her duster in her pocket.*

Said of a person who uses her pocket-handkerchief instead of a duster.

7. *An owl always thinks its own young ones the prettiest, and a rook the whitest.*

That is, every parent thinks its own child the best.

8. *Better a little fire to warm 'ee than a great one to burn 'ee.*

A warning against striving for too much. (See T. Hardy's *A Changed Man* (1913), p. 58.)

9. *Better be at the end of a feast than at the beginning of a fray.*

Meaning that it is better to be content with a little that is good than to take part in a dangerous or risky undertaking.

10. *Better wed over the mixen than over the moor.*

Query, implying that it is safer to marry some one from your own neighbourhood than a stranger from a distance. (See T. Hardy's *Far from the Madding Crowd*, chap. xxii.)

11. *Burn your bonds first of "nickies" (wood-faggots) or else you'll never get rich.*

Advice to use method in your work.

12. *Don't be between two parishes at meal times.*

Meaning that you will lose your dinner if you are.

13. *Don't fall before you're pushed.*

A piece of advice not to anticipate troubles.

14. *Don't make fish of one and fowl of another.*

That is, treat all alike ; especially applicable to children.

15. *Forced put is no choice.*

A local rendering of there being no virtue in necessity.

16. *Fore pay is the worst pay.*

That is, never pay before the work is done, in case it may be indifferently executed.

17. *Half of the washing is to wipe in the water and wash in the towel.*

An allusion to hurried and ineffective washing.

18. *Hang the dog that has no excuse.*

Meaning that it must be a very bad case if no justification can be found for it.

19. *He is too fond of looking at his little finger.*

Said of a drunkard.

20. *He'll say anything but his prayers, and for them he'll whistle.*

A disparaging remark.

21. *He that is to be poor must be poor.*

Implying that it is useless to fight against what is inevitable.

22. *He took his pigs to a fine [the wrong] market.*

Said of anyone who has been ruined or disgraced.

23. *I live too near a wood to be frightened by an owl.*

Said of an ineffectual attempt to startle a person.

24. *If a man has one pig he makes it fat ; and if he has one child he spoils it.*

This carries its own explanation.

25. *If you begin where your father left off you will end where your father began.*

A warning to young people on starting life.

26. *If you chop seasoning too fine it will choke you.*

An ironical way of expressing an impossibility.

27. *If you make songs about yourself you can't blame other people for singing them.*

A reminder to persons who endeavour to make themselves attractive or admired so that they may be talked about. (See T. Hardy's *Under the Greenwood Tree,* part v, chapter i, p. 252.)

28. *If you must grow cucumbers boil them and throw them on the dunghill.*

An allusion to their supposed unwholesomeness or uselessness.

29. *If you sing before breakfast you'll cry before night.*

Meaning that too much hilarity can never last.

30. *It's a foul bird that dirties its own nest.*

Said when members of a family expose their own failings to strangers or the public.

31. *Keep an old house dry and an old man wet.*

A bibulous allusion as to what is best for each.

32. *Laziness [idleness] is not worth a farthing [fig] unless it's well followed.*

A local rendering of the well-known proverbial expression: " If a thing is worth doing it is worth doing well."

33. *Money got over the devil's back is sure to go under the belly o'en (of him).*

Said of anyone getting money in a dishonest way; it will soon be lost, or do the person no good.

34. *More nice than wise.*

Said of anybody who is too fastidious.

35. *Most people can see through a turnpike gate when it is open; you can see through a barn door.*

A satirical expression applied to a conceited person.

36. *Never hold with the hare and run with the hounds.*

An allusion to the impossibility of being friends with both parties.

37. *Never make a man your friend till you've seen the smoke come twelvemonths out of his chimney.*

A warning against hasty acquaintanceships.

38. *Never marry anybody outside the sound of your parish bells.*

A warning against hastily marrying a stranger.

39. *Never open the door on the first of March to keep the fleas out all the year.*

The meaning is obscure.

40. *Not too poor to have time to sing.*

Said of persons who are comfortably off. (See T. Hardy's *Under the Greenwood Tree,* part v, chapter ii, p. 270.)

41. *Play with your play-fellows.*

That is, support those who support you.

42. "*That snuddle's over,*" *as Matthey Rawlinson said when he had buried his wife* (Marshwood).

Applied to any fuss or mess (called " snuddle " in this district of Dorsetshire) being over.

43. *That will never pay the old woman her ninepence.*

Said of too low an offer for an article.

44. *That won't happen till I am looking up at the daisy mores* (*roots*).

Said of anything that is not likely to take place soon. More literally, not till you're in your grave with the turf above you.

45. *There never was but one good step-mother, and her the pigs ate.*

A local expression of the opinion so generally entertained of the *injusta noverca.*

46. *There's a difference between staring and stark mad.*[1]

Implying that a thing is not quite so bad, or so good, as it might be.

47. *They like all the water to run in their own ditch.*

Said of selfish people.

48. *Those who change their minds often never die crazy.*

Implying that it is obstinate people who suffer most on being forced to change a conclusion once arrived at.

[1] *Conf.* Ford's *The Lover's Melancholy,* Act II, Scene ii.

49. *Two heads are better than one even if one is a calf's head.*

Meaning that two opinions are better than one, though one of them may not be worth much.

50. *We can't all live in Fore Street.*

Signifying that there must be different positions in life.

51. *What the eye doesn't see the heart doesn't think* [*grieve*].

The meaning is obvious.

52. *What you see wrong in another mend in yourself.*

Another way of expressing the advice given in St. Matthew, chapter viii, vv. 3–5.

53. *When your character is made you may lie a-bed.*

Implying that when your reputation is once established it is afterwards kept up without much trouble.

54. *Whoever will take a pin will take a large thing.*

Possibly intended for a rhyming couplet, implying that dishonesty usually begins by stealing trifles.

55. *You can't yawn after a person you don't like.*

Meaning that you are more likely to follow the example of those with whom you are in sympathy.

56. *You'd spoil a new eighteen-penny knife scraping an ounce of fat off their bones.*

A satirical reference to lean people. Sometimes used with reference to mean or stingy ones.

57. *Your eyes are larger than your stomach.*

Said of a greedy child who has taken on its plate more than it can eat.

58. *Your head will never save your heels.*

A rebuke for thoughtlessness or forgetfulness.

III. Proverbial Sayings

(i) **Metaphors**

1. *A hare and a pound of butter isn't dear at a shilling.*

An allusion to the dry nature of a hare, which requires a lot of basting when being cooked.

2. *A queer Christian, like the Devil's head in a cowl.*

Said of an insincere or hypocritical person. (See T. Hardy's *Far from the Madding Crowd*, chapter viii.)

3. *A silver new nothing.*

Nothing. Said of a promised present.

4. *As busy as a cat in a tripe shop.*

An allusion to a person being very busy without any satisfactory result.

5. *As much need as a toad has of a side-pocket.*

Spoken of anything that is quite unnecessary.

6. *Blindman's holiday.*

When it is too dark to do anything rest is justifiable—as it is to the blind.

7. *Bowing and scraping like a bull at a bank.*

Implying an affectation of extreme politeness.

8. *Cats are like mothers-in-law, more attached to the house than to the people who are in it.*

The meaning is obvious.

9. *Don't be like a pig, no good to anybody till he's cut up and you've got his flitch.*

Said of a stingy old man.

10. "*Every one to his liking,*" *as the old woman said when she kissed her cow.*

A local rendering of the old saying that there's no accounting for taste.

11. *Every whip and turn.*

A term applied to the frequent repetition of a thing.

12. *Furze is out of bloom when kissing is out of fashion.*

That is, never.

13. *Greasing the fat sow.*

Bestowing gifts upon the rich.

14. *He has eaten too much pig's marrow.*

Said of a talkative or indiscreet person who speaks of what he should not. What the exact significance of "pig's marrow" is I do not know.

15. *He is one of those who hangs up his fiddle behind the door.*

Said of a person who is very amiable except when at home.

16. *He was born on a Wednesday.*

Said of a person who squints, because he looks both ways for Sunday. (Wednesday being the middle day of the week.)

17. *High tail on end.*

Said of a person in an excited state.

18. *I wouldn't trust him further than I could throw a bull by the tail.*

That is, no distance ; not at all.

19. *In the twinkling of a cock-sparrow's eyebrow.*

Said of anything done very quickly.

20. *Just like the parson's barn.*

That is, the tithe barn ; never so full but that it could take a bit more.

21. *Laurence has got hold of you.*[1]

Said of a lazy person. Barnes, in his *Glossary* (1886), p. 77, *s.v.* " Larrence = Lawrence ", says that from some cause which he has not yet found Lawrence is in some parts of Dorsetshire the patron or personification of laziness. An old lady correspondent in West Dorset has suggested to me that the saying is derived from a very lazy man of that name who used to live at Beaminster.

22. *Like a devil's " cow "*[2] *in a dish of butter-milk.*

Said of anything ridiculously small in proportion to its surroundings.

23. *Like a tomtit on a quarter of horse-flesh.*

Another expression denoting a ridiculous contrast in size.

24. *Like chips in a porridge, neither good nor hurt.*

Said of any harmless, useless sort of person.

25. *Next never-come tide* [*time*].

That is, a doubtful or indefinite period.

26. *No more brains than a turnip.*

Spoken of a very stupid person.

27. *Not to have all his buttons on.*

Said of a person of weak intellect.

28. *One onion is enough for a whole parish.*

A tribute to the far-reaching properties of this wholesome vegetable.

[1] *Conf.* Local Proverbs, *s.v.* Beaminster, *ante*, and Rhyming Proverbs, *post*.

[2] A flat kind of beetle ; the little spotted red insect called " Lady-bird ".

29. *Plant pears for your heirs.*

An allusion to the fact that pear trees are a long time before they bear fruit.

30. *Saturday-Sunday work.*

This, pronounced drawlingly, indicates a rebuke for dawdling in your work.

31. *Set the fox to keep the geese.*

Said of one who may have intrusted property to the keeping of another, who, from circumstances of character, is likely to be unfaithful.

32. *Sewn with a red-hot needle and burning thread.*

Said of needlework insecurely or carelessly done.

33. *Short and sweet, like a donkey's gallop.*

An allusion to the slow pace of that animal.

34. *Some folks are always behind, like a cow's tail.*

A gibe at unpunctual persons.

35. *Spring cauliflowers' style.*

Making a good deal out of a little, or a fuss out of nothing.

36. *The black dog is on his back.*

Said of anyone who is in a bad temper.

37. *The dustman is coming.*

Said when children rub their eyes on feeling sleepy, as if inconvenienced by something in them.

38. *The kettle is crocking.*[1]

A local variant of the more general expression: "The pot calling the kettle black." Said when a person finds fault with another when he does the same thing himself.

39. *The still sow eats the lou' (loud) sow's meat.*

Meaning that a quiet person often comes off best.

40. *The vu'st bird, the vu'st ëass.*[2]

The first bird, the first earthworm. A dialect form of the well-known proverb: "First come, first served."

41. *There's our cat and another.*

Said in rebuke of an exaggerated statement.

[1] A "crock", ordinarily the name of an earthen vessel, is applied to an iron pot in some parts of Dorsetshire (Barnes's *Glossary*, 1863).

[2] Barnes's *Grammar and Glossary*, 1863, p. 37.

42. *They don't shut ploughs.*[1]

That is, they cannot agree.

43. *To get out of the way of the waggon.*[2]

To go one's way ; to go upstairs.

44. *To swallow the anchor.*

To change or give up one kind of occupation or work for another.

45. *To turn your toes up.*

To kill you ; or meaning when you are dead.

46. *Two-legged blackbirds.*

Human fruit-stealers.

47. *Two-legged foxes.*

Human thieves.

48. *What a tail our cat's got!*

An exclamation evoked by the sight of unwonted finery or conceit, or by the expressions of a boaster.

49. *Worth a Jew's eye.*

A term of comparison.

50. *You want to pick out my gizzard.*

Said to a prying, inquisitive person.

(ii) Similes

1. *As big as a Dorchester butt* (Halliwell).
2. *As dapper as a dunnick* (*hedge-sparrow*).
3. *As dead as a nit* [*or nits*].
4. *As drunk as lords.*
5. *As fast as a donkey's gallop.*
6. *As lazy as Ludlam's dog.*
7. *As lively as a lark.*
8. *As lively as a maggot.*
9. *As long as a fiddle.*
10. *As mad as a cappel-faced bull.*[3]
11. *As meek as Moses.*
12. *As merry as a cricket.*

[1] *Conf.* "shut," Barnes's *Glossary*, 1863.

[2] See Barnes's *Poems*, "Father Come Hwome," p. 129 (last line).

[3] *i.e.* with white muzzle. *Conf.* Barnes's *Glossary*, 1863, *s.v.* "capple-cow." See also T. Hardy's *Under the Greenwood Tree*, pt. ii, chap. viii, p. 147.

13. *As nervous as a cat.*
14. *As plain as houses.*
15. *As plain as a pike-staff.*
16. *As proud as a louse.*
17. *As ragged as a ram.*
18. *As rotten as tinder.*
19. *As scatter-brained and thirtingill* [1] *as a chiel.*
20. *As sour as a grig* [*rig*].
21. *As thin as a rail.*
22. *As wet as muck.*
23. *As wry as a badger.*
24. *To grin like the teeth of a rake.*
25. *To run like a skitty* [*land-rail*].
26. *To yap like a sheep-dog.*

(iii) Rhyming Proverbs

Several of our Dorsetshire proverbial sayings take the form of rhyming couplets or verses, which I have thought it better to place together here in a separate section.

1. *A son is a son till he takes him a wife ;*
A daughter's a daughter all the days of her life.

Implying that a son's affection is more easily alienated from his parents than a daughter's.

2. *A whistling woman and a crowing hen*
Are neither good to God nor men.

(A variant reads in the second line : *nor outdoor nor 'ithin.*)
An allusion to the estimate in which females who adopt masculine attributes are held.

3. *Barnaby Bright,*
The longest day and shortest night.

Said of St. Barnabas's Day, which occurs shortly before the summer solstice.

4. *Good for the bider,*
Bad for the rider.[2]

Said of deep alluvial soil, which is remunerative to the inhabitants but inconvenient to travellers.

[1] ? or *thirtover* (Barnes's *Glossary*) = perverse. See T. Hardy's *Under the Greenwood Tree*, pt. i, ch. iii, p. 21.

[2] See Barnes's *Grammar and Glossary*, 1863, p. 37.

5. *He that would care for his eyes and brain*
Will never eat an onion again.

It was popularly supposed that an onion was bad for the brain, as well as causing the eyes to smart.

6. *If " ifs " and " ans "*
Were pots and pans,
What would poor tinkers do ?

An allusion to the frequency of these expressions of excuse.

7. *If you want to see the King and Queen*
You must cut the oats when they are green.

A somewhat obscure warning against incurring loss or waste. If oats are not cut before they are quite ripe there is a risk of their falling out of the husks.

8. *If youth did know what age did crave,*
How many pence there would be save.

A warning against extravagance in young people.

9. *Leazy Laurence, let me goo,*
Don't hold me zummer an' winter too ! [1]

An exclamation uttered when one feels unusually lazy or disinclined to work.

10. *Sluggard's guise,*
Lwoth to bed and lwoth to rise.[2]

Said of a sluggard.

11. *Them as would thrive*
Must rise at five ;
Them as has thriven
May lie till seven.

Another form of Proverb No. 53, *ante*.

12. *To eat an apple going to bed*
Will make the doctors beg their bread.

An allusion to the supposed wholesomeness of eating a winter, or keeping, apple at bed-time.

13. *When there's no arm aching*
There's no heart breaking.

A consolation to those who have no children.

[1] *Ibid.*, p. 67.
[2] *Ibid.*, p. 86.

14. *If a partridge had but a woodcock's thigh*
'Twould be the finest bird that ever did fly;
If a woodcock had but a partridge's breast
'Twould be the finest bird that ever was drest.

15. *Green and white,*
Forsaken quite;
Pink and blue,
Will never do;
Pink and green,
Fit for a queen.

A Dorset form of a not uncommon "colour" proverb.

16. *Thatch me well and keep me dry,*
Hearts of oak I will defy.

Spoken of alder-poles when peeled for rafters.

(iv) **Weather Proverbs**

There are still some proverbs foretelling or denoting changes in the weather which I have thought it better to deal with separately under the subject of "Weather-lore" in Chapter VIII.

CHAPTER XI

BALLADS AND SONGS

I SUPPOSE all the ballads and songs known to or sung by those resident within the geographical limits of any particular county can no more be said to be the product of that county than can the proverbs customarily to be found within its borders. I think the best way, therefore, will be to notice here those folk-songs which are to be found within the boundaries of Dorsetshire, and which may fairly be said to belong to it, either from having been generally sung by its people or as containing distinct reference to locality or dialect which would tend to render any other source improbable.

The Rev. Herbert Pentin, honorary secretary of the Dorset Field Club, published in vol. xxvii, p. 24 (1906) of the *Proceedings* of that Society a paper upon " Old Dorset Songs ", to which source I am indebted for several of the songs comprised in this chapter.

In the introductory portion of his paper Mr. Pentin makes the following interesting remarks which are worth recording here. He says :

" Of course, we cannot shut our eyes to the fact that the old traditional songs are fast dying out. Boys educated at a National School think it almost beneath their dignity to sing the ungrammatical, unrhythmical and unpoetical songs in which their fathers and forefathers delighted. They do not know that the bad grammar, the uneven rhythm, and the poor rhyme often mark the most ancient songs—songs composed not infrequently by villagers themselves, and corrupted as the years have passed away ; old-time roystering ale-house songs with their nonsense choruses ; songs sung by the wandering minstrels of days gone by ; songs from the old ballad-sheets of the pedlars. And yet I notice that these same boys, when they sing in public, repeat the title of their songs at their conclusion, thus unconsciously keeping up a custom started by the old ballad-singers of long ago."

The first of these Dorset ballads that I came across was during a short visit I once paid to the Chetham Library at Manchester, upwards of forty years ago, when consulting Halliwell's *Catalogue of Ballads and Broadsides* in that library. It was called *The Dorsetshire Garland*, or, *The Beggar's Wedding*. No date was affixed to it. It was lengthy and I had not time then to take a copy of it. The Rev. Canon Mayo, however, in the *Somerset and Dorset Notes and Queries*, vol. vii, p. 115 (1901), has supplied my want, and has given a copy of the words. This is what he says about it:

"The following ballad, in my possession, is roughly printed on a leaf of hand-made paper, measuring 14½ in. by 9½ in., in four columns about 7½ in. high, each column being separated from its neighbour by a line of ornament. It is evidently meant for sale by chapmen in the street, or at Fairs. The subject may suit, indeed, any other county, but as the scene is laid in Dorsetshire these lines may be worth recording in the pages of *Somerset and Dorset Notes and Queries*."

It would seem, therefore, to come within the canons I have laid down for inclusion in this chapter.

THE DORSETSHIRE GARLAND,

OR

THE BEGGAR'S WEDDING.

PART I.

All you that delight in a jest that is true,
Give ear to these lines I unfold to you;
I'm sure you will smile when the same you hear,
This frolic was acted in fair Dorsetshire.

Now a noble knight of renown lived there,
Who had a daughter of beauty most clear;
Hard by liv'd a merchant who had riches store,
Who had but one son whom he did much adore.

The knight and the merchant being neighbours near,
In friendship they liv'd, and lov'd each other dear.
Now they had agreed, these infants so dear,
Should be man and wife when come to riper year.

The merchant fell sick, and his lady likewise,
They sent for the knight with tears in their eyes,
Saying, From the world we soon must part,
And leave our baby the joy of our heart

I hope if we leave our dear child to your care,
With all our estate and worldly affair,

You'll take care of him when we're laid in the grave,
Nay furthermore grant us the thing that we crave;

That you do not break your promise to me,
But give your fair daughter his bride to be.
But if he should die 'ere he to age do come,
Then all that I leave him is to be your own.

To the Church of England I'd have him brought,
And to serve his Maker let him be taught,
That we may meet in heaven above.
Dear Sir, said the knight, for the friendship and love

That has pass'd betwixt us I'll take special care
How I do bring up your young son and heir;
Now if that the Lord so long gives me life,
My daughter shall be your son's sweet wife.

So then for the babies they sent for with speed,
And the merchant said, Now my heart does bleed,
For to leave them behind, but it must be done,
Death calls me hence, and my glass is run.

His will being made, I'm content, as he did say,
And kissed the babes with lips cold as clay,
So both in one moment did yield up their breath,
The happiest couple that lived on earth.

The merchant and his wife both laid in one grave,
He takes home the child and kept it most brave;
So the knight's daughter and the merchant's son
Became the public talk around the town.

These children loved each other so dear,
As this covetous knight began to fear;
His promise he now accounts but a jest,
How he must perform, which disturbed his rest.

My daughter, said he, is a beauty most bright,
She will be fit for a lord or a knight.
But ten thousand pounds is left to the boy,
I must find means his life to destroy.

PART II.

He hired a beggar the child to kill,
So the innocent babe, thinking no ill,
As they both at sport were busy at play,
The treacherous knight with a false laugh did say,

Come, Jemmy, will you go and take the air ?
And I, worthy Sir, said the daughter so fair,
For to gather dazies with Jemmy will go.
But her father answer'd, It must not be so ;

You must stay at home till he comes back again.
So this innocent child, like a lamb to be slain,
Did go with the beggar many a long mile,
Who at length to him did speak with a smile ;

Pray where are you going, Sir, tell unto me,
Must I no more pretty Susan to see ?
So his innocent talk made the beggar relent,
So home to his wife with the child away went,

And told her the story ; the woman then said,
Lo ! he's a fine creature and a well-favour'd babe ;
So a-begging with us I pray let him go,
We'll call him our son, let us order it so.

But five years of age was this merchant's son,
Yet he for the loss of his Susan did mourn ;
So the beggarman's wife to her husband did say,
Come let us contrive to steal Susan away.

It is but justice to cheat the cruel man,
That wants this innocent for to trapan ;
So the beggar to Dorset then instantly went,
For to steal young Susan was resolute bent.

He brought her ten miles, till they came to a town,
And stripp'd off her clothes as she mightn't be known,
And over a hedge he threw them indeed,
And homewards at night did hasten with speed.

In two or three hours he arrived at his cell,
Where a noble legion of beggars did dwell ;
Where now I must leave those beggars so young,
And return to the knight who did bitterly mourn.

An hue and cry he sends to every town,
For finding his daughter there's five hundred pound.
They brought him the clothes as found in the field,
Which made him believe his daughter was kill'd.

Now, heavens ! he said, I see it is just,
This innocent babe whom I had in trust,
His blood cries for vengeance, I have my desert ;
I have lost my daughter, the joy of my heart.

So now let us leave this base traytor to mourn,
Who wander'd about like one that's forlorn;
And turn to young Jemmy and Susan also,
Who along with the rest now a-mumping[1] did go.

Now the beggar them for his children did own,
And most dutiful children that ever was known,
Which pleas'd him so well, to Doll he did say,
The money that was gave me this babe to slay,

He shall have for his portion, and twice as much more,
And since that each other they do so adore,
If they do live to the age of eighteen,
We'll have the best wedding that ever was seen.

For Jemmy and Susan in marriage shall join,
Do not me controul for this frolic of mine,
A score of bold suitors I swear shall be there,
We will keep this wedding in fair Dorsetshire.

We will give it out upon such a day,
A brave beggar's wedding there is to be,
The gentry will be eager to see such a sight,
And, if he is living, that base perjur'd knight.

When that this wedding is done and all o'er,
I'll take this young couple unto their own door,
And make him a present of his daughter fair,
And take to him Jemmy his son and heir.

Old Doll she was pleased to hear him say so,
So merrily out they a-cruising did go.
For thirteen long years they at this rate did run,
At length the fixed time for the wedding was come.

Part III.

The richest attire that ever was bought,
With silver and gold it was richly wrought,
For the bridegroom and bride they did then prepare,
And took their journey into Dorsetshire.

A score of the best that did belong to the tribe,
They took along with them to credit the bride,
The lame with their crutches, the halt and the blind
Were placed in great order to follow behind.

[1] Conf. *Mump*—" one who is wont to beg of her neighbours." Barnes's *Glossary*, 1886. Also Halliwell: *s.v. Mump*—to beg or cheat (West.).

And having been two or three days in the town,
The fame of this wedding it spread up and down.
The rich and the poor were all curious to see,
And many resolv'd the bride's guest to be.

They hired the noblest hall in the town,
That rich and the poor might get room to sit down,
But Jemmy and Susan were both kept secure,
'Till they in their splendour appear'd at the door.

Some hundreds of people stood by for to gaze,
At the sight of the couple were struck in amaze;
For she did appear like an angel divine,
And he did the rest of his sex far outshine.

Old Doll and her husband did follow the bride,
With a budget of good bread and cheese by her side,
And after came hopping the blind and the lame,
Such a wedding in England was ne'er before seen.

This couple were not ashamed of their guest,
Because they nothing did know of their birth,
But joined in marriage they back did return;
And now for the pastime they had, Sir, at home.

They furnished the table with good wedding cheer
They mump'd on the road to fair Dorchester,
Good rhine of fat bacon, and old musty cheese,
And noggins of ale as much as you please.

Dinner being over starts up one of the guests
And pulled out his bag-pipes and played up the best,
The lame and the blind went to dancing the hay,[1]
And the gentry flock'd as they would to a play.

Amongst the rest came this treacherous knight,
Fixing his eyes on his daughter so bright,
His heart did flutter, and throb in his breast
His spirits were seized, and his mind opprest.

Old Doll cry'd, We must have a jig of the bride,
Come, play up a merry horn-pipe she cry'd,
Which Susan performed with so much grace,
That she won the praise of every one in the place.

Nay come, said the old man, 'tis a child of my own,
Come, jovial piper, strike up t'other tune;
A health to the bridegroom let's pass round the room,
Tho' a beggar brought up he's a merchant's son born.

[1] A round country dance (Halliwell).

The knight hearing this stept up to the bride,
Let me speak to you, fair creature, he cry'd ;
If you have a mark of a rose on your breast,
Then you are my daughter I vow and protest.

She showed him the mark ; he immediately cry'd,
Take home the bridegroom and the sweet bride.
For this is my joy that's been missing so long,
And her dear joy the merchant's young son.

Bring the guests with you unto my home,
I'll kindly receive you, and when I have done
I'll inform the world of my treacherous deed.
Who can deny what the heavens decreed ?

The cripples snatched up their crutches and run
To see what great miracles there had been done.
Her father confessed the whole matter that night.
All praised the beggar that saved the babe's life.

All people upbraided him for his base crime.
With grief he dyed within a short time,
And left this young couple six thousand a year,
Who are styled the beggars of fair Dorsetshire.

Old Doll and her husband in splendour did dwell,
This couple they loved them very well ;
You misers that are of a covetous mind,
Strive not to prevent what the powers design'd.

I think this ballad is a very good example of the kind spoken of by Mr. Pentin. Though evidently corrupt and modernized—the names of the hero and heroine being painfully so—it bears traces of a respectable antiquity. In its early stages it has a strong resemblance to a well-known old story of the " Babes in the Wood ", yet ends very differently and in quite a melodramatic manner. It contains several archaic and provincial expressions ; and though, as I have said, no date is fixed to it, yet from one of the incidents mentioned in Part III, namely " dancing the hay "—a dance no longer known, I believe, in the West of England—it is possible to suggest a period not less remote than the seventeenth century. Halliwell, in his *Archaic and Provincial Dictionary* (1852), explains this as a " round country dance ", and gives a reference to Howell's *England's Helicon*, p. 228 (1660) :—

" Shall we go daunce the *hay* ? "

Mr. C. J. Wallis in *Notes and Queries* (Ser. v, x, 297) (1878), mentions " An Old Story ", which, he tells us, was done into verse and sung by the peasantry of Dorset when George III was king. The ditty was a very long one, and Mr. Wallis could remember but a few verses only. Perhaps the deficiency can be supplied. He says :—

" Discarding all preliminary matter, I hasten to introduce the hero—a faithless swain on murderous deeds intent,—who perfidiously prevails upon the lady of his love to elope from ' her own father's hall ' :—

She mounted on her milk-white steed,
And he on a dapple-grey ;
They rode till they came to the lone seashore,
Three hours before it was day.

" At this point an abrupt halt is made, and the lady is peremptorily invited by her cavalier to dismount. Then follows the command :—

' Doff off, doff off your silken gown,
And deliver it unto me,
For I think it not fit such a fine garment
Should rot all in the salt sea.'

" And so it fares, *seriatim,* with each of the luckless lady's vestments until the ultimate delicately interesting snow-white garment is reached, which the incarnate fiend standing before her grossly calls her ' holland smock ' :—

' If I'm to doff my holland smock,
Pray turn thy back unto me,
For I think it not fit such a ruffian
A naked woman should see.'

He turned his back towards her,
And bitterly did she weep ;
She caught him round the middle so small
And tumbled him into the deep.

" Then came repentance, with its usual unfortunate tardiness :

He dropped high, he dropped low,
Until he came to the side.
' Take hold of my hand, my pretty Polly,
And I will make thee my bride.'

" The lady prudently declines to take the hand thus insidiously offered :—

' Lie there, lie there, you false-hearted man,
Lie there instead of me ;
For six pretty maidens you have drowned here,
And the seventh hath drowned thee.'

"After this very startling revelation the lady—so recently inspired by courage and prudence—coldly turns her back upon her quondam lover and returns to 'her own father's hall.'"

Mr. W. J. Bernhard Smith, at the same page, suggests that this story is probably from the ballad of "The Outlandish Knight", printed in *Ballads, Songs, etc., of the Peasantry*, by Robert Bell.

3. The next song is a dialect one, which sufficiently bespeaks its origin. In 1882 a correspondent "W. B." (under which initials I think we can easily trace the "Dorset Poet"—William Barnes—) in the then recently started Folk-Lore Column of the *Dorset County Chronicle*, asked for the full words of an "old Dorset song" of which he gave three verses. Another correspondent, from memory, added a couple more, and eventually, the full song in eight verses, under the title of "Roben's Cöortèn", was supplied by an anonymous correspondent. It is in dialect form, with such variations as indicate a somewhat wide range, and runs as follows :—

ROBEN'S CÖORTÈN.

"As I be thee mother, and thou bëest my zon
Coom listen to pëarent's advice.
Put on thee best clothes and thee fine yaller hose,
And goo out and zeek thee a wife, thee must,
Aye, thee must, that thee must,
Thee must goo out and zeek thee a wife, thee must."

Then Roben put on his very best clothes
Which were nayther ragged nor torn ;
His best Zunday clothes, and his fine yaller hose,
And he looked like a gen'leman born, 'er did,
A'a', 'er did, that 'er did,
'Er looked like a gen'leman born, 'er did.

As Roben were walkèn along th' röad,
Not mindèn the t'other fine folk,
He happened to kiss the wife of a priest,
An' she had 'en clapped into the stocks, she did,
A'a, she did, that she did,
She had 'en clapped into the stocks, she did.

The next one that Roben wer' smiten to,
Wer' th' butcher's fat därter called Grëace ;
He hadn't a-zaid twenty-four words or more,
When she hit 'en a slap in th' fëace, she did,
A'a, she did, that she did,
She hit 'en a slap in the fëace, she did.

"O! öoman, O! öoman, thee sure must be mad,
To beäte such a gallant as I,
Th' blood from my nose ha' spoiled my best clothes,
And never I will get me a wife, I wunt,
Nay, I wunt, that I wunt,
I never'll seek me a wife, I wunt.

If thëase be the wäay I goo zeek me a wife,
I'll never goo zeek me another,
But zingle I'll bide all the days o' me life
And I'll goo hwome to my mowther, I 'ooll,
A'a, I 'ooll, that I 'ooll,
I'll goo hwome to my mowther, I 'ooll."

When she zaw 'en a coomèn along th' road,
Her heart wur for yoother's quite glad;
She called 'en her bwoy, her darlèn, her jwoy;
"Why, Roben, how quickly thou'rt wed, thou art,
A'a, thou art, that thou art,
Why Roben, how quickly thou'rt wed, thou art."

"Now, mowther, I tell 'ee 'tis noo such a thing,
I wur never zoe 'shëamed in my life;
I have spoiled my best clothes and my fine yaller hose,
An' I'll never goo zeek me a wife, I wunt,
Nay, I wunt, that I wunt,
I'll never goo zeek me a wife, I wunt."

Somewhat later, "B.", in the "Folk-lore Column", referring to the above song, said that the mention of the yellow "hose" in "Roben's Cöortèn" betokens that that song was written about the time of the foundation of the Bluecoat School of Christ's Hospital, when the yellow hose, yet worn by the boys, was in full fashion. This would make it appear that the song was written about the middle of the sixteenth century. I can scarcely imagine, however, that it was necessary to go so far back as that for its origin, for the wearing of "yaller hose" by old-fashioned folk surely can be traced to a very much later period than that.

The same writer, at the same time, supplied the words of another courting song, which he said he had heard sung in Dorchester many years previously by an old man and his sister who had been asked in to a Christmas dinner. He stated that while singing the woman walked *floutingly* round the room with the man after her till the middle of the last verse, at the end of which they walked off "a-hitched up". The words are as follows :—

HE :

"I will give you a silken gownd,
Nine yards long to trail on the ground,
If you'll be my love and my only dear,
And go walking with me anywhere."

SHE :

"I'll not accept of a silken gownd,
Nine yards long to trail on the ground,
I'll not be your love and your only dear,
And go walking with you anywhere."

HE :

"I'll give you the keys of the little chest,
And all within that is now possest,
If you'll be my love and my only dear
And go walking with me anywhere."

SHE :

"I'll not accept the keys of the little chest,
And all that within is now possest;
I'll not be your love and your only dear
And go walking with you anywhere."

HE :

"I'll give you the very keys of my heart,
To bind us together till death us do part,
If you'll be my love and my only dear,
And go walking with me anywhere."

SHE :

"I will accept the keys of your heart,
To bind us together till death us do part,
I will be your love and your only dear,
And go walking with you anywhere." [1]

"B. B." in the *Somerset and Dorset Notes and Queries* (1905) (vol. ix, p.272) gave the words of an old song which had been lately repeated to him from memory by an old woman who had never learnt to read or write, nor had ever quitted her native Dorset village of Yetminster. She told him that the children used to sing this "when she was a very little maid, not four years old". The lines were :—

When Adam was first created
And Lord of the Universe crowned,
His happiness was not completed
Until that a helpmate was found.

[1] These two last songs are also given in Mr. Pentin's paper.

Then Adam was laid in a slumber
And God took out part of his side;
And when he awoke he was wondered,
For he held a most beautiful bride!

"She was not took out of his feet, Sir,
By Man to be trampled upon;
Nor was she took out of his head, Sir,
To reign and triumph o'er Man.

But she was took out of his side, Sir,
His equal and partner to be;
So now they're united together,
Let Man be the top of the tree!"

The following ballad partakes of a more legendary character—indeed it is styled "The Legend of St. Gabriel's"—I have a note that it appeared in the pages of *Once a Week*, but I can give no more exact reference, and can only say that if so it must have been a good many years ago. The account went on to say that the "ruins of the little chapel of St. Gabriel's which bear testimony of the truth of at least some part of the legend (well known amongst the country people of the neighbourhood) are still to be found in a parish of the same name situated at the foot of Golden Cap, the highest range of beautiful cliffs bordering the coast of Dorsetshire between Lyme Regis and Bridport."

I myself heard a very similar version of the legend read at a meeting of the Dorset Field Club in the summer of 1887 by the then incumbent in charge of Stanton St. Gabriel, the late Rev. C. R. Baskett, a member of the Society—the rest of us standing by the chapel ruins situated a few fields away from the present church. A few years previously, I remember, a massive old oak beam which had, no doubt, formed part of the rood screen in the old chapel, and had been lying neglected for many years, had been rescued from the ruins by Mr. Baskett, who was then curate of Whitechurch Canonicorum, the mother church, and restored to a similar position in the new chapel or church of St. Gabriel's.

The words of the legend are as follows:—

THE LEGEND OF ST. GABRIEL'S.

The waves beat high about the ship,
A goodly ship and strong;
The captain sends a cheering word
Th' affrighted crew among.

The waves beat wild upon the ship,
And howling blows the wind;
And the crew can read in the captain's face
The anguish of his mind.

The vessel drifts on the open sea,
Her masts, her compass, gone;
And the foaming, seething billows now
Are fearful to look upon.

"Oh! Captain, give me the ship's small boat,"
Young Bertram loud he cried.
"Oh! give me straight the ship's small boat
To save my fair young bride."

"I will not give thee the ship's small boat,
To sink in such a sea;
For be thy bride or drowned or saved
It shall not part from me."

"Oh! Captain, change that cruel word,
For the ship is lost I wot;
But the little boat may ride and float
Where the vessel riseth not."

The captain looked at the broken ship;
He looked at the lady pale;
He heard the roaring of the sea
And the howling of the gale.

"Ay, take the boat, and the Saints thee save,
And bring thee safe to shore;
For of crew or captain never a man
Shall live to tread it more."

Then Bertram took his bride in his arms,
Into the boat leapt he;
But the waves dragged down the doomèd ship
To the prison house of the sea.

The ship's small boat rides well—rides well—
Over the waves so high;
The lady she trembles and weeps for fear,
And moans with piteous cry.

She beareth weight of precious freight,
Of gold and gems good store;
She beareth Bertram and his bride
Back to old England's shore.

"Oh! hush thee," Bertram said, "dear love,
And pray on God," quoth he;
"Pray good St. Gabriel, send us help,
In this necessity."

Then he aloud, and she at heart,
The selfsame words they spake:
"Oh! save us, Christ, as thou did'st save
On Galilean lake."

"Oh! save us, Gabriel, saint adored,
And still this raging sea;
And whereso'er the boat be cast
We'll raise a shrine to thee.

A beauteous altar, gold bedeck'd,
Where night and morn shall shine,
A silver lamp to tell to all
This gracious deed of thine."

And through the night he prayèd thus,
But loud the wind did rage;
And the awful anger of the sea
Did not with dawn assuage.

The second night he prayèd thus:
And as he closed each prayer
His bride grew pale and wrung her hands
And wept in dire despair.

The third night that he prayèd thus
His voice was weak and worn;
But stars on high gemm'd all the sky
And calmly broke the morn.

"Now praise we good St. Gabriel,
My bonnie bride and I.
My dearest love, so still and pale,
Why do'st thou silent lie?"

He kissed her lips, he called her name,
But answer gave she none;
He wept aloud with bitter cry,
"Dear love, my life is gone."

He spied upon th' horizon clear
A line of unknown land,
And knew that the gentle flowing tide
Would drift them to the strand.

And ere the sun had sunk behind
The waste of watery store,
With signs his burdened boat he drew
Upon the desolate shore.

A rugged coast, a belt of sand,
A cavern dark and dree,
With sea-mews sending as they wheel'd
Their cries across the sea.

He paced the belt of red-ribbed sand,
He clomb the rugged cliff;
He looked below on his pale, pale bride,
And on the broken skiff.

He kneel'd him down on the barren rock,
With his face toward the sea—
"Oh! Gabriel, send me help to keep
The vow we vowed to thee."

And while he spake, from far and near,
The people of the land
Came running o'er the bleak sea-shore
Across the ribbed sea-sand.

They lifted the lovely lady high,
As in the boat she lay;
They bare her up the pathway steep,
Nor rested by the way.

They took the granite from the cliff,
And quarried marble fine;
They hew'd, they built from night to morn.
And raised a goodly shrine.

They made an altar, and beneath
They laid the lady fair,
And lighted there a lamp that gleamed
Like the gleams on her golden hair.

Another chapel to this day
Braves the rough storm wind well,
And proves the vow fulfill'd, I trow,
To good St. Gabriel.

The remainder of the songs I include in this chapter—nine in number—are from Mr. Pentin's paper already mentioned, and comprise one agricultural, one nautical, one drinking song, and the rest are courting or love songs. As Mr. Pentin says, some are but Dorset versions of songs commonly sung elsewhere. I regret that my collection of such songs is not a larger one, but with the advent of the newly established " Folk-Song Society " it is to be hoped that more Dorset ones will be unearthed, together with the tunes accompanying them.

The first of these is called :

TURMUT-HOEING

'Twas on a jolly summer's morn, the twenty-first of May,
Giles Scroggins took his turmut hoe, with which he trudg'd away ;
For some delight in haymakin', and some they fancies mowin',
But of all the trades that I like best, give I the turmut-hoein'.

Chorus.

For the fly, the fly, the fly be on the turmut,
And it's all my eye for we to try to keep fly off the turmut.

Now the next place as I went to work it were at Farmer Tower's,
He vowed and sweared and then declared I were a first-rate hoer.
Now the next place as I went to work I took it by the job,
But if I'd ha' knowed it a little afore I'd sooner been in quod.
(*Chorus.*)

When I was over at yonder farm they sent for I a-mowin',
But I sent word back I'd sooner have the sack than lose my turmut-hoein'.
Now all you jolly farming lads as bides at home so warm,
I now concludes my ditty by wishing you no harm.
(*Chorus.*)

The next is a nautical one called " The Crocodile ", which, Mr. Pentin says, comes from Buckland Newton.

THE CROCODILE

Now listen, you landsmen, unto me, to tell you the truth I'm bound,
What happened to me by going to sea, and the wonders that I found.
Shipwrecked I was once off Perouse and cast upon the shore,
So then I did resolve to roam the country to explore.

Chorus.

To my rit fal lal li bollem tit ! to my rit fal lal li dee ! (*bis*).

'Twas far I had not scouted out when close alongside the ocean
I saw something move, which at first I thought was all the world in motion ;
But steering up close alongside I found 'twas a crocodile,
And from his nose to the tip of his tail he measured five hundred mile.
(*Chorus.*)

'Twas a crocodile, I plainly could see he was not of a common race,
But I was obliged to climb a high tree before I could see his face;
And when he lifted up his jaw (though perhaps you may think 'tis a lie)
He reached above the clouds for miles three score and almost touched the sky.

(*Chorus.*)

While up aloft the wind was high, it blew a gale from the south,
I lost my hold and away did fly right into the crocodile's mouth.
He quickly closed his jaws on me, and thought he'd got a victim,
But I ran down his throat d'ye see? and that's the way I tricked him.

(*Chorus.*)

I travelled on for a month or two till I got into his maw,
Where I found of rum kegs not a few and a thousand fat bullocks in store.
Of life I banished all my care, for of grub I was not stinted,
And in this crocodile I lived ten years and very well contented.

(*Chorus.*)

This crocodile being very old, one day, alas! he died.
He was ten long years a-getting cold, he was so long and wide.
His skin was eight miles thick, I'm sure, or very near there about,
For I was full ten years or more a-cutting my way out.

(*Chorus.*)

And now I'm once more got on earth I've vowed no more to roam.
In a ship that passed I got a berth, and now I'm safe at home.
And if my story you should doubt, should you ever travel the Nile,
It's ten to one you'll find the shell of that wonderful crocodile.

(*Chorus.*)

The Prickly Bush

"Just *bret* still and tarry for a while,
Methinks I see my father dear coming over yonder stile.
Oh, father dear, have you silver or gold to set my body free,
For to keep my body from the *cafe* cold ground, and my neck from the gallows' tree?"
"Oh, no, I have no silver or gold to set thy body free;
But I am come for to see you hung, and your neck to the gallows' tree."

(*Chorus.*)

Oh, the prickly bush: it pricks my heart full sore.
If ever I get out of the prickly bush, I'll never get in any more.

Mr. Pentin tells us that the above verse is repeated four times more with the successive substitutions of "mother," "sister," "brother," and "true love" for "father"; but in the case of the "true love" she replies:

"Oh yes, I have both silver and gold to set thy body free;
I am come not for to see you hung, nor your neck to the gallows' tree."
(*Chorus.*)

Oh, the prickly bush: it pricked my heart full sore.
But now I'm out of the prickly bush, I'll never get in any more.

Mr. Pentin says that this is a Dorset version of a well-known song, and rightly characterizes "bret" and "cafe" as "two curious words." They may be so to Dorset ears; but its origin, I think, should be sought for in the north.

THE KING'S FIRST COURSE

I went unto the King's first course,
How I did knock and ring!
And the very, very first that answered me
Was the high and lofty King.
(*Chorus.*)
Ri fal de dal de diddle di de ri fal de dal di de.

"What do you want of me, fair maid,
What do you want of me?"
"There is a man in your first course
That has a-robbed me."
(*Chorus.*)

"What has he robbed you of, fair maid?"
The King he said to me.
"Has he robbed you of any of your houses or land,
Or of any your gold?" cried he.
(*Chorus.*)

"He has not robbed me of houses or land,
Or any of my gold," cried she,
"But the finest flower that my garden grows,
Of that he has robbed me."
(*Chorus.*)

"What will you know him by, my fair maid,
What will you know him by?"
"I will know him by the cape of his coat
And the winking of his eye."
(*Chorus.*)

He called his soldiers by his side,
By one, by two, by three.
Sweet William used to be the very, very first,
But the last to come was he.
(*Chorus.*)

"I'll give you houses, I'll give you land,
  I'll give you gold," cried he,
"If you will fancy some other young man,
  And will not fancy me."
(*Chorus.*)

"I don't want your houses, I don't want your land,
  Nor any of your gold," cried she;
"But all I want, and all I'll have
  Is thy sweet and whole bodee."
(*Chorus.*)

So the very first town that we went through
  We bought the gay gold ring;
And the very next town that we went through
  We set the bells to ring.
(*Chorus.*)

The Lost Lady

'Twas down in the valley this damsel did dwell;
She lived with her uncle, as all know-for well.
'Twas down in the valley where violets were gay
Three gipsies betrayed her and stole her away.

Long time she'd been missing and could not be found;
Her uncle he searchèd the country around.
He came to her trusty [1] between hope and fear;
The trusty made answer "She has not been here."

The trusty spoke up: "Her courage was bold;
I fear she's been lost for the sake of her gold.
We'll have life for life, sir," the trusty did say
"We'll send you to prison and there let you stay."

He travelled through England, through France, and through Spain.
(He ventured his life on the watery main.)
He came to a house where he lodged for a night,
And in that same house was his own heart's delight.

She saw him, she knew him, she fled to his arms,
She told him her grief while engaged in her charms.
"Why did you *disbine* me, my dearest?" cried he.
"Three gipsies betrayed me and stole me away."

"Your uncle's in England, in prison does lie,
And for your sweet sake he's condemnèd to die."

[1] Trustee.

"O, take me to England, my dearest," she cried;
"One thousand I'll give you, and will be your bride."

When she came to old England her uncle to see,
The cart it was under the high gallows' tree.
"O pardon, O pardon, O pardon, I crave.
See, see, I'm alive your sweet life for to save."

And straight from the gallows they led him away;
The bells they did ring, and the music did play;
Each house in the valley with mirth did abound,
As soon as they heard the lost lady was found.

Mr. Pentin considers this Dorset version of the song evidently a corrupt one, and suggests that some verses are missing. The word "disbine" in the fifth verse is new to me, and as I cannot find it in the late Dr. Joseph Wright's most comprehensive *English Dialect Dictionary,* I think it is probably a corruption.

I'm a Man that's done Wrong to my Parents

I'm a man that's in trouble and sorrow,
That once was light-hearted and gay;
Not a coin in this world can I borrow,
Since my own I have squandered away.
I once wrongèd my father and mother,
Till they turnèd me out from their door,
To beg, starve, or die, in the gutter to lie,
And ne'er enter their dwelling no more.
(*Chorus.*) I'm a man that's done wrong to my parents,
And daily I wander about,
To earn a small mite for my lodging at night.
God help me, for now I'm cast out!

Then my father will say when he meets me,
"You beggar, you still are at large,
And mind, sir, that you don't come near me,
Or by heaven I will give you in charge."
My mother, poor thing's broken-hearted;
To meet me she oft times will try,
For to give me a crown with her head hanging down
And a tear rolling out of her eye.
(*Chorus.*)

I'd a sister that married a squire,
She'll ne'er look nor speak unto me,
Because in this world she's much higher,
And rides in her carriage so free.

Then the girl that I once loved so dearly
Is dying broken-hearted, they say;
And there on her bed she is lying near dead,
And now for her outcast doth pray.
(*Chorus.*)

Kind friends, now from me take a warning
From what I have just said to you,
And I hope in my dress you won't scorn me,
For you don't know what you may come to.
And I try to be honest and upright,
And do all the good that I can;
And I try all I know to get on in this world
And prove to my friends I'm a man.
(*Chorus.*)

This song, credited with a Dorset origin, Mr. Pentin says is not infrequently sung by tramps; and was heard recently in the streets of Weymouth.

THE PUNCH BOWL

O come listen awhile and I'll give you a song
In the praise of good brandy and Jamaica get rum;
Strong beer and good cider through England doth run;
Sweet orange and lemons from Portugal come.
(*Chorus.*) Give me the punch ladle, I'll fathom the bowl;
Give me the punch ladle, I'll fathom the bowl;
I'll fathom the bowl, I'll fathom the bowl;
Give me the punch ladle, I'll fathom the bowl.

My wife will come in, and will sit at her ease;
She'll pay what she'll call for, and drink what she please;
She'll drink till she's black in the face as a coal.
Give me the punch ladle, I'll fathom the bowl.
(*Chorus.*)

My father is dead, and he lies in the seas,
What matter of that if he lies at his ease?
A clear crystal fountain through England doth roll.
Give me the punch ladle, I'll fathom the bowl.
(*Chorus.*)

Mr. Pentin states that for this song and the next one—evidently a more modern song—he was indebted to the rector of Stour Provost, who obtained them from an aged parishioner.

SALLY IS THE GIRL FOR ME

Last week I was twenty one;
My master set me free;
And now I've money plenty,
I'm just going to have a spree.

(*Chorus.*) For she has got such winning ways
To spend her money free;
And here's good liquor, come and drink.
Oh! Sally is the girl for me.

Her waist, that was so slender;
Her ankle was so small;
If 'twasn't for her heel
She'd have no foot at all.
(*Chorus.*)

If all the girls in our town
Was melted into one,
I'd marry them all if I'd think fit,
Or else I'd let them run.
(*Chorus.*)

To see her on a Sunday,
As through the streets she'd walk,
You'd think it was Victoria
Just landed in New York.
(*Chorus.*)

Sary Sikes

To me, said mother t'other day,
"Why, Gyles, you seem to pine away!"
"Yes, mother, as I grows old I grant
I feel as 'ow there's summat I want.
There's Sary Sikes, the girl I likes,
Of her I'm thinking all my life;
She looks so sweet, and is so meek.
How fat I should get if I had her for wife!"
(*Chorus.*) Tooral, looral, looral looral, etc.

"Lord, love the boy," my mother said,
"Why don't 'e go and court the maid?
For every Jack there is a Jill."
"So there, mother, then so I will."
Myself I drest in all my best,
A nosegay sweet in my button-hole hung,
I saddled my hoss, and jumped across,
And as I cantered along I sung:
(*Chorus.*)

I soon got up to Farmer Sikes;
I hitched my hoss and in I hikes.[1]
All were abroad, so quite at ease
I helped myself to bread and cheese.

[1] Hastens.

I drank some beer, and then did steer
To look for Sary (my heart in a flutter);
When in the dairy, like a fairy,
There was my Sary a churning of butter.
(*Chorus.*)

"Lor' Gyles," said she, "why who'd a-thought
Of seeing thee! Why, what has brought
Thee here to-day?" Said I, "Of course
I was brought hither by my horse.
O, Sary Sikes, 'tis you I likes;
Yes, Sary, you're my only joy."
She looked so coy, and said "O, fie!
What is it you want, you foolish boy?"
(*Chorus.*)

"Why, Sary, I wants to fix in life,
And you I wish to be my wife."
"Lor', Gyles, you don't mean that, I know."
"Yes, Sary, 'pon my soul I do."
Then kiss, consent, without any fuss,
Without any fuss, with her aprin thus,
She wiped her mouth and gave me a buss.
(*There is a line missing here.*)
(*Chorus.*)

Then off we went a-squeezin' hands
To tell the parson about the banns.
When we came back we did find means
To make our dinner off bacon and greens.
We're married now, and I somehow
Am only happy with my wife;
I love her and press her, and cry "God bless her,"
I was never so happy all the days of my life.

Mr. Pentin concludes his selection of songs with a version of the National Anthem as sung in Dorsetshire in 1809, commencing "God save great George our King".

Besides the ballads and songs given above are those which are sung at particular times or seasons of the year, such as harvest-home, hay-making and sheep-shearing gatherings. These appear in the accounts given of those festivities in Chapter II.

In concluding my somewhat scanty account of Dorsetshire ballads and songs I would refer my readers to a small volume of poems by the late Sir William Smith Marriott, Bart., entitled *Olden and Modern Times*, published in 1855, in which besides

"A Tribute to Dorset" (mainly a panegyric upon several well known places in the county) appears some half dozen "Songs of Dorset", of which only two seem to be of any value for my purpose here as illustrating two pieces of folk-lore to which I have already referred. They are "The Haunted Hare" and "The Fairy Ring". They are each preceded by a short statement of the particular form of superstition they illustrate.

The Haunted Hare

Says the author: "There is a legend of Dorset that an old witch in the shape of a hare haunts the downs and hills at night; . . . and that nothing will take effect against her but a silver bullet; which he must indeed be 'a stalwart man and true' to have courage to use, especially as it's only at the dead of night she can be seen." The earlier verses tell us that the game-keeper had on several occasions attempted to shoot this particular hare, but without success; his effort being followed by the hag's jeering cry—"Keeper, shoot better!" Apparently, at last, he had provided himself with a better charge. The last verse gives the result.

"At length o'er his bones did his flesh 'gin to creep,
As the moon darting forth from a cloud shewed THE HARE—
And the same haggard voice o'er the wind seemed to sweep:
'Now, keeper, shoot better—shoot away, but—Beware!'

"Both barrels went off—that moment a cry
And a horrible, sulphurous smell rose around—
But neither the hare nor the witch could he spy
When gladly, but firmly, he strode from the ground." [1]

The Fairy Ring

This song is prefaced by the following remarks: "From the old and well known legend which is commonly supposed to be true in the west of England that a wish formed previous to the ceremony of dancing three times round a 'fairy ring' is likely to be fulfilled with the year." Each verse gives the following chorus or refrain:

"Oh! prythee come and dance with me
Around the ring where fay
And elfish sprites in revelry
Their nightly gambols play." [2]

[1] See Chapter VII, p. 234.
[2] See Chapter VII, pp. 260–1.

Place Rhymes

To the above collection of ballads and songs I will add a few local or place rhymes.

(1) **Bindon** (Wool).

Wool streams and Coombe Keynes wells
Fordington rogues stole Bindon bells.

This rhyme is current in the district of Wool in perpetual memory of the act of the Fordington men who stole the bells in the western tower of Bindon Abbey.[1]

(2) **Dorchester**.

When Hardy's Monument is plainly visible from Dorchester the weather-wise give vent to their poetic feeling in the following:

When Hardy's monument is plainly seen
There'll soon be heavy rain I ween.[2]

(3) **Hambledon**.

The clubmen of Dorset who were defeated at Hambledon Hill in 1645 by Cromwell carried on their banners the device :

If you offer to plunder our cattle,
Be assured that we'll give you battle.

(4) **Poole**.

The busy people of Poole boastfully announce that

Poole was a thriving town
When Liverpool was a furzy down.

(5) **Parkstone**.

The prophets of Parkstone insist :

Wareham was, Poole is, and Parkstone is to be
The most important place of all, and the biggest of the three.

The name of their town has been substituted by Swanage men for that of Parkstone.

(6) **Lyme Regis**.

The good people of Lyme Regis praise their town in this verse :

At Lyme Regis Devon takes the band
Of Dorset's fairest spot of land.
With liberal heart they both combine
To make a Paradise of Lyme.

[1] See Chapter IV, p. 151.
[2] See Chapter VIII, p. 269.

King Charles II and his ill-fated son, the Duke of Monmouth, are both said to have made this promise to Lyme:

Lyme although a little place
I think is wondrous pretty;
If 'tis my fate to wear the crown
I'll make of it a city.

(7) **Knowlton.**

Knowlton bell is a-stole
And thrown into White Hill Hole.
All the devils in hell
Could never pull up Knowlton bell.[1]

[1] See Chapter IV, p. 165.

CHAPTER XII

CHILDREN'S GAMES AND RHYMES

WHILE the late Rev. William Barnes was lying on what proved to be his death-bed,[1] I more than once discussed with him various matters of local folk-lore and antiquarian interest common to us both, an occupation in which he was ofttimes fond of indulging.

At one of these interviews he put into my hands a scrap-book of printed manuscript folk-lore jottings, amongst which I found an account of several games and rhymes, with the directions or rules under which each game was played by Dorsetshire children. Besides these the scrap-book contained a long letter written to Mr. Barnes early in 1874 by Mr. Amos Otis, of Yarmouth, Mass., U.S.A., a gentleman who evidently took a great interest not only in the folk-lore of New England, but in that of the old country as well, in which he acknowledged the receipt of some three or four games which the Dorset poet would seem to have sent him, and in which he pointed out the similarity to several in his own country. To these games I shall presently refer. With this letter was a cutting from the *Yarmouth Register* of February, 1874, containing a paper contributed by Mr. Otis to that journal, in which an account of those games appeared, together with some interesting observations on the general subject of the folk-lore and children's games of Dorsetshire and New England. At this time I had myself collected some items of a similar nature, which I had intended to weave into the larger subject of Dorset folk-lore generally, but the placing of this new material at my disposal immediately decided me to form a separate chapter upon "Children's Games and Rhymes". So, as a means to this end, I contributed a paper on this subject to the Folk-lore Society's *Journal* in 1889 (vol. vii). This paper is now incorporated in this chapter, together with the numerous additions I have since been able to make to it.

Since I contributed this paper to the *Folk-lore Journal* Mrs. A. B. Gomme (now Lady Gomme, the widow of my old friend

[1] He died in the autumn of 1886, a period of the year at which in one of his poems he beautifully expressed a wish that it might be his lot to die.

Sir Lawrence Gomme, F.S.A.) has brought out, in 1894, her important work, in two volumes, on *Traditional Games*, a work which has considerably widened our view as to the value of our children's games, in which she gives all their variants and different ways of playing them so far as she has been able to collect them. Her classification of these is similar in its main lines, though on a more elaborate scale, to that adopted by Miss Burne in her *Shropshire Folk-lore*, and followed by myself. Amongst these games is to be found a goodly number of those I have gathered together here, and as her authority for which she refers to the *Folk-Lore Journal* as above.

In the preface to her book Lady Gomme has made some valuable remarks on the subject of children's games in connection with folk-lore generally, in which she considers them not only from the point of view as a means of amusement, but for obtaining an insight into many of the customs and beliefs of our ancestors. " Children," she remarks, " do not invent, but they imitate or mimic very largely, and in many of these games we have, there is little doubt, unconscious folk-drama of events and customs which were at one time being enacted as a part of the serious concerns of life before the eyes of children many generations ago." And she calls in aid Professor E. B. Tylor, who in his well known work, *Primitive Culture* (1871), vol. i, chapter iii, p. 65, says : " If the games of children and of grown-up people be examined with an eye to the ethnological lessons to be gained from them, one of the first things that strikes us is how many of them are only sportive imitations of the serious business of life." Lady Gomme elaborates this and other cognate theories in her lengthy " Memoir on the Study of Children's Games ", with which she concludes her second volume.

I would recommend Lady Gomme's book to the attention of those who desire to know the fullest details as to how each game is played, and the widest signification given to its action.

Such, then, is the value of children's games from the point of view of folk-lore and anthropology. But this I must leave to others to deal with. My work is but to endeavour to provide the material—and from a Dorset source alone—from which these deductions may be rendered possible.

Although it may be true, as Mr. Otis says in his paper before mentioned, that the fairy stories, the charms, and the games that pleased the children of the Pilgrims now delight not only the children of New England but of Dorsetshire and many other counties in Old England; that in our out-door sports no change seems to have occurred; that *ball, hail-over, hide-and-hoop,* or *hide-and-seek, prison, prison-bar, pitch-forks, pins, I espy,* or *hide-and-hoop with tag to it, bunch of maggots,*[1] and many other games, have come down to the present time with little or no change from a remote antiquity; and that the same may be said of the charms, the dances, and games in which the girls take a part—still I have found no little trouble in obtaining exact information as to what the games of our country children are at the present day, and how they are played. The children now-a-days seem to me to be more shy and more reluctant to afford information on the subject than they were in former days, and ofttimes when one comes suddenly upon a party of them playing at their games in a country lane or corner of a field (especially if you happen to belong to the class known as "gentry") they will either break off their game altogether, or, if they continue it, they do so in a subdued and half-hearted kind of way that shows to you more eloquently than words that your room would be far preferable to your company. In short, it is rapidly becoming as difficult to get satisfactory information out of children as it is to elicit by an artfully-veiled cross-examination anything from "the oldest inhabitant" of a parish, who you have every reason to believe is the store-house of many a tale of superstition or witchcraft.

It may be that the greater facilities of communication that railways have now established between so many of the larger towns and the country districts have brought new and noisier games in the place of the simpler and old-world amusements of our grandparents' days, for one hears it frequently said that "them gëames is a-dièn out a'together", and, in the words of a critical elder (as told to me by a correspondent), that "them childern, seemin' to I, döant play nothèn the gëames we user't to do when *I* wer to schoöal!" I cannot help thinking, however, that the rapid spread of education and the institution of Board

[1] Scarcely any of these games, I think, exist in Dorsetshire at the present day—at all events under these names.

Schools in the country districts have much to do with this bashfulness and shyness on the part of the school children with regard to their games. They are beginning to think there is something almost to be ashamed of in their old-fashioned ways and sayings; and I verily believe that if it were not for the school-treats, where the restraint of personal supervision of the teachers is to a great extent relaxed or altogether removed, school children would soon be the last, instead of the first, to whom one should go for the study and information on this interesting subject. I am told that in some parts of Germany, school-teachers (who are ahead of us in this as in most other things) are instructed to call upon the children in their classes to recount any stories of folk-tales which they may happen to know, and such tales when told, you may depend upon it, are carefully noted down and stored up for future tabulation. Could not some such system be brought to bear in our English country schools, whereby the games and pastimes of the young might be collected and preserved? If not taken out of their play-hours, I do not think the time covered by this inquiry would be grudged even by the children themselves. But, if this is to be done, it must be done quickly; it is more than probable that *their* children will have none to tell!

I have myself endeavoured to follow somewhat the principles of this plan, by obtaining the assistance of one or two ladies who have been in the habit of giving more or less of their time to visiting the cottagers in their homes, and who would therefore know more of their families and their habits and modes of life than would the ordinary residents in a parish. The children, it is only reasonable to suppose, would be more likely to confide in those—although of a higher station in life—whom they frequently see about them, and would not hesitate, I think, to make some little return, such as I have suggested, to those who have shown by their actions that they take more than ordinary interest in the homes and in the lives of the poor.

The result of my experiment in my own particular district of West Dorset has been, on the whole, fairly satisfactory, and is responsible for several of the games or their variants which appear in the following pages.

These words were written more than thirty years ago. It has

taken just twenty years to verify them in a remarkable manner. In a very interesting article in the *Times* of 15th February, 1909, upon the "Value of Play", we learn from the late Mrs. Humphry Ward of the admirable efforts that are being made to teach the children of the London poor how to play their games, and to illustrate them with appropriate dance and song, in other words, "folk-music." The subject is itself much too large, even were I a musician, to be included in an already very long chapter on "Children's Games". Yet that it must take a very large share in such games is evident from what Miss Burne says in her address, as President of the Folk-Lore Society for 1909, upon the necessity for the systematic study of folk-lore; an address, which was printed in *Folk-Lore* of the following year (vol. xxi), where, at p. 35, she says: "Ten years ago no one knew that there was any folk-music in England. The Folk-Song Society was founded. Not long ago I found the secretary of the Society surrounded by the MSS. of a thousand airs from Dorset alone, which were awaiting classification and sifting." I must be content to leave that subject to the Folk-Song Society. So long as the children continue their games the folk-music will survive with them. Some day, perhaps, we may see the proper airs and tunes for many of the choral and other games here described duly recorded for us, where now they but linger in our memories like the half-forgotten fragrance from an old *pot-pourri* jar.

There are already signs that our children's games are bearing good fruit from a folk-lore point of view. I learn that there is now an English "Folk-Dance Society". I take the following from an interesting article in the *Morning Post* of 30th September, 1920, on the "Folk-Dance Revival":—

"It is not only a pleasure but an inspiration to witness the tremendous popularity which has crowned the efforts of the English Folk-Dance Society, now holding their Christmas vacation school at the South-Western Polytechnic Institute at Chelsea. Upwards of five hundred and fifty students from every corner in the country have flocked to this winter's session, while half that number again have been unable to obtain admission owing to the lack of sufficient accommodation. Classes in Folk-Singing, Children's Singing Games, Morris, Country, and Sword Dancing, are being held daily throughout this week, and informal lectures are delivered by the director, Mr. Cecil J. Sharp, on the theory, history, folk-lore, and artistic significance of the songs and dances."

When I had collected my materials the classification of them was the next difficulty, and for some time I was at a loss how to proceed on this score, but finally decided upon following that used by Miss Burne in her excellent and exhaustive work on *Shropshire Folk-lore* (the first part of which was published in 1883), and adapted it, so far as I was able, to my own materials.

Under this arrangement the games are divided into: (i) Choral; (ii) Dramatic; (iii) Games of skill; (iv) Christmas and indoor games; (v) Rhymes, which I have again subdivided into (a) Rustic, (β) Nursery or Domestic, (γ) Counting out, or "lot" rhymes; and (vi) Riddles. To Miss Burne also I am principally indebted for the resumé of the special characteristics that belong to the first four sections at all events.

At the same time, whilst I have omitted many games that are obviously known to be common to every county, and which are to be found in every book dealing with the subject of games, I fear I cannot claim for those I have recorded any absolute originality or peculiarity to my own county, for, as we know, these games or their variants are largely spread over many counties. Like many other branches of folk-lore they are not to be confined within the area of geographical or other artificial limitations. On the other hand, were we to discard everything that is to be found beyond the boundaries of one particular county, a large mass of most interesting material would be left unchronicled altogether. By these games children keep up the continuity, so to speak, of a phase of social life the value of which is only beginning to be understood. In the words of Miss Burne, "They imitate the doings of their elders; and they even keep alive in the strangest manner things practised by their elders in former generations, but long since dropped by them as foolish and idle, if not superstitious, customs. The children's games of to-day show us, as in a mirror, the occupations and manner of life of our forefathers. They had their origin in the festive songs and dances of rustic pagandom, in the early beginnings of masque and drama, and in the obscure rites of divination and magic which attended the ancient popular assemblies." Viewed from such a standpoint, the study of children's games and rhymes no longer appears trivial or unworthy the attention of serious persons, and believing as I do that such a study cannot but prove not only interesting and amusing, but useful and instructive to the intelligent inquirers after the manners and customs of their fore-elders, I will now proceed to discuss in detail the various sections of the games I have been able to collect.

I. Choral Games

These are played out of doors by parties of boys and girls, though, inasmuch as boys are very often nowadays kept distinct from the girls during play-hours they are usually played by girls only. There is nothing, as Miss Burne says, of the *game*, properly so called, about them—nothing, that is to say, of winning or losing. They consist for the most part of circular dances, accompanied by songs, in which one player is called out after another, desired to choose a lover, kissed or embraced, and promised all kinds of good fortune.

(i) *Sally Water*

The first of these is the well-known *Sally Water* (or *Walker*). A party of children forms a circle, in the middle of which one of them, a girl, kneels alone ; the rest, taking hands, slowly move round and sing :—

> Sally, Sally Water
> Sprinkle in the pan ;
> Rise, Sally, rise, Sally, (*she rises*).
> And choose a young man.
> Choose [or bow] to the east,
> Choose [or bow] to the west,
> And choose [or bow to] the pretty girl [or young man]
> That you love best.

Another version has :—

> Choose for the best one,
> Choose for the worst one,
> Choose for the pretty girl
> That you love best.

The girl in the centre then selects her favourite, who is taken by her within the circle, where they kiss each other, the rest moving round in a circle the while. In some parts of Dorsetshire they here sing :—

And now you're married I wish you joy;
First a girl and then a boy;
Seven years after son and daughter;
And now, young people, jump over the water.

The one that first knelt down now rejoins the circle, leaving the one she had chosen in the centre, who in turn, in response to the same invitation by the chorus, chooses his or her favourite. This is repeated until the whole party have had their turn or are tired out. (*Symondsbury.*)

(ii) *Little Girl of Mine*

This is similar to *Sally Water*, and played in the same way.

Here's a pretty little girl of mine,
She's brought me many a bottle of wine;
A bottle of wine she gave me too;
See what this little girl can do.
On the carpet she shall kneel
(*Here the child must kneel.*)
As the grass grows on the fiel';
Stand upright on your feet;
(*Here the girl rises up.*)
And choose the one you love so sweet.

Here the girl must select her favourite from the ring and lead her to the centre, whilst the others, moving round, continue their song:—

Now you are married I wish you joy;
First a girl and then a boy;
Seven years after, son and daughter;
Pray, young couple, kiss together.

Here the two must kiss and separate; the first girl going to form part of the ring, whilst her companion takes her place in the centre, and the game goes on as before. Boys and girls often play this together, and then the words are changed to suit the circumstances. (*Symondsbury.*) [1]

The following somewhat peculiar variant of this last was contributed by Miss M. G. A. Summers, of Hazelbury Bryan, to the *Dorset County Chronicle*, in April, 1888.

[1] A very similar version of this is played by the children in the neighbourhood of Chard, in the adjoining county of Somerset.

I had a bonnet trimmed wi' blue.
Why dosn't wëare it ? Zo, I do ;
I'd wëare it where I con,
To tëake a walk wi' my young mon.
My young mon is a-gone to sea,
When he'd come back he'll marry me.
Zee what a purty zister is mine,
Doan't 'e think she's ter'ble fine ?
She's a most ter'ble cunnèn too,
Just zee what my zister can do.
On the carpet she can kneel,
As the grass grow in the fiel'.

The sister kneels in the centre of the circle, and they all dance round her, saying :—

Stand upright upon thy feet
And choose the prettiest you like, sweet.

She chooses one, and after she has caught her they go through the game again.[1]

(iii) *What are you weeping for ?*

The children form a ring, and one of them (a girl) is chosen to stand in the centre, and pretends to cry, whilst the rest move round her, singing :—

Pray, Sally, what are you weeping for—
Weeping for—weeping for ?
Pray, Sally, what are you weeping for,
On a bright shiny day ?

The girl in the middle answers :—

I am weeping for a sweetheart—
A sweetheart—a sweetheart.
I am weeping for a sweetheart,
On a bright shiny day.

The chorus replies :—

Pray, Sally, go and get one—
Go and get one—get one.
Pray, Sally, go and get one,
On a bright shiny day.

Here the girl in the centre must choose a boy (a girl if she prefers), the others still circling round and singing :—

[1] The game of *Sally Water* is common to many counties. *Conf.* variants in Miss Burne's *Shropshire Folk-lore*, p. 509 ; see *Folk-lore Record*, vol. v, p. 88, for a contribution from a Surrey source, and *Folk-lore Journal*, vol. i, p. 385, for a Derbyshire one.

Pray, Sally, now you've got one—
You've got one—got one ;
Pray, Sally, now you've got one,
On a bright sunny day.

The pair then kiss or embrace each other as the others continue :—

One kiss will never part you—
Never part you—part you ;
One kiss will never part you,
On a bright sunny day.

The game then recommences as before, with a different girl in the middle.

The Rev. Charles E. Seaman, writing from Stalbridge Rectory, sends the following variant to *Somerset and Dorset Notes and Queries* (vol. iv, p. 64) :—

"Here is another [singing game] which I witnessed last summer [1893]. It was played at that time by girls alone, but seems to demand the presence of the "uninteresting" sex.

A girl assumes a lachrymose attitude in the middle of a ring of playmates, when they proceed to sing :—

Poor Sally is a-weeping,
A-weeping, a-weeping,
Poor Sally is a-weeping,
On a bright summer day.

Pray tell me what you're weeping for—
Weeping for—weeping for ?
Pray tell me what you're weeping for,
On a bright summer day.

(*Sally loq.*) I am weeping for a sweetheart—
A sweetheart—a sweetheart.
I am weeping for a sweetheart,
On a bright summer day.

(*Omnes.*) Pray stand up, and choose one—
Choose one—choose one.
Pray stand up, and choose one,
On a bright summer day.

Sally does as she is told. Another girl takes Sally's place, and the game goes on as before.

(iv) *Rosy Apple, Lemon, and Pear*

The children form a ring, and one of them is chosen to stand in the middle, as in the last game, whilst the rest circle round and sing :—

Rosy apple, lemon, and pear,
A bunch of roses she shall wear;
Gold and silver by her side,
Choose the one shall be her bride.

Take her by her lily-white hand,
(Here the one in the centre chooses one from the ring to stand by her.)
Lead her to the altar;
Give her kisses, one, two, three,
To old mother's runaway daughter.

On these words being uttered, the one who was first standing in the middle must run away and take a place in the ring as soon as she can. The second one remains in the centre, and the game is repeated over and over again until all have been chosen. (*Symondsbury.*)[1]

(v) *Isabella*

Mr. Seaman also sent the following singing game to *Somerset and Dorset Notes and Queries* (iv, p. 265) (1895) :—

A child is placed inside a ring of playmates who go round singing :—

Isabella, Isabella, Isabella so fair,
Last night when I departed,
I left her broken-hearted.
On the mountains (*bis*)
I left the fair girl.
Take a [and ?] choose, love, (*ter.*)
Farewell.

She chooses, and the pair walk off together out of the ring, to the strains of:

Go for a walk, love, (*ter.*)
Farewell.

They return when bidden by the words:

Come back, love (*ter.*)
Farewell.

but start again to the accompaniment of:

Go to church, love, (*ter.*)
Farewell.
Say your prayers, love, (*ter.*)
Farewell.

[1] For a Hampshire version, with very slight variance, see *Notes and Queries*, Ser. VIII, vii, 383.

On the return of the supposed matrimonialists, the bride is summoned to:

Show your ring, love, (*ter.*)
Farewell.

and raises her finger, while her partner is directed to:

Take a kiss, love, (*ter.*)
Farewell.

They salute each other. The one last chosen stays in the ring, the other joins the circle, and the game begins again.[1]

(vi) *Here we go round the Mulberry Bush* [2]

The children form a ring, and, taking hands and slowly moving or dancing round the while, sing:—

Here we go round the mulberry bush—
The mulberry bush—the mulberry bush;
Here we go round the mulberry bush,
Of a cold and frosty morning.

The children then unloosen hands, and, pretending to wash their faces with their hands, sing:—

This is the way we wash our face—
Wash our face—wash our face;
This is the way we wash our face,
Of a cold and frosty morning.

They then quickly take hands again, and dance round, singing as before:—

Here we go round the mulberry bush, etc.

They next make pretend they are brushing their clothes as they sing:—

This is the way we brush our clothes—
Brush our clothes—brush our clothes;
This is the way we brush our clothes,
Of a cold and frosty morning.

A similar pantomime is gone through to represent brushing their boots, combing their hair, or any other act that may happen to strike their childish fancy, each verse ending with the refrain:—

Here we go round the mulberry bush, etc.

[1] A variant of this was sent me in 1896 from the adjoining county of Somerset, as played by the children in the neighbourhood of Chard.

[2] Sometimes called the *gooseberry* bush, as in a variant in the *Folk-lore Record*, vol. iv, p. 174, from a West of Scotland source.

The two last verses are generally those describing their going to and their coming from school, the former being signified by covering their faces with their hands, and the latter by unbounded skipping and jumping testifying to the exuberance of their joy, during which the ring is broken up, and, as often as it is thought desirable, the game recommenced.

Another version, which has the appearance of a fragment merely, is as follows :—

All round the mulberry bush,
Maidens all together,
Give a kiss and take a kiss,
And curtsey all together. (*Symondsbury.*)

(vii) *Walking Round the Village*

There is another choral, or singing game, in which the children having formed a ring, their leader walks round outside it, singing the following verses. When she has finished she joins the ring and another of her playmates takes her place, when the game continues till all have had their turn.

Walking round the village,
(*Repeated two or three times.*)
As you have done before.

In and out the windows,
(*Repeated as before.*)
As you have done before.

Stand and face your lover,
(*Repeated as before.*)
As you have done before.

Follow me to London,
(*Repeated as before.*)
As you have done before.

There seems to be something wanting in the setting to this game, but as I have had only the words sent me and have never seen it played in Dorsetshire, I am unable to supply it. I have, however, a very strong recollection of having once seen a very similar game played, and with very similar words, by white children in Levuka, the old capital of Fiji, in the early nineties. I was much surprised at finding one of our old English children's games in such surroundings, and watched it and some other games with great interest; but I cannot remember now that any other than this one seemed to have any Dorset connection. It had probably come from one of the neighbouring colonies of Australia or New Zealand, where many of the children of the white residents of Fiji have gone to school. The tune still seems to linger in my ears, but not being a musician I am unable to set it to music. It reminds me of the well-known refrain, " So early in the morning."

(viii) *Kiss in the Ring*

In order to play this universally popular game a ring is formed, and one of the players (usually a girl), carrying a handkerchief, commences to walk slowly round the outside of the ring, repeating these words :—

I sent a letter to my love,
And on the way I dropped it;
And one of you has picked it up
And put it in your pocket.

Touching each one with her handkerchief as she passes, she says: " Not you," " Not you," " Not you," etc., till the favoured individual is reached, when it is changed to " But you ! " and his or her shoulder lightly touched at the same time. The first player then runs round the ring as fast as she can, pursued by the other, who, if a capture is effected (as is nearly always the case), is entitled to lead the first player back into the centre of the ring and claim a kiss. The first player then takes the other's place in the ring, who in turn walks round the outside, repeating the same formula.

A variant under the title of *Drop the Handkerchief*, commenced in the same way as the last, is as follows :—

I wrote a letter to my love;
I carried water in my glove;
And by the way I dropped it—
I dropped it—I dropped it—I dropped it, etc.

This is repeated until the handkerchief is stealthily dropped immediately behind one of the players, who should be on the alert to follow as quickly as possible the one who has dropped it, who at once increases her speed and endeavours to take the place left vacant by her pursuer. Should she be caught before she can succeed in doing this she is compelled to take the handkerchief a second time. But if, as it more usually happens, she is successful in accomplishing this, the pursuer in turn takes the handkerchief, and the game proceeds as before. (*Symondsbury.*)

In this last it will be noticed there is no kissing, and I am assured by several persons who are interested in Dorset children's games that the indiscriminate kissing (that is, whether the girl pursued runs little or far, or, when overtaken, whether she objects or not) with which this game is ordinarily associated, as played now both in Dorsetshire and in other counties, was not indigenous to our county, but is merely a pernicious aftergrowth or outcome of later days, which had its origin in the various excursion and holiday fetes, which the facilities of railway travelling had instituted by bringing large crowds from the neighbouring towns into the country. I am told that sixty years ago or so such a thing was unknown in the country districts of Dorsetshire, when the game then usually indulged in was known merely as *Drop the Handkerchief.*[1]

(ix) *My little Dog Buff*

This game, which is but a variant of these last and seems to partake somewhat of the nature of a "counting-out" rhyme, is best played by a party consisting of as many boys as girls, who must join hands and form a ring.

The eldest boy or girl must choose whom he or she likes to go outside the ring, who must thereupon go round the circle carrying a handkerchief, with which he or she touches each one in passing, and saying or singing the following lines :—

Mr. Monday was a good man,
He whipped his children now and then,
When he whipped them he made them dance,
Out of Scotland into France;
Out of France into Spain,
Back to dear old England again.
O.U.T. spells "out,"
If you please stand out.

[1] Lady Gomme in her book on *Traditional Games* (1894), vol. i, p. 112, notes and comments on the distinction I have here drawn as to the way in which this game and its congener *Kiss in the Ring* were orginally played in Dorsetshire.

I had a little dog and his name was "Buff",
I sent him after a penn'orth of snuff,
He broke the paper and smelled the stuff,
And that's the end of my dog "Buff".

He shan't bite you—he shan't bite you—he shan't bite you, etc.—he *shall* bite you all over.

This is so arranged that on coming round to the one he or she loves best the handkerchief is thrown upon that one, and with the words "he *shall* bite you all over" the speaker runs away, pursued by the other as soon as the handkerchief is secured. The pursuit is kept up until the first one is caught, when the two return to the centre of the ring and kiss each other. The pursuer then takes the place of the captive in the ring and goes round singing as before.

The game is repeated until all have had their turn or have had enough of it.

(x) *Cat after Mouse.* Sometimes called *Threading the Needle*

This game is played by children forming a ring, with their arms extended; one — the "mouse" — goes outside the circle and gently pulls the dress of one of the players, who thereupon becomes the "cat", and is bound to follow wherever the mouse chooses to go—either in or out of the ring—until caught, when he or she takes the place formerly occupied in the ring by the "cat", who in turn becomes "mouse", and the game is recommenced.

(xi) *Green Gravel*

A party of boys and girls joins hands and forms a ring. A boy or girl stands in the middle and says or sings this verse:—

Green gravel, green gravel, the grass is so green,
The fairest young lady that ever was seen;
Ah! Mary, ah! Mary, your true love is dead;
I send you a letter to turn round your head.

As soon as the boy or girl has sung this verse, and called out the name of one of the ring, the one so called upon must turn his or her back to the inside of the circle, and, still holding hands as before, continue the game facing outwards; and so on until all have been called upon and have their backs to the centre, when the whole ring dances round in a chorus.

In some parts of Dorsetshire the game is called *Silly Gravels*, and the girl is called upon as :

Oh ! Silly, oh ! Silly, your true love is dead,
I send you a letter to turn round your head.[1]

This was one of the games Mr. Barnes had sent an account of to Mr. Amos Otis, as I have already mentioned, and in Mr. Otis's reply he says it is called the *Needle's Eye* in New England.

(xii) *Wall-flowers*

This is a very similar game to the last, and a very popular one. The children form themselves into a ring, and as they dance round say or sing :

Wally, wally, wall-flower,
A-growèn up so high,
All we children be sure to die,
Excepting (*naming the youngest*),
'Cause she's the youngest,
Oh ! fie ! for shame ! fie ! for shame !
Turn your back to the wall again.

The youngest child now turns round, still retaining the hands of her companions, but with her face in an opposite direction to theirs. This is gone through again until all have their faces on the outside of the circle, when they reverse the order, and gradually resume their old positions.[2]

Another version is as follows :

Wall-flowers, wall-flowers, growing up so high,
We are all living [children], and we shall all die,
Except the youngest here. (*naming her.*)
Turn your back to overshed. (?) (*repeated three times.*)
(*Symondsbury.*)

II. Dramatic Games

These, too, are games which are principally played by girls out of doors. The players are not called by their own names, but personate characters, such as a mother and her daughter, dukes, knights, fox and geese, hen and chickens, etc. Their ditty is a dialogue, not a song ; and a great deal of dramatic

[1] *Conf.* the Shropshire variant in Miss Burne's book, p. 510. See also *Folk-lore Record*, vol. v, p. 84, for a Surrey one.

[2] Conf. *Shropshire Folk-lore*, p. 513.

effect is often given to their acting. Instead of dancing in a ring, they form lines, facing each other. We still have nothing of winning or losing, except in those games of this class where, as in the case of *Oranges and Lemons*, the game ends by one party pulling the other over a boundary or division line.

(i) *Oranges and Lemons*

This is a very favourite game with Dorset children, and can be played by any large number of them. Two of the tallest of the party are chosen to be " Orange " and " Lemon " ; but the rest must not know which child is " Orange " and which is " Lemon ". The two stand facing one another, and taking each other hold by both hands (the right hand of the one taking the left of the other, and *vice versâ*) raise them as high as their shoulders. The rest of the party then form into a line or string, one behind the other, holding only the frock or jacket of the one immediately in front of them, and in this form pass once round " Orange " and " Lemon ", who are standing erect in the midst. They then creep underneath their raised arms, singing meanwhile :

Oranges and Lemons,
Say the bells of St. Clemen's.
I owe you five farthin's,
Say the bells of St. Martin's.
When shall I pay you.
Monday, Tuesday, Wednesday,
Thursday, Friday, Saturday,
Or Sunday ?

It should be so arranged that the end of the line should be about to pass under the improvised archway just when they come to the word " Sunday ", then the raised arms drop and enclose within their grasp the last one of the line. This one they keep fast, whilst the others pass on still singing as before. The captive then is asked which she will have " Orange or Lemon ? " This should be asked and the answer given in a whisper, so that none of the others can hear. On her making her choice she is told to go behind the one she has selected and clasp her round the waist. By this time the rest of the children ought to be ready to pass under again, and again the last one of the line is caught at the word " Sunday ". This is repeated until all are caught. The new captives in turn select their favourites—Oranges or Lemons—and take up their positions behind their leaders, according as they have chosen. Then begins the tug-of-war between the Oranges and Lemons, each still holding on firmly by the waist of the one in front. Whichever side pulls the other over wins the game. (*Symondsbury.*)

A variant of the rhyme which obtained at Broadwinsor many years ago is as follows:

I owe you five farthings.
When will you pay me,
To-day or to-morrow ?
Here comes a candle to light you to bed ;
Here comes a chopper to chop off your head.

Another is from the borderland of Dorset and Devon, by Uplyme:

Orange or limon, the bells are so chimmin',
I owe you five farthings, and when shall I pay you ?
When I get rich, like a little tommy-tit.
Here comes a candle to light you to bed ;
Here comes a chopper to chop off your head.

These last two lines form the usual conclusion to these variants.[1]

(ii) *Fox and Goose*

One of the party called the " Fox " takes one end of the room or corner of a field (for the game was equally played indoors or out) ; all the rest of the children arrange themselves in a line or string according to size—one behind the other, the smallest last—behind the tallest one, called " Mother Goose ", with their arms securely round the waist of the one in front of them (as in the last game), or sometimes by grasping the dress.

The game commences by a parley to this effect :

MOTHER GOOSE (to Fox) : " What are you after this fine morning?"
Fox : " Taking a walk."

[1] *Conf.* the London version as sung by the school children of the parish of St. Clement's Danes, and in which its old peal of bells, having been repaired and rehung in March, 1920, will in future take its daily part; thus making actual and permanent the traditional association of the game with St. Clement's. (See an interesting article in the *Morning Post* of 1st April, 1920, as to this.) See also *Folk-lore Record*, vol. v, p. 86, for a Surrey variant; the *Folk-lore Journal*, vol. i, p. 386, for a Derbyshire one. Also Halliwell's *Nursery Rhymes*, No. cclxxxi.

M. G.: "With what object?"
Fox: "To get an appetite for a meal."
M. G.: "What does [will] your meal consist of?"
Fox: "A nice fat goose for my breakfast."
M. G.: "Where will you get it?"
Fox: "Oh! I shall get a nice morsel somewhere; and as they are so handy, I shall satisfy myself with one of yours."
M. G.: "Catch one if you can."

A lively scene follows. The Fox and Mother Goose should be pretty evenly matched, the "mother" with extended arms seeking to protect her "brood", whilst the Fox, who tries to dodge under, right and left, is only allowed in case of a successful foray or grasp to secure the last of the train. Vigorous efforts are made to escape him, the "brood", of course, supplementing the "mother's" exertions to elude him as far as they are able, but without breaking the link. The game may be continued until all in turn are caught.

The game was sometimes called *Hen and Chickens.* A good illustration of the way in which it was played may be obtained from the charming picture, bearing this title, by G. D. Leslie, R.A., which was exhibited in the Royal Academy in 1881.[1]

(iii) *The Sheep-fold*

This is a somewhat similar game to the last. The children form in a ring, kneeling on the ground. One kneels in the centre, and another walks round on the outside. The one in the middle says:

"Who's that walking round my sheep-fold?"

The one on the outside answers:

"Only little Jacky Jingle."

The inside one then says:

"Don't you steal any of my fat sheep."
"Only this very small one"

is the reply, and with that the outside child carries away the biggest child in the ring, and so on until all the children are taken.

(iv) *When first we went to School*

The children form a circle, and moving round and round to the right, sing:

[1] See *Folk-lore Journal*, vol. i, p. 386, for a variant from a Derbyshire source.

When first we went to school—to school—to school—
How happy was I !
(*Each girl here takes the side of her dress or skirt by the right hand and just lifts it, singing the while* :)
'Twas this way, and that way,
How happy was I !

Next I went to service—to service—to service—
How happy was I !
(*The dress is now let go, and sometimes an imitation o scrubbing or sweeping with a long broom is introduced, as they sing* :)
'Twas this way, and that way,
How happy was I !

Next I had a sweetheart—a sweetheart—a sweetheart—
How happy was I !
(*Here they break the ring, and walk round in couples, singing* :)
'Twas this way, and that way,
How happy was I !

Next I got married—got married—got married—
How happy was I !
(*Still walking round in couples.*)
'Twas this way and that way,
How happy was I !

Next I had a baby—a baby—a baby—
How happy was I !
(*Here their arms swing to and fro as they walk round, as if nursing or trying to quieten a baby.*)
'Twas this way, and that way,
How happy was I !
(*At the conclusion of this verse the circle is re-formed.*)

Next my husband died—he died—he died—
How sorry was I !
(*Here they put their pinafores to their eyes, crying.*)
'Twas this way, and that way,
How sorry was I !

Next my baby died—she died—she died—
How sorry was I !
(*Still crying.*)
'Twas this way and that way,
How sorry was I ! (*Symondsbury.*) [1]

[1] *Conf.* several Shropshire variants in *Shropshire Folk-lore*, p. 514. Also *Notes and Queries*, Ser. x, viii, 206, for an account of a similar "action game" as witnessed at a Sunday-school treat at Exmouth, co. Devon.

(v) *Garden Gate*

One girl is chosen from the group to represent the mother, and the rest, as her daughters, stand in front of her. The eldest of them is selected to address the mother.

DAUGHTER: "Mother, mother, may I go to play?"
MOTHER: "No! daughter, no! for fear you should stay."
D.: "Only as far as the garden gate,
To gather flowers for my wedding day."
M.: "Make a fine curtsy, and go your way."

Upon this they all curtsy and scamper off, appearing delighted at being allowed to go, and before out of hearing of the mother exclaim, "Now what shall we do?" and proceed to plan some mischief or game to play as soon as they are out of sight. Presently they return to the mother looking rather crestfallen, pretending they have stayed away too long; then the mother asks them sharply:

"Now where have you been?"
D.: "Up to Uncle John's."
M.: "What for?"
D.: "Half a loaf, half a cheese, and half a pound of butter."
M.: "Where's my share?"
D.: "Up in cupboard."
M.: "'Tisn't there then!"
D.: "Then the cat eat it."
M.: "And where's the cat?"
D.: "Up on the wood." (*i.e. the faggots.*)
M.: "And where's the wood?"
D.: "Fire burnt it."
M.: "Where's the fire?"
D.: "Water douted it."
M.: "Where's the water?"
D.: "Ox drank it."
M.: "Where's the ox?"
D.: "Butcher killed it."
M.: "And where's the butcher?"
D.: "Behind the door cracking nuts, and you may eat the shells of them if you like."[1]

Here the mother becomes very indignant and runs after her daughters, endeavouring to catch them, which they use strenuous efforts to avoid. This game was played in the neighbourhood of Blandford in the "forties".

[1] A great deal of this is similar to the widely-known story of the "Old Woman and her Pig".

A version, very similar to the last, called *May I go out to* *lay*? is played in much the same way.

The DAUGHTER says: "Please may I go out to play?"
MOTHER: "How long will you stay?"
D.: "Three hours in a day."
M.: "Will you come when I call you?"
D.: "No."
M.: "Will you come when I fetch you?"
D.: "Yes."
M.: "Make then your curtsies and be off."

The girls then scamper off as before, and as they run about the field keep calling out: "I won't go home till seven o'clock!" "I won't go home till seven o'clock!" After they have been running about for some five or ten minutes the mother calls "Alice" (or whatever the name may be) to come home, when the one addressed will run all the faster, crying louder than before, "I won't go home till seven o'clock!" Then the mother commences to chase her until she catches her, and when she gets her to any particular place in the field where the others are playing, she says:

"Where have you been?"
D.: "Up to grandmother's."
M.: "What have you done that you have been away so long?"
D.: "I have cleaned the grate and dusted the room."
M.: "What did she give you?"
D.: "A piece of bread and cheese as big as a house, and a piece of plum cake as big as a mouse."
M.: "Where's my share?"
D.: "Up in higher cupboard."
M.: "It is not there."
D.: "Up in lower cupboard."
M.: "It is not there."
D.: "Then the cat have eat it."
M.: "Where's the cat?"
D.: "Up in heath."
M.: "Where's the heath?"
D.: "The fire burnt it."

The rest is the same as in the last. The mother then chases the daughters as before.

(vi) *The Duke of Rideo* [or *Riddeo*]

In this game the children stand in a group; one is chosen for the Duke, and he [or she] must stand opposite to and at some little distance from the rest of the party, who say or sing:—

"Here comes the Duke of Rideo—
Of Rideo—of Rideo—
Here comes the Duke of Rideo,
Of a cold and frosty morning."

The Duke answers:

"My will is for to get married—
To get married—get married—
My will is for to get married,
Of a cold and frosty morning."

Chorus:

"Will any of my fair daughters do—
Fair daughters do—daughters do-o-o?
(*The word "do" must be said in a drawling way.*)
Will any of my fair daughters do,
Of a cold and frosty morning?"

Duke:

"They are all too black or too proudy,
They sit in the sun so cloudy,
With golden chains around their necks,
That makes them look so proudy."

Chorus (indignantly):

"They're good enough for you, Sir!
For you, Sir! for you, Sir!
They are good enough for you, Sir,
Of a cold and frosty morning."

Here the Duke steps forward and says or sings:

"I'll walk the kitchen and the hall,
And take the fairest of them all;
The fairest one that I can see
Is Miss —— (*naming her*)
So Miss —— come to me."

The one chosen then becomes a Duke, and the game is repeated, the chosen ones, each in turn, becoming Dukes, until there is only one of the party left, when they sing:

"Now we've got this pretty girl——
This pretty girl—this pretty girl—
Now we've got this pretty girl,
Of a cold and frosty morning."

Whilst singing this last verse they come forward and claim the last girl, and embrace her as soon as they get her over to their side. (*Symondsbury.*)

Sometimes the game is played by three girls standing on one side and as many as they like on the other. It then bears the name of *Here comes three Dukes a-riding.*

The three girls walk to and fro and say:

"Here comes three dukes a-riding—a-riding—
This cold and frosty morning."

The other girls say:

"Pray what may your fortune be?"

To which the three reply:

"My fortune is to get married—get married, etc."

The dialogue then proceeds much the same as before.

The following variant of this game, called *A Young Man that wants a Sweetheart,* was one of those that Mr. Barnes sent an account of to Mr. Otis, and appeared in the *Yarmouth Register* (Mass.) for February, 1874, before alluded to.

The players consisted of a dozen boys standing hand in hand on one side, and a dozen girls standing in a row facing them. The boys commence by singing as they dance forward:

"There's a young man that wants a sweetheart—
Wants a sweetheart—wants a sweetheart—
There's a young man that wants a sweetheart,
To the ransom tansom tidi-de-o.

Let him come out and choose his own—
Choose his own—choose his own—
Let him come out and choose his own,
To the ransom tansom tidi-de-o."

The girls reply:

"Will any of my fine daughters do—
Daughters do—daughters do?
Will any of my fine daughters do,
To the ransom tansom tidi-de-o?"

Boys:

"They are all too black and brawny,
They sit in the sun uncloudy,
With golden chains around their necks
They are too black and brawny."

Girls:

"Quite good enough for you, Sir!—
For you, Sir!—for you, Sir!—
Quite good enough for you, Sir!
To the ransom tansom tidi-de-o."

Boys :

" I'll walk in the kitchen, and walk in the hall,
I'll take the fairest among you all,
The fairest of all that I can see,
Is pretty Miss Watts, come out to me.
Will you come out ? "

Girls :

" Oh, no ! oh, no ! "

Boys :

" Naughty Miss Watts she won't come out—
She won't come out—she won't come out—
Naughty Miss Watts she won't come out,
To help us in our dancing.
Won't you come out ? "

Girls :

" Oh, yes ! oh, yes ! "

(vii) *Gathering Nuts away*

The players should be divided into two equal divisions (each from eighteen to twenty in number if possible) and between them should be drawn a mark or boundary line upon the ground. The two parties stand opposite one another ; and the one on the right-hand side, joining hands, advances up to the line and retires again, singing :

" Here we come gathering nuts away—
Nuts away—nuts away—
Here we come gathering nuts away,
On a bright and sunny morning."

[1] Mr. W. W. Newell, in his *Games and Songs of American Children* (New York, 1884), reviewed in *Folk-lore Journal*, vol. ii, p. 243, says that the " Knights of Spain ", which he gives as the American variant of this game, is still acted, not only throughout England and the United States, but also in Spain and Sweden, in Italy and Ireland, among the Baltic Finns and the Moravian Sclavs. He believes that it was originally based on the idea of a courtship conducted in the strictly mercantile spirit which probably pervaded the next stage of marriage-making after the primitive carrying off of the bride. *Conf.* also two variants in *Shropshire Folk-lore*, pp. 516–17, called " The Knights of Spain ", and " Here comes three Dukes a-riding ". See also *Folk-lore Record*, vol. iii, p. 170, for an Essex variant, and vol. v, p. 89, for a Welsh one. Also Halliwell's *Nursery Rhymes*, No. cccxxxiii.

On the conclusion of this verse, the opposite party, which had been standing, hand in hand, perfectly still and silent, now advances in turn to the boundary line and retires again, singing :

" Pray, who will you send to fetch them away—
To fetch them away—fetch them away ?
Pray, who will you send to fetch them away,
On a cold and sunny morning ? "

The first party, who in the meanwhile had remained quiet and silent in its turn, now advances again as before, singing :

" We'll send Miss Bishop to fetch them away—
To fetch them away—fetch them away—
We'll send Miss Bishop to fetch them away,
On a bright and sunny morning."

As soon as this verse is finished the other party says, " Will you come ? " and on their opponents replying " Yes," the first girls on either side stand up to the boundary line, and taking each other's right hand commence to pull against each other, assisted by those behind, much in the same way as in *Oranges and Lemons* (*ante*), and the side which succeeds in pulling the other over the mark wins the game.

A variant of this game, called *Here we come gathering nuts to-day*, in which two children named in the verse are deputed to pull each over instead of the whole sides contending, is played by the school children at Symondsbury, in West Dorset, and as there are other interesting variations in it, I give it in full.

Two leaders are chosen, who proceed to pick their sides by alternately selecting them from the group of children till all have been chosen. Then the two parties, with their leaders at the end, each holding hands, stand in a line facing each other, with a distance of two or three yards between them. One party, still holding hands, advances towards the other, singing the while :

" Here we come gathering nuts to-day—
Nuts to-day—nuts to-day—
Here we come gathering nuts to-day,
So early in the morning."

On its retirement, the other line advances and retires in the same way, singing :

"Pray, whose nuts will you gather away—
Gather away—gather away?
Pray, whose nuts will you gather away,
So early in the morning?"

Before the first line advances again, an understanding has to be arrived at as to whose nuts are to be asked for from the opposite party, when it again approaches and retires, singing:

"We'll gather Miss A——'s nuts away—
Nuts away—nuts away—
We'll gather Miss A——'s nuts away,
So early in the morning."

To this the other party, again advancing and retiring as before, replies:

"Pray, who will you send to take them away—
To take them away—take them away?
Pray, who will you send to take them away,
So early in the morning."

Again a consultation must be held in the ranks of the first party as to which of their number is considered fairly equal in strength to endeavour to draw or pull over Miss A——, and when one has been decided upon they once more advance, singing:

"We'll send Miss B—— to take them away—
To take them away—take them away—
We'll send Miss B—— to take them away,
So early in the morning."

Thereupon A. and B., the two children before named, now advance, and clasping each other by the right hand, each endeavours to pull or draw her opponent over to her own side, a boundary line having generally been drawn at equal distances between the contending parties. As soon as one is drawn over, she has to be "crowned" immediately by the conqueror putting her hand on her head; for if this is not done at once the captive is at liberty to return to her own party. On the crowning taking place, the captured one takes up her position at the end of the line, and henceforth is considered to belong to the side of her conqueror. The game is now recommenced in the same way as before; but the second line advances first this time, and so on alternately until one side has drawn all the others over to it, or one has become too weak to continue the game.

Another version runs:

Here we come gatherin' nuts away.
Here we come gatherin' nuts away,
On a could and frasty marnen.[1] (*Hazelbury Bryan.*)

(viii) *English and Romans*

Miss A. L. Colfox gives in *Somerset and Dorset Notes and Queries*, vol. xi, p. 75, a game (the words of which she took down some years ago from a Bridport woman), in which the children advance and retire in two lines as in the previous games.

The first line asks: "Have you any bread and wine? We are English soldiers."

Second line answers: "Yes, we have some bread and wine; we are Romans."

1st: "Will you give us some of your's? We are English."
2nd: "No, we won't give any of our's; we are the Romans."
1st: "Then we'll tell the magistrate; we are English."
2nd: "We don't care for the magistrate; we are the Romans."
1st: "Will you come and have a fight? We are the English."
2nd: "Yes, we'll come and have a fight." (*They fight.*)

Miss Colfox refers to a similar game quoted by Mr. Cecil Sharp from a Somersetshire source, only instead of "magistrate" they had "king", and followed it with another couplet:

"We will ask the highest priest."

This Mr. Sharp traces down to a case of excommunication, where the appeal is made, first to the king, then to "the highest priest"—*i.e.* the Pope.

(ix) *The Lady of the Land*

An account of this game, which for want of a better appellation I call by the above title, is contained in the *Somerset and Dorset Notes and Queries*, vol. i, part v, pp. 133–4 (1889). In this two girls are chosen, the one to represent a lady and the other a mother, who is supposed to be taking her children out to service. She has one or more of them in each hand, and leads them up to the lady, saying or singing:

"Here comes the Lady of the Land,
With sons and daughters in her hand;
Pray, do you want a servant to-day?"

[1] The game is called *Nuts in May* in *The Peasant Speech of Devon*, by Sarah Hewett, 1892, p. 41.

The lady answers:

"What can she do?'

The mother replies:

"She can brew, she can bake,
She can make a wedding cake,
Fit for you or any lady in the land."

The lady then says:

"Pray leave her."

The mother then leaves her child and says:

"I leave my daughter safe and sound,
And in her pocket a thousand pound,
And on her finger a gay ring,
And I hope to find her so again."

This is repeated until all are similarly disposed of. A few days are supposed to pass, after which the mother calls to see her children, when the lady tells her she cannot see them. At last she insists upon seeing them, and the children are all "sat down" behind the lady, and the mother asks one child what the lady has done to her; and she tells her "that the lady has cut off her nose, and made a nose-pie and never give her a bit of it". Each one says she has done something to her and made a pie, and when all have told their tale "they all turn on her and put her to prison".

The following variant was contributed by Miss M. G. A. Summers, of Hazelbury Bryan, to the *Dorset County Chronicle* (April, 1889), to whom I am also indebted for the next two games.

One child takes seven or eight others whom she pretends are her children. Another child, presumably a mistress in want of servants, stands at a distance. The first child advances, holding the hands of her children, saying:

"There camed a lady from other land,
With all her children in her hand—
Please do you want a servant, marm?"

The supposed mistress answers:

"Leave her."

The mother before retiring says:

"I leaves my daughter zafe and zound,
And in her pocket a thousan' pound,
And on her finger a goulden ring,
And in her busum a silver pin.

I hopes when I return,
To see her here with you.
Don't'e let her ramble ; don't'e let her trot ;
Don't'e let her car' [1] the mustard pot."

Just as the woman and her children are supposed to be out of hearing the mistress says :

" She shall ramble, she shall trot,
She shall carry the mustard pot."

This is gone through again until the mistress has engaged all the children as her servants, when she is supposed to let them all out to play with the mustard pots, which are represented by sticks or stones, in their hands.

(x) *Queen Anne*

A large party of children form themselves into two ranks ; to one of these parties is given a ball. The rank to whom the ball is entrusted all hold their hands behind their backs, so that the opposite party should not know who has the ball in her possession.

The first rank advances and retires, saying :

" Queen Anne, Queen Anne,
She sot in the sun ;
So fair as a lily,
So white as a nun ;
She had a white glove on,
She drew it off, she drew it on.'

Those in the second rank, who have nothing in their hands, say :

" Turn, ladies, turn."

The opposite party turns round, saying :

" The more we turn, the more we may,
Queen Anne was born on Midsummer Day ;
We have brought dree letters from the Queen,
Wone of these only by thee must be seen."

The other party replies :

" We can't rëade wone, we must rëade all,
Please (*naming some one*), deliver the ball."

If they guess the right person, they change sides and go through the game as before.[2]

[1] Carry.

[2] See *Folk-lore Record*, vol. v, p. 87, for a variant from a Surrey source. *Conf.* also Halliwell's *Nursery Rhymes* (ed. 1846), No. ccxxxvi.

(xi) *Old Woman from the Wood* [1]

This is also called *Dumb Motions.*

Here again the children form themselves into two ranks, as in the last game.

The first rank says:

> " Here comes an old 'oman from the wood."

The second party answers:

> " What cans't thee do ? "

First Party:

> " Do anythin'."

Second Party:

> " Work away."

This the children proceed to do, some pretending to sew, some to wash, some to dig, some to knit, without any instruments to do it with. If the opposite guess what they are doing they change sides.

These last two games, Miss Summers believes, are very old ones, and have been played by several generations in the village of Hazelbury Bryan.

(xii) *How many miles to Gandigo* ?

This is another of the games mentioned in the *Yarmouth Register* as having been sent to Mr. Otis by Mr. Barnes. It is played by as many as like, standing two and two, opposite each other, each of them taking with the right hand the right hand of the other; then the two that are the king and queen say or sing:

> " How many miles to Gandigo ? "

The others answer:

> " Eighty-eight, almost or quite."

The king and queen reply:

> " Can I [we] get there by candle-light ? "

Chorus:

> " Yes, if your legs are long and light."

King and Queen:

> " Open the gate as high as the sky,
> And let the king and his queen go by."

[1] Called in Sussex *A Man across the Common.*

Then all the other pairs hold up their hands as high as they can, and the king and queen run through the archway and back again, and so on with the next pair, and other pairs in turn.

According to Mr. Otis this game is known as the *Quaker's Dance* in New England, where the last line runs :

"And let King George and his queen go by."[1]

(xiii) *Basket*

In this game the children all follow one who is styled the "mother", singing :

"I'll follow my mother to market.
To buy a silver basket."

The mother presently turns and catches or pretends to beat them.

The following three games were contributed by F. M. P. to the *Somerset and Dorset Notes and Queries*, vol. i, pp. 172–3 (1889), and hail from the borderland of Dorset and Devon by Uplyme.

(xiv) *Wolf in the Church-yard*

The children go out to school and think they see a ghost in the churchyard. The mother says : "'Tis only your father's shirt and stockings ; go on to school again." The mother then goes with them, and the wolf catches some of them and hides them behind him. Then they go to school again, and come back again and say : "Oh ! mother, there's a ghost in the churchyard !" Again she goes with them, and the wolf catches some more of them and hides them behind him as before. Then they say : "Where's my sheep ?" He answers, mentioning any place, as "on the hill". Whereupon they all cry "mah !" and run off.

(xv) *Old Woman*

One girl of the party is chosen to represent an old woman, and the rest ask her :

"What's the time, ole dumman, to-day ?"
OLD WOMAN : "One o'clock."

[1] *Conf.* a variant in *Shropshire Folk-lore*, p. 522, called "How many miles to Barley Bridge," which is played more in the manner of "Oranges and Lemons," ending in one party pulling against the other. See *Folk-lore Record*, vol. v, p. 88, for a Welsh variant. Also Halliwell's *Nursery Rhymes*, No. cccxxviii (ed. 1846), No. ccxxx.

This is repeated until " six o'clock " is reached, when they all exclaim :

" What d'e want six for ? "
O. W. : " To light the fire."
CHORUS : " What d'e want to light the fire for ? "
O. W. : " To roast my chicken."
CHORUS : " Where be going to get them ? "
O. W. : " Out of your yard, if I can get them ? "
(*She tries to catch the " chicken " girls.*)

This is all repeated till several are caught.

In the last round, after the Old Woman has said " To roast my chicken " the others say :

" Where's my chicken ? "

The Old Woman mentions some place or other.

" I don't know whether they be to then."
CHORUS : " What've got behind 'e ? "
O. W. : " Seven sacks of barley meal."
CHORUS : " Your boots is dirty.
Your stockings is dirty.
Your feet is dirty.
The blood'll come through.
The blood'll come through."
O. W. : " I'll take them off,
I'll take them off.
I'll cut them off.
Rub it up in a thousand blankets.
Rub it up in a thousand more blankets."

The others then all cry " mah ! " and run off as the game comes to an end.

(xvi) *My Fair Lady* [1]

In this game it would seem as if the children form a ring, or rows, and repeat alternately the following quaint and not unrhythmical lines :

London Bridge is falling down—
down—down—down—
My fair lady. Bricks and mortar 'll build it up—
up—up—up—
Bricks and mortar 'll soon fall down—
down—down—down—
Iron bars 'll build it up—
up—up—up—

[1] *Conf.* variant in *Shropshire Folk-lore*, pp. 518–19, there called *Gay Ladies.*

Iron bars 'll soon fall down,
down—down—down—
My fair lady. *Penny horse* (?) 'll build it up—
up—up—up—
Penny horse 'll soon fall down—
down—down—down—
My fair lady. What have this poor prisoner done ?—
done—done—done— done—done—done—
My fair lady. Stoled my locks and broke my keys—
keys—keys—keys— keys—keys—keys—
My fair lady. Half a sovereign he must pay—
pay—pay—pay— pay—pay—pay—
Half a sovereign he must pay, my fair lady.

One of the party, who seems to have been caught " inside ", then says:

Half a sovereign I'd'n got—
got—got—got—
My fair lady. Off to prison he must go—
go—go—go—
My fair lady. Off to prison he must go—

The one who was caught inside then asks:

" Wur's my ship ? " (sheep).

The others answer:

" I zeed 'em out een the vi'ld " (field).

The first replies, and the game ends very similarly to the last:

" I don't know where they be to then.
What've got behind 'e ?
How many bwys (or gurls) is behind 'e ?
Vive ar zix zacks o' barley me-al."

Thereupon they all cry " mah ! " and run off.[1]

III. Games of Skill

As Miss Burne says,[2] these are usually played by boys; and here the element of loss or gain comes uppermost, though sometimes something of a dramatic form may still be traced. The use of implements of play, such as bats and balls, comes in here for the first time. The governing principle of this class of games is doubtless to be found in young men's natural delight in sportive

[1] See *Notes and Queries*, Ser. VIII, i, 210, for a similar game played in Sussex with the refrain " My fair lady ", in which children representing robbers appear, and who at the end run away and are pursued.

[2] See *Shropshire Folk-lore*, p. 506.

trials of strength and skill. In the following game these two qualities are predominant.

(i) *Lamploo*

The following account of this game, which was a favourite schoolboy amusement in the west country half a century ago, is contributed by Σ to the *Somerset and Dorset Notes and Queries* (vol. i, p. 125) (1888).

"A goal having been selected and bounds determined, the promoters used to prepare the others by calling at the top of their voices:

"Lamp! Lamp! Laa-o!
Those that don't run shan't play-o!"

Then one of the 'spryest' lads is elected to commence, thus: first touching the goal with his foot or leaning against it, and clasping his hands so as to produce the letter W in the dumb alphabet, he pursues the other players, who are not so handicapped, when, if he succeeds in touching one without unclasping his hands, they both make a rush for the goal. Should either of the other boys succeed in overtaking one of these before reaching that spot, he has the privilege of riding him 'home' pick-a-back. Then these two boys (*i.e.* the original pursuer and the one caught) joining hands, carry on the game as before, incurring a similar penalty in case of being overtaken as already described. Each successive boy, as he is touched by the pursuers, has to make for the goal under similar risks, afterwards clasping hands with the rest, and forming a new recruit in the pursuing gang, in whose chain the outside players alone have the privilege of touching and thus adding to their numbers. Should the chain at any time be broken, or should the original pursuer unclasp his hands, either by design or accident, the penalty of carrying a capturer to the goal is incurred, and was always enforced. Of course, a great deal of mirth is caused by a big boy capturing a little one, and having to ride him home; by cleverly dodging a fast runner, as a hare does a greyhound, and by other events in a game, success in which is the result of superior agility.

In West Somerset the pursuing boys after starting were in the habit of crying out the word 'brewerre' or 'brewarre'; noise appearing to be quite as essential to the game as speed." [1]

Another correspondent to the same periodical (vol. i, p. 142) says that an almost identical game was played at the King's

[1] See *Shropshire Folk-lore*, p. 523, for a very similar game called *Stag-warning*.

School, Sherborne, some fifty years ago. It was called *King-sealing*, and the pursuing boy was obliged by the rules to retain his hold of the boy seized until he had uttered :

One, two, three, four, five, six, seven, eight, nine, ten,
You are one of the king-sealer's men.

If the latter succeeded in breaking away before the couplet was finished the capture was incomplete.

Mr. A. Matthews, of Dewlish School, Dorchester, has sent me a somewhat similar version of this game, which is called *Stag*. A leader is chosen to start the game. He usually recites a rhyme, with his hands closed ; after which he runs after his fellows and tries to touch one of them with closed hands. Whoever is so touched joins hands with him and together they continued the game until all are touched. The leader is always at one end, and the last one touched at the other, whose privilege it is to commence the next game.

(ii) *Marrels*

The ancient game of " nine men's morris " is yet played by the boys in Dorsetshire. The boys of a cottage, near Dorchester, had a while ago carved a " marrel " pound on a block of stone by the house. Some years ago a clergyman of one of the upper counties wrote that in the pulling down of a wall in his church, built in the thirteenth century, the workmen came to a block of stone with a " marrels " pound cut on it. " Merrels " the game was called by a mason.[1]

I have been unable to find out from any Dorset source how this game was played, but probably it was much in the same way as it is described to have been played in the Midlands in Brand's *Popular Antiquities* (ed. 1813, vol. ii, p. 297), where we are told that the shepherds and other boys dig up the turf with their knives to represent a sort of imperfect chess-board. It consisted of a square, sometimes only a foot in diameter, sometimes three or four yards. Within this was another square, every side of which was parallel to the external square ; and these squares were joined by lines drawn from each corner of both squares and the middle of each line. One party, or player, had wooden pegs, the other stones, which, placed by turns in the angles,

[1] See Barnes's *Glossary* (1886).

and playing alternately, they moved in such a manner as to take up each other's "men" as they were called; and the area of the inner square was called the "pound", in which the men taken up were impounded. He who could play three in a straight line might then take off any one of his adversary's where he pleased, till one, having lost all his men, lost the game. These figures were by the country people called "nine men's morris", or "merrils", and were so called because each party had nine men. These figures were cut upon the green turf, or leys, as they were called, or upon the grass at the end of ploughed lands, where in any rainy season it never failed to happen that, in the words of Shakespeare (*Midsummer Night's Dream*, act ii, scene 2):

"The nine men's morris is filled up with mud."[1]

Mr. H. J. Moule, in *Notes and Queries*, Ser. VIII, xii, 28, says that a similar board, but without the diagonal lines, is in full swing in Dorsetshire at this day. Nine bits of chalk and nine of coal are the "men". He calls it "marnull".

(iii) *Hop-frog*

This is a very curious amusement. You must bend as though about to sit on a *very low* stool; then spring about with your hands resting on your knees.

(iv) *Cat-and-kitten*

The common game of "tip-cat" was so-called by Dorset children. The long stick represented the "cat" and the small piece the "kitten".

It was also sometimes called *Cat and Dog* or *Cat* simply. For the following description of how it is played in his neighbourhood, I am indebted to Mr. A. Matthews, who is also responsible for the remaining games of this section, of which he sent a list to the *Dorset County Chronicle* in May, 1889, but from want of space no details were given. These details he was kind enough to give me subsequently, and of which I have here made full use:

"Two play at this game, or more if desired. A ring about a yard in diameter is made on the ground, and the implements

[1] See Strutt's *Sports and Pastimes* (ed. 1831), p. 317, where the game is fully described, and an engraving of a "merelles" table also appears.

of play are a stick and a short piece of wood bluntly pointed at each end. One lad takes the stick and another the " cat ". The latter goes to an agreed distance and tries to toss the " cat " into the circle. If he succeeds his opponent is " out ". If he fails in placing the " cat " within the circle, the boy with the stick proceeds to hit it upon one of the pointed ends, which makes it hop or rebound. Whilst in the air he hits it as far as he can away from the ring. This is done three times, except in the event of the " cat " happening to be tossed *on* the ring, when the striker has but one hit. Then his opponent says: 'How many?' (*i.e.* how many feet do you say it is from the ring to the 'cat'?). 'Fifty,' says the other, or any number he fancies it is over, but not less than five. The distance is then measured by placing the heel against the ring and the other foot in front of that, and so on; care being taken that the heel touches the toe, and that an exact line is taken. The striker looks to the former, and the bowler to the latter. If the distance turns out to be less than the stated number the striker is out, but if greater the striker remains in and deposits his number as the nucleus of his score. He can be got out in either of the following ways: (i) By being tossed out; (ii) by falling short of the right number of feet; (iii) by not succeeding in hitting the " cat "; (iv) by his opponent succeeding in catching the " cat " when struck. The game is won by the player whose score first reaches the *maximum* decided upon at the commencement of the game.

(v) *Cat-in-hole*

" This may be called a 'double-wicket' version of the last. Sides are chosen of equal numbers. Two holes are made in the ground about 10 yards apart. Two go in to hit with sticks, one at each hole; and two bowl with a small piece of stick about six inches long called a 'cat'—one from either end. If the 'cat' is hit runs are obtained as in cricket. The striker is put out by being caught from a hit, or 'stumped' by having the 'cat' placed in the hole.

" This is a capital substitute for cricket in places where circumstances do not admit of the latter being played."

(vi) *Last Tat* or *Touch*

" A lad starts and runs after his playmates. Whoever is touched takes his place, and so on."

(vii) *Cross Tag*

" This is an improvement upon the last. The one who is to chase the rest must do so with closed hands, and name someone he intends chasing. The others endeavour to cross his path, and as soon as anyone does so the boy run after is at once relieved and the pursuer must follow the nearest one to him who has crossed the line, who, if he be touched, restarts the game by taking the place of the pursuer. It is believed that the hands are clasped in order that the chaser—whose part is thus rendered more difficult—may be more readily distinguished."

(viii) *Dibs*

"This is sometimes called *Five stones*, from the number of stones required in the game, and may be played singly or with an opponent. Five round pebbles are chosen and placed on a slab of pavement, for instance. The player takes one up and tosses it in the air, endeavouring whilst the pebble is in the air to take up another and catch the first when it descends, with No. 2 in the same hand. One of these two is then placed in the left hand. The same stone if next tossed up as before, and No. 3 treated in the same way, and if the catch is made placed in the left hand. This is followed until the fifth is picked up. So far the player is said to be in the 'ones' or 'oneses'. The five stones are next scattered on the slab and left as they settle. One stone is next taken, no matter which, and tossed into the air, when *two* stones must now be taken up—no matter how far apart they may happen to be—before the other is caught. If the player does not succeed in taking up the two he stops, and if he has an opponent the latters follows on, the first player remembering that he is in the 'twoses'. If two are taken up successfully they are placed aside as before, and the stone tossed up again whilst the remaining two are similarly treated. The five stones are then again scattered gently on the slab, and the game proceeds as before, except that *three* stones are now snatched up. The fourth stone, the odd one, is allowed to be taken up. The stones are now placed carefully together, not scattered, and the one is once more tossed up, being picked up from the rest, and the game is finished by the four stones being successfully snatched up before the other is caught. Whoever reaches the end first is declared the winner.

"The game is sometimes commenced by tossing *all* the stones in the air and catching as many as possible on the back of the hand as an introduction. All use the same stones if several are playing. This is principally a girls' game."

(ix) *Hop-scotch*

"This game is played by first planning out an oblong diagram on the ground or floor, divided into some half dozen compartments, numbered in sequence. The first player chooses a flat stone, and, standing on one leg at a little distance in front of No. 1, tosses it into that compartment. He or she then hops into No. 1 and with the foot that is on the ground kicks the stone out of the compartment towards the starting point. The stone must come straight out and not lodge on a line; if it does, the player is 'out', and an opponent follows on. If the difficulties be successfully negotiated, No. 2 must be treated in the same way, and the stone must be pitched plainly within the division lines. The game is continued by the stone being tossed into No. 3, and afterwards kicked out again. Care must be taken not to touch a line with the foot, or the same penalty would follow as when the stone lodges on the line. This is followed up until the sixth and last space has been tossed into, and the stone carefully and straightly kicked out again to the starting point. The raised foot may be rested in the third and sixth spaces. This again is a great favourite with the girls."

(x) *Duck-stone*

" For this game a brick is required, and as many large stones or medium-sized flints as there are boys playing. One boy commences the game by placing his 'duck' (stone) upon the brick A and stands there, whilst all the others, one after another or in a volley, fire at the stone upon the brick from the line BB to try and knock it off. If they miss, their 'ducks' go up to line CC. If no one succeeds in [dis]lodging the 'duck' A, all the players will be beyond line DD. They may *kick* their 'ducks'

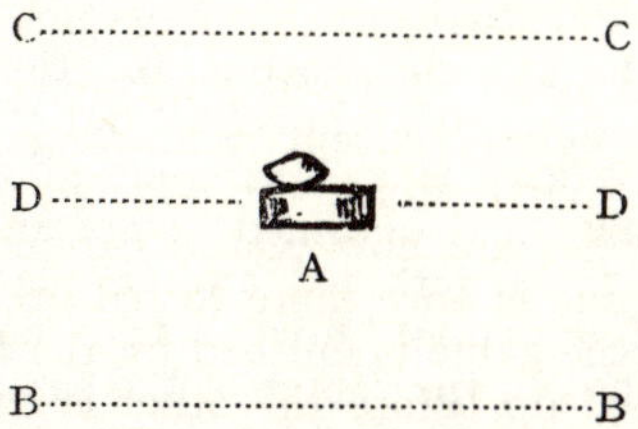

as far as line DD, but not touch them unless the 'duck' A is off its pedestal. If any one should touch his own 'duck' with his hands he must pick it up and reach line BB before the lad at A can catch him. If he is caught with his 'duck' in his hand before reaching home (BB) he places his 'duck' upon the pedestal in place of the one there previously. If any one should happen to knock the 'duck' A from off the brick, those whose 'ducks' are round about CC may pick them up and run, and the boy at A cannot touch them whilst his 'duck' is off. His duty is to see that his 'duck' is safe."

(xi) *Blandford Ring*

"This is a game at marbles said to be peculiar to the district whence its name is taken. A large ring is drawn with chalk or a stick on the floor or ground, and a smaller one in the centre of this called a 'pound'. The lads divide for partners (or two can play) and place so many marbles each within the 'pound'. In their proper turns—first decided upon by guessing or tossing—the players shoot gently towards the inner ring, and endeavour to knock out a 'shot'. If any one's 'taw' rests on the line or within the ring, then instead of afterwards shooting from where his marble settled, he will have to shoot again from the outer ring. If a player knocks a 'shot' out of the 'pound' he will take precedence (the 'shot' knocked out remaining where it rested) and fire at the nearest marble and endeavour to drive it out of the larger ring, when it would be his. A skilful player would do this and make his 'taw' stand in the place of the 'shot' by spinning. If he does not succeed in knocking the 'shot' out of the outer ring, he must shoot at it again, and only stops shooting at it when he has either missed it or has knocked it out of the ring. When it is knocked out of the ring he shoots again at whatever he likes, either at an opponent's 'taw' or a 'shot'; or he might dribble or 'drilly' (*i.e.* shoot slowly along the ground) as near as he could to the 'pound', when of course he would be nearer the 'shots'; or he might shoot close to a 'shot' and there wait his turn, for he is not to shoot twice in succession unless he hits the marble, and then he must follow up the same one until he either knocks it out of the ring or misses it. If a player's 'taw' is knocked out of the ring, and the owner of that 'taw' had obtained possession of any 'shots' they would have to be forfeited and be placed once more in the 'pound'. If anyone's 'taw' settles on the line of the 'pound' or within it in the course of the game, the owner of it has to go 'home' (*i.e.* to the outer ring again), unless there happens to be only one 'shot' in the 'pound', when this rule does not hold good. Those who hold most 'shots' win the game, and take the lead in the next.

"The following are phrases used in the game:

"*Knuckles up, i.e.* knuckles *off* the ground—cried by an opponent.

"*Knuckles down, i.e.* knuckles *on* the ground; claimed for instance when the 'shot' is low or behind a rising.

" *Movingses* (movings), *i.e.* moving any obstruction, such as a loose stone, etc.

" *No movingses, i.e.* no moving anything.

" These phrases are used by both parties. Whichever side claims them first the other is bound in honour to concede them."

(xii) *Hat or Cap Game*

To the following hat or cap game no name is affixed.

" A number of lads place their caps, crown downwards, at the base of a wall or fence. The boy whose cap is first tosses a ball into whosoever's cap he wishes from a certain specified distance. The boy into whose hat the ball happens to be tossed throws it at one of the lads who all beat a retreat. If he hits one of them, that one has a pebble placed in his cap ; if the thrower misses he has to have a pebble placed in his cap ; or if the tosser fails to place the ball (within three tries) in any hat he has to receive a stone. When one gets three stones or pebbles he is ' out ' and must stand aside till the game is finished. The one whose hat outlives the others has the pleasure of being ' punisher '. Each lad in the order of his going out has to stand with the back of his hand against the wall or fence, and the ' punisher ' from a certain distance throws at the palm of his hands with all his might half a dozen times. If the ' punisher ' hits any other part of the lad's body he receives the remainder of the punishment himself at the close of the game. If the boy ' bobs ' (*i.e.* drops) his hand he receives ' double 'lowance '. A hollow indiarubber ball is generally used for this purpose but sometimes a tennis ball."

The following interesting account of schoolboy games in a middle-class day-school in Dorsetshire at the beginning of the last century, which formed the subject of a paper called " School Days in a Country School " in *Longman's Magazine* for March, 1889, was contributed by Mr. Edmund Gosse from the unpublished papers of his father, the late Mr. Philip H. Gosse, F.R.S., depicting the latter's childhood at school in Poole in 1818.

" Slight as they are,' says Mr. Edmund Gosse, " and desultory, they give very realistically and vividly a sketch of conditions which are extinct to-day as the dodo is, and almost as remote ; nor am I aware that there exists any similar trivial record of life among boys of a country day-school at the beginning of the present century."[1]

The following extracts from this very interesting paper fittingly find a place in a record of Dorset children's games.

" We played games in the streets as well as in the playground. The thoroughfares of Poole were not so crowded with passengers as to make this practice any public nuisance. Scourge-tops, peg-tops, and humming-tops were all patronised; the last-named, however, chiefly within doors.

" Marbles of course upon the pavement; of these we used chiefly three sorts. The most highly prized were the 'alleys' of veined white marble, highly polished, the purest having often pink veins. Those of a yellow sort were called 'soap-alleys'. Others, made of a compact blue or grey limestone, went by the name of 'stoners'. There was also an inferior sort rudely moulded out of red and white clay, and baked, which were named 'clayers'.

" A game called 'Long-galls' (? goals) was a favourite with the boys, but I never heard of it elsewhere than in Poole. I never cared for it; it was something like 'prisoner's base'. Another, named 'ducks off',[2] consisted in setting on a large flat stone a round stone as big as one's fist, which from a certain distance one strove to knock off by bowling at it a stone of similar size. Two boys or more did this in turn, with certain conditions and results determined by rules.

" Birds-nesting, egg-stringing, squailing at birds, flinging stones at anything or nothing, throwing a flat stone across water to produce 'ducks and drakes', these of course were common. We used the term 'jellick'—no doubt a corruption of 'jerk'—to denote a mode of projecting a stone as the arm came suddenly against the ribs, or, by a more fantastic trick still, against the thigh of the lifted right leg.

" Saturday afternoon was our only holiday, and in summer bathing in the sea was in vogue on these occasions. We never used the word 'bathe' however, but invariably 'get into water', and this strange periphrasis never seemed strange to me until after I had left Poole."

[1] Mr. E. Gosse must have forgotten William Howitt's delightful *Boys' Country Book*, published in 1839, giving most charming scenes of school-boy life in the beautiful Derbyshire Peak district.

[2] Still played, Mr. Thomas Hardy tells me, as " cobs off " in the interior of the county. (Note by Mr. E. Gosse.)

IV. Christmas and Indoor Games

The class of games known as indoor games was generally played at Christmastide or in the long winter evenings, but occasionally these games were played at other seasons of the year, and sometimes, when the weather permitted, even out of doors. It is this difficulty which prevents one from classifying children's games absolutely into " out-door " and " in-door ". In these a distinctly mirthful character predominates, and in many of them the element of winning and losing has so strongly asserted itself that humorous penalties are ofttimes imposed on the losers. Those games with forfeits attached to them are, Miss Burne thinks, a decidedly later stage of development. Many of these games have a word-formula attached to them.

(i) *Mending the Shoe*

A party of children, thirty or forty in number if possible, must sit in a ring or half-circle on the floor (or, if the weather admit of it, on the grass) as closely as they can together, with both their hands hidden under their legs, so as to be able to pass the shoe from one to the other without being noticed. One of the party, who carries a shoe or slipper, is selected to go round and ask one of the group sitting in the ring, " Please can you mend my shoe ? " who answers, " Yes." The shoe is then handed over, and the first one proceeds : " When can I have it again ? " To which the other replies : " To-morrow, about 12 o'clock." The inquirer then says, " Thank you, good morning, and I'll be off," and leaves for a moment, but presently, having counted " one, two, three, four, five, six, seven, eight, nine, ten, eleven, twelve," returns and asks the one who had received the shoe to be mended if her shoe is done, when the girl will say in answer " I passed it to my next-door neighbour ". The inquirer then goes to the next person and says, " If you please I am come for my shoe," and will be told by each one she asks that " my next-door neighbour has got it." If the questioner is not very sharp and manages to detect by the movement of the arms where the hidden shoe is, she may have to go round the ring five or six times, or even more, in quest of it. If any one is detected with the shoe in her possession she will have to take the place of the girl in the middle and go through the same formula.

This is a very favourite game with children, and is sometimes kept up with great spirit for an hour or more.

A very similar game is called *The Cobbler*, and is played in much the same way. One of the party says :

"Cobbler, cobbler, mend my shoe,
And get it done by half-past two."

Then as the rest sit in a ring on the floor or grass, she leaves her shoe and goes outside the circle, calling once or twice to know if the shoe is finished.

After being told two or three times that the shoe is not quite finished, the owner of the shoe gets impatient and demands it, but it cannot be found as those seated are secretly passing it from one to another. A scramble ensues, and the one that is discovered with the shoe has to take the other's place outside the ring.

It is also, and perhaps more commonly, known as *Hunt the slipper*.[1]

(ii) *Hidy-buck*

Barnes in his *Glossary* (1863) gives this as a local name for the game of *Hide and Seek*.[2]

(iii) *Truckle the Trencher*

This used to be a standard game for winter evenings. A circle was formed, and each one was seated on the floor, every player taking the name of a flower. One player stood in the midst and commenced to spin the trencher round on the floor as fast as possible, at the same time calling for one of the flowers represented by the other players seated in the ring. The bearer of the name had to rush forward and seize the trencher before it fell to the ground, or else pay a forfeit, which was redeemed in the usual manner at the close of the game.

This game was entered into with the greatest vivacity by staid and portly individuals as well as by their juniors.

(iv) *Buff*

The players in this game sit in a circle and the one who is selected to commence takes a stick or poker and knocks on the

[1] And "The Lost Slipper" *in Shropshire Folk-lore*, p. 525.
[2] Conf. *Hide-fox* (*Hamlet*, Act iv, sc. 2).

floor, when the person who is sitting next to him or her on the left-hand side exclaims :

" Who's there ? " [or " Who is it ? "]

The first player answers :

" Buff."

Second Player :

" What says Buff ? "

First Player :

" Buff says ' Buff ' to all his men,
And I say ' Buff ' to you again."

Second Player :

" I think Buff smiles."

First Player :

" Buff neither laughs nor smiles,
But gives the staff to you again."

And suiting the action to the word, " Buff " hands the stick or poker to the next player, who is bound to receive it, and becomes " Buff " in turn. Should the first player, however, at any time during the foregoing dialogue smile before the staff is actually handed over, a forfeit is incurred.[1]

(v) *Fool, fool, go to School*

A number sit in a row. Some one is selected to represent a dunce or fool, and is sent out of the room, or out of ear-shot. Then each of those sitting down adopt the name of some bird, fish, or animal. This done the " fool " is readmitted and the spokesman says :

All the birds in the air,
All the fishes in the sea,
Go and find me a —— (*naming one of the children's nom-de-plume*).

If the " fool " fails to find the right one after three guesses he is beaten " home ". If he selects the right one he claims him on his side.

FORFEITS

As a means of lightening this already long chapter, I have included the playing of " forfeits ", mostly obtaining at Christmas-time, amongst the other customary amusements and children's games prevalent during that period. See Chapter II, p. 75.

[1] *Conf.* variant in *Shropshire Folk-lore*, p. 526.

V. Rhymes

These I have subdivided into (*a*) Rustic, (*β*) Nursery or Domestic, (*γ*) Counting out, or "Lot" rhymes.

The first were sometimes used merely as a rhyme or jingle attached to a game or trick; sometimes as a means of divination by which children—both boys and girls—would attempt to foretell their future life, or to gain a peep into their matrimonial future; sometimes by way of invocation to or apostrophe upon some object of natural history in which they were interested, or upon which they were experimenting; and sometimes apparently without reference to any special subject or object.

Those of the second class appear to be mostly confined to very young children, and nearly all that I have come across were applicable to the case of the mother or nurse and the infant on her knee.

The third class—the "counting-out", or "lot" rhymes, as they are called in Dorsetshire [1]—was commonly used by country children as a means of selecting by chance or lot those of their number upon whom is first to fall the burden or honour of playing a disagreeable or a distinguished part in their games. I would refer those who are interested in comparing the "counting-out" rhymes of various countries to Mr. H. C. Bolton's exhaustive work on the subject, called *The Counting-Out Rhymes of Children* (published in New York in 1888), from which I gather that variants of several of those I give here are common in the United States of America, and especially in New England; a circumstance which perhaps it is only natural to expect from the large share that Dorsetshire is known to have had in contributing to the early settlers of that colony.

(*a*) *Rustic*

It is the custom in agricultural districts for boys and men to keep birds off cornfields until the seeds are up, and the stalks high enough for protection. For this purpose an old gun is sometimes provided, or sometimes "clackers", [2] but more often the "bird-keepers" have to depend solely upon their own vocal powers. At such times songs or rhymes sung in a loud voice

[1] Called "chapping out" or "titting out" in Scotland.

[2] A kind of rattle.

are frequently indulged in, and the following, heard by a passer-by in the neighbourhood of Halstock, is given as a specimen :

Vlee away blackie-cap,
Don't ye hurt meäster's crap
While I vill my teätie-trap,
And lie down and teäk a nap.[1]

In the rural districts of Dorsetshire the country folk have a great affection and veneration for the robin and the wren, and the following couplet affords proof of this :

The robin and the wren
Are God Almighty's cock and hen.

To which is sometimes added :

The martin and the swallow
Are God Almighty's bow and arrow.

In some parts the poor people say :

If 'twere not for the robin and the wran,
A spider would overcome a man.

Children sometimes catch large white moths or "millers", and, having interrogated them on their taking of toll of flour, make them plead guilty and condemn them in these words :

Millery, millery, dousty poll,
How many zacks hast thee a-stole ?
Vow'r-an'-twenty, an' a peck—
Hang the miller up by's neck.

This has been said to have reference to the unfair way in which the monkish owners of tithes exacted their dues of corn or flour ; or to the exorbitant charges they made in granting permission to the people to grind their own corn at the monastery or abbey mill.

Children often catch lady-birds,[2] and, placing them on the tips of their fingers, encourage them to fly away by the following words :

Leädy-bird, leädy-bird, vlee away home,
Your house is a-vire, your children wull burn [roam].

So, too, it is a common amusement of theirs, having set fire to a piece of paper, to watch the running fiery spots as it burns—called by them "passons an' clarks"—and see which will run

[1] See *Notes and Queries* (Ser. II, vii, 313).
[2] Sometimes called "God Almighty's Cow."

last—parsons, the large ones, or clerks, the small ones. (See Barnes' *Glossary* (1863), p. 74.)

The supposed virtues of plants and flowers for purposes of weather prognostications, or for foretelling future events or fortunes, are widely known and believed in amongst our country children, and abundant scope is afforded them by the flowery hedgerows of Dorsetshire for indulging in the harmless amusements connected with these beliefs. The kernels or pips of pomaceous fruit are often playfully shot from the thumb and forefinger, as the young folks repeat:

Kernel, come, kernel, hop over my thumb
And tell me which way my true love will come.
East, west, north, or south,
Kernel, jump into my true love's mouth.

Sometimes the pips are placed in the fire, when the children, as they anxiously watch the effect, exclaim:

If you love me, pop and fly;
If you hate me, lay and die.

The pimpernel, called the poor man's weather-glass, is often apostrophised as follows:

Pimpernel, pimpernel, tell me true,
Whether the weather be fine or no.
No heart can think, no tongue can tell,
The virtues of the pimpernel.

A ball consisting of cowslip blossoms tied in a globular form called a "tissty-tossty", is often used by children as a means of divining their future, when the following lines are repeated whilst they play with it:

Tissty-tossty, tell me true,
Who shall I be married to?

The names of A, B, C, etc., are mentioned until the ball, which is being tossed about, drops. And again:

Tissty-tossty, four and foarty,
How many years shall I live hearty?

The numbers one, two, three, four, etc., etc., are called out until the ball drops as before.

As a mere game it is played by one of the children who holds the "ball" calling out: "Tissty-tossty, one, two, three," and then, as she throws the ball, calls out the name of one of the children standing round in a circle to catch it. If this one should fail to catch it she in turn tosses the ball. If she succeeds, the ball is returned to the one who threw it, who continues to toss it until someone fails to catch it. The game is continued until they are tired, or until all have had their turn in tossing the ball.

In addition to pretending to tell the time by blowing off the seeds of the dandelion—each puff counting as an hour—children, and especially girls, seek to divine their future prospects of marriage by pulling off the petals of a flower or a flowering stalk of grass, whilst repeating some variant of the well-known lines :

Tinker, tailor, soldier, sailor,
rich man, poor man, beggarman [or gentleman], thief.

One more particularly apposite to agricultural districts was : " Rich man, poor man, farmer, ploughman, thief."

As to the rhymes used on the occasions of the scattering of hemp seed and the placing of their shoes in the form of a T on going to bed on Midsummer Eve by Dorset maidens for purposes of divination, see Chapter I, *s.v.* " Midsummer Eve ".

The following lines were often used by children in the endeavour to charm snails out of their holes :

Snail, snail, come out of your hole,
Or else I'll beat you so black as a coal.

It was customary when a crow or rook was seen to shout :

Crow, crow, get out of my sight,
Or else I'll have your liver and light,

and it was always thought that however far off the bird might be it would immediately obey.

Dorset children are not alone in their aversion to " tell-tales ", and the following is one rendering of a not uncommon rhyme :

Tell-tit ! tell-tit !
Shall have your tongue a-slit ;
And every dog in parish,
Shall have a little bit.

The following rhyme is used by children who have occasion to make a division of anything, whilst they hide the article behind them and say :

Handy-pandy,
Jack-a-dandy,
Which hand will you have ?

It is also used as a formula inviting a small wager, when a child hides a marble or other trifle in one hand, and holds out both fists; when if the other guesses right he wins the marble, or if wrong he pays one.[1]

A variant runs:

Handy-pandy, Jack-a-dandy
Loves plum-cake and sugar-candy.
He bought some at a grocer's shop,
And out he came a-hop-hop-hop.

The following rhyme was often heard among school children, sung to a particular tune:

Went out in garden,
Picked up a pin,
And asked if any one was in.
No one in, and no one out,
Out in the garden walking about.

The same, with the following:

Turn about, and wheel about,
And do just so;
And every time we turn about,
And jump Jim Crow.

Children running races were started by the following rhyme:

One to make ready,
Two to prepare,
Three to be off,
And *four* to be there.

Another more commonly known form, perhaps, was:

One to stop,
Two to stay,
Three to make ready,
And *four* away.

Few children would at first recognize in the following queer couplet that the sweet woodruff (*Asperula odorata*), called by the rustics "woody-ruffy", was intended:

Double u, double o, double d, e,
R, o, double u, double f, e. (*Woodderowffe.*)

The following couplets relating to the combination of colours would afford some light as to the canons of taste adopted by Dorset country children in these matters:

Pink and blue
Will never do.

[1] This infantine form of gambling, says Miss Burne (*Shropshire Folk-lore*, p. 530), is alluded to as "handy-dandy" in *Piers Plowman*, and also in *King Lear*.

Pink and green
Fit for a queen.

Green and white,
Forsaken quite.

It is unlucky to wear a wedding dress of this last combination of colours.[1]

That rhymes were as common in the amusements of schoolboys as in that of girls we may learn from the following account of some rhyme games given by Mr. Gosse from the same source I have before stated.[2] He there states that rude doggerel rhymes were repeated on occasions among the boys and learned from one another.

Thus a boy would come suddenly behind another, and seizing him by the shoulder proceed to dig his knee into the posterior of the other at every line of the following :

I owed your mother
A pound of butter ;
I paid her once—
I paid her twice—
I paid her three times over,

the last line accompanying a kick of double vehemence.

The word FINIS at the end of books was turned into the following poetic flight :

F for Finis,
I for Inis,
N for Nuckley Bone,
I for Johnny Waterman,
S for Samuel Stone.

And a variant I have heard is :

F for Fig,
I for Igg,
N for Nickle Bones (Nickley Boney),
I for John the Waterman,
S for Sally Stones (Stoney).[3]

The next the boys no doubt learnt from their little sisters, since the imagery, as Mr. Gosse says, is of a decidedly feminine cast :

[1] See *Notes and Queries*, Ser. IX, ix, 490, where I have noted this.
[2] See *ante*, p. 375.
[3] Conf. *Shropshire Folk-lore*, p. 575.

My needle and thread
Spells Nebuchadned ;
My bodkin and scissors
Spells Nebuchadnezzar ;
One pair of stockings and two pairs of shoes
Spells Nebuchadnezzar the king of the Jews.[1]

One boy meeting another would address him with these queries, the other giving the replies :

" Doctor, Doctor, how's your wife ? "
" Very bad upon my life."
" Can she eat a bit of pie ? "
" Yes, she can as well as I."

Sometimes, when there were several children, the rest of the party would run round and try to catch the one that gives the answer, and would punish him or her in some way previously arranged if the answer were given rudely.

Having gathered a tuft of the shepherd's purse (*thlaspibursa pastoris*), so abundant by waysides, a boy would invite his unsuspecting fellow to pull off one of the triangular capsules. Then he would immediately cry :

Pick-pocket, penny nail,
Throw the rogue into gaol,

suiting the action to the word by catching him hold and dragging him off.

There were certain tricks or catches that could be practised on the same person only once. Of this kind were two insidious verses always held in reserve for a fresh boy. One of the initiated would attack the newcomer with an invitation to play at a petty game, saying :

Now I'll begin : I one my mother.

The other is to reply :

I two my mother.

And they run the cardinals in alternation till the unsuspecting urchin comes to :

I eight my mother.

Immediately the artful tempter shouts :

Here's a wicked footer ! He says he hates his mother !

[1] For a Scottish variant see *The Games and Diversions of Argyleshire*, by Dr. Maclagan, p. 258, 1901.

Or the device would be varied thus. The dialogue would run down the alphabet, beginning :

I'll go to A,
I'll go to B,

till the stranger in due course comes to :

I'll go to L,

when, as before, a cry of affected surprise is raised :

Lor' ! What do you think ? He says he'll go to hell !

In both cases the trifling difference of the absence of the aspirate is considered as being of no moment.

A similar catch which I give from another source is attempted by the questioner beginning :

I went up one stair.
Ans. : Like I.
I went up two stairs.
Like I.
(And so on to the sixth stair.)

I went into a room.
Like I.
I looked out of the window.
Like I.
I saw a monkey——

Here of course the answer is still desired to be " Like I ", but if the boy that is being practised upon be not taken unawares, he turns the tables on his questioner by replying " Like *you* ".[1]

Here is another similar catch.

Question. I am a gold lock.
Answer. I am a gold key.
Q. I am a silver lock.
A. I am a silver key.
Q. I am a brass lock.
A. I am a brass key.
Q. I am a lead lock.
A. I am a lead key.
Q. I am a monk lock.
A. I am a monkey.[2]

or Q. I am a don lock.
A. I am a donkey !

[1] *Conf.* similar version in Halliwell's *Nursery Rhymes* (ed. 1846), No. ccx.
[2] See Halliwell's *Nursery Rhymes* (ed. 1846), No. cci.

(β) *Nursery or Domestic*

William Barnes, in his "Fore-say" (p. 14) says of these: "Game rhimes used by children in their round games are a kind of folklore of the lower level of life, though they are mostly called 'nursery' rhimes, as some of them are wont to be sung by mothers and nurses to children in the lap. I am ready to believe that those which are clearly rather game verses than nursery rhimes are made by clever children, since if the girl is mother to the woman there is wit in girls or boys as in their elders; and many play-games that are good may, as such, have come down in a stream of childhood folklore, while others may have been lost."

The rhymes in which children indulge in their nursery games and amusements are of great variety, and range from lines which are intended to represent a story, or a series of questions and answers such as I have first mentioned to a mere collection of nonsense verses, from which it is impossible to evolve any connected thread or idea whatever.

The following is often said by boys and girls as a general rhyme, but in some districts of Dorsetshire it is adopted as a nursery one, when the nurse or other person on taking off a child's boots pretends to knock nails into its foot, saying:

"[John Smith] fellow fine,
Can you shoe this horse of mine?"
"Yes, good sir, that I can,
As well as any other man.
Here's a nail and here's a prod,
And now, good sir, your horse is shod." [1]

For an inquiry as to a nursery song commencing:

Man of the sea,
Come listen to me;
For Alice, my wife,
The plague of my life,
Has sent me to beg a boon of thee—

see *Notes and Queries* (Ser. VIII, vol. i, p. 293) (1892), where it is stated by the late Mr. H. J. Moule, of Dorchester, to have been a nurse's song in those parts sixty years ago.

[1] *Conf.* two variants of this rhyme in Gregor's *Folk-lore of North East of Scotland.*

The next is common, with its variants, to many counties:

One, two, buckle my shoe;
Three, four, open the door;
Five, six, pick up sticks;
Seven, eight, lay them straight;
Nine, ten, a good fat hen;
Eleven, twelve, let them delve;
Thirteen, fourteen, maids a-courtin';
Fifteen, sixteen, maids a-kissin'; [maids in the kitchen;]
Seventeen, eighteen, maids a-waitin'; [I'm a-waitin';]
Nineteen, twenty, my stomach's empty;
Please, mother, give me some dinner.[1]

Also the following:

Rain, rain, go away,
Come again another day,
—— and I want to play.
[A—— B—— wants to play.]

Great A, little a,
Bouncing B,
The cat's in the cupboard,
And can't see me.

Jack be nimble, Jack be quick,
Jack jumped over the candle-stick.

Where's Jim, in his skin,
He jumped out, and I jumped in.

Cut the bread.
How can I cut it without any knife?
How can I marry without any wife?

A common amusement is to tap the forehead of a young child whilst saying:

Knock at the door,
And peep in;
(*Pulling up the eyelids.*)
Lift up the latch,
(*Raising up its nose.*)
And walk in.
(*Putting a finger into its mouth.*)

Sometimes it is repeated in this form:

Knock at the door,
(*Tapping the forehead.*)

[1] *Conf.* similar lines in Gregor's *Folk-lore of North East of Scotland*, p. 20. Also Halliwell's *Nursery Rhymes* (ed. 1846), No. xxxv.

Ring at the bell,
(*Pulling a lock of hair, or sometimes an ear.*)
Lift up the latch,
(*Raising the nose.*)
And walk in.
(*Putting a finger in the mouth.*)
[or, peep in.]
(*Lifting up the eyelids.*)

A similar and equally common amusement practised on a young child or infant to its invariable and infinite delight, was to take hold of its toes, one by one, beginning at the big toe, and say:

This little pig went to market,
This little pig stayed at home,
This little pig had roast beef,
This little pig had none,
This little pig cried, " Wee ! wee ! wee ! " all the way home.

A similar one—only generally played on the fingers instead of the toes—is the following:

" I went to the woods," says this pig.
" What to do there ? " says this pig.
" To look for my mother," says this pig.
" What to do with her ? " says this pig.
" To kiss her—to kiss her—to kiss her—" says this pig.

Another popular finger game was to bend the thumb backwards and forwards whilst saying:

Dance, thumbkin, dance.
Dance, ye merry men, every one.
(*Moving all the fingers.*)
But, thumbkin, dance alone.
(*Moving the thumb only as before.*)

The fore-finger and the rest of the fingers in rotation then take the turn of the thumb, alternating as before, to the words:

Dance, foreman, dance.
Dance, ye merry men, every one,
But, foreman, dance alone.

Dance, middleman, dance.
Dance, ye merry men, every one,
But, middleman, dance alone.

Dance, ring-man, dance.
Dance, ye merry men, every one,
But, ring-man, dance alone.

Dance, little man, dance,
Dance, ye merry men, every one,
But, little man, dance alone.[1]

Sometimes the nurse, having taken off the little one's shoes and socks, would turn its feet to the fire and say:

Shoe the little horse, and shoe the little mare,
But let the little colt go bare, bare (*touching each foot*).

Another well-known way of amusing a little child is to pat its hands or feet, and repeat:

Pat a cëake, pat a cëake, bëaker's man,
Mëake me a cëake as fast as you can,
Pat it and prick it, and mëark it with T,
And put it in oven for [baby] and me.

An equally popular amusement was to seat a child on your crossed foot, and repeat:

This is the way the little girl walks,
(*Moving the foot gently.*)
This is the way the little boy trots,
(*A little faster.*)
This is the way the lady canters,
(*Faster still.*)
This is the way the gentleman gallops.
(*As fast as possible, and ending by tilting off the rider.*)

The following variant has a more rustic sound:

Little boys and girls walk, walk, walk;
Farmers go trit trot, trit trot, trit trot;
Ladies go canter, and canter, and canter;
Gentlemen go gallop, and gallop, and gallop,
And then they fall off.
(*Here the action being suited to the words the infantile rider invariably comes to the ground.*)

Here is another:

Father, mother, and Uncle Jan [Sam]
Rode to B—— on a black ram,
Down fell father—and down fell mother,
(*Here let the child slip off your foot.*)
And away rode Uncle Jan [Sam].

(γ) *Counting-out, or "Lot" Rhymes*

These rhymes were especially in vogue in those games, Mr. Gosse says, in which one lad was set in antagonism to the

[1] Conf. *Shropshire Folk-lore*, p. 528.

rest, or had to be " he "—as it was termed—such as the game of " touch ", where the individual was determined by all standing in a ring while one within repeated the following nonsense, touching a boy in succession at every word ; and so going round and round the circle, when the one on whom the last word fell was " he ".

One-ry, oo-ry, ick-ry, an,
Bipsy, bopsy, Solomon San. [Little Sir Jan.]
Queery, quawry,
Virgin Mary,
Nick, tick, tolomon tick,
O. U. T. out,
Rotten, totten, dish-clout,
Out jumps " He ".

The next is one from the borderland of Dorset and Devon by Uplyme, and is used in playing the common game of " tig " or " touch ".

Mary at her garden gate
Eating cherries off her plate ;
Two, four, six, eight,
Mammy, daddy, dish-clout,
O.U.T. spells " out goes he " (*or " she " as the case may be*).[1]

The following are some further examples which I have obtained from various sources, several being from William Barnes's scrap-book of folk-lore jottings which he gave me, as I have already mentioned.

Hoky, poky, wangery, fum,
Polevee (?), ke, ky, bulum, kum,
Wungery, fungery, wingery, wum,
King of the Cannibal Islands.

One a zoll, zen a zoll, zig a zoll, zan,
Bobtail vinegar, tittle tol tan,
Harum, scarum, Virgin Marum,
Blindfold.

Onery, youery, ickery, Ann,
Phillisy, phollissy, Nicholas Jan,
Queeby, quanby, Irish Mary,
Buck.[2]

[1] See *Somerset and Dorset Notes and Queries*, vol. i, p. 174.

[2] *Conf.* a Romany variant of this one quoted in Mr. Bolton's book before mentioned.

Onery, twory, Dickery, Davy,
Harry mo crackery, nickery, navy,
Usque dandum, merry cum time,
Humbledy, bumbledy, twenty-nine.

Hokey, pokey, winkey, wum,
How d'ye like your tëaties done ?
All to pieces, that's the fun—
Can't ye now jest gie I wone ?

Ena, mena, mina, mo,
Keska, lena, lina, lo,
Eggs, butter, cheese, bread,
Stick, stock, stone dead.
O. U. T. spells "out"—
And out goes "she".

A correspondent in *Somerset and Dorset Notes and Queries*, vol. xiii, 184–5, states that the apparently unmeaning and cabalistic words *eena, mena, mina, mo*, etc., have been commonly assumed to have formed part of an ancient priestly ritual, either connected with the selection of a victim for the sacrifice or of the expulsion of some one from a tribe. But he is more inclined to think that the words are not numerals at all, but are an invocation to the ancient Assyrian gods.

The following old favourite is well known :

Dickory, dickory, dock,
The mouse ran up the clock,
The clock struck one, the mouse ran down,
Dickory, dickory, dock.

Another less common :

Whippence, whoppence,
Half a groat, want two-pence,
More kicks than half-pence.

A correspondent in the *Dorset County Chronicle* in April, 1889, said that many years ago a thoroughly Dorset rustic was heard singing to a little child the following curious conglomeration of nonsense verses, which seem to form a collection of counting-out rhymes in themselves :

Oon, two, dree, vour,
Bells of Girt Toller (Great Toller),
Who can mëake pancëake
'Thout fat or vlour ?

"Gargy, Pargy, how's yer wife?"
"Very bad upon my life"
"Can she ait a bit o' pie?"
"Ees, sa well as you or I."[1]

Zee zaw, Margery Daw,
Swold her bed an' laid in straw,
Wadden she a dirty slut,
Da zell her bed and lay in dirt?

'Pon my life an' honner!
As I was gowine to Toller,
I met a pig a'thout a wig,
'Pon my life an' honner!

The two following rhymes may fittingly come in here:

Oh dear! sad!
The maid is married I ought to have had!
If she idden married she's bespoke,
And my poor heart is almost broke!

I wish I was where I do wish,
In the sea in a gret bowl dish;
If the dish turned up and I turned down
I would'en be there for a thousand poun'.

The following lines, which strike a deeper note, are given me as "children's verses":

What are heavy?
Sea and sorrow.
What are brief?
To-day and to-morrow.
What are frail?
Spring blossoms and youth.
What are deep?
The ocean and truth.

VI. Riddles

Very much akin to the tricks or catches before mentioned under "Rustic Rhymes", and often quite as amusing, are the riddles that children especially are so fond of asking each other, particularly those which contain a catch in themselves.

The following is a thoroughly rustic but somewhat coarse example, which as in the other cases is generally attempted to be played upon children upon first going to school.

[1] Conf. *ante*, p. 386.

Which would you rather have, a rusty rag, a sunburnt cake, or a blackbird under the bush ?

To the initiated these alternatives signified a rusty piece of bacon, a piece of dried cow-dung, and the devil ! Great merriment was caused should the unsuspecting urchin choose either of the two latter.

As I was going over —— Bridge I saw something in the hedge. It had four fingers and one thumb, and was neither fish, flesh, fowl, or bone ?

(*Answer* : A glove.)

Elizabeth, Betsy, and Bess went over the water to seek a bird's nest. They found four eggs in the nest, and took one egg each. How many did they leave in the nest ?

(*Answer* : Three. The three names being those of only one person.)

Stick, stone, and a feather
Went over the water together.
Stone sank, stick swam,
What was the name of the other ?

(*Answer* : Feather.)

As white as milk, an' 'tisn' milk ;
As green as grass, an' 'tisn' grass ;
As red as blood, an' 'tisn' blood ;
As black as ink, an' 'tisn' ink ?

(*Answer* : The four stages of a blackberry.)

Long legs, crooked thighs,
Little head, and no eyes ?

(*Answer* : A pair of tongs.)

There is a little house ; and in that little house there is a little room ; and in that little room there is a little shelf ; and on that little shelf there is a little cup ; and in that little cup there is something I would not take all the world for ?

(*Answer* : The heart's blood.) [1]

Under the water, over the water, and never touches the water.

(*Answer* : A woman crossing a stream with a pail of water on her head.)

There was a thing just four weeks old,
And Adam was no more ;
Before that thing was five weeks old,
Adam was fourscore.

(*Answer* : The moon.)

[1] Conf. *Shropshire Folk-lore*, p. 574.

There was a king met a king
In a narrow lane;
Said the king to the king,
"Where have you been?"
"I have been a-hunting
The buck and the doe."
"Will you lend me your dog?"
"Yes, I will do so.
"Call upon him, call upon him."
"What is his name?"
"I have told you twice,
And won't tell you again."
(*Answer*: "Bean.")[1]

Little Miss Etticott,
In a white petticoat,
And a red nose;
The longer she stands,
The shorter she grows.
(*Answer*: A lighted candle.)

The answer to the following riddle or puzzle is to be found by altering the punctuation, when it will be seen that the whole sense is completely changed.

I saw a fish-pond all on fire;
I saw a house bow to a squire;
I saw a parson twelve feet high;
I saw a cottage near the sky;
I saw a balloon made of lead;
I saw a coffin drop down dead;
I saw two sparrows run a race;
I saw two horses making lace;
I saw a girl just like a cat;
I saw a kitten wear a hat;
I saw a man who saw these too;
And said though strange they all were true.[2]

In *Notes and Queries* (Ser. X, ii, 182, 1904 and again at Ser. XII, viii, 283, 1921), I compare this form of versification with the lines written to Dame Custance by Ralph Roister Doister in the play of that name—our first English comedy—written by Nicholas Udall, or Uvedale, *c.* 1540, probably to be acted by his scholars

[1] These last two riddles, with slight variations, are also to be found in Gregor's *Folk-lore of North East Scotland.*

[2] For another specimen of the same kind see Halliwell's *Nursery Rhymes* (ed. 1846), No. cccclxxxv.

at Eton, of which school he was at that time *Magister Informator* (head master).

I think I cannot do better in closing this last section of Dorsetshire children's games and rhymes than refer my readers to one of William Barnes's most humorous dialect poems, entitled " Riddles ", which contains some excellent specimens of that kind of ingenious word-puzzling which affords so much amusement to the youth of both sexes. These are best seen in the first complete edition of the poems, published by Kegan Paul and Co. in 1879 and again in 1888, as it contains several riddles which are not be to found in the earlier editions.

FINIS

INDEX

A

Abbottsbury customs—
Wishing at St. Catherine's Chapel, 102.
Fishing customs, 103.
Flower custom ("Garland Day"), 104.
Abortion in cows (charm), 226.
Adder, 245.
(The) Agglestone (Studland) legend, 172.
Allhallowtide or Hallow E'en, 48.
Blandford bell-ringing custom, 48.
Animal-lore, 232–7.
Apple tree, 250.
Apple tree wassailing, 251.
Ascension Day. See Holy Thursday, 34.
Ash tree, 252.
Ass, 232.

B

Bagley House [Baglake ?] (Bridport) ghost story, 142.
Ball, Kicking the, 27, 112.
BALLADS AND SONGS, 307.
The Dorsetshire Garland, 308.
An Old Story, 314.
Roben's Cöortèn, 315.
An old Dorchester song, 316.
An old Yetminster, 317.
The Legend of St. Gabriel's, 318.
Turmut-hoeing, 322.
The Crocodile, 322.
The Prickly Bush, 323.
The King's First Course, 324.
The Lost Lady, 325.
I'm a Man that's done wrong to my Parents, 326.
The Punch Bowl, 327.
Sally is the Girl for me, 327.
Sary Sikes, 328.
The Haunted Hare, 330.
The Fairy Ring, 330.
Barnes's [William] "Fore-say", 1.
Batcombe Down Cross, 143.
Batcombe proverb, 290.
Beaminster ghost story, 144.
Beaminster proverb, 290.
Beating the Bounds or Perambulation of Boundaries on Holy Thursday, 34.
Bridport, 37.
Chideock, 36.
Marnhull, 37.
Melcombe Regis, 36.
Radipole, 36.
West Lulworth, 36.
Wyke Regis, 38.
Bed charm, 228.
Bed superstition, 273.
Bee, 245.
Beetle, 246.
Bellows, 274.
Bell-ringing customs, 182, 273.
Bell-ringing superstition, 182.
Bergamot, 255.
Bettiscombe Skull superstition, 146.
Bincombe Music Barrow, 151.
Bindon Abbey Bells, 151.
Bindon place rhyme, 331.
Bingham's Melcombe (witchcraft), 214.
Bird, 237.
Bird-lore, 237–45.
BIRTH, DEATH, AND MARRIAGE CUSTOMS AND SUPERSTITIONS, 177–200.
Birth customs and superstitions, 177.
Alliterative naming of children, 179.
Days of the week, 178.
Dipping in spring, 179,
Groaning drink, 177.
Hardening of infants, 179.
Lucky omens, 178.
Unlucky omens, 178.
Bishop Caundle bell tolling custom, 182.
Bishop's Caundle, 104.
Blackdown Dolmen superstition, 152.
Blackmore Vale, White Hart Silver, 152.
Blandford bell-ringing custom, 48.
Blandford Hocktide custom, 105.
Church penance custom, 105.
Boils (charm), 220.
Boot, 274.
Box, 255.
Bradpole proverb, 290.

Bramble, 255.
Bridport, 105.
  Flower service, 105.
  Robin Hood Ale, 105.
Bridport flower service, 41.
Bridport May Queen and Maypole dance, 38.
Bridport proverb, 291.
Broadway, 106.
  Candle auction, 106.
Broadwinsor proverb, 291.
Bronchitis (charm), 224.
Bullock, 232.
Butter-making (charm), 224.

C

CALENDAR CUSTOMS AND SUPERSTITIONS, 17–52.
  New Year's Day, 19.
  Twelfth Day, 19.
  Candlemas Day, 19.
  St. Valentine's Day, 20.
  Lent, 28.
  Mothering, or Mid-Lent, Sunday, 29.
  Palm Sunday, 29.
  Good Friday, 29.
  Easter, 32.
  Hock- or Hoke-tide, 33.
  Holy Thursday or Ascension Day, 34.
  May Day, 38.
  Oak Apple—or Royal Oak—Day, 42.
  Midsummer Eve, 44.
  Allhallowtide or Hallow E'en, 48.
  Guy Faux Day, 49.
  Christmas Eve, 50.
Calf, 233.
Came (Winterborne), 108.
  Induction Service, 108.
Candle, 274.
Candlemas Day, 19.
Candlemas Day weather-lore, 263.
Cat, 233.
Cattistock, 108.
  Feast Day, 108.
Cattistock Maypole, 39.
Cattle, 233.
Cerne Abbas Giant, 154.
Cerne Abbas Maypole, 39.
Cerne Abbas St. Austin's Well, 158.
Cerne Mill Stream, 159.
Chantmarle ghost story, 160.
Chardstock Flower and Maypole Dance, 38.
Charity customs (Corfe Castle), 112.
CHARMS, 11, 218.
  Definition of, 218.
Charms against—
  Abortion in cows, 226.
  Bed charm, 228.
  Boils, 220.
  Bronchitis, or Whooping-cough, 224.
  Butter-making, 224.
  Consumption, 224.
  Cramp, 224.
  Epilepsy, 223.
  Fits, 223.
  Headache, 224.
  Jaundice, 224.
  King's evil, 227.
  Loo, or looer, in cows, 226.
  Nose-bleeding, 220.
  Quarter-evil in calves, 226.
  Quinsy, 222.
  Rheumatism in pigs, 227.
  Rupture, 222.
  Scriptural riddle or charm, 230.
  Shingles, 220.
  Snake bite, 220.
  Sore eyes, 222.
  Stye, 221.
  To find a drowned corpse, 228.
  To keep witches out of the house, 229.
  To prevent fishing boats from being bewitched, 230.
  To test love and friendship, 228.
  To treble money, 229.
  Toothache, 219.
  Troublesome infants, 255.
  Warts, 220.
  Worms, 221.
Cheselborne, 109.
  Treading in the Wheat, 109.
Cheselborne Giant's Grave, 161.
Chideock—
  Beating of Bounds, 36.
CHILDREN'S GAMES AND RHYMES, 333–97. See Games.
Children's Rhymes. See Rhymes.
Children's Riddles, 394.
Christening palm (or pane), 282.
Christmas weather-lore, 266.
Christmas Eve customs, 50.
"Christmasing" or Dole custom, 49.
Christmastide customs, 75–101.
  Forfeits, 75.
  Forfeit rhymes, 78.
  Mummers, 83.
Clothes, 274.
Club Walking. See Whitsuntide Club Walking, 58.

Cobwebs, 275.
Cock, 237.
Cock-fighting, 27.
Cock-squailing, 26.
Colt, 233.
Combe Keynes, 109
Tithing custom, 109.
Comfrey, 255.
Confirmation, 275.
Consumption (charm), 224.
Corfe Castle, 110.
Quarrymen's customs, 110.
Kicking the ball, 112.
Charity customs, 112.
Harden's Charity, 112.
Corfe Castle King Edward the Martyr legend, 162.
Corn, 275.
Corpse (drowned, to find) (charm), 228.
Counting out, or " lot " rhymes, 391.
Cow, 226, 234.
Cowslip, 255.
Cramp (charm), 224.
" Crocodile, The " (ballad), 322.
Cuckoo, 238.
Culliford Tree Music Barrow, 162.
Cunning man, 215.
Curfew bell, 134.
Curfew plot custom at Ibberton, 113.
Curfew plot custom at Mapouder, 115.
Curfew plot custom at Stoke Abbott, 134.

D

Daffodil, 256.
Days of the week, 178 (births), 267 (weather-lore), 275 (generally), 286 (sneezing).
Death customs and superstitions, 180.
Death omens : Articles of domestic use, bees, birds, dogs, plants, church bells and clocks, deaths at Christmas, knockings at night, shivering, 180-4.
Death-bed and corpse customs and superstitions, 184-6.
Dipping infants in spring, 177.
Divination. See Matrimonial Oracles, 188.
Dock, 256.
Dog, 234.
Dolmen Superstition (Blackdown), 152.
" Dorchester Garland " (ballad), 309.
Dorchester " overlooking ", 206, 210.
Dorchester place rhyme, 331.
Dorchester proverb, 291.
" Dorchester song (A)," 316.
Dream, 276.
Drowned Corpse (to find) (charm), 228.
Duck, 239.
Dumb Maids' Plot (Evershot), 162.

E

Ear, 276.
East Knighton (witchcraft), 207.
Easter, 32-3.
Easter cakes, 32–3.
Easter weather-lore, 266.
Eggardon proverb, 291.
Egg-shell, 276.
Epilepsy (charm), 223.
Ever-green, 256.
Evershot Dumb Maids' Plot, 162.
Evil Eye, definition of, 205. See Witchcraft.

F

Fairy, 276.
" Fairy Ring, The " (ballad), 330.
February weather-lore, 264.
Fire, 277.
Fishing-boats (charm), 230.
Fits (charm), 223.
Fly, 247.
Folke Church legend, 163.
Folk-lore, Definition of, 1, 17.
Folk-medicine, 218.
Limitation of, 16.
Classification of, 17.
Forfeits and Forfeit rhymes at Christmas, 75, 78.
Fork, 278.
Frampton Monastic legends, 163.
Funeral customs, 187.
Furmity, 29, 33.
Furze, 256.

G

Game Rhymes (Children's), 14, 380–94.
(α) *Rustic*, 380.
(β) *Nursery or domestic*, 388.
(γ) *Counting out, or " lot "*, 391.
GAMES (CHILDREN'S) AND RHYMES, 333–97.
Classification of, 338.
(i) Choral ; (ii) Dramatic ; (iii) Games of skill ; (iv) Christmas and

indoor games; (v) Rhymes: (α) rustic, (β) nursery or domestic, (γ) counting out, or "lot" rhymes; (vi) Riddles.
I. Choral Games:
Sally Water, 339.
Little Girl of Mine, 340.
What are you weeping for? 341.
Rosy Apple, Lemon, and Pear, 342.
Isabella, 343.
Here we go round the Mulberry Bush, 344.
Walking round the village, 345.
Kiss in the ring, 346.
My little Dog Buff, 347.
Cat after Mouse (or *Threading the Needle*), 348.
Green Gravel, 348.
Wallflowers, 349.
II. Dramatic Games:
Oranges and Lemons, 350.
Fox and Goose, 351. (Or *Hen and Chickens*.)
The Sheepfold, 352.
When first we went to School, 352.
Garden Gate, 354.
The Duke of Rideo, 355.
Gathering Nuts away, 358.
English and Romans, 361.
The Lady of the Land, 361.
Queen Anne, 363.
Old Woman from the Wood, 364.
How many miles to Gandigo? 364.
Basket, 365.
Wolf in the Churchyard, 365.
Old Woman, 365.
My Fair Lady, 366.
III. Games of Skill:
Lamploo, 368.
Marrels, 369.
Hop-frog, 370.
Cat-and-kitten (or *Cat and Dog*, or *Cat*), 370.
Cat-in-hole, 371.
Last Tat (or *Touch*), 371.
Cross Tag, 371.
Dibs, 372.
Hop-scotch, 372.
Duck-stone, 373.
Blandford Ring, 374.
Hat or Cap Game, 375.
IV. Christmas and Indoor Games:
Mending the Shoe, 377.
Hidy-Buck, 378.
Truckle the Trencher, 378.
Buff, 378.
Fool, fool, go to School, 379.
Games of Forfeits, 75.
Ghost, 278.
Good Friday, 29.
Good Friday Bread, 29.
Plants, 31.
Bees, 31.
Nails, 31.
Soapy water, 31.
Good Friday weather-lore, 266.
Goose, 239.
Groaning drink, 177.
Guisers. See Mummers.
Guy Faux Day customs, 48.
Portland Bonfire custom, 49.

H

Hair, 279.
Hallow E'en. See Allhallowtide, 48.
Hambledon place rhyme, 331.
Hampreston haunted church, 163.
Hardening of infants, 179
Harden's Charity (Corfe Castle), 112.
Hare, 234.
Harvest Home customs, 64.
Harvest Home songs, 70.
"Haunted Hare, The," 330.
Hawkchurch (witchcraft), 213.
Hay-making customs, 62.
Haythorne haunted chapel, 164.
Headache (charm), 224.
Heather, 256.
Hemp, 256.
Hen, 239.
Herb-lore, 15.
Hiring, 280.
Hock- or Hoke-tide customs, 33.
"Hocking" men and women, 33.
Holnest church legend, 164.
Holt ghostly apparition, 164.
Holy Thursday customs, 34.
Beating of Bounds or *Perambulation of Boundaries*, 34.
Horse, 235.
Horseshoe, 235.
Houghton proverb, 291.

I

Ibberton curfew plot, 113.
"I'm a Man that's done wrong to my Parents" (ballad), 326.
Infants (charm), 255.
Insect and Reptile lore, 245-50.

Invocation to Woden at Harvest Home, 71.

J

Jack-o'-lent, 28.
January weather-lore, 264.
Jaundice, 224.
Journey, 280.

K

Kettle, 280.
Kicking the Ball custom, 27, 112.
King Edward the Martyr legend (Corfe Castle), 162.
King-evil (charm), 227.
"King's First Course, The" (ballad), 324.
Kingston Russell spectral coach, 165.
Kinson haunted gate, 165.
Knife, 280.
Knowlton bell legend, 165.
Knowlton place rhyme, 332.

L

Ladder, 281.
Lady-bird, 247.
Leek, 257.
"Legend of St. Gabriel's" (ballad), 318.
Leigh Witches' Corner, 166, 212.
Lent, 28.
Lent-crocking, 21.
Lily, 257.
Liverwort, 257.
LOCAL CUSTOMS, 102–41.
LOCAL LEGENDS AND SUPERSTITIONS, 142–76.
Long Burton bell omen, 166.
Loo (or looer) in cows (charm), 226.
"Lost Lady, The" (ballad), 325.
Lot or counting out rhymes, 391.
Louse, 246.
Love and friendship test (charm), 228.
Luck, 281.
Lulworth (West).
  Feeding custom, 113.
  Perambulation of Bounds, 36.
Lychett charm, 166.
Lychett spectral coach, 167.
Lyme Regis, 113.
  Cobb Ale Feast, 113.
Lyme Regis black dog legend, 167.
Lyme Regis place rhyme, 331.
Lyme Regis proverb, 292.

M

Magpie, 239.
Mapouder curfew plot custom, 115.
March weather-lore, 265.
Marriage customs and superstitions, 188–200.
Martin, 241.
Maskers. See Mummers.
Matrimonial Oracles (*even ash leaf divination, hemp seed throwing, crossed shoes, letters of alphabet, cowslip ball*), 188–90.
May weather-lore, 266.
Michaelmas weather-lore, 266.
MIDSUMMER EVE CUSTOMS, 44.
  Hempseed throwing, 45.
  Crossed shoes, 46.
  Letters of Alphabet, 46.
  Church porch death omen, 47.
Midsummer weather-lore, 266.
Milton Abbey, 115.
  Annual Fair, 115.
  King Athelstan's Chapel, 116.
MISCELLANEOUS CUSTOMS AND SUPERSTITIONS, 273–87.
Money, 281.
Money (to treble money) (charm), 229.
Month, 281.
Moon, 281.
Moon weather-lore, 267.
Moreton Palm Sunday and Good Friday church decorations, 32.
Moth, 247.
Mothering, or Mid-Lent, Sunday customs, 29.
Mottoes, 10.
Mouse. (See Shrew-mouse.)
Mummers (Christmas), 83.
Mummers (Cornish), 84.
Mummers (West Dorset), 87.

N

Nail, 282.
NATURAL HISTORY SUPERSTITIONS, 232–61.
  (i) Animal-lore, (ii) bird-lore, (iii) insect and reptile lore, (iv) plant-lore.
  I. ANIMAL-LORE, 232.
  Ass, Bullock, Calf, Cat, Cattle, Colt, Cow, Dog, Hare, Horse, Mouse, Pig, Rabbit, Shrew-mouse, Weasel.

II. Bird-lore, 237.
Bird, Cock, Cuckoo, Duck, Goose, Hen, Magpie, Martin, Owl, Peacock, Raven, Robin, Rook, Swallow, Wood-pecker, Wood-pigeon or *Ring-dove, Wren.*
III. Insect and Reptile Lore, 245.
Adder, Bee, Beetle, Fly, Lady-bird, Louse, Moth, Slow-worm, Snail, Snake, Spider, Toad, Wasp.
IV. Plant-lore—
Apple tree, Ash tree, Bergamot, Box, Bramble, Comfrey, Cowslip, Daffodil, Dock, Ever-green, Furze, Heather, Hemp, Leek, Lily, Liver-wort, Nettle, Nut, Oak tree, Oats, Pear tree, Pimpernel, Plant, Rose, Sloe, Thorn, Toad-stool, Tree, Wheat, Wood.
Netherbury churchyard legend, 168.
Netherbury proverb, 292.
Nettle, 258.
New Year's Day, 19.
New Year's Day weather-lore, 263.
Nose-bleeding (charm), 220.
Nursery rhymes, 388.
Nut, 258.

O

Oak Apple — or Royal Oak — Day customs, 42.
Oak tree, 258.
Oats, 259.
" Old Story, An " (ballad), 314.
Omens (birth), lucky 178, unlucky 178.
Omens (death). See Death omens, 180.
Omens, Magpie, 177.
Ooser (Dorset), a mask, 97.
Overlooking, 205. See Witchcraft.
Owl, 241.

P

Pack Monday Fair (Sherborne), 129.
Palm, or pane, 282.
Palm Sunday customs, 29.
Parkstone place rhyme, 331.
Peacock, 243.
Pear tree, 259.
Perambulation of Boundaries. See Beating the Bounds, 34.
Piddleton Christmas Dole, 117.
Pig, 235.
Pimpernal, 259.
Place rhymes, 331.
Plant, 259.
Plant-lore, 250–61.
Poole place rhyme, 331.
Poole proverb, 292.
Portland (i) *Bonfire custom*, 49.
(ii) *Reeve staff*, 118.
(iii) *Marrying the Land*, 120.
(iv) *" Church gift,"* 121.
(v) *Land system*, 122.
(vi) *Courtship and marriage customs*, 198.
(vii) *The " Jump "*, 123.
(viii) *Binding Day*, 124.
Portland cock legend, 169.
Poundbury Field, Annual stocking of, 124.
" Prickly Bush, The " (ballad), 323.
Proverbs and Proverbial Sayings, 5, 288–306.
Classification of, 289.
(i) *Proverbs proper*, 295.
(ii) *Proverbial Sayings*, 299.
Metaphors, 299.
Similes, 303.
(iii) *Local Proverbs and Proverbial Sayings* :
Local Proverbs :
Batcombe, 290.
Beaminster, 290.
Bradpole, 290.
Bridport, 291.
Broadwinsor, 291.
Dorchester, 291.
Eggardon, 291.
Houghton, 291.
Lyme Regis, 292.
Netherbury, 292.
Poole, 292.
Shaftesbury, 293.
Shapwick, 293.
Stourpaine, 294.
Stour Provost, 294.
Wareham, 294.
Proverbs (rhyming), 304.
Proverbs (weather), 264.
Pucknoll " Garland Day ", 104.
" Punch Bowl, The " (ballad), 327.
Purbeck—
Purbeck Marblers, 100.
St. Aldhelm's Chapel (*Wishing and Flower customs*), 124.
Purbeck (witchcraft), 207.

Q

Quarrymen's customs (Corfe Castle), 110.
Quarter-evil in calves (charm), 226.
Quinsy (charm), 222.

R

Rabbit, 235.
Radipole Perambulation, 36.
Raven, 243.
Rempstone right-of-way custom, 125.
Repetition of events, 283.
Rheumatism in pigs (charm), 227.
Rhymes (children's game), 14, 380.
Rhymes (counting out, or "lot"), 391.
Rhymes (forfeit) at Christmas, 78.
Rhymes (nursery), 388.
Rhymes (place), 331.
Rhymes (rustic), 380.
Rhymes (weather), 264.
Rhyming proverbs, 304.
Riddles (children's), 394.
Ring-dove. See Wood-pigeon.
"Roben's Cöortèn" (ballad), 315.
Robin, 243.
Rook, 244.
Rose, 260.
Royal Oak Day. See Oak Apple Day, 42.
Rupture (charm), 222.
Rustic rhymes (children's), 380.

S

St. Austin's Well (Cerne Abbas), 158.
"St. Gabriel's (Legend of)" (ballad), 318.
St. Thomas's Day customs, 49.
Christmasing, 49.
Thornford Tithe custom, 50.
St. Valentine's Day customs, 20.
"Sally is the girl for me" (ballad), 327.
Salt-cellar, 283.
Sampler, 283.
"Sary Sikes" (ballad), 328.
Scissors, 285.
Scriptural riddle or charm, 230.
SEASONAL CUSTOMS, 53–101.
Christmastide, 75.
Harvest Home, 64.
Hay-making, 62.
Sheep-shearing, 53.
Whitsuntide Club-walking, 58.
Shaftesbury Bezant custom, 125.
Shaftesbury proverb, 293.
Shapwick proverb, 293.
Sheep-shearing customs, 53.
Sheep-shearing songs, 53.
Sherborne, 128.
Bell-tolling custom, 128.
Pentecost Money, 129.
Children's Christmas Pence, 129.
Pack Monday Fair, 129.
Sherborne (witchcraft), 209.
Shillingstone Maypole, 40.
Shingles (charm), 220.
Shipton Gorge (witchcraft), 214.
Shivering, 285.
Shoe, 286.
Shrew-mouse, 236.
Shrove Tuesday customs, 21.
Skimmington riding, 192.
Skull superstition (Bettiscombe), 146.
Sloe, 260.
Slow-worm, 248.
Snail, 248.
Snake, 249.
Snake bite (charm), 220.
Sneeze, 286.
Snow, 286.
Songs. See Ballads and Songs.
Soot, 286.
Sore eyes (charm), 222.
Spade, 286.
Spells, 218.
Spider, 249.
Spitting, 286.
Spring superstition, 173, 179.
Stairs, 286.
Stalbridge—
Lent-crocking, 24.
Crookern and Hunting the Buck customs, 133.
Stalbridge ghost story, 170.
Stalbridge witchcraft, or "overlooking", 205.
Stanton St. Gabriel legend, 318.
Stoke Abbott, 133.
Flaxhorn custom, 133.
Curfew Plot custom, 134.
Stoke Abbott phantom coach, 171.
Stoke Abbott songs and customs at Harvest Home, 73–5.
Stone, 287.
Stourpaine proverb, 294.
Stour Provost proverb, 294.
Studland Agglestone legend, 172.
Stumbling, 287.

Sturminster Marshall—
Smoke-hole (or hold) tenure, 136.
Land customs, 136.
Stye (charm), 221.
Swallow, 244.
Swanage marblers' custom of kicking football, 112.
Swyre " Garland Day ", 104.
Symbols, 10.
Cock-fighting, 27.
Cock-squailing, 26.
Kicking the Ball, 27.
Lent-crocking, 21.
Symondsbury songs and customs at Harvest Home, 68–72.
Symondsbury spring superstition, 173.

T

Thorn, 260.
Thornford Tithe custom, 50.
Toad, 249.
Toad Fair, 216.
Toad-stool, 260.
Toothache (charm), 219.
Towel, 287.
Tree, 261.
Troublesome infants (charm), 255.
" Turmut-hoeing " (ballad), 322.
Twelfth Day, 19.

U

Upwey auction by candle custom, 138.

V

Visitor, 287.

W

Walditch spring superstition, 173.
Wareham borough custom, 139.
Wareham proverb, 294.
Warts (charms), 220.
Washing, 287.
Wasp, 250.
Weasel, 236.
Weather on particular days of the week, 267.
Weather at particular times of the year, 263.
Weather portents—
Fine weather, 271.
Wet weather, 268.
Weather rhymes and proverbs, 264.
Weather-lore, 262–72.
Classification of, 262.
Wedding customs, 191.
West Dorset (" overlooking "), 209.
Wheat, 261.
White Hart Silver (Blackmore Vale), 152.
White witch, 215.
Whitsuntide Club Walking, 58.
Whooping-cough (charm), 224.
Wife sale, 197.
Wimborne—
(i) *Cock-fighting*, 139.
(ii) *Cake custom*, 140.
Wimborne haunted barns, 173.
Wimborne St. Giles ghost story, 174.
Winterbourne Abbas stream superstition, 174.
Wise woman, 215.
WITCHCRAFT AND CHARMS, 201–31.
Witchcraft generally, 201–5.
Instances given, 205–18.
Witches (charm), 229.
Witches' Corner (Leigh), 166, 212.
Woden (Invocation to) at Harvest Home, 71.
Wood, 261.
Wood-pecker, 244.
Wood-pigeon, 244.
Wool—
Smoke-pence custom, 140.
Dog fair, 141.
Wool spectral coach, 174.
Work, 287.
Worms (charms), 221.
Wort-lore, 15.
Wren, 244.
Wyke Regis Bound Stone perambulation, 141.

Y

Yetminster song (A), 317.

Printed by Stephen Austin & Sons, Ltd., Hertford.